The Complete Idiot's Com… Reference

FrontPage 2000 T…

cut here

…ar

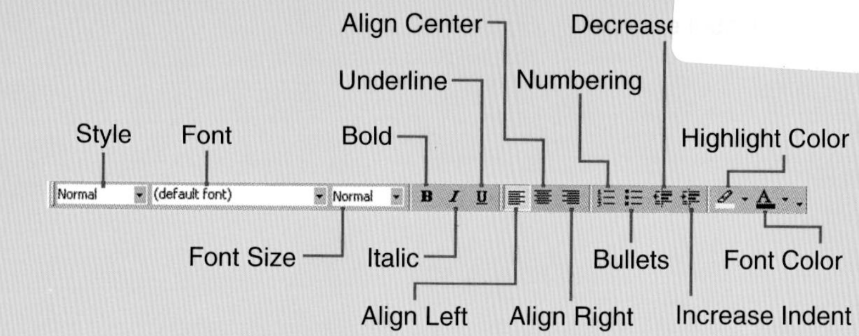

The Standard Toolbar

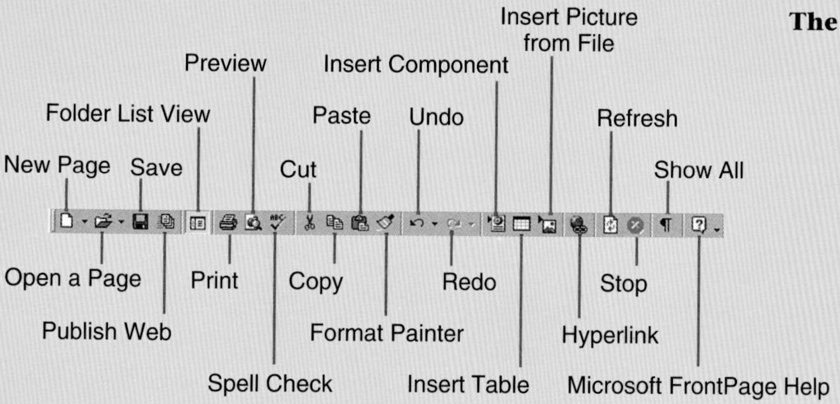

The Tables Toolbar

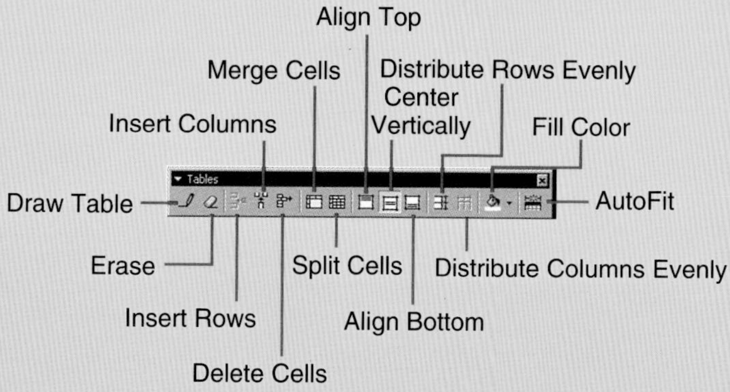

QUE®

FrontPage 2000 Keyboard Shortcuts

Keyboard shortcuts for FrontPage 2000's top-level menus are accessed by pressing Alt+ except where indicated.

Ctrl+PgDn cycles between FrontPage Views (Normal, Source, and Preview)

File Menu

New	Ctrl+N
Open	Ctrl+O
Close	Ctrl+F4
Save	Ctrl+S
Save **A**s	
Preview in **B**rowser	
Print	Ctrl+P
E**x**it	

Edit Menu

Undo	Ctrl+Z
Redo Last Action	Ctrl+Y
Cu**t**	Ctrl+X
Copy	Ctrl+C
Paste	Ctrl+P
Delete	Del
Select A**l**l	Ctrl+A
Find	Ctrl+F
R**e**place	Ctrl+H

View Menu

Reveal T**a**gs	Ctrl+/
Refresh	F5

Insert Menu

Break	
Horizontal **L**ine	
Date and **T**ime	
Symbol	
Comment	
Na**v**igation Bar	
Page Ba**n**ner	
C**o**mponent	
Database	
For**m**	
Advanced	
Picture	
File	
Boo**k**mark	
Hyperlink	Ctrl+K

F**o**rmat Menu

Font	
Paragraph	
Bullets and Num**b**ering	
P**o**sition	
Dynamic HTML **E**ffects	
Style	
Style Sheet **L**inks	
Theme	
Share**d** Borders	
P**a**ge Transition	
Bac**k**ground	
Remove Formatting	Ctrl+Shift+Z
Propert**i**es	Alt+Enter

Tools Menu

Spelling	F7
Thesaurus	Shift+F7

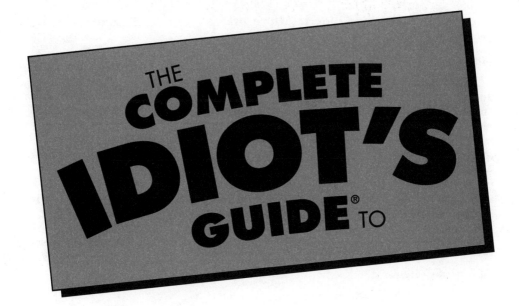

THE COMPLETE IDIOT'S GUIDE® TO

Microsoft® FrontPage® 2000

by Elisabeth Parker

QUE®

201 W. 103rd Street, Indianapolis, IN 46290

The Complete Idiot's Guide to Microsoft® FrontPage® 2000

International Standard Book Number: 0-7897-1806-5

Library of Congress Catalog Card Number: 98-88241

Printed in the United States of America

First Printing: May 1999

01 00 99 4 3 2 1

Trademarks

All terms mentioned in this book that are known to be trademarks or service marks have been appropriately capitalized. Que cannot attest to the accuracy of this information. Use of a term in this book should not be regarded as affecting the validity of any trademark or service mark.

Warning and Disclaimer

Every effort has been made to make this book as complete and as accurate as possible, but no warranty or fitness is implied. The information provided is on an "as is" basis. The author and the publisher shall have neither liability nor responsibility to any person or entity with respect to any loss or damages arising from the information contained in this book.

Executive Editor
Mark Taber

Acquisitions Editor
Randi Roger

Development Editor
Deidre Hayes

Managing Editor
Lisa Wilson

Project Editor
Rebecca Mounts

Copy Editor
Sean Medlock

Indexer
Larry Sweazy

Proofreader
Gene Redding

Technical Editors
Keith Giddeon
Pamela Rice Hahn

Interior Design
Nathan Clement

Cover Design
Mike Freeland

Layout Technicians
Brian Borders
Amy Parker

Editorial Assistant
Amy Patton

Contents at a Glance

Contents

Part 1: On Your Mark, Get Set, Go!

Part 3: You've Got the Look: Designing Pages Like the Pros 115

About the Author

Elisabeth Parker is the author of several computer books, including *The Microsoft Word Exam Cram* (Coriolis), *The Little Web Cam Book* and *The HotDog Pro Visual QuickStart Guide* (Peachpit Press), and *Home Page Improvement* (IDG Books). She lives in San Francisco with her husband and fellow computer book author, Richard Grace, and Puddy, the fat, lazy cat. For more information, or just for grins, visit her home page at `http://www.byteit.com/`.

Dedication

To my husband, Richard Grace.

Acknowledgments

Special thanks to:

- *Judd Winick, the artist behind the clever cartoons in this book.*
- *The Microsoft Beta team, who graciously dispensed betas and information.*
- *Randi Roger and Bob Correll, two of the editors for this book.*
- *Dave Fugate, my agent.*
- *My husband, Rich Grace, the computer hardware and networking guru of the household.*

Tell Us What You Think!

As the reader of this book, *you* are our most important critic and commentator. We value your opinion and want to know what we're doing right, what we could do better, what areas you'd like to see us publish in, and any other words of wisdom you're willing to pass our way.

You can fax, email, or write me directly to let me know what you did or didn't like about this book—as well as what we can do to make our books stronger.

Please note that I cannot help you with technical problems related to the topic of this book, and that due to the high volume of mail I receive, I might not be able to reply to every message.

When you write, please be sure to include this book's title and author as well as your name and phone or fax number. I will carefully review your comments and share them with the author and editors who worked on the book.

Fax: 317-581-4666

Email: office_que@mcp.com

Mail: John Pierce
Publisher
Que
201 West 103rd Street
Indianapolis, IN 46290 USA

Part 1

On Your Mark, Get Set, Go!

Congratulations! You'll soon be the proud owner of a Web site that makes your friends, family, and boss say, "Wow! How did you do that?" Whether you want to unleash your creative self, promote your business or favorite cause, or communicate better with your co-workers, FrontPage 2000 gives you everything you need.

Maybe you've shied away from building a Web site because it seems too darned technical. Or perhaps you're a Web whiz who's skeptical that such a user-friendly program can really offer the advanced features you want. Either way, you'll find that there's no limit to what you and FrontPage can do!

But first, you need to get up and running. Sure, FrontPage is user friendly and all that. But it still means doing something on a computer—and we all know what that means! The chapters in this section will acquaint you with FrontPage and guide you through building your first Web pages.

So what are you waiting for? Let's get started!

Chapter 1

Get Ready to Rock with FrontPage 2000

In This Chapter

- What are Web sites, servers, and URLs?
- The Internet vs. an intranet
- Introduction to FrontPage
- Five cool things you can do with FrontPage

Welcome to the Wild, Wild Web

You've done some Web surfing and now you want a Web site of your own. Or maybe you need to set one up at work. FrontPage makes it easy for you to build professional-looking Web sites right away. So let's talk about Hypertext Markup Language and coding... just kidding! With FrontPage, you can skip all that dreary technical stuff. But first, it helps to understand a little bit about how the Web works. (Just a *little* bit, I promise!)

Web Pages and Web Sites

Web pages are HTML documents. *HTML* stands for *Hypertext Markup Language*—a set of codes used to format Web pages so Web browsers can display them. When you create two or more Web pages and link them together, you've got a Web site. Do you have to learn HTML? Good heavens, no! FrontPage makes designing Web pages as easy and intuitive as creating word processing documents. It generates all the codes for you. Chapter 3, "Fooling Around with Web Pages," explains how Web pages work. If you're curious, you can even take a peek at the HTML tags behind the Web page.

One Web Page Coming Up! A Bit About Servers

Hey, You've Got a Web Server!

As you'll learn while reading this book, FrontPage is also a Web server program.

Web pages live on servers—superfast computers with huge amounts of disk space. Servers stay connected to the Internet 24 hours a day and do nothing but serve up data. *Data* is Ancient Geek for "everything and the kitchen sink," including Web pages, email messages, pictures, applications, and everything else that gets stored on computers. When you check your email messages or click a link in your Web browser, you request data from a server. And the server gives it to you. Well, most of the time. Servers run different programs to handle different types of files.

What the Heck's a URL, Anyway?

`http://www.thecompanyname.com/`. It seems like everyone and their dog has a URL these days, and pretty soon you'll have one too. Or perhaps you already do. *URL* stands for *uniform resource locator*. Just as your home has a street address, a Web page has an Internet address. When you enter a URL in your browser's location window or click a link, the URL tells the browser where to go.

Let's take a typical URL, such as `http://www.thecompanyname.com/Website/webpage.htm`. The different parts of the address stand for the following:

- `http//` This stands for *Hypertext Transfer Protocol*, a set of standards that tells computers how to handle Web pages. When you type a URL or follow a link beginning with `http://`, it tells the `thecompanyname.com` server to display a Web page.

- `www` Indicates a World Wide Web server. There are many different types of servers, including news, file transfer protocol (FTP), and email servers. Nowadays, most browsers don't make you type the `http://www` part of a URL. You can just type `thecompanyname.com` and your browser assumes you want to see a Web page.
- `thecompanyname.com/` This is the *server domain*, or the name of the server hosting the Web site. There are many types of domains, including `.com` for commercial businesses, `.edu` for educational institutions, `.org` for non-profit organizations, `.net` for ISPs, and `.gov` for government agencies.
- `Website/webpage.htm` Servers store folders and documents just like regular computers. `Website` is the name of a folder, and `webpage.htm` is the name of an HTML document inside the folder. By the way, people who've been using computers for a long time often say "directory" instead of "folder," but both words mean the same thing.

So, are you ready to run your own server? Me neither. That's what Internet service providers (ISPs) and Web hosting companies are for. When you get Web space on a server, you can register and pay for a domain name (`yourcompanyname.com`) without the hassle of actually running a server. For more about ISPs and Web hosts, see the "Getting Connected" section later in this chapter.

You Can Have a Domain Name Too!

How does `www.yourcompanyname.com` sound? Your ISP or Web hosting company can tell you how to get your own domain name. Most people and companies don't *really* have their own servers, so these types of domain names are called *virtual domains*. Most ISP and Web hosting companies can help you register and set up your domain. Registering a domain costs $35.00 per year, and you pay for your first two years in advance. You can register and pay for a domain name yourself from Internic's Web site at `http://rs.internic.net/`. Internic is the main agency that handles domain names and servers on the Internet. Or, for an extra charge, you can have your provider register your domain name for you.

What's an Intranet?

So far, we've only talked about servers on the Internet. But companies, schools, and other organizations have servers too. Unlike Internet servers, these servers run on *closed networks*, which means only people in the organization can get information from them. *Intranets* are internal networks that work like the Internet and the World Wide Web. You can view Web pages with daily announcements, download files, send messages to coworkers, and participate in discussion groups as easily as you do on the Internet—and with the same applications. With FrontPage, you can set up your own office intranet.

Getting Connected

Connecting to the Internet is easier than ever these days. Plug in a 28.8Kbps (kilobits per second) or faster modem to your computer, and let your ISP do the rest. In many cases, your Internet account will include space on the server for your Web site.

By the way, ISPs and Web hosting companies are *not* the same thing. Web hosting companies *only* host Web sites; they don't provide dial-up access. Instead, they offer a wider range of server features, including FrontPage server extensions and secure server access so you can safely process credit card orders online. Only a few companies manage to provide reliable Internet access *and* good Web hosting. You'll need both services to create and publish your own Web site.

Finding a FrontPage-Friendly Web Host

When you're finding a home for your home page, make sure your ISP or Web hosting company offers *FrontPage server extensions*. (When companies support FrontPage, their main page usually mentions it.) While FrontPage 2000 no longer requires that FrontPage Server Extensions be in place for you to publish your site, the extensions do offer you more versatility. What are FrontPage server extensions? FrontPage lets you do lots of neat stuff that used to require programming—like creating a Web site search form. Sure, you can use FrontPage to create pages destined for a non-FrontPage server, but you'll miss out on a lot of the cool stuff. For a list of FrontPage-friendly Web hosts, visit Microsoft's list at `http://microsoft.saltmine.com/frontpage/wpp/list/`.

Start It Up! Getting Acquainted with FrontPage 2000

Now let's fire up FrontPage and take it for a spin. To launch it, click the Start button, select Programs from the Start menu, and select Microsoft FrontPage from the Programs menu. When FrontPage launches, it displays a blank Web page. When you work on a Web page, FrontPage displays the page as it would appear in a Web browser, as shown in the following figure. FrontPage provides toolbar buttons, Web site management tools, and a host of other nifty features to help you build and maintain your Web site.

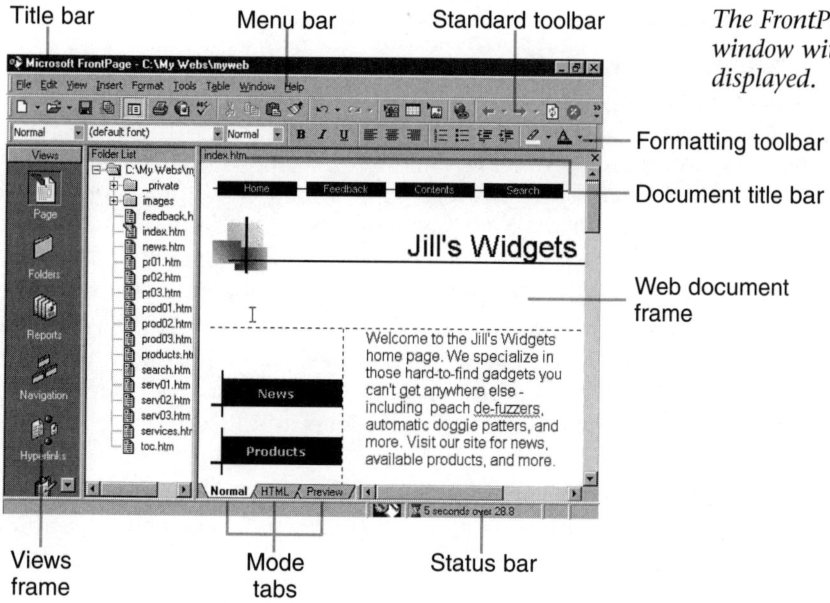

The FrontPage application window with a page displayed.

A Whole New Look

If you upgraded from a previous version of FrontPage, check out FrontPage 2000's new facelift. It sports new Microsoft Office toolbars and a more intuitive look and feel.

Using Page Views to Get Information About Your Web Site

All Web editing programs help you create Web pages, but only FrontPage makes it so easy to manage and keep track of everything. Even if you only have a few Web pages and graphics at first, you'll be amazed at how quickly your Web site grows! The Views frame on the left side of the application window contains a list of icons that you can click to get information about your Web site.

The FrontPage Views frame offers the following options:

- *Page* Click the Page icon when you want to design and edit Web pages. FrontPage automatically appears in the Page view when you launch the program. Technogeeks call these types of automatic program settings *defaults*. The Page view displays three frames. The first frame contains the Views list, the second contains the Folder List so you can see other files and folders on your Web site, and the third displays the Web page that you're working on. You can open folders and files directly from the Folder List by double-clicking them. Chapter 3 introduces you to working with Web pages in the Page view.
- *Folders* For a more detailed list of your folders and files, click the Folder icon. When you switch to the Folder view, you can select a folder from the folder list by clicking on it. When you do, the list of files within that folder appears in the third frame. For more about working with folders and files, see Chapter 24, "You and Your Web Files."
- *Reports* Wonder how many files you have on your Web site? Click the Reports icon to have FrontPage generate a detailed summary. You can check for broken links, pages that may take too long to download, older files that you may have forgotten about, and more. Chapter 25, "Testing, Testing, One, Two, Three: Checking Your Web Site," tells you more about generating reports and analyzing your Web site.
- *Navigation* To display a graphical view of how your Web site is organized, click the Navigation icon. The Navigation view looks a lot like a flow chart and organizes your pages hierarchically. For more information about organizing your Web site and using the Navigation view, see Chapter 7, "Think Links: Adding Links to Your Pages."
- *Hyperlinks* Visitors find their way around Web sites by clicking on links. To see how you've organized the links for your Web site and which links go where, click the Hyperlinks icon on the Views list. For more about links, see Chapter 7.
- *Tasks* Have trouble remembering things and staying organized? Join the club! FrontPage gives you a task list so you can remind yourself of all the things you need to tweak and finish. To display the task list, click the Tasks icon on the Views list. Chapter 28, "Keeping Track of It All with the Task List," tells you more about how to use the Tasks feature.

Don't worry if you don't fully understand all of the Views options yet. This section simply tells you how to display them. You'll learn more later in the book.

Fiddling with Frames in the Application Window

FrontPage arranges the application window in frames so you can work quickly without having to hunt and peck for different features. You can adjust the frame sizes by clicking on a frame border (which turns the cursor into a double I-beam with right and left arrows) and dragging your mouse to the right or left. The number of frames and what they contain depends on which Views option you select, as explained in the previous section.

Where's the FrontPage Explorer?

If you've used previous versions of FrontPage, remember that you had to use two application windows to create your pages: the FrontPage Explorer and the FrontPage Editor. In FrontPage 2000, Microsoft has combined these two applications. Now you can do all of your work in one application window.

Tooling Around with Toolbars and Menus

Psst! Look back at the previous figure, do you recognize the toolbars? If you use Microsoft Word, you'll probably recognize your old friends, the Standard toolbar and the Formatting toolbar. Even if you're new to the world of Uncle Bill (Gates), you'll catch on quickly. FrontPage also has a menu bar located below the title bar at the top of the application window. You can select features and commands from the menu bar (and sometimes you have to), but most of the time it's easier to use the toolbars.

FrontPage also has other toolbars up its sleeve, but it doesn't want to clutter your workspace with them. Instead, they appear only when you need them. For example, when you insert an image, the Picture toolbar appears. Look at some of the toolbars that FrontPage offers:

- *Standard* Contains buttons for basic tasks like opening and saving files, checking spelling, and creating tables and links. The Standard toolbar automatically appears beneath the menu bar when you launch FrontPage.
- *Formatting* Enables you to select fonts, text styles, colors, and other text-formatting options by selecting text and clicking the buttons. The Formatting toolbar automatically appears beneath the Standard toolbar when you launch FrontPage.

- *DHTML Effects* *DHTML* stands for *Dynamic HTML*. It enables version 4.0 and higher browsers to display animated graphics and text effects. The DHTML toolbar appears only when you create and edit DHTML page components, as explained in Chapter 20, "Gee-Whiz Pages with Animated Special Effects."
- *Navigation* Appears and provides options when you display your Web site in the Navigation view, as explained in Chapter 7.
- *Pictures* Appears when you insert or edit images so you can work with pictures, as explained in Chapters 8, "The Picture-Perfect Web Page: Placing and Tweaking Images," and 9, "Spiffing Up Pictures."
- *Positioning* Appears when you position and layer text and graphics, as explained in Chapter 9.
- *Reporting* Appears and provides options when you choose Reports from the Views list, as explained in Chapter 25.
- *Style* Appears and provides options to modify the style for selected HTML tags, as explained in Chapter 15.
- *Tables* Appears when you create or edit tables, as explained in Chapter 12, "Table It! Arranging Text and Images with Tables."

You can also display toolbars by right-clicking the selection bar (raised vertical line) on the right edge of the menu bar, Standard toolbar, or Formatting toolbar, selecting a toolbar from the shortcut menu, and releasing the mouse button. To remove a toolbar, right-click a selection bar, select the toolbar from the shortcut menu (it should have a check mark next to it), and release the mouse button.

Keeping Tabs on Pages: Normal, HTML, and Preview

Most people like building Web pages in Normal mode so they can view the page as it would appear in a browser and use toolbar buttons and dialog boxes. And believe it or not, some people prefer to enter all the HTML tags themselves. With FrontPage, you can work whichever way you prefer.

When you create and edit Web pages in the Page view, you can click the tabs below the Web page display to view a page in three different ways:

- *Normal* For placing and arranging text, images, and other page elements the WYSIWYG way. WYSIWYG, pronounced "whizzy-wig," stands for What You See Is What You Get. The Normal view displays pages mostly as they would appear in the browser, but with some modifications that make it easier for you to work and tell page elements apart. To work in Normal mode, leave the Normal tab selected.
- *HTML* Reveals the techie source code behind the pretty pages. If you want to learn HTML or tweak your HTML source code by hand, Chapter 3 tells you more about working with Web pages. To work in HTML mode, click the HTML tab.
- *Preview* Displays your page exactly as it would appear in a Web browser like Internet Explorer. You cannot edit your page while in Preview mode. To preview your page, click the Preview tab.

Status Conscious: The Status and Title Bars

Take a peek at FrontPage's title bars and the status bar. Both give you information about the Web page you're currently working on (the *current page*). The main title bar, which appears at the top of the application window, displays the name of the current FrontPage Web and the folder. (You'll learn more about FrontPage Webs in Chapter 2, "Instant Web-Site-O-Matic: Spinning FrontPage Webs.") In addition, a smaller, gray title bar appears above your Web document and displays the filename (such as `index.htm`). You can also glance at the status bar in the lower-right corner of the application window to see how long the current page takes to download when people visit from the Web.

Want to See What FrontPage Is Doing?

If you want to see which HTML coding tags FrontPage inserts in your pages without actually having to view the source code, choose Reveal Tags from the View menu with the Normal tab selected.

Five Cool Things You Can Do Only with FrontPage

Wheeeeeee! FrontPage lets non-techies do the coolest things. Unless you want to hire a programmer, there are quite a few things that normal people like us can do *only* with FrontPage... and a FrontPage-friendly Web host.

Help!

Help is just a mouse-click away. Whenever you forget something or run across something you're not familiar with, click the Help button on the Standard toolbar or choose Help from the menu.

- *Start a discussion group* Fire up the Discussion Web Wizard and set up your own Web bulletin board. Visitors can post messages and respond to other people's messages. Whether you want to provide customer support or invite people to come and chat about gardening, discussion groups are useful and fun. For more on setting up discussion groups, read Chapter 23, "Switchboard Central: Setting Up a Discussion Web."
- *Make your Web site searchable* Search engines and Internet directories like Excite (`http://www.excite.com/`) and Yahoo! (`http://www.yahoo.com/`) are cool. Wouldn't it be great if your visitors could find information on your Web site that easily? Thanks to the FrontPage Search Form Web Bot, you can set up a search engine for your own Web site. For more about FrontPage components and building your own search form, check out Chapter 19, "A Grab Bag of Helpful Doodads: FrontPage Components."

- *Publish and share files at work* If you and your co-workers use Microsoft Office, you're in luck. FrontPage is now part of Office 2000. With it, you can easily communicate, collaborate, and share documents, spreadsheets, databases, and presentations. Hey... when it's this easy to work online, why not telecommute from home? Chapter 18, "A Match Made in Redmond: FrontPage and Microsoft Office 2000," tells you more about using FrontPage with Microsoft Office.
- *Impress friends and others with groovy special effects* Try some hover buttons that change color when a visitor passes his mouse pointer over it. Or some cool animated DHTML text and graphics that assemble themselves into a spiffy layout when your page loads. Some Web programs let you do similar things, but FrontPage makes it so-o-o-o-o easy. Your friends and coworkers will scratch their heads and say, "Wow! How did you *do* that?" Shhhh! Don't tell them about Chapter 20.
- *Give your Web site an instant face-lift* Thanks to FrontPage themes, you can change the look and feel of your entire Web site in seconds. Chapter 4, "Poof! You're a Designer with FrontPage Web Themes," talks about FrontPage's Web themes in greater detail.

And to think—this is just the tip of the iceberg. Want to set up GIF animations, 3D buttons, or a hit counter? FrontPage helps you do these things and more.

The Least You Need to Know

- FrontPage helps you create and manage your Web site quickly by putting some of the frequently used menu choices on the toolbars. They're just one click away.
- FrontPage gives you several ways to view and manage your Web site: the Page view (to create and edit pages), the Folders view (to organize your files), the Reports view (to analyze your files), the Navigation view (to help link your pages together), the Hyperlinks view (to see how your files are related to each other), and the Tasks view (to keep you organized).
- In the Page view, FrontPage lets you look at your Web page in three different modes. The Normal mode lets you create your page while seeing it the way it would appear on the Internet. The HTML mode lets you see the HTML source code used to create your page. The Preview mode lets you try out the advanced features you've added to your page.

Chapter 2

Instant Web-Site-O-Matic: Spinning FrontPage Webs

In This Chapter

- What are FrontPage Webs?
- Creating Web sites with wizards and templates
- Starting a Web site from scratch
- Importing an existing Web site from the Web or from your computer
- Five cool ideas for using FrontPage2000

Rome wasn't built in a day, but your Web site can be. Sure, you might not want to rush things, but it's nice to know that you can build a functioning, slick-looking Web site in record time if you need to. Whether you're a complete novice or already have a Web site set up, FrontPage gives you all the tools you need. You can even use the FrontPage wizards to help you set up instant Web sites.

What Are FrontPage Webs?

FrontPage Webs are folders that contain Web pages, images, and other files. Ho hum, that sounds just like any ol' Web site. So what makes a FrontPage Web different from all other Webs? FrontPage works as a Web server that keeps track of all your files and helps you add cool and useful features without any programming. But FrontPage can only do these things with Web sites that are set up as FrontPage Webs.

A Web site in FrontPage is called a FrontPage Web. If you already have a Web site, you can turn it into a FrontPage Web by importing it. If, like most people, you plan to host your site on someone else's server, you also need a Web hosting company that supports FrontPage so its Web server can do all the things that your FrontPage Web server does.

Help! What Comes First?

Don't know where to begin with your Web site? Not to worry, FrontPage can help you build the basic framework. Whether you want to put your business online, publish a personal page so Grandma can download photos of the kids, or pursue a pet project, the wizards and templates provided can help you get started. A Web wizard takes you through a series of dialog boxes that ask questions about what you want on your Web site, and then it builds a set of basic Web pages for you. A template creates a FrontPage Web without asking you any questions. Whichever way you create your Web, all you have to do is open the pages and insert your own text and pictures.

Picking the Right FrontPage Web

FrontPage is packaged with the following types of Webs:

- *One Page Web* FrontPage creates a Web with one blank Web page to get you started.
- *Corporate Presence Web* A wizard helps you create a typical company or small business Web site, with pages for products, news, and press releases, and for gathering feedback and searching the Web site for information.
- *Customer Support Web* FrontPage creates a Web site with a feedback form, discussion group, search form, product information, and other pages and features that help businesses support their customers online.
- *Discussion Web* A wizard helps you create a Web site especially for hosting an ongoing discussion, with a form for submitting messages, an automatically updated table of contents with titles and links to each message, and a searchable archive of older messages. For more about setting up a discussion Web, see Chapter 23, "Switchboard Central: Setting Up a Discussion Web."
- *Empty Web* FrontPage creates a Web site with no documents or images, just the framework.
- *Imported Web* A wizard takes you through the steps of importing an existing Web site from your computer, network, or a server. The "But I Already Have a Web Site! Importing Web Sites into FrontPage" section of this chapter tells you how.

- *Personal Web* FrontPage helps you create a typical personal Web site with pages for hobbies or interests, photographs, and favorite links.
- *Project Web* FrontPage creates a Web site that helps people work together as a team and keep track of who does what. Features include a schedule page, search form, automatically updating table of contents, discussion Web, and status page.

Creating FrontPage Webs

To create a FrontPage Web:

1. Select New from the File menu, and then select Web.
2. When the New dialog box appears with the Web Sites tab selected, as shown in the following figure, select the type of Web site you want to create. A description of that Web site type appears in the Description area.

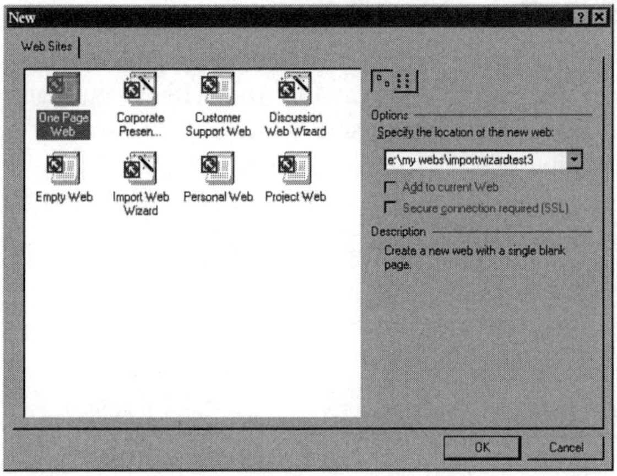

Pick a Web, any Web! The New dialog box with different types of Webs to select from.

3. Enter the *directory path* to where you want the new Web to be located in the Specify the location of the new Web box. In most cases, you can enter `C:\My Webs\Name-of-Your-Web`.
4. Click the OK button.
5. Fill in the information for each dialog box and move forward by clicking the Next button.
6. When you finish filling out your information, a dialog box appears with the Choose Web Theme button displayed. Skip themes for now (we'll get to them in Chapter 4, "Poof! You're a Designer with FrontPage Web Themes") and click the Finish button.
7. A dialog box appears and asks if you want the wizard to display the task list when you finish. Leave the check box selected and click OK.

What's a Directory Path?

A *directory path* is kind of like a URL—it points to the location of a file or folder in relation to your hard drive. By default, FrontPage creates Webs in the My Webs folder on your main drive (usually the C drive). If you're hooked up to a network, ask your administrator which drive and folder you should use.

Starting Your Web from Scratch

"Wizard? I don't need no stinkin' wizard!" If that's your attitude, join the club. Some people *enjoy* designing their own Web sites, gosh darn it, and with FrontPage, you can do that too. To create your Web site from scratch, select New from the File menu and then select Web. When the New dialog box appears, pick the One Page Web template. This creates a blank page that you can start off with. If you have pictures and other files that you plan on using, you need to import them into your new Web, as explained in Chapter 24, "You and Your Web Files."

But I Already Have a Web Site! Importing Web Sites into FrontPage

If you already have a Web site set up, you still need to import it into a FrontPage Web. This enables you to use FrontPage components and take advantage of FrontPage's Web site management features. Whether you store your Web site on an Internet Web server, on your computer, or on a network, the handy-dandy Import Web Wizard makes importing your Web site a breeze.

Don't Worry, Your Source Code's Safe!

If you've avoided previous versions of FrontPage because you've heard it messes around with the source code, not to worry. FrontPage 2000 keeps the source code for your existing pages intact.

Getting Files from Your Web Site

You've already got a site up and running on the Web, but now you'd like to use FrontPage. No problem. Just connect to the Internet and then fire up the Import Web Wizard.

To import your Web site from the Internet:

1. Connect to the Internet. Then, from within FrontPage, select New from the File menu and select Web.
2. When the New dialog box appears with the Web Sites tab selected, click on Import Web Wizard. You could also select Import from the File menu to automatically open the Import Web Wizard.
3. Enter the directory path to where you want the new Web to be located in the Specify the location of the new Web box. In most cases, you can enter `C:\My Webs\Name-of-Your-Web`.
4. Click the OK button.
5. The Import Web Wizard - Choose Source dialog box appears and asks you where your Web site is located. Click the From a World Wide Web site radio button and enter your URL in the Location window.
6. Click the Next button to display the Import Web Wizard - Choose Download Amount dialog box. Deselect all of the check boxes. Otherwise, FrontPage may only download part of your Web site. Take a look at the Technical Note below if you're trying to import a Web that you didn't create.
7. Click the Next button to display the Import Web Wizard - Finish dialog box, and then click the Finish button to begin downloading your Web site.

Import a Web, Any Web!

You can import *any* Web from the Internet, not just one that you've created. That comes in handy if you need to make changes to someone else's pages.

When your Web site finishes downloading, the Import Web Wizard returns you to the FrontPage application window and opens your newly imported Web. When you finish revamping your Web site, you can publish it to your server again, as explained in Chapter 26, "Don't Just Let It Sit There! Publishing Your Web Site."

Why Limit Download Amounts?

Well, in most cases, you shouldn't. But the amount of time it takes to import a Web site will depend on your connection speed and the number of files you have. If you have a large Web site with hundreds of files buried in folders seven levels deep, you might not agree with me. Especially if you don't need to update or change certain files very often.

Clicking the Limit to this page plus check box and picking a number from the Levels below scrolling list limits the number of folder levels the wizard downloads. For example, if you enter the number 3 and your Web site has a folder buried four levels deep, the Import Wizard won't download it.

Clicking the Limit to check box and entering a number in the KB box prevents the wizard from downloading more than 500KB worth of files.

Clicking Limit to text and image files tells the wizard to download only Web pages and images. If you only need to work with your Web files, this can save you some download time and disk space.

Getting Files from Your Computer or Network

To import a Web site from your computer or a computer on a network:

1. Select New from the File menu and then select Web.
2. When the New dialog box appears with the Web Sites tab selected, click Import Web Wizard.
3. Enter the directory path to where you want the new Web to be located in the Specify the location of the new Web box. In most cases, you can enter `C:\My Webs\Name-of-Your-Web`.
4. Click the OK button.
5. The Import Web Wizard - Choose Source dialog box appears and asks you where your Web site is located. Click the From a source directory of files on a local computer or network button.

6. Click the Browse button to display the Browse for Folder dialog box (shown in the following figure), which displays all of the computers and storage devices (drives) connected to your computer so you can access folders on your Zip disk, CD-ROM, or other computers on your network. Locate and select your Web folder, and click OK to return to the Import Web Wizard - Choose Source dialog box.

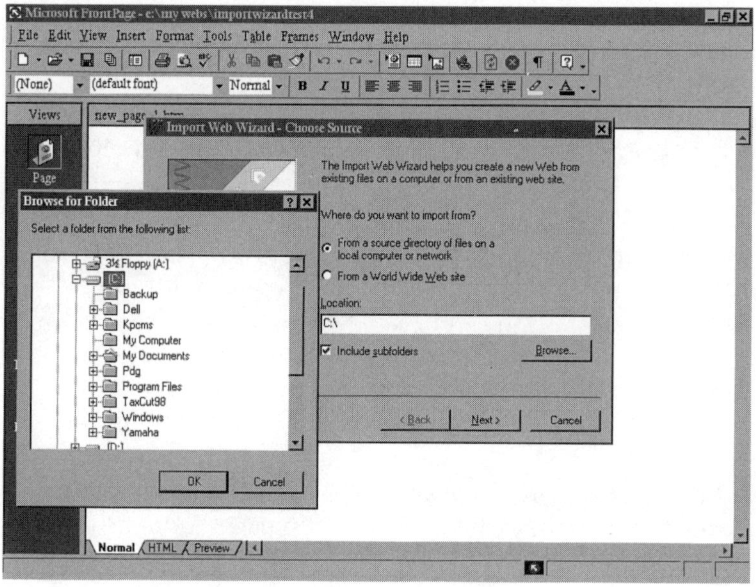

The Browse for Folder dialog box.

7. Click the Include subfolders check box to tell the Import Web Wizard to include all of the folders inside your Web site folder.
8. Click the Next button to display the Import Web Wizard - Edit File List dialog box. Here you can scroll down the list of files and decide whether to include all of them in your new Web. To leave a file out of your Web, select a file and click the Exclude button. To review your list after excluding files, click the Refresh button.
9. When you finish reviewing your list, click the Next button to display the Import Web Wizard - Finish dialog box. Then click the Finish button to import your files.

When the Import Web Wizard finishes importing your Web site to FrontPage, it returns you to the FrontPage application window and opens your Web for you. When you finish revamping your Web site, you can publish it to your server again, as explained in Chapter 26.

Some FrontPage Web Terminology

FrontPage wizards and templates are designed to help you, but they don't always speak in plain English. Here are some terms you might come across while creating your FrontPage Web:

- *Main pages* FrontPage creates a page for each category that you select, such as Contents, Products, What's New, and Feedback. Because each page represents a main section of your Web site, FrontPage refers to them as *main pages*. If you want to change the page titles and the banners and navigation buttons that go with them, see Chapter 4.
- *Search form* Allows visitors to search your Web site for files by keyword. You can find out more about Search forms in Chapter 19, "A Grab Bag of Helpful Doodads: FrontPage Components."
- *Feedback form* A Web form that gathers information from visitors and sends the information to you in an email message. Chapter 13, "Form and Function: Building Online Forms," shows you how you can build your own forms.
- *Tab-delimited vs. Web page format* You can have form results sent to you as an attached tab-delimited text file so you can import them into a database, or in HTML format so you can read them straight from the email message. Learn more about databases in Chapter 22, "If You've Got it, Flaunt it: Putting Your Access Databases on the Web."
- *Discussion forum* Also referred to as a *Web bulletin board*, a discussion forum allows visitors to leave messages for each other on a Web page. For more on setting up a discussion forum, see Chapter 23.

Five Cool Ideas for Building Web Sites with Web Wizards

You can be creative, even if you use the Web wizards. Don't let the descriptions stop you. The wizards help you get started, but you can turn your Web site into anything you want. Chapter 4 tells you how to create your own look by changing and customizing themes, and Chapter 7, "Think Links: Adding Links to Your Pages," describes how to change the navigation bars.

FrontPage wizards and templates are ideal for creating the following types of sites:

- *Start an online club* Whether you're interested in books, gardening, fine wines, antiques, or Beanie Babies, you can find some like-minded people and start a club. The Discussion Web Wizard helps you build an online community where people can drop in and have an ongoing conversation.

- *Promote your home business or creative projects* The Corporate Presence Wizard? Don't let the stuffy-sounding name scare you off. With a few changes, you can use the Corporate Presence Wizard to promote your home business, art gallery, or band.
- *Launch an online zine* If you've always wanted to publish your own magazine, now's your chance. With the Project Web, you can even collaborate with other writers and keep track of who does what.
- *Keep family and friends up to date* The Personal Web looks pretty blah at first, but it's a good fixer-upper. Use it to display favorite family photos and keep in touch with friends and relatives who live far away.
- *Build Super-Duper Web combos* Put as many types of Webs in your site as you want. With FrontPage, the sky's the limit. After starting out with a basic Web, you can add folders with nested sub-Webs, as explained in Chapter 27, "You're the Boss! Becoming a Web Site Administrator."

The Least You Need to Know

- *FrontPage Webs* In FrontPage, Web sites are called Webs. A Web is a collection of Web pages, images, and other files.
- *Creating FrontPage Webs* FrontPage comes with several Web wizards and templates to help you get your Web set up. To spin a new Web, display the New dialog box, choose the type of Web you'd like to create, choose a location for it, and click the OK button.
- *Getting started with the wizards and templates* FrontPage has wizards and templates that help you create common types of Web sites, such as for business or personal use. When you choose the Corporate Presence, Customer Support, Discussion, Personal, or Project Web options from the New dialog box and click OK, a wizard takes you through a series of easy steps.
- *Creating your Web site* If you create a One Page Web or an Empty Web, you'll need to start your Web site from scratch. Chapter 3, "Fooling Around with Web Pages," gets you started with creating new Web pages.
- *Importing an existing Web site as a FrontPage Web* If you've got an existing Web site that you'd like to work on, the Import Web Wizard helps you get your files from a folder on your computer, a network, or a remote server. When the wizard finishes, it opens the imported Web for you.

Chapter 3

Fooling Around with Web Pages

In This Chapter

- Taking a look at Web page ingredients and HTML source code
- Creating new Web pages
- Opening, creating, saving, printing, and closing Web pages
- Giving your Web page a title
- Jazzing up Web pages with color schemes, images, and watermarks
- Five cool color schemes you can try

So what are you waiting for? Take FrontPage for a spin. This chapter tells you a bit about Web pages, what they're made of, and how they work. You can then cut to the chase and learn about how to work with Web documents and create basic Web pages. If you know how to use a word processing program, like Microsoft Word, you'll get the hang of things pretty quickly.

What Web Pages Are Made Of

Frogs and snails and puppy dog tails… whoops, wrong book. Web pages are made of text, links, pictures, and just about everything else. FrontPage also makes it easy for you to add multimedia (Chapter 17, "Strut Your Stuff: Sound, Video, and More"), animation (Chapter 20, "Gee-Whiz Pages with Animated Special Effects"), hit counters (Chapter 19, "A Grab Bag of Helpful Doodads: FrontPage Components"), and other cool stuff to your Web pages. But let's stick to the basics for now.

A Web page almost always contains the following elements:

- *Title* When you view a Web page in a browser, the page title appears on the Web browser's title bar. The "What's in a Name? Changing Your Page Title" section of this chapter explains how this works.
- *A Color Scheme* You can display a *patterned background* on your page (like the left side of the page shown in the following figure) or a solid-colored background, and you can choose text and link colors, as explained in the "Color My Web Page: Changing Background, Text, and Link Colors" section of this chapter.
- *Pictures* FrontPage makes it easy to add pictures to your Web pages. It even converts your existing images to the `.GIF` and `.JPEG` formats used on the Web, and comes with a clip art collection. For more about pictures, read Chapters 8, "The Picture-Perfect Web Page: Placing and Tweaking Images," and 9, "Spiffing Up Pictures."
- *Navigation bar* Navigation bars should appear consistently on pages throughout a Web site so that visitors can find their way around. After all, you wouldn't want to leave them stranded, would you? A navigation bar can consist of a row of graphical buttons (like the ones shown in the following figure), an image map, or text, with links to other pages on the Web site. Navigation bars are explained further in Chapter 7, "Think Links: Adding Links to Your Pages."
- *Text* In spite of all the hype about graphics and multimedia, most Web pages contain at least a few lines of text. As you'll learn in Chapter 5, "Entering Text and Fiddling with Fonts," entering text on a Web page works pretty much the same way as with your other applications.
- *Links* Think links! Links are what makes the Web cool and different from everything else. Just click a word or picture that looks like it's meant to be clicked on. Your browser displays another page, launches a multimedia file, runs a program, or starts downloading a file. Chapter 7 tells you how to link your words and graphics.

You don't need a fancy Web page with lots of bells and whistles to attract visitors and get your message across (although FrontPage has everything you need to add all the frills you want). But you do need well-organized information that visitors can read without squinting, links and navigation bars, and a picture or two to liven things up.

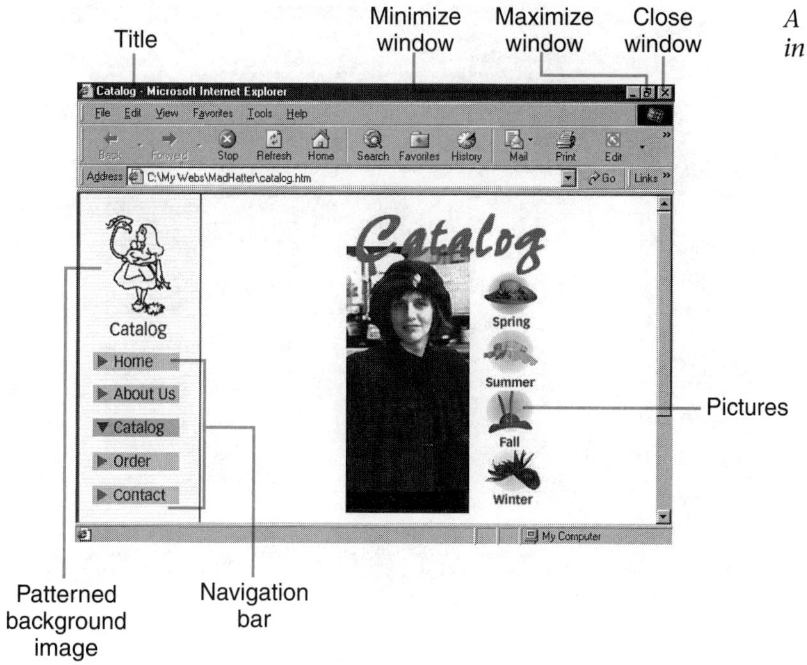

A basic Web page displayed in Internet Explorer.

Starting a New Web Page

And now, the part you've been waiting for: starting a new Web page from scratch. FrontPage even comes with some cool prefab templates with popular types of page layouts that you can use to get started. The pages come with dummy text and sample images, which you can replace. If you want to create a blank, unformatted page, select the Normal template. The New dialog box also helps you create Web sites with frames and style sheets. These topics are covered in Chapters 11, "Get Framed! Building a Web Site with Frames," and 15, "Now You're Stylin'! Using Style Sheets."

To create a new Web page:

1. Select New from the File menu and then select Page from the cascading list; the New dialog box, displaying the page templates, appears. (You can use the Ctrl+N key combination, but that just opens a new blank page.)
2. With the General tab selected, select a template option. A preview of the template's layout appears in the Preview box, as shown in the following figure.
3. Click the OK button.

When your new Web page is displayed, you can add your own text and images and format them however you want.

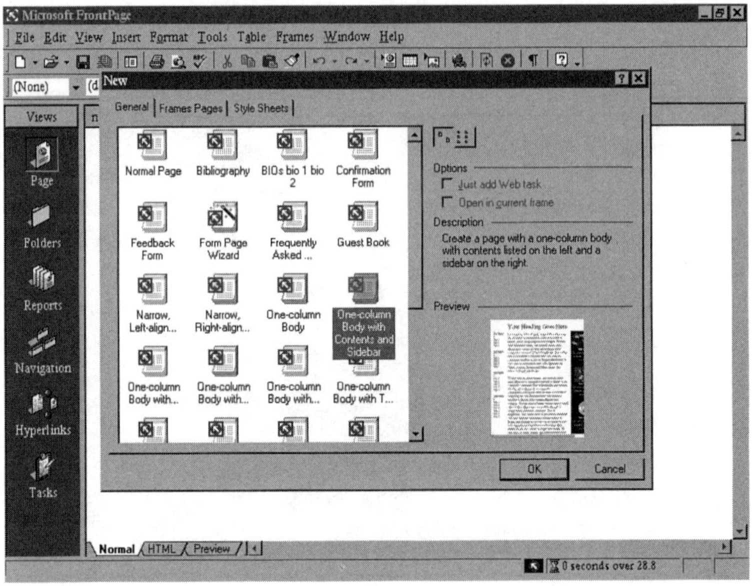

The New dialog box with a template selected and a preview displayed.

Try the New Toolbar Button

If you wind up using themes on your Web site, as discussed in Chapter 4, "Poof! You're a Designer with FrontPage Web Themes," you can create a new Web page by clicking the New toolbar button. FrontPage automatically applies the theme. If your Web site doesn't have a theme, clicking the New toolbar button creates a blank, unformatted Web page, what is referred to as a Normal Page in the New dialog box.

Saving a New Web Page

"Save your work," computer teachers always say. And this goes for Web pages too. Creating and saving a new Web page works a little differently than creating and saving a plain old file. In addition to naming your document, you can also give your page a *title*. If you don't want to bother with that now, you can go back and change your page's title at any time, as explained in the "What's in a Name? Changing Your Page Title" section later in this chapter.

To save a new Web page:

1. Click the Save button on the standard toolbar, or use the Ctrl+S key combination, to display the Save As dialog box. This dialog box only appears when you're saving a new Web page or when you select Save As from the File menu.
2. Enter a filename in the File Name box and select Web Pages from the Save as type pull-down list. You don't need to enter a filename extension (like `.htm` or `.html`) because FrontPage does it for you.

Play the Name Game!

Web folders and document names should never have any spaces in them, but you can use dashes (-) or underscores (_) instead, as in `About-Us.htm`. Also, if you decide not to use a Web wizard, remember that you absolutely *must* name your main page `index.htm`, `index.html`, `default.htm`, or `default.html`. Those document names designate a document as the main page (only one page should have a main page name). It's also better to keep your file and folder names short so you can see your documents more easily on the Folder list.

3. To create a title for your Web page, click the Change button to display the Set Page Title dialog box.
4. Enter a title for your page in the Page Title box and click the OK button to return to the Save As dialog box. (If you aren't sure what you want to name your page, you can skip steps 3 and 4 and create a page title later.)
5. Click the Save button.

Saving an Existing Web Page

Saving existing Web pages is a lot easier because all you have to do is select Save from the File menu, Ctrl+S, or click the Save button on the standard toolbar. You can also save an existing Web page with a different filename by selecting Save As from the File menu and following steps 2-5 in the preceding numbered list.

Why Does FrontPage Open a New Application Window When I Save My File?

Because you saved your file to a different folder on your computer or network instead of the current folder. Chapter 2, "Instant Web-Site-O-Matic: Spinning FrontPage Webs," tells you how to work with FrontPage Webs.

Printing Out a Page

Printing a Web page? Whatever happened to the "paperless office"? Well, sometimes it's nice to see your work on paper. You can print files in FrontPage the same way you print files in most Windows applications. Click the Print button on the Standard toolbar or select Print from the File menu. When the Print dialog box appears, choose your options and click OK. FrontPage even adjusts the printer settings so your layout fits on the printed page.

Previewing a Web Page Printout

Don't like taking chances? Feel free to preview your Web page before printing it out by selecting Print Preview from the File menu. The Print Preview window enables you to move from page to page (if your Web document takes more than one page to print completely) by clicking the Next Page and Previous page buttons, and you can print the file by clicking the Print button. You can also look at two pages at a time by clicking the Two Page button, take a closer look by clicking the Zoom In button, and zoom out again by clicking the Zoom Out button. To exit the Print Preview window and return to your Web page, press the Esc key or click on the Close button.

Closing a Web Page

Web pages are fun, but everyone has to close their documents sometime. To close a Web page, select Close from the File menu or click the document's Close box for the Web page window frame. You can also use the Ctrl+F4 key combination to close a Web page.

Opening a File in FrontPage

FrontPage wouldn't be very useful if it didn't let you open files, would it? In addition to Web pages, FrontPage lets you open and work with Microsoft Office files too. Chapter 18, "A Match Made in Redmond: FrontPage and Microsoft Office 2000," tells you more about FrontPage and Word documents, Excel tables and charts, PowerPoint presentations, and Access databases.

Watch It!

When closing a file, don't click the X to the right of the application title bar or you'll exit FrontPage by mistake.

To open a file:

1. Click the Open button on the Standard toolbar, select Open from the File menu, or use the Ctrl+O key combination to display the Open File dialog box.
2. Select the type of file you want to open (such as Web pages) from the Files of Type list at the bottom of the Open File dialog box.
3. Browse for the folder your file is located in from the Look in box.
4. Select the file from the list and click the Open button.

If you aren't familiar with the file types listed on the Files of Type list, don't worry for now. You'll learn more about them throughout the book, especially in Chapter 18, which talks about Microsoft Office files.

A Peek Under the Hood: Viewing HTML Source Code

Psst! Wanna see some source code? Take a peek by opening a Web page in FrontPage and clicking the HTML tab. The following figure shows the source code behind the page shown in the previous figure. Seen enough? Click the Normal tab to return to the graphical page view. *HTML source code* consists of the text and markup tags that make up a Web. Because FrontPage generates all of the source code for you, you never have to look at a single HTML tag if you don't want to.

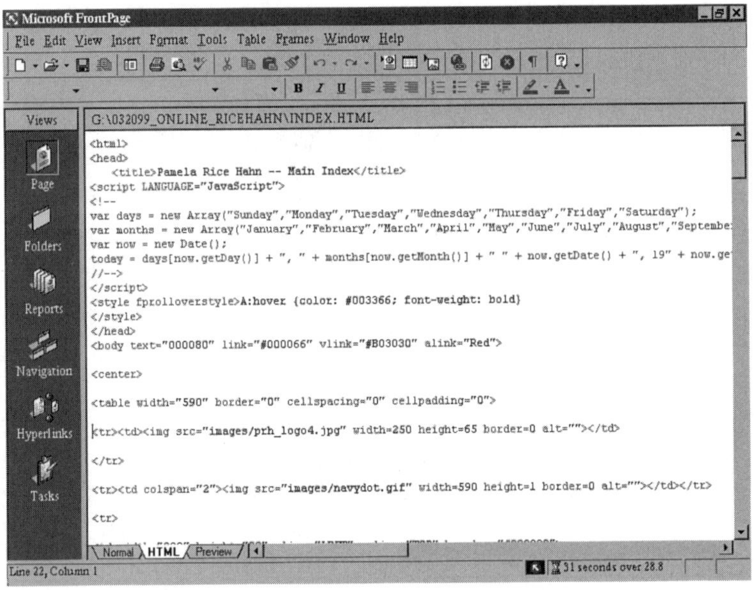

A Web page shown in FrontPage's HTML source code view.

Unmasked! Revealing Your HTML Tags

If you still want to read HTML but the HTML source code view looks like complete gobbledygook to you, try displaying HTML tag markers in the Normal page view so you can see them in context. To display HTML tags for your page elements, select Reveal Tags from the View menu. Although the tag markers (shown in the following figure) don't tell you everything you need to know about HTML, they can help you get the basic idea. To get rid of the HTML tag markers, go back to the View menu and select Reveal Tags again to remove the check mark next to it.

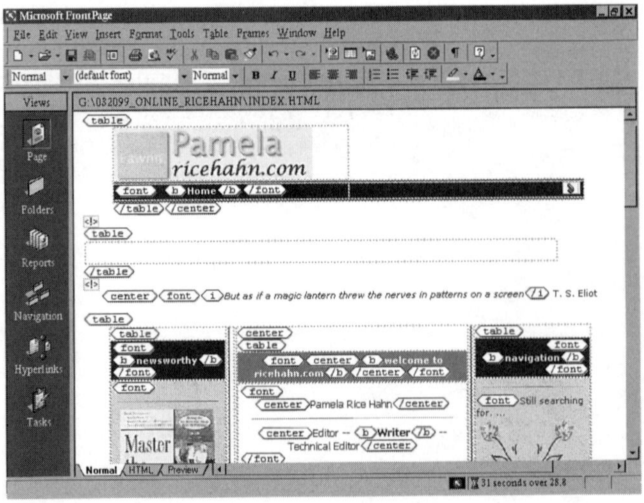

Web page with HTML tags revealed.

If you know HTML and want to work directly with your source code, FrontPage can still help you work faster. You can format text and insert images and tables quickly by using the toolbar buttons, even when you're in the HTML page view. (If you don't know HTML but would like to learn, pick up *The Complete Idiot's Guide to HTML 4.0* by Paul McFedries.)

What's in a Name? Changing Your Page Title

If you didn't title your page when you saved it, as described in the "Saving a New Web Page" section earlier in this chapter, you can do it now. After all, when people visit your pages, you probably want the browser title bar to display something more descriptive than `New_Page_1`. FrontPage also uses titles to generate labels for navigation bars, as you'll see in Chapter 7.

You can change the titles for your pages anytime you want. To change a page title, select Properties from the File menu to display the Page Properties dialog box. You can then enter a new page title in the Title box and click OK to return to your Web page. Find out how to edit page titles without opening the actual page from the Folders view, as explained in Chapter 24, "You and Your Web Files."

Color My Web Page: Changing Background, Text, and Link Colors

Too old for coloring books? Color your Web page instead. All Web pages contain color schemes that determine the colors for the background, text, and hyperlinks. You'll want to create your own color schemes for your pages or FrontPage will apply the default color scheme for you. It's more fun to be creative, isn't it? Create your color schemes with style sheets, as explained in Chapter 15.

FrontPage gives you lots of options for creating color schemes, so let's take things one at a time. First we'll run through the basic steps of setting the color scheme for your Web page. The following sections cover details like how to pick colors and create custom colors, add a patterned background, display a watermark, and copy a color scheme from another Web page.

To change the color scheme for a Web page:

1. Select Background from the Format menu to display the Page Properties dialog box with the Background tab selected, as shown in the following figure.

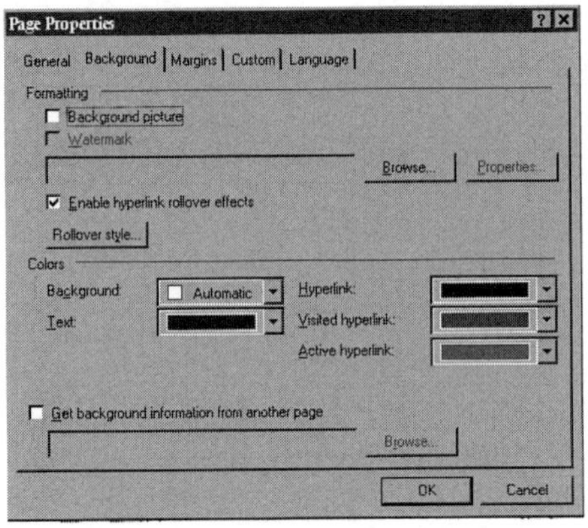

The Page Properties dialog box with the Background tab selected.

2. To pick a *solid background color* for your Web page, click the Background box to display the pull-down color menu and select a color. This option determines your page's background color.
3. To choose a *text color* on your page, click the Text box to display the pull-down color menu and select a color. This option determines the color of all of the headings, paragraphs, and other unlinked text on your page. Chapter 5 tells you more about working with text.
4. To choose a color for your *hyperlinks*, click the Hyperlink box to display the pull-down color menu and select a color. This option determines the color of your page's linked text and the borders around linked graphics (if you choose to display borders, as explained in Chapter 8).
5. To choose a color for your *visited hyperlinks*, click the Visited Hyperlink box to display the pull-down color menu and select a color. This determines the color that links change to when visitors have already followed them. For more about creating links, see Chapter 7.
6. To choose a color for your *active hyperlinks*, click the Active Hyperlink box to display the pull-down color menu and select a color. This determines the color that links change to *while* you click on them.
7. When you finish selecting options, click the OK button to apply your color scheme and return to the Web page.

You can also use the Page Properties dialog box options to apply hyperlink rollover effects, which change the color and font for your text links when you pass your mouse pointer over them, as discussed in Chapter 7.

Picking Colors: Web-Safe Colors and Custom Colors

When you choose colors for your Web page, the pull-down color menus mentioned in the previous section can seem a little confusing at first. What the heck *are* all these things, and where can you get *more* colors? Not to worry—you'll get the hang of it after you try a few.

Select the following options to apply colors to your page:

- *Automatic* Leave this option selected if you want to keep FrontPage's default color setting.
- *Standard Colors* The pull-down color menu provides a convenient little palette of the most popular background, text, and link colors. To select one of these colors, click one of the squares.
- *Document's Colors* Displays currently selected text and link colors, in case you want to use one of the colors for a different element.
- *More Colors* Click this option to display the Colors dialog box, which contains the complete palette of 216 *browser-safe* colors. To select a color and return to the Page Properties dialog box, click on a color and then click the OK button.
- *Custom Colors* To pick a custom color, click the Custom button to display the Color dialog box, select a color from the Basic Colors palette, and click OK to return to the Colors dialog box. You can also create custom colors by clicking a color on the color swatch, adjusting the brightness with the slider, clicking the Add to Custom Colors button, and clicking the OK button.

Keep It Safe: Choose the Right Colors

Different computer systems (such as Windows 3.x, Windows 95 or 98, Macintosh, and UNIX) don't display all colors the same way. This means that your beautiful colors might look funny—or downright awful—on someone else's computer. You can avoid this problem by sticking with browser-safe colors.

Copying a Color Scheme from Another Web Page

Once you come up with a color scheme you like, you can apply it to other Web pages quickly and easily. To copy a color scheme to the current page, display the Page Properties dialog box with the Background tab selected, select the Get Background and Colors from Page radio button, click the Browse button to display the Current Web dialog box, select a Web page, click OK to return to the Page Properties dialog box, and then click the OK button to apply the color scheme and return to your Web page. You can only select files from the current Web, as explained in Chapter 2.

Adding a Background Image

Background images make it easy for even non-designers to add a dash of pizzazz to a Web page. If you've ever wallpapered a room or tiled a floor, you already have some idea of how background patterns work. When you add a background image, the Web browser repeats the image across your page to form a pattern. You can add your own images as backgrounds by importing them into your FrontPage Web. Find out more in Chapter 2.

Microsoft FrontPage also comes with a clip art gallery with background images you can use. The FrontPage clip art gallery comes with all kinds of artwork you can use, as explained in Chapter 8.

To select a background image from the FrontPage clip art gallery:

1. Select Background from the Format menu to display the Page Properties dialog box with the Background tab selected.
2. Click the Background Image checkbox to select it, and then click the Browse button to display the Select Background Image dialog box.
3. Click the Clip Art button to display the Clip Art Gallery dialog box.
4. Scroll down through the Category list and select Web Backgrounds.
5. Click on a pattern, and then select Insert Clip (the first option) from the pop-up menu to choose a pattern and return to the Page Properties dialog box.
6. Click the OK button to apply the background and return to your Web page.

To add your own background image:

1. Select Background from the Format menu to display the Page Properties dialog box with the Background tab selected.
2. Click the Background Image checkbox to select it, and then click the Browse button to display the Select Background Image dialog box.
3. Browse for a image in your Images directory, select the image, and click the OK button to return to the Page Properties dialog box.
4. Click the OK button to apply the background and return to your Web page.

Displaying a Watermark

Have you ever written letters on fancy paper with an image or embossed stamp in the middle of the page? These are called *watermarks*, and they're not just for paper any more! As with background images, watermarks are displayed in the background. But instead of repeating as a pattern, they appear as a single image in the middle of the Web page.

To add a watermark to your Web page, display the Page Properties dialog box with the Background tab selected, click the Watermark checkbox to select it, click the Browse button, and proceed as if you were inserting a background image.

Try the Shortcut Menu!

When you want to change your page title or colors, click anywhere on the page with your right mouse button and select Page Properties from the shortcut menu. Isn't that easier than selecting Properties from the File menu?

Five Cool Color Schemes You Can Try

Sure, you want your Web pages to look attractive and professional, but they should also reflect your personality or your organization's image. FrontPage comes with ready-to-use page designs called themes, as covered in Chapter 4.

If you'd rather try your hand at designing your own color scheme, try the following ideas:

- *Cutting Edge* Black background, white text, aqua links, fuchsia followed links, and yellow active links.
- *Earth Tones* Tan background, brown text, navy blue links, olive followed links, black active links.
- *Slick and Professional* White background, black text, red links, gray followed links, blue active links.
- *Tons O' Fun* Pale yellow background, black text, red links, blue followed links, fuchsia active links.
- *By the Sea* Navy blue background, lime links, aqua followed links, purple active links.

When you select colors from the Colors dialog box, the name of the color name appears in the Name box so you can make sure you've picked the right color. For more Web design tips, see Chapter 10, "Elements of Style: Web Design Basics."

The Least You Need to Know

- *Starting a new Web page*: To start a new Web page from a template (FrontPage comes with many), click New from the File menu. To start a blank new Web page, select the Normal Page template or use the Ctrl+N key combination.
- *Opening, saving, and closing Web pages*: To open a Web page, click the Open button or use the Ctrl+O key combination. To save a Web page, click the Save button or use the Ctrl+S key combination. To close a Web page, select Close from the File menu, Ctrl+F4, or click the Close box.
- *Changing Web page titles*: The title for your Web page appears on the browser's title bar when people view your page online. To change a Web page's title, display the Page Properties dialog box, click the General tab, and type your text in the Title box.
- *Creating and applying Web page color schemes*: Color schemes determine the colors for the text, links, and background of a Web page. To create a color scheme for a Web page, display the Page Properties dialog box, click the Background tab, and choose your colors.
- *Adding backgrounds and watermarks to Web pages*: A Web page background is a single image that tiles across a Web page to form a pattern. A watermark is a single picture that appears in the background of a Web page. You can add a background or watermark to a Web page from the Page Properties dialog box with the Background tab selected.

Part 2

Dive In! The Water's Fine!

Wow! You've learned to spin a FrontPage Web and set up a Web page or two. That's a lot of progress for just three chapters! Now you can dive in and start adding some content. While surfing the Web, you've probably come across exciting pages with multimedia and interactive bells and whistles. With FrontPage 2000, you can create your own gee-whiz Web sites. But first, let's start with the basics: text, pictures, and links.

If you've ever used a word processing program like Microsoft Word, you'll catch on quickly. You may have even noticed that FrontPage 2000's toolbar buttons and menus look an awful lot like the ones in your word processor. When you think about it, that makes perfect sense. After all, like word processing documents, Web pages are made mostly of text and pictures.

This part will tell you how to create instant page layouts with FrontPage themes, work with text, format lists, set up links, add pictures, and add special effects to your pictures. Once you've mastered these basic Web page elements, the rest will be easy.

Chapter 4

Poof! You're a Designer with FrontPage Web Themes

In This Chapter

- Picking FrontPage themes for your pages
- Applying special effects to themes
- Customizing theme colors, graphics, and font styles
- Changing banner and global navigation button text
- Five cool Web themes to check out

Yikes! Designing a Web page can seem overwhelming for non-arty types. If your creative style leans more towards writing or getting things organized than designing pages, let FrontPage themes come to the rescue.

Pick a Theme, Any Theme

So what's on the menu? FrontPage themes offer an all-you-can-eat buffet of color schemes, textures, and graphics to tempt even the pickiest palate. Whether you're creating a Web site for your party-planning service or your church group, you can pick the right look. So go ahead and take FrontPage themes for a spin. The following sections tell you how.

Instant Makeover! Applying a Theme to Your Whole Web Site

If you used a Web wizard, as explained in Chapter 2, “Instant Web-Site-O-Matic: Spinning FrontPage Webs,” your Web site already has a theme. But that doesn’t mean you have to *like* it. FrontPage makes it easy to change the look and feel of your Web site.

To apply a theme to an entire Web site:

1. Select Theme from the Format menu to display the Themes dialog box, as shown in the following figure.

The Themes dialog box with the default options selected.

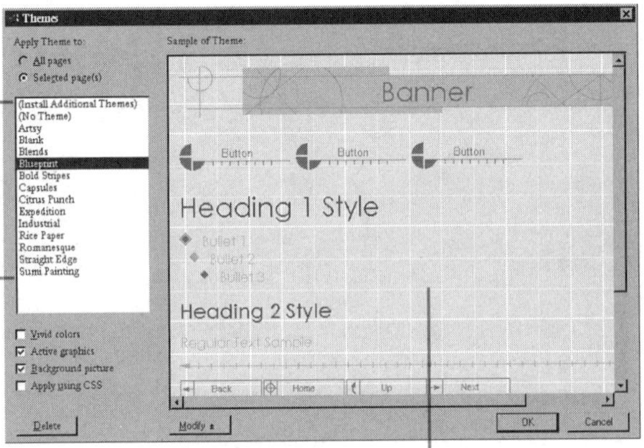

2. Select the All Pages radio button from the Apply Theme to option.
3. Pick a theme from the scrolling list to display a preview in the Sample of Theme window.
4. You can also select additional options for your theme, as explained in the following sections.
5. When you finish choosing options, click the OK button to apply your theme.

When you’re ready for an instant Web site makeover, apply a new theme. Voilà! A whole new look. (Now if I could only apply a new theme to my apartment!)

More Goodies! Applying Special Effects to Themes

Want brighter colors, a nice patterned background, or cool active graphics that change color when you pass your mouse pointer over them? When you select a theme from the Themes dialog box, you can also apply special effects to it by selecting options from the checkboxes below the scrolling list of themes. FrontPage allows you to select as many special effects as you want, and previews them in the Sample of Theme window.

FrontPage themes offer the following special effects:

- *Vivid colors* Brightens up the background and text colors.
- *Active graphics* Turns your navigation buttons into images that respond to visitors. For example, they change color when you pass your mouse cursor over them, or when the button links to the current page.
- *Background Picture* Replaces the solid-colored background with a patterned background image.
- *Apply using CSS* Applies text formatting for the theme with style sheets, rather than regular HTML. This requires no extra work on your part because the theme generates the style sheets for you. If you plan to use style sheets on your Web site (see Chapter 15, "Now You're Stylin'! Using Style Sheets"), you should select this checkbox.

If you later want to change your special effects, you can return to the Themes dialog box and do so.

Applying a Theme to Selected Pages

You may want all of your Web pages to look the same so your visitors don't get confused. (For a crash course in Web design, see Chapter 10, "Elements of Style: Web Design Basics.") But rules are made to be broken, and maybe you'd like all of your pages to look different for some reason. FrontPage lets you use as many themes in your Web as you want.

You can apply a theme to one page or just a few pages from within the Folders page view. Click Folders on the Views list to switch to the Folders view, select the pages you want to change, and display the Themes dialog box. From there, click the Selected Pages radio button before you apply the new theme. You'll then need to apply shared borders. See the "Creating Shared Borders for Your Web" section below.

Selecting More Than One Web Page in the Folders View

To select multiple Web pages, click the files while holding down the Ctrl key. To deselect a file, click it again while holding down the Ctrl key. To select a group of consecutive files, click the first file on the list, hold down the Shift key, and then click the last file in the list.

Psst! Want Some More Themes?

FrontPage comes with only a few of its themes loaded. Maybe somebody in Redmond thinks "less is more," but, then again, many of us think "more is more." So how do you get the whole enchilada? Tell FrontPage to install the rest of your themes, of course—don't worry, it only takes a few seconds. Put your FrontPage CD-ROM in the CD-ROM drive, display the Themes dialog box as you normally would, and select Install Additional Themes from the list. Click Yes in the Install Additional Themes? Microsoft FrontPage dialog box. A status dialog box is displayed until the themes finish installing. And voila! Now you have more choices.

The Best of Both Worlds

The FrontPage team over at Microsoft has finally figured out a way to offer more bells and whistles without hogging up too much of your precious hard drive space. When you install FrontPage 2000, you install only the basic package. Now you can install more themes, clip art (Chapter 8, "The Picture Perfect Web Page: Placing and Tweaking Images"), and components (Chapter 19, "A Grab Bag of Helpful Doodads: FrontPage Components") from the CD-ROM when you need them.

Creating Shared Borders for Your Web

In order for FrontPage to automatically apply your theme to the rest of your pages and to any new pages you create, you need to create shared borders for your Web. Shared borders is a FrontPage feature that saves you work by automatically applying elements of your page design to your other pages. Chapter 3, "Fooling Around with Web Pages," tells you how to set up new pages. Chapter 14, "Don't Like What You See? Designing Your Own Page Template," explains shared borders in greater detail.

To apply shared borders to your Web:

1. Select Shared Borders from the Format menu to display the Shared Borders dialog box.
2. Choose the All pages radio button from the Apply to list.
3. Click OK.

If you created a theme for just a few of the pages on your Web site, you can also create shared borders for only those pages.

To apply shared borders to selected pages on your Web:

1. Hold down the Ctrl key and select your pages from the Folder List by clicking on them, one by one.
2. Choose Shared Borders from the Format menu to display the Shared Borders dialog box.
3. Choose the Selected Pages radio button from the Apply to list.
4. Click OK.

As You Like It: Customizing Themes

Couldn't find a theme that suited you? Picky, picky, picky. But, hey, you have every right to be picky—after all, it's *your* Web site. So dive in! With FrontPage, you can customize theme colors, graphics, and font styles to your liking. First, let's walk through the basic steps of changing a theme. For details on theme elements and making specific changes, read the following sections.

To customize your themes:

1. Select Themes from the Format menu to display the Themes dialog box.
2. Click the Modify button and then click the Colors, Graphics, or Text button to modify that part of the theme. Maybe you like everything about the theme except the font in the headings. Click the Text button, choose Heading from the Item list, pick the font you like, and click OK. What if you want to change the background color? Click the Colors button, select a new background color, and so on. It's easy.
3. When you finish making your changes, click OK to return to the Themes dialog box.
4. Click OK to apply the changes to your theme. A Warning dialog box appears and asks if you want to save changes to your theme.
5. Click the Yes button.

Not for the Faint of Heart!

Before you start customizing a theme, keep in mind that doing so requires some design and Web know-how. Fortunately, FrontPage lets you preview those changes before you apply them and make them permanent. By first viewing the color combinations, you can make sure they coordinate and that your text is visible against the new background selection.

FrontPage saves the changes to the theme and changes your pages. If you later decide that you don't like your changes (it's an artist's prerogative to be fickle!), you can always change them again.

Understanding Themes and Page Elements

What make themes tick? Themes divide page elements into three categories (colors, graphics, and styles) and then apply settings to each element. In order to tweak your theme, you need to select a page element category, pick a page element from one list, and then select your changes from another list. The following sections tell you how to change theme elements for each category, and the following figure shows an example of a themed Web page and some common theme elements.

Web page with the Blueprint theme and theme elements displayed in a Web browser.

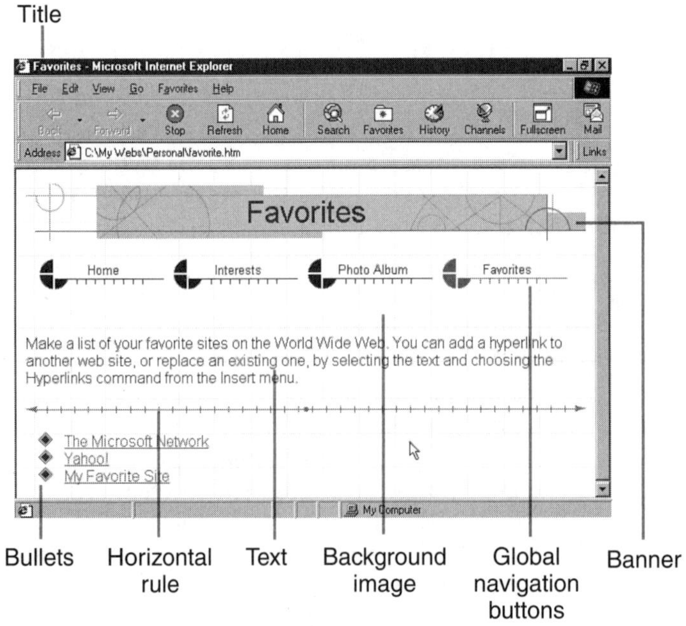

Changing Theme Colors

Don't like your text, links, solid-colored background, and banner text colors? To change them from the Themes dialog box, click the Modify button and then the Colors button. When the Modify Theme dialog box appears, click the Custom tab to display the Item and Color pull-down lists. You can then select page elements from the Item list, and pick new colors from the Color list. If you want more color choices, select More Colors from the Color list and pick a color as you would when creating page color schemes, as explained in Chapter 3. When you finish picking colors for different page elements, click OK to return to the Themes dialog box.

You can change colors for the following page elements:

- ➤ *Background* The solid background color for the page. For more about page backgrounds, see Chapter 3.
- ➤ *Banner text* The text inside the large horizontal graphics that head up each page.

- *Body* Font styles for paragraph and bulleted list text. For more about bulleted lists, see Chapter 6, "Making a List, Checking It Twice."
- *Different types of links* For definitions of hyperlinks, followed links, and active links, see Chapter 7, "Think Links: Adding Links to Your Pages."
- *Headings* Level 1 to Level 6 headings. For more about headings, see Chapter 5, "Entering Text and Fiddling with Fonts."
- *Table Border* To modify the color of the border around a table. For more information on tables, see Chapter 12, "Table It! Arranging Text and Images with Tables."

Changing Theme Graphics

Themes come with different types of graphics, including background images, banners, bullets, navigation buttons, and more. But you can also substitute your own images if you want. From the Themes dialog box, click the Modify button, and then click the Graphics button. When the Modify Theme dialog box appears, select an image type from the Item menu and click the Browse button to browse for an image. Replace as many images as you like from the Item menu. When you finish replacing theme images, click OK to return to the Themes dialog box.

You can substitute the following types of graphics:

- *Background Picture* The image that creates a patterned background on a page, as explained in Chapter 3.
- *Banner* The large horizontal graphic that appears at the top of each page.
- *Bullet List* The graphics used as bullets for bulleted lists. For more about setting up lists, see Chapter 6.
- *Global Navigation Buttons* The buttons used in the navigation bars for main section pages on the site. For more about navigation bars, see Chapters 7 and 14.
- *Horizontal and Vertical Navigation* Secondary navigation buttons or text used for listing pages within a section. Depending on the theme layout, these are either Horizontal Navigation or Vertical Navigation elements.
- *Horizontal Rule* The graphic used as a page divider.
- *Quick Buttons* Special navigation buttons that say Home, Next, Previous, and Up.

Before Your Replace Any Graphics!

You will need to know about creating and editing images, and adding them to Web pages. Your replacement graphics should be the same size as the original theme graphics in order for the theme to look right.

Changing Theme Styles

Tired of looking at those newfangled modern fonts? Go ahead and switch back to good ol' Times Roman, or whichever font you want. From the Themes dialog box, click the Modify button and then the Styles button to display the Modify Themes dialog box. Select a text element from the Item menu and choose a font. For more options, click the More Text Styles button. For more about fonts, see Chapter 5, and for more about styles, see Chapter 15.

Editing Banner Graphic Titles

The banner graphic displays the page title at the top of the page. Why not call your pages something like fun like "Welcome to My World"? FrontPage theme banners have generic titles, but you can spice them up. Click the banner with your right mouse button and select Page Banner Properties from the shortcut menu to display the Page Banners Properties dialog box. Select Image from the Properties list, and then enter your new text in the Page Banner Text box. You can also change your banner image to a text heading by selecting the Text radio button. When you finish, click OK to apply the changes.

Changing Navigation Bar Labels

Sure, it's nice of the Web wizard to create navigation bars for you, but you might want to re-label them. FrontPage generates navigation button labels from page titles, and you can change them in the Navigation view. Select Navigation from the Views list to display the pages and page titles, click your right mouse button on a page title, and select Rename from the shortcut menu. FrontPage highlights the page title so you can enter a new name. For more about working with navigation bars, see Chapter 7.

Five Cool Web Themes to Check Out

Ally McBeal has her own theme, so why shouldn't you? Okay, maybe you don't have anyone to write a song for you and follow you around everywhere you go. But you can still pick Web site themes to fit your personality—or even whatever mood you're in today.

FrontPage offers lots of attractive themes, but you can check out five of my favorites if you want:

- *Blueprint* Professional-looking, yet cool
- *Poetic* Freeform and flowing
- *Blends* Bold and zesty
- *Citrus Punch* A morning eye opener
- *LaVerne* Friendly with a certain retro charm

The Least You Need to Know

- *Picking Web themes* FrontPage comes with a variety of professionally designed themes for instant Web sites. To create a theme to your Web, display the Themes dialog box and pick a theme from the list to display a preview of the theme in the Sample of Theme window.
- *Adding special effects to Web themes* From the Themes dialog box, you can also choose the check boxes labeled Vivid Colors, Active Graphics, a Background Image, or to Apply Theme Using CSS (style sheets).
- *Using themes for selected pages* You can also use different themes throughout your Web site. To apply a theme to selected pages on your Web site, select the pages from the Folder List, display the Themes dialog box, and choose a theme.
- *Applying shared borders to make your theme work* In order to make your themes work, you need to apply shared borders to your Web. Apply shared borders with the Shared Borders dialog box. See Chapter 14 for details.
- *Getting more themes* You can install more themes by putting your FrontPage CD-ROM in the CD-ROM drive, displaying the Themes dialog box, and selecting Install Additional Themes from the list.
- *Understanding theme elements* Themes consist of a background color or image, banner, global navigation buttons, text, bullets, and horizontal rules. In addition, themes determine the font styles and text formatting for Web pages.
- *Customizing FrontPage themes* Once you've set up your themes, you can change the colors, graphics, and font styles from the Themes dialog box. However, customizing themes can get tricky. A better method for creative types is to design your own template, as covered in Chapter 14.
- *Changing banner titles* To edit the banner graphic titles for your pages, select each banner, display the Page Banner Properties dialog box, choose Image from the Properties list, and type your new text in the Page Banner text box.
- *Editing global navigation button labels* To change the labels on your global navigation buttons (also called navigation bars), choose Navigation from the Views list to display the Navigation page view, and change the titles for each page. The global navigation button labels will change along with the page titles. For more about working with navigation bars in the Navigation view, see Chapter 7.

Chapter 5

Entering Text and Fiddling with Fonts

In This Chapter

- Creating paragraphs and line breaks
- Selecting, deleting, and moving text
- Importing text from a file
- Applying text styles
- Using the Format Painter
- Inserting signs, lines, and other special characters
- Spell checking, finding, and replacing text
- Five cool text-formatting tricks

When the World Wide Web first got started, people joked about how you could use any fonts you liked, as long as you only liked Times Roman and Courier. Whew! Times sure have changed. Although the Web still has its limitations, you can do all kinds of cool things to jazz up your text nowadays. Add a dash of color or try a few fonts. The sky's the limit—well, almost. With FrontPage, you can do almost everything you can do with your word processor.

Version NEW! 2000

More Like Word

If you use Microsoft Word, you'll find that FrontPage even has many of the same toolbar buttons and functions. Microsoft has integrated FrontPage into the Office 2000 software family, making it easier than ever to use. For more about working with FrontPage and Microsoft Office, read Chapter 18, "A Match Made in Redmond: FrontPage and Microsoft Office 2000."

Bossing Text Around: Entering and Editing Text

Text doesn't look fancy, and nobody ever seems to talk about it. (After all, do any glamorous high-tech companies ever shake up the stock market or make the evening news because their application helps people create or look at text?) Nonetheless, try to imagine a Web page—or anything else people create with computers—that doesn't have any text.

Yep, for all the hype about multimedia, animation, and other stuff on the Web, you'll still wind up entering and editing text a lot. Fortunately, FrontPage gives you all the tools you've come to expect with your other applications. So go ahead and create headings, align text, spell check, search and replace, copy and paste, and do all the other things you normally do when creating your Web pages. The following figure shows a few basic text elements that you'll learn how to work with in this chapter.

A few basic text elements displayed in the FrontPage application window with the paragraph markers turned on.

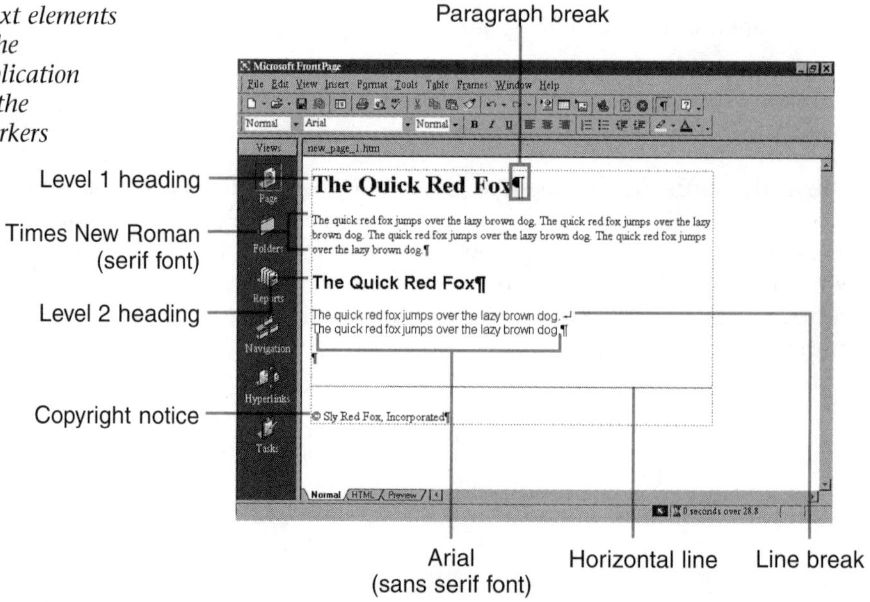

Paragraphs and Line Breaks: What's the Diff?

Your high school English teacher probably told you that a paragraph contains two or more sentences. Forget that when you create Web pages. FrontPage thinks of a paragraph as a line of text (or several sentences) with an extra space above and below it. Every time you press the Enter key, you start a new paragraph.

When you're typing away and want to begin a new line without creating a new paragraph, you can insert a line break by pressing the Shift key and holding it down while pressing the Enter key. When you create a line break, the text retains the formatting of the current paragraph.

Turn Your Paragraphs On

Sometimes it's easier to see what you're doing when you display the paragraph formatting on the page. To display the paragraph formatting, click the Show All button on the Standard toolbar. To turn off the paragraph formatting display, click the Show All button again. This feature does not affect how your Web page displays in the browser.

Selecting Text

You probably already know how to select text, but it's still worth mentioning just in case you're *very* new to the computer thang. To select text, place your cursor (it looks like an I-beam) in front of the text you want to select, left-click, drag the cursor across the text, and then release the mouse button. To select a word or a link, place your mouse pointer in front of the word or link and double-click the mouse button.

Yuck, I Don't Want That! Deleting Text

When you're having a bad day and hate everything you write, deleting text is wonderfully cathartic. Try it sometime! To delete text, select it and press the Delete key or the Backspace key.

Copying and Pasting Text

Why type things over and over again when you can copy and paste them instead? To copy and paste text, select it and click the Copy button on the Standard toolbar (or use the Ctrl+C key combination). Then place your cursor where you want to copy the text and click the Paste button on the Standard toolbar (or use the Ctrl+V key combination).

Try Drag and Drop

When you're moving text somewhere in the current document, you can drag and drop it. Select the text, click on it, and use your mouse to drag it to the new location when the arrow cursor appears.

Moving Text to Another Location

You can move blocks of text to a different part of the current document, or to a different document, by cutting and pasting. Remember nursery school? I used to love cutting and pasting things. (I'm surprised the teacher didn't take my scissors away!) With computers, cutting and pasting works sort of the same way—you cut something out and stick it somewhere else. To move text, select it and press the Cut button on the Standard toolbar (or use the Ctrl+X key combination). Then place your cursor where you want to place the text and click the Paste button on the Standard toolbar (or use the Ctrl+V key combination).

Load It In, Charlie! Importing Text from Another File

If you're creating a Web site for an organization or your home business, you probably have stuff already on your computer that you'd like to include on your Web site—a mission statement, a product list, or an annual report. With FrontPage, you can put word processing documents, spreadsheets, and even text from other Web pages on your Web page lickety-split. FrontPage can even handle some document and spreadsheet types that weren't created with Microsoft Office applications.

To import text from a different file:

1. Place your cursor where you want to insert the text.
2. Select File from the Insert menu to display the Select File dialog box.
3. Browse to find the file you want and then click the Open button. To search for a specific type of file (such as a Word document), select the file type from the Files of Type list. If you're not sure of the file type, select All Files.
4. Select the file and click OK.

For Desktop Publishers

If you're a graphic designer migrating Web-wards, you probably want to put some of your portfolio pieces online. Although FrontPage can't import QuarkXPress and PageMaker files, there's still hope.

If you have a recent version of Quark or PageMaker, you can export your files as HTML documents and then import those Web pages and graphics into your FrontPage Web, as explained in Chapter 24, "You and Your Web Files." You'll probably need to do a lot of tweaking of these files because both Quark and PageMaker really make a mess of things when it comes to Web pages.

You can also export your text from Quark or PageMaker as `.RTF` (rich text format) files, import the text into your page (or pages), bring the images into your Web separately, and re-create your designs as Web pages.

If you use drawing programs like Adobe Illustrator, Macromedia Freehand, or CorelDRAW, you can also use special plug-ins so people can view your work on the Web. Chapter 17, "Strut Your Stuff: Sound, Video, and More," covers file types that require plug-ins.

Formatting Paragraphs

What's the difference between Web pages and word processing documents? Not much, if you use FrontPage. Paragraph formats are different than character formats, as you'll see in the "A Little Font Magic: Playing with Fonts" section later in this chapter. *Paragraph formats*, such as alignment, indents, and HTML text styles, are applied to the entire paragraph—not just a word or two (unless the word stands alone as a paragraph).

You can find the paragraph and text formatting options on the Format menu or the shortcut menu (by right-clicking on the paragraph). Even better, the Formatting toolbar (shown in the following figure) has several of these formatting options.

Formatting toolbar.

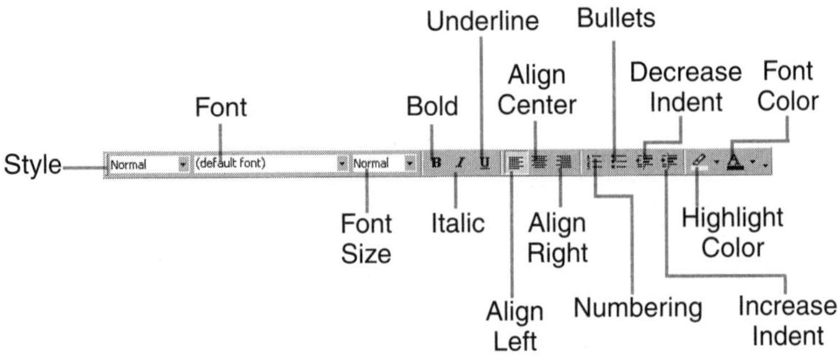

Aligning Text

Life sure would be boring if all text automatically aligned to the left. Aligning text places it horizontally in relation to the rest of the page. To align text to the left, center, or right, click the Align Left, Align Center, or Align Right button on the Formatting toolbar. You can also align text by right-clicking the selected text, selecting Paragraph from the shortcut menu, and then choosing an option from the Alignment menu.

Indenting Text

Indenting text can make important items like quotations stand out. To indent text, place your cursor on a line or paragraph and click the Increase Indent button on the Formatting toolbar. You can increase your indent by clicking the Increase Indent button again. And if you get overzealous with your indenting, you can fix things by clicking the Decrease Indent button.

For more options, you can right-click the selected text and choose Paragraph from the shortcut menu to display the Paragraph dialog box. You can then select items from the Indentation menus to adjust the indentation of the left margin, right margin, and first line of the selected paragraph.

Inserting Blank Spaces

Spacing text can be tricky on the Web. You can insert spaces with the spacebar until you're blue in the face and things still might not line up correctly. You can try pressing the Tab key, but when you view your page on the browser, you'll learn the unpleasant fact that there ain't no such thing as tabs on the Web. FrontPage *will* let you insert a few spaces before a paragraph as an indentation and add space between words in a paragraph using the spacebar. But if you really want to line up text and images on a Web page, you'll need to create tables, as explained in Chapter 12, "Table It! Arranging Text and Images with Tables."

Applying HTML Text Styles

You can apply a text format in FrontPage the same way you would with Microsoft Word—by placing your cursor on the line of text that you want to format and selecting a style from the Styles list on the Formatting toolbar. When you select a style, FrontPage applies it to the entire paragraph even if you only select one word.

You can choose from the following HTML styles or create your own, as described in Chapter 15, "Now You're Stylin'! Using Style Sheets:"

- *Normal text* Use for normal paragraph text.
- *Formatted* Also called *preformatted* text, this applies a monospaced font, like Courier, to your text.
- *Address* This style is generally applied to the contact and copyright information, usually located at the bottom of a Web page.
- *Headings* FrontPage and HTML support six different heading levels.
- *Lists* This style is applied to all numbered, bulleted, and table of contents-type lists with definition terms and definition descriptions, as explained in Chapter 6, "Making a List, Checking It Twice."

Try Style Sheets!

If plain old HTML doesn't give you the kind of text formatting and layout options you want, try using style sheets, as explained in Chapter 15.

Removing Text Formatting

Don't like the text formats you've applied? Get rid of them! To strip the formatting from a line or paragraph, select it, click on the Format menu, and select Remove Formatting from the pull-down list.

Inserting a Horizontal Line

Horizontal lines (also called *horizontal rules* or *page dividers*) come in handy when you want to separate different sections of your page from one another. To insert a horizontal line, select Horizontal Line from the Insert menu.

Don't like the looks of your line? Feel free to change its width, height, alignment, and color by clicking it with your right mouse button and selecting Horizontal Line Properties from the shortcut menu. When the Horizontal Line Properties dialog box appears, you can change settings for the following:

- *Width* Select a number from the list, and then select the Percent of Window or Pixels radio button to determine which unit of measurement you want to use and then enter a number in the box.
- *Height* This is a funny term to use because this setting actually controls the line's thickness. To adjust the thickness of your line, select a number from the list.
- *Alignment* Click a radio button to align your horizontal line to the left, center, or right of the page.
- *Color* You can add a dash of color to your page by picking a color from the Color list.
- *Solid Line (no shading)* By default, horizontal lines are shaded so they appear to be embedded in the page. To display your line as a solid line, click the check box.

What Are Pixels?

No, pixels aren't those cute little space critters you cooed over while watching *Star Wars*. They're the unit of measurement used on the Web and in the computer graphics world in general. Computers display text and graphics as tiny little dots, sort of like those Roy Lichtenstein comic book prints from the '60s. The actual size of a pixel depends on your computer screen, but if you have an application like Microsoft Word that comes with a ruler, each inch on that ruler represents about 72 pixels.

A Little Font Magic: Playing with Fonts

When you get your first computer, it's hard to stop playing with all the fonts. Many people get so excited that they write letters to all their friends and circulate memos around the office, using five or 10 fonts on each page! It's terrible from a design standpoint, but it can sure be fun. With FrontPage, you can still play with fonts. But remember that Web pages don't work like the printed kind. If your visitors don't have the same fonts installed on their systems, they'll see boring old fonts instead of the fabulous ones you picked out.

You can avoid this problem by sticking to fonts that most people have on their systems, like Times Roman, Arial, Helvetica, Trebuchet, and Verdana. Meanwhile, there are plenty of cool things you can do with fonts that everyone can see—like resizing and coloring them in. The following three sections talk about character styles that you can apply to a letter, word, or several words without changing the entire paragraph.

Changing the Font and Font Size

When you apply HTML paragraph styles from the Style list, it formats your text according to default text sizes and your color scheme settings (as explained in Chapter 3, "Fooling Around with Web Pages"). But you can override these settings to make your headings and text stand out. The Formatting toolbar's just a quick mouse-click away.

To change a font, select the text and then pick a font from the Font menu. To adjust the font size, select the text and choose a font size from the Size list. FrontPage even lists Web text sizes (levels 1-6, with 1 as the smallest) with their equivalent point sizes since most software programs measure text sizes in *points*.

Adding a Dash of Color with Font Colors and Highlighting

Publishing documents in live Technicolor used to be complicated and expensive, but the Web lets you use all the colors you want. You can add a dash of color to your language or create a highlighter-pen effect for text that you want to emphasize.

To color in your text, select it, click the little arrow next to the Font Color toolbar button on the Formatting toolbar. Then select a color from the color palette. To highlight your text with a color, select the text, click the little arrow next to the Highlight Color button on the Formatting toolbar, and select a color from the color palette.

You can read more about selecting colors in the "Color My Web Page: Changing Background, Text, and Link Colors" section of Chapter 3.

Applying Bold, Italics, and Underlines

As with most applications, FrontPage lets you apply bold, italic, and underline styles to your text. Select your text and click the Bold, Italic, or Underline button on the Formatting toolbar. (By the way, underlining text on a Web page is not recommended. Web surfers expect underlined text to function as a link, and they get pretty annoyed when they click on the text and nothing happens!)

Superscripts, Subscripts, SmallCaps, Etc.: Applying Special Character Effects

Need some more special character effects, like small caps, superscript, and subscript? Imagine publishing scientific documents without superscript text! If you don't see the special effect you're looking for, select your text, click it with your right mouse button, and select Font from the shortcut menu to display the Font dialog box. There, now that's more like it!

To apply special character effects, select a check box from the Effects list and click the OK button. The Font dialog box even provides a Preview window so you can see how your choices look before applying them.

Copying Text Formats with the Format Painter

Once you've decided how you want your text to look, who wants to keep selecting text and applying paragraph and text styles over and over again? Nobody. Why bother when the Format Painter can do the work for you? To copy formatting from one paragraph to another, select the text that contains the formatting you want to copy, click the Format Painter button on the Standard toolbar, and then click your cursor (it turns into a paint brush) on the text you want to reformat.

The Standard toolbar is shown in the following figure.

The Standard toolbar.

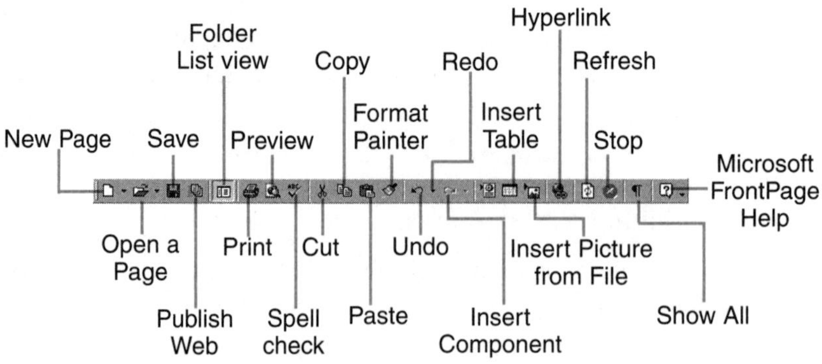

To copy formatting from one paragraph to several paragraphs, select the text that contains the formatting you want to copy, double-click the Format Painter button, and then click on all the paragraphs you want to reformat. To turn the Format Painter off, click the Format Painter button again.

Signs, Symbols, and Special Characters

Sooner or later, everyone winds up using symbols and special characters in our documents. After all, your Web site belongs to you or your organization, and you should include copyright and trademark notices when appropriate. A © or ® symbol looks much more professional than writing out the words "Copyright" or "Registered Trademark." And what will your future employers think of your Web résumé if you spell the word incorrectly, without the accents over the e's?

To insert a special character, choose Symbol from the Insert menu. When the Symbol dialog box appears, click a symbol, click the Insert button, and then click the Close button.

Whoops! Can I Undo That?

Yikes! Just one little mistake and you've made a mess of everything! Let Undo come to the rescue. Click the Undo button on the Standard toolbar, select Undo from the Edit menu, or use the Ctrl+Z key combination, and your page is good as new. Oh, you didn't mean to undo that? No problem. Just click the Redo button on the Standard toolbar, select Redo from the Edit menu, or use the Ctrl+Y key combination. (Now, how do you undo that excessively honest comment you made about your significant other's outfit this morning?)

Time for a Spell Check

You've put lots of hard work into your Web site—don't let those pesky typos slip through and embarrass you when you show your Web site to the world! FrontPage comes with a spell check feature so you can make your pages letter perfect.

To run a quick spell check, click the Spelling button on the Standard toolbar to display the Spelling dialog box, as shown in the following figure. Or display the Spelling dialog box by pressing the F7 key or select Spelling from the Tools menu. When FrontPage catches a misspelled word, it displays the word in the Not in Dictionary box with a list of suggested corrections below it. To change the spelling, select a word from the Suggestions list or enter the correct spelling yourself in the Change To box, and then click the Change button.

What if the word isn't really misspelled? You can click the Ignore button. Or, if you use the word frequently, add it to the dictionary by clicking the Add button. FrontPage will recognize the word from now on. You can also keep FrontPage from flagging the same words over and over again by clicking on the Ignore All or Change All button.

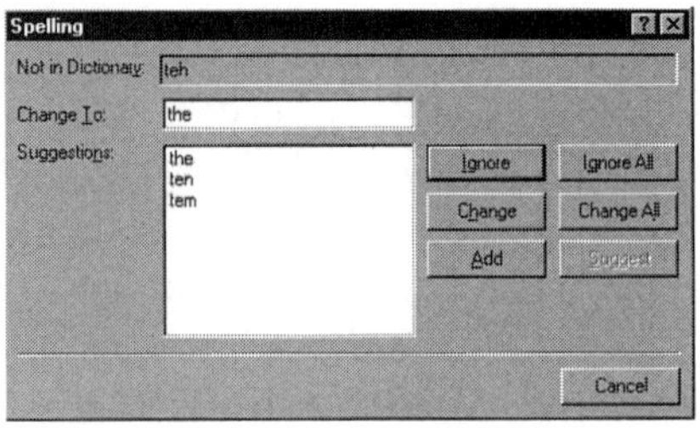

The Spelling dialog box.

Searching for Text

Scrolling through documents to locate a snippet of text can get awfully dreary. Luckily, FrontPage comes with a Find feature so you can quickly find text on the current page or your entire Web site.

To locate a word or phrase in a single page, select Find from the Edit menu, or use the Ctrl+F key combination, to display the Find dialog box. (The following figure shows a picture of the Replace dialog box, which looks similar.) Enter a word or phrase in the Find box, and click a radio button from the Direction list to determine whether to search upwards or downwards in the document. To search for the next place where the word or phrase appears, click the Next button. When FrontPage finishes searching your page, a dialog box appears to tell you.

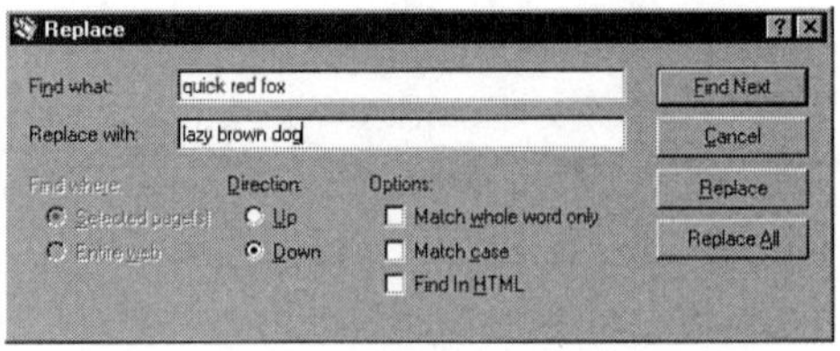

The Replace dialog box.

You can narrow your search options by clicking the Options list check boxes. Match Whole Word Only searches for both upper- and lowercase versions of your word or phrase, and Match Case searches for words and phrases with the exact same combination of upper- and lowercase letters. Find in HTML comes in handy if you know HTML because it lets you search for bits of source code. You can also search all of the pages on your Web by clicking the Entire Web radio button.

Search and Replace Your Whole Web!

FrontPage also lets you find and replace text throughout your entire Web site. You can do this by clicking the Entire Web radio button. Chapter 25, "Testing, Testing, One, Two, Three: Checking Your Web Site," talks more about putting the final touches on your Web site.

Searching and Replacing Text

FrontPage not only helps you find words and phrases, it also makes it easy to replace them with different text. To search and replace text, select Replace from the Edit menu, or use the Ctrl+H key combination. This displays the Replace dialog box, which looks a lot like the Find dialog box and offers the same options. Enter a word or phrase in the Find What box, and then enter the replacement text in the Replace With box.

To replace all of your words or phrases in one fell swoop, click the Replace All button. To search and replace items one by one, click the Find Next button. When FrontPage locates and selects the text, you can either click the Replace button to replace the text and move on to the next item, or you can click the Find Next button to leave the item unchanged and move on to the next item.

Five Cool Text-Formatting Tricks

With a little imagination and experimentation, you can add visual interest to your pages with a few text tricks.

- *Jumpin' headings!* Give your headings a jumpy look by making each letter a different size, or by alternating different fonts. This looks cool when done right. But keep in mind that *too* many jumpy headings can look distracting.
- *Try some ASCII art* *ASCII* stands for *American Standard Code for Information Interchange* and is pronounced "ask-ee." It's plain, unformatted text that anyone can read no matter what computer or browser they use. By using formatted text, you can turn boring old ASCII text into a work of art. For some cool ASCII art examples, visit Joan Stark's ASCII Art Gallery at `http://www.geocities.com/SoHo/7373/`.

- *Add a scrolling text marquee* You can create a scrolling text marquee that makes your text scroll across your page like a live news feed, as explained in Chapter 20, "Gee-Whiz Pages with Animated Special Effects."
- *Turn characters and symbols into graphics* Keyboard characters and symbols can be used to create graphics. Experiment with different colors and sizes. Try typing a row of asterisks and using them as a page divider instead of a horizontal line. Some of the symbols can look pretty interesting too.
- *Learn some more type tips and tricks* Microsoft's Typography site at `http://www.microsoft.com/typography/` has lots of information about text on the Web.

The Least You Need to Know

- *Entering and selecting text* To enter text, place your cursor on the page and start typing. To select text, place your cursor before the text you want to select and drag it across the text.
- *Importing text* You can add text from other Web pages and word processing documents by placing your cursor where you want to place the text, selecting File from the Insert menu, and selecting a document.
- *Formatting text* You can select text and then apply font and paragraph styles from the Formatting toolbar. You can also display the Paragraph or Font dialog box from the Format menu for more options. Font formats include the font, size, style (bold, italic, or underline), and color. Paragraph formats include the style (such as Heading 1), alignment, and indent.
- *Editing text* You can select text and then make edits from the Standard toolbar or the Edit menu. Editing functions including copying, cutting, pasting, and deleting. In addition, you can use the Format Painter to copy font and paragraph formats from one paragraph to the next, or delete text by selecting the text and pressing the Delete key.
- *Other helpful tools* You can add symbols and special characters from the Symbol dialog box, run a spell check from the Spelling dialog box, search for text from the Find dialog box, and replace words and phrases from the Replace dialog box.

Chapter 6

Making a List, Checking It Twice

In This Chapter

- Creating bulleted lists and choosing bullet styles
- Using graphics as bullets
- Creating numbered lists and choosing number styles
- Setting up definition lists
- Building lists within lists
- Making and previewing collapsible lists
- Five cool ways to use lists

Whenever you see a magazine announcing their Top Ten Whatevers, can you resist picking it up and taking a look? I can't. People love lists, so the media obliges us and keeps cranking them out. If you disagree with their choices, well, kvetching about lists is almost as fun as reading them.

Lists also make it easier for people to absorb facts, figures, and tasks. That's why people who present information every day, like teachers, public speakers, and "How To" book writers, use lots of lists. Now that you've got some information of your own to present on your Web pages, you can make lists too, as shown in the following figure.

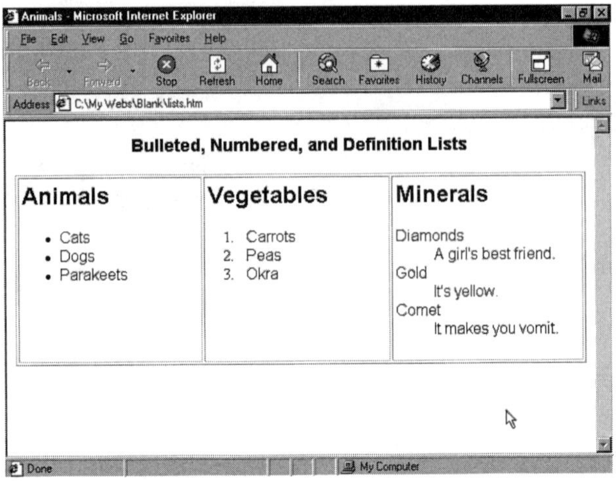

Examples of a bulleted, a numbered, and a definition list.

Get the Point? Making Bulleted Lists

Want to tell your customers about your latest products, or point people to your favorite links and explain why you like them? Bulleted lists can do the trick. The bullets draw the eye to your most important points, and if people want more information, they can follow your links or scroll down the page.

To begin a bulleted list, click the Bullets toolbar button, or select Bulleted List from the Style list on the Formatting toolbar, and begin typing. When you press the Enter key, FrontPage adds another bullet so you can begin a new list item. So now you might be wondering: if FrontPage adds a new bulleted list item every time you press the Enter key, how do you end your list? Not to worry. FrontPage won't doom you to an eternity of entering bullets—just press Enter twice and you're out.

You can also format existing text as a bulleted list. Select the text and either click the Bullets toolbar button or select Bulleted List from the Style list on the Formatting toolbar.

Creating Paragraph Space Between List Items

If your list items each contain a sentence or two, you can separate them so they're easier to read. Oddly enough, to create the illusion of paragraph spaces between list items, you need to add a line break. Otherwise, you wind up with an extra bullet or number floating in space. To create a line break, place your cursor at the end of a list item and press the Enter key while holding down the Shift key.

Picking a Bullet Style

If you get tired of looking at little solid-colored dots, try little outlined circles or solid-colored squares instead. Select your list, click on it with your right mouse button, and select List Properties from the shortcut menu. FrontPage displays the List Properties dialog box with the Plain Bullets tab already selected for you, as shown in the following figure. Pick the bullet style you like, click the OK button, and you're done.

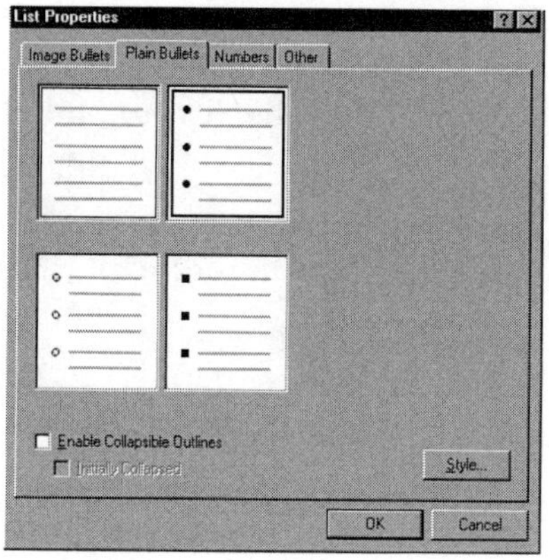

The List Properties dialog box displayed with the Plain Bullets tab selected.

But wait—did you notice the Style button in that dialog box? If you click on it, the Modify Style dialog box appears so you can use style sheets to format the text in your bulleted list. Style sheets let you do all kinds of stuff you can't do with ordinary HTML Web text. We'll talk more about style sheets in Chapter 15, "Now You're Stylin'! Using Style Sheets."

Using Images for Bullets

Why use normal bullets at all, when you can have spiffy graphics instead? Small shapes and icons make great bullets, and the FrontPage Clip Art Gallery even comes with some freebies you can use. To give your bulleted list a facelift, let's make another trip to the List Properties dialog box.

If your Web page has a theme, you've got it easy. From within the List Properties dialog box, select the Picture Bullets tab and click the Use pictures from current theme radio button and click the OK button, and FrontPage adds color-coordinated bullet graphics for you.

Don't Like Clicking Your Right Mouse Button?

Right-clicking is easier for most people, but you can also display the List Properties dialog box by selecting Bullets and Numbering from the Format menu.

If you'd rather pick your own image, hang on! You've only got a couple more steps to go. Choose the Specify Picture radio button, and then click on the Browse button to display the Select File dialog box. From here, you can browse your Web for a graphic or click the Clip Art button to take a tour through the Clip Art gallery.

You've Got Their Number: Creating Numbered Lists

Now that you know how to create bulleted lists, setting up numbered lists is a cinch because they work the same way. You can use numbered lists to rank things in order of importance, or to teach people how to do something step by step.

To begin a numbered list, click the Numbering toolbar button, or select Numbered List from the Style menu, and start typing away. To turn ordinary paragraphs or lines of text into a numbered list, select the text and either click the Numbering toolbar button or select Numbered List from the Style menu.

Picking a Number Style

Some people like to lead off with a 1, 2, 3, while others prefer Roman numerals or letters. Feel free to number (or letter) your lists however you please. Select your numbered list, click on it with your right mouse button, and select List Properties from the shortcut menu. FrontPage displays the List Item Properties dialog box with the Numbers tab already selected for you, as shown in the following figure. Pick a number style, click the OK button, and you're done.

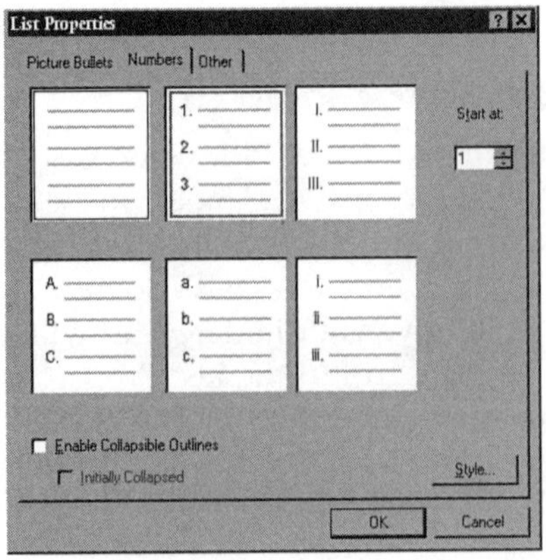

List Properties dialog box displayed with the Numbers tab selected.

You can also choose which number will start your list—a helpful feature for building lists within lists, as explained in the "Mixing It Up: Lists Within Lists" section later in this chapter. To start your list with a number other than 1, click the up or down arrow button next to the Start At list until you find the number you want.

Creating Definition Lists

Definition lists are different because they're actually made with two different list styles. This format works perfectly when you need to list short titles or sentences followed by longer paragraphs on the next line. The *definition term* aligns on the left with the rest of the page, followed by a *definition,* which indents underneath the definition term.

To begin a definition list, select Defined Term from the Style box (the drop-down menu box to the left of the font style box) on the Formatting toolbar. Type a line of text and then press the Enter key. FrontPage automatically applies the Definition style and indents the next line. Type a paragraph or so of text and press the Enter key. See? FrontPage returns you to the Definition Term style so you can enter your next set of definition list items.

To format existing text as a definition list, click on the line of text that you want to format as a defined term (aligned at the left of the page) and select Defined Term from the Style list. Then click on the paragraph of text that you want to format as a definition (indented) and select Definition from the Style list. Continue until you finish formatting your definition list.

Mixing It Up: Lists Within Lists

Why limit yourself to only one kind of list? Some documents, like the table of contents shown in the following figure, call for lists within lists (also called *nested lists*) and different types of lists. Feel free to experiment. You can also indent your nested lists by selecting them and clicking the Increase Indent button on the Formatting toolbar.

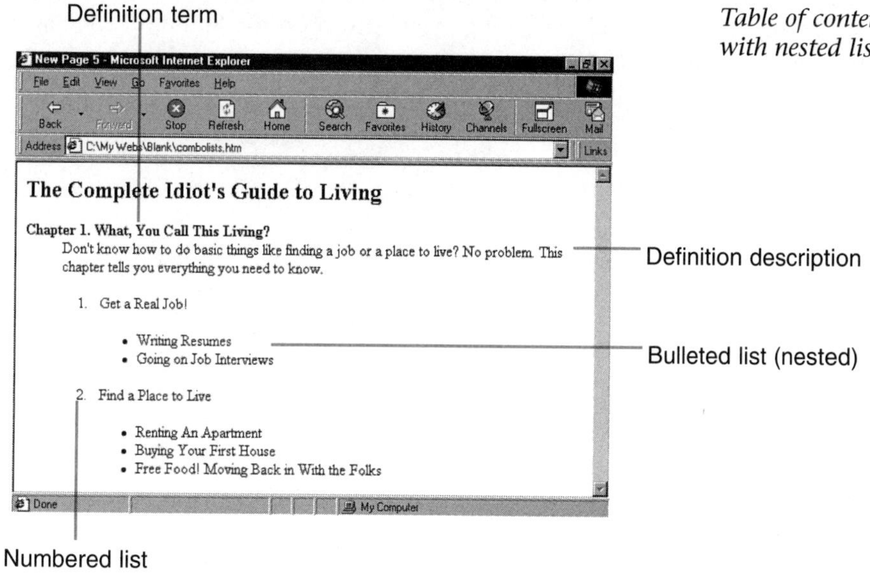

Table of contents page with nested lists.

Making Collapsible Lists

Printed documents don't respond to users. They just sit there waiting for you to read them and turn the pages. Interactivity is part of what makes the Web so cool. Collapsible lists look impressive and also save you some valuable *screen real estate* (the amount of space available to display your Web page elements before your visitors have to scroll down). When your page appears in a browser window, only the first item in a collapsible list is displayed. When you click the first list item, the rest of the list appears. This is also called *expanding* the list. Click the first list item again, and the list disappears again. This is also called *collapsing* the list.

Best of all, collapsible bulleted and numbered lists are incredibly easy to create. To set up collapsible lists, do the following:

1. Create a bulleted or numbered list.
2. Select the list items you want to collapse and click the Increase Indent button on the Formatting toolbar twice. This indents the list items below the top list item and applies a different bullet or number style to the indented items.
3. Select the indented list items and display the List Properties dialog box.
4. Click the Enable Collapsible Outlines check box. When you do, the Initially Collapsed check box becomes active. Click that check box to make sure that all of your lists start out collapsed, and then click OK.
5. Repeat steps 1-4 to collapse the rest of your list items.

Previewing a Collapsible List

Ready to see your collapsible list in action? Although it won't be displayed in the Normal page view, you can try it out by clicking the Preview tab and viewing your page in Preview mode. You can also preview your page in a Web browser, as shown in the following figure, by clicking the Preview button on the Standard toolbar or selecting Preview in Browser from the File menu.

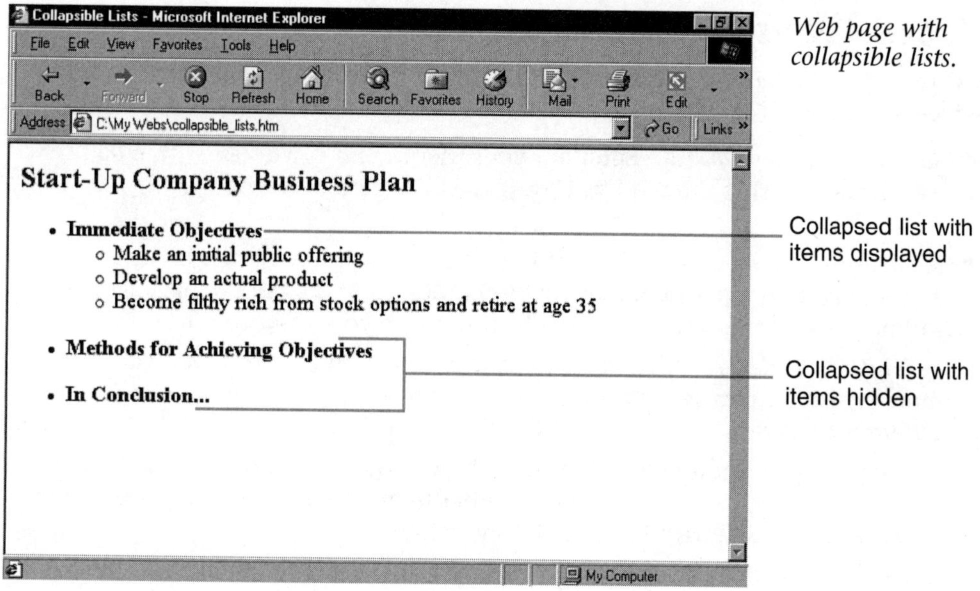

Web page with collapsible lists.

Changing a List to a Different Kind of List

You can apply a different list format to any list at any time. Select the entire list, click the right mouse button and open the List Properties dialog box, click a tab for the type of list you want to create, pick a style, and click the OK button. To apply the default style numbers or bullets, click the Numbering or Bullets toolbar button.

Removing List Formatting

If you decide your text doesn't look so good as a list after all, go ahead and remove the formatting. Select your list and display our old friend, the List Properties dialog box. With the Plain Bullets or Numbers tab selected, click on the unformatted list style on the upper-left and click on the OK button. This removes all bullets, numbers, and definition list formatting without stripping out your other text styles.

Five Cool Ways to Use Lists

Lists are pretty basic, but don't let that stop you from being creative. Try the following ideas on for size:

- *Start your own top ten list* Entertain your friends and coworkers with a daily, weekly, or monthly top ten list. Hey, if David Letterman can do it, why can't you?
- *Make lists of hover buttons* Lists of links that change color when the user passes a mouse pointer over them look really cool. Chapter 20, "Gee-Whiz Pages with Animated Special Effects," tells you how to make your links roll over.
- *Use different bullet or number styles for nested lists* You can make nested lists more stylish (and easier to read) by using different bullet or number styles for different list levels.
- *Frame 'em* Create framed Web pages, where you can click on lists of links in one frame to display a new page in another frame. Chapter 11, "Get Framed! Building a Web Site with Frames," tells you how.
- *Be creative with bulleted list images* You can use image bullets creatively to get your point across to your visitors. For example, if you include lists of files and folders for your company intranet, try some folder and file icons. Chapter 8, "The Picture-Perfect Web Page: Placing and Tweaking Images," tells you where to get free clip art on the Web.

The Least You Need to Know

- *Types of lists* With FrontPage, you can set up bulleted lists, numbered lists, and definition lists. Bulleted lists are indented, and list items are preceded with a bullet. Numbered lists are indented, and list items appear in numerical order. Definition lists consist of main list items followed by indented descriptions for each main list item.
- *Collapsible lists* Collapsible lists are like regular bulleted or numbered lists, except that only the top list item appears when the page first loads. Visitors can then expand the list to display the remaining list items by clicking the top list item, and then collapse the list by clicking the top list item again.
- *Creating bulleted and numbered lists* To create a list, type a list of items, select the list, and then click the Numbering or Bullets list toolbar button, or select Numbering from the Format menu, to display the Numbering dialog box.
- *Setting up definition lists* To create a definition list, type a list of main items followed by descriptive text. Format each main list item as a definition by selecting the text and choosing Defined Term from the Style menu on the Formatting toolbar. Then format each description by selecting the text and then choosing Definition from the Style menu on the Formatting toolbar.
- *Collapsing a bulleted or numbered list* To collapse a bulleted or numbered list, select the list items beneath the first list item and click the Increase Indent button on the Formatting toolbar twice. Then select the entire list, display the Numbering dialog box, and click the Enable Collapsible Outlines and Initially Collapsed check boxes. Collapsible lists work only when you click the Preview tab or preview the Web page in a browser.
- *Choosing bullet and number styles* You can change the bullet and number styles for your lists by displaying the Numbering dialog box, clicking the appropriate tab, and choosing an option. You can also use your own images as bullets.

Chapter 7

Think Links: Adding Links to Your Pages

In This Chapter

- Making links to local and remote Web sites
- Setting up links within a document
- Creating email links
- Viewing pages in the Hyperlinks view
- Adding hyperlink rollover effects
- Creating a navigation bar

Following links is kind of like using a telephone's auto-dial buttons to make a call—only much cheaper! Just press a button (or an image, or some text) and off you go. Just as telephone numbers are associated with auto-dial buttons, Web page addresses are associated with links so you can open a Web page with a single click instead of typing the whole URL. Fortunately, you'll find that creating links is much easier than programming your telephone's auto-dial buttons… or, for that matter, your VCR.

Hello? Is Anyone Out There? Linking to Other Web Sites

No man or woman is an island, so you'll probably want to make links to other people's Web pages. You can use links to point visitors to useful resources that relate to the material on your Web page, introduce them to friends and relatives who have Web sites set up, or tell the world about your favorite places to visit on the Web. Outside Web sites are also called *remote* Web sites because your computer isn't directly connected to them.

New, Improved Linking!

If you've used previous versions of FrontPage, you'll sure appreciate FrontPage 2000's easier-to-use Create HyperLink dialog box! For example, when you're creating email links, click the Make a Hyperlink That Sends Email button and type an email address when the Create Hyperlink dialog box appears.

To link to someone else's Web site, select the text or image you want to link, and then click the Hyperlink button on the Standard toolbar to display the Create Hyperlink dialog box. You can then enter a Web site address in the URL box and click on the OK button. Web site addresses must begin with `http://` (as in `http://www.website.com/`). FrontPage even puts it in the URL box so you won't forget! If you aren't sure of the Web page's URL, you can click the Use your Web Browser to Select a Page or File button to launch your Web browser so you can browse for the page.

Create Hyperlink dialog box.

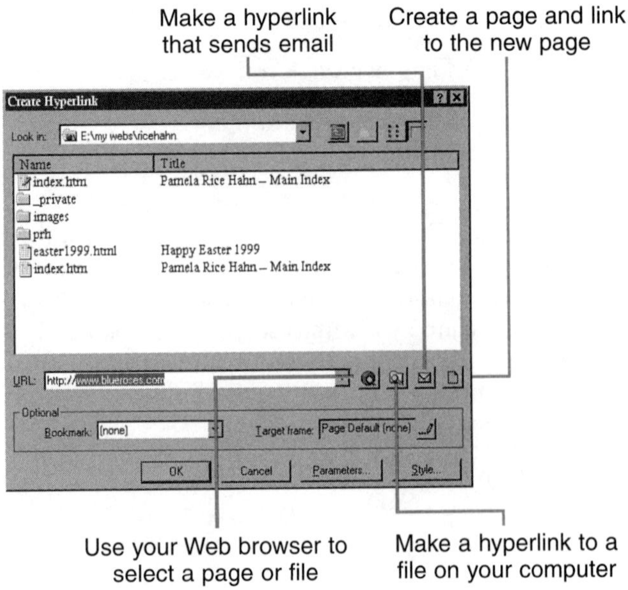

Linking to Web Pages on Your Web Site

Linking to pages on your own Web site can be easier because you don't have to remember any URLs—you can browse for your files instead. To link to a page on your Web, select your text, display the Create Hyperlink dialog box, select the file, and click the OK button. If you've stored your Web page in a different folder, you can select a folder from the Look in list.

How Do You Say "URL"?

Please don't say "Earl" unless you want people to think you're the pet bear in *The World According to Garp*! Say "You are ell" instead.

Linking to Local Files

You can link to pages in other folders on your computer or network—these are also called *local files*. To link to a local file, display the Create Hyperlink dialog box and click Make a hyperlink to a file on your computer. When the Select File dialog box appears, you can browse for a file, select it, and click the OK button to return to the Create Hyperlink dialog box.

If you link to a page on your office intranet, you might want to talk to your network administrator before making links. Depending on how he or she set the network up, the Web sites you want to link to may have their own local URLs, such as `http://theserver/department/sales.htm`. Even if those pages aren't on the Internet, you should still link to them as if they are. For more about server administration, see Chapter 27, "You're the Boss! Becoming a Web Site Administrator."

Watch Your Local Links!

If you plan to host your site on a remote Internet server, like your ISP or Web hosting company, *don't* link to local files! Otherwise, your links won't work because they'll point to files on your computer instead of files on the Web. You should import the files into your FrontPage Web first, as explained in Chapter 24, "You and Your Web Files."

Linking to Areas Within a Document

In general, a Web page should not be longer than a screen or two of stuff because people don't like to scroll (for more design tips, see Chapter 10, "Elements of Style: Web Design Basics"). But sometimes you might need to create longer documents. For example, if you're a writer who wants to make samples of your work available online, it doesn't always make sense to split up your short stories or press clippings into separate Web pages. Fortunately, long documents don't *have* to make visitors scroll. You can create links to areas within the same Web page so people can navigate easily. The following sections tell you how to set up targets (bookmarks) and make links to them.

If You Use Netscape Navigator...

Don't confuse *Netscape* bookmarks with *FrontPage* bookmarks. Netscape bookmarks are like Internet Explorer favorites—URLs that you can save and visit again. FrontPage bookmarks are targets that let you link to areas of a Web page, as you'll see in the following sections.

Setting Up the Target

To create a link to an area in your document, you first need to make a bookmark (Microsoft's word for what the Webmeisters call *targets*). Select the text that you want to target, and choose Bookmark from the Insert menu. When the Bookmark dialog box appears, as shown in the following figure, enter a one-word name in the Bookmark Name box (bookmark names cannot have spaces in them) and click the OK button.

The Bookmark dialog box also comes in handy when you need to move around your document quickly while you work on it. To jump to a bookmarked area of your document, display the Bookmark dialog box, select a bookmark from the Other Bookmarks on this Page box, and click the Go button. You can also rename a bookmark by selecting it and typing a new name in the Bookmark Name box.

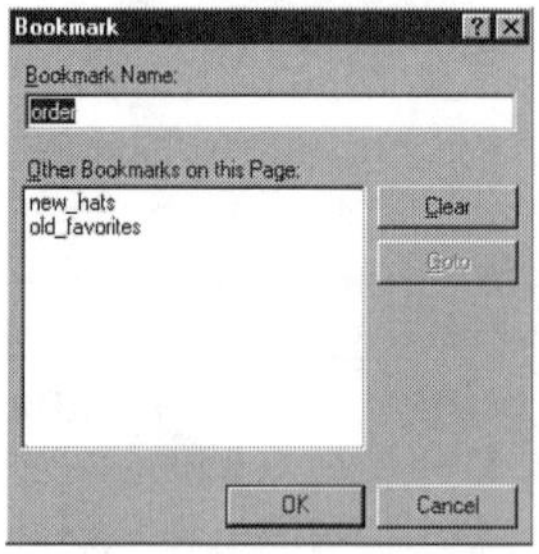

The Bookmark dialog box.

Making the Link

Once you've created a few bookmarks, you can create links for them. To link to a bookmark, display the Create Hyperlink dialog box, select a bookmark from the Bookmark list, and click the OK button. To help visitors navigate through a long document, you can provide a linked table of contents at the top of the page, and then provide a link back to the top of the page every few paragraphs or so. You can also link to bookmarks in other pages on your Web. When you select a Web page to link to, you can then pick a bookmark from the Bookmark list, as shown in the Create Hyperlink dialog box figure earlier in this chapter.

Send Email! Creating an Email Link

Email links make it easy for visitors to communicate with you and give you feedback about your Web site. When you click on an email link, your email application launches and a message window appears with the email address entered so you can fire off a message. To create an email link so visitors can respond to your Web page, select the text and display the Create Hyperlink dialog box. Then click the Make a Hyperlink That Sends Email button to display the Create Email Hyperlink dialog box, enter your email address in the Type an Email Address box, and click OK. When you return to the Create Hyperlink dialog box, click on the OK button to apply the link.

Where Do My Links Go: Viewing Web Pages in the Hyperlinks View

Links are the glue that holds Web pages together. Without links, Web pages wouldn't go anywhere, and then they wouldn't be any fun. You can take a peek at how your Web pages are linked together in the Hyperlinks view, as shown in the following figure. To display your Web site in the Hyperlinks view, click on the Hyperlinks icon from the Views menu.

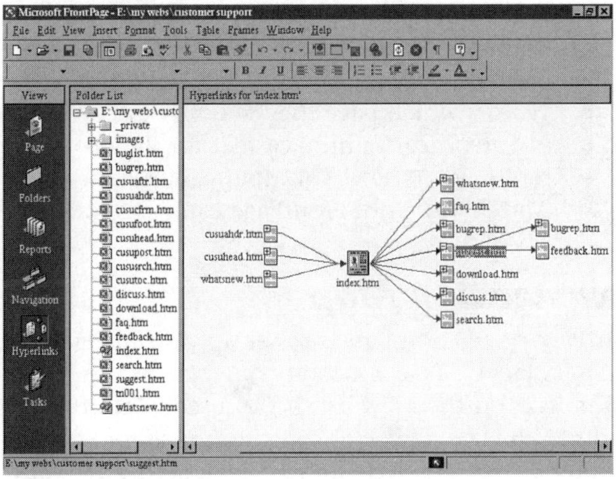

A Web site displayed in the Hyperlinks view.

FrontPage displays the current page with arrows pointing to linked pages with filenames. If a plus sign (+) appears in the upper-right corner of a document icon, you can click it to see where that document links to. Or you can click a minus sign (-) to collapse a link display. Links to remote Web sites are indicated with a full URL and a little globe icon.

Animating Your Text Links

How would you like to make your text links change color when the user rolls his mouse cursor over them? In Web-speak, these are called *rollovers*. To activate your links, select Background from the Format menu to display the Background dialog box—our old friend from Chapter 3, "Fooling Around with Web Pages." Select the Enable Hyperlink Rollover Effects check box and click on Rollover Style to display the Font dialog box. Then pick a new color for your links to change to when a mouse rolls over the link (you can also apply character effects—like bold and italics—or even choose different font styles) and click OK. When you return to the Properties dialog box, click OK. Then click the Preview tab and check out your new rollovers!

If You've Applied a Theme to Your Web Page

You cannot change your page's background properties. However, you can create rollovers by setting up animated hover buttons, as covered in Chapter 20, "Gee-Whiz Pages with Animated Special Effects."

Showing Visitors the Way with Navigation Bars

Navigation bars are groups of image links or text links that appear consistently throughout a Web site so visitors can find their way around. Larger Web sites usually have several sets of navigation bars, with a main navigation bar that appears on all pages and links to major sections of the site, and others that appear only within each section and link to pages within that section. Navigation bars also tell visitors which page they're on by displaying a different graphic, or unlinked text for the link to the current page. Whew! That sounds like a lot of work! And it was, until FrontPage came around.

Viewing Your Web's Navigation Map

The first step in creating FrontPage navigation bars is to set up your navigation map (also called a *jump* map in Web parlance). Take a look at your Web in the Navigation view by clicking the Navigation icon on the View list. If you used a FrontPage wizard to build your Web, the wizard has already created a navigation map for your pages, as we touched on briefly in Chapter 2, "Instant Web-Site-O-Matic: Spinning FrontPage Webs."

A Web site with a navigation map in place looks similar to a customer service Web site shown in the following figure. If you've imported your Web site or created it from scratch, rather than using a Web wizard, you'll see only one item that says Main Page. That's okay because you can set up navigation map yourself, as explained in the following section. Navigation maps look a lot like genealogical charts—and in fact, FrontPage does use the terms *parent* and *child* to describe relationships between different pages on a Web.

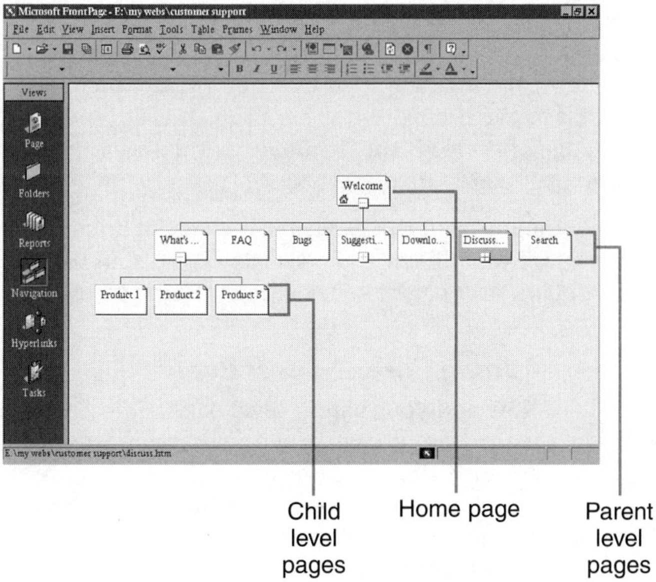

The customer service Web site displayed in the Navigation view.

A navigation map consists of the following levels:

- *Home page* The grandmother of all the documents on your Web site, this is the main (top-level) page. The home page is always named `index.htm`, `index.html`, `default.htm`, or `default.html`, and it should link to each of your main section (parent-level) pages.
- *Parent-level pages* The pages for each of the main sections on your Web site, such as Favorite Links or Products.
- *Child-level pages* The pages that parent-level (main section) pages link to. For example, if you have a Products section (a parent-level page), and then you create a page for each product, the product pages are child-level pages.

As with human families, Web page relationships can get complicated! For example, a child-level page can also be a parent for another set of Web pages.

Building a Navigation Structure

Unless you created your Web site with a wizard, you'll need to map your Web site in order to use navigation bars. This is also called building a *navigation structure.* If you've used a wizard to create your Web site, it has already set up the navigation structure for you. You don't *have* to map your Web site (unless you plan to use themes), but being able to place FrontPage navigation bars on your pages can save you a lot of work. You can either create a new Web site from scratch from the Navigation view while building your navigation structure, or you can create a navigation structure from your existing Web pages.

Creating New Pages for Your Navigation Structure

You don't yet have all the pages that you want to include in your navigation structure? Go ahead and create a new page for each item that you plan to include on your navigation bar, and then switch to the Navigation view. You can leave your pages blank for now, because FrontPage only needs the documents and page titles. (Don't forget to title your pages, as explained in Chapter 2.)

You can also create new pages straight from the Navigation view. Right-click the page that you want to link the new page to, and then choose New Page from the shortcut menu. FrontPage will create a blank new page one level down from the selected page.

Adding Parent-Level Pages

Now add your parent-level pages. Select your first main section page (the one that you would want to appear first in a list of links) from the Folder List, and drag it onto the Home Page item in the Navigation window frame. The home page may have a different name, depending on how you titled your pages, but it always appears with a little house icon. When FrontPage inserts the page below the Home Page icon, go ahead and add your other pages to your navigation map.

You can change the order in which pages appear by selecting a page and dragging it to the left or right. To add child-level pages (if you have any), select a page from the Folder List and drag it onto a page in the navigation window frame.

Attention, Theme Users!

If you plan to use themes, you need to map your Web site. Themes come with built-in navigation bars, and they generate the global navigation button labels and links from your Web's navigation structure. For more about themes, see Chapter 4, "Poof! You're a Designer with FrontPage Web Themes."

Adding Child-Level Pages

Once you create your parent-level pages, you can create child-level pages the same way. Select a page from the Folder List and drag it onto the parent-level page that you want it to go with. The child-level pages will appear below their respective parent-level pages.

Sharing Your Borders

Before you can put a navigation bar on your Web site, you need to apply shared borders to your pages. To apply shared borders to a Web site with a theme, see Chapter 4. To add shared borders and navigation bars to pages that don't use themes, see Chapter 14, "Don't Like What You See? Designing Your Own Page Template."

If you used one of the FrontPage Web wizards to create your Web, as covered in Chapter 2, your Web pages already have shared borders, a theme, and navigation bars.

Inserting a Navigation Bar

Once you've created a navigation structure for your site, you can add navigation bars to your pages. Place your cursor where you want to insert the navigation bar, and then select Navigation Bar from the Insert menu to display the Navigation Bar Properties dialog box, as shown in the following figure. Select your options and click the OK button.

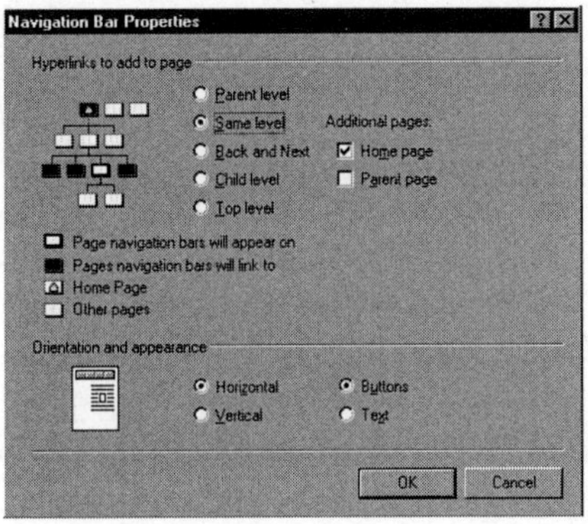

The Navigation Bar Properties dialog box.

The Navigation Bar Properties dialog box offers the following options:

- ➤ *Hyperlinks to add to page* You can choose to link to pages at the parent or child level, or to pages on the same level. If you want visitors to view your pages in a particular sequence, click the Back and Next radio buttons to insert buttons that link to the previous and next page, respectively.
- ➤ *Additional pages* You can also provide links to the main (home) page and the parent page.
- ➤ *Orientation and appearance* Select Horizontal to arrange your links in a row, or Vertical to arrange them in a column. Select Buttons if you want to use images for your links, or select Text if you want to use text links.

Plan Your Web Site the Old-Fashioned Way!

Sketching out a jump map (also called a *navigation map*) with a pen and paper can help you figure out where everything should go.

When you insert your navigation bar (or bars), they should look similar to the ones shown in the following figure.

The Catalog Web page on the Mad Hatter Web site, with same-level and child-level navigation bars.

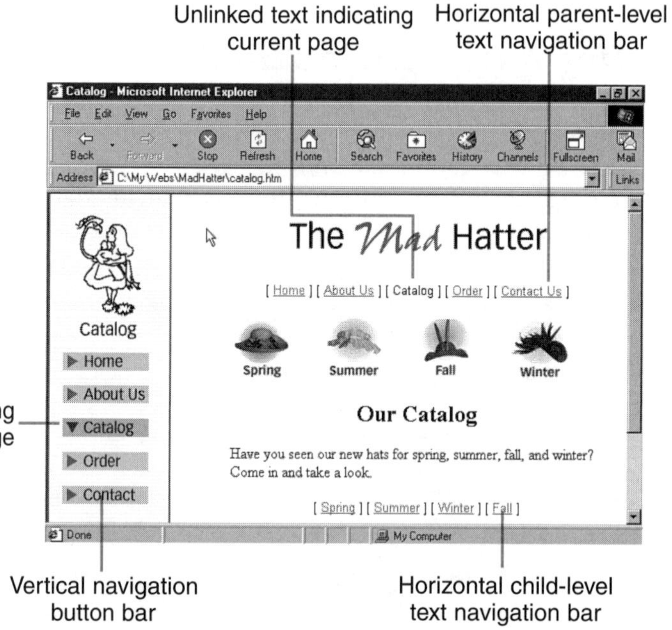

Adjusting the Navigation View

Ooof, it's kind of crowded in here! Larger Web sites sometimes don't quite fit into the Navigation View window. But you can *make* them fit with some help from the Navigation toolbar. The Navigation toolbar should appear automatically, but if it doesn't, you can select Toolbars from the Tools menu and then select Navigation. To zoom in or zoom out, select an option from the Zoom list. You can also switch between landscape (horizontal) and portrait (vertical) displays by clicking the Portrait/Landscape button.

Five Cool Ways to Use Links

This chapter talks about how to make basic text links to Web pages. As you read this book, you'll find out that you can do all kinds of other neat things with links too.

Here are a few nifty little link tricks:

➤ *Make an image map* Image maps are regular pictures with clickable *hot spots*—parts of the image you can click on to follow links. Chapter 16, "X Marks the Hot Spot! Making Image Maps," tells you how to make image maps.

- *Create link lists with Netscape bookmarks* Thinking of adding lists of your favorite links to your pages? If you use Netscape Navigator, you already have a list. Netscape stores your bookmarks (as defined earlier in this chapter) as an HTML document that you can import into a Web page and touch up a bit. Netscape bookmarks are located in your Netscape folder, which is usually located in your Programs folder. Depending on which version of Netscape you have, you might have to dig a little bit to find your bookmark file.
- *Link with images* You can also turn images into links. Chapter 8, "The Picture-Perfect Web Page: Placing and Tweaking Images," tells you how.
- *Link to files* As you'll find out in Chapters 17, "Strut Your Stuff: Sound, Video, and More," and 18, "A Match Made in Redmond: FrontPage 2000 and Microsoft Office 2000," you can link to just about any type of file you want. If the user has the right plug-in, he'll be able to view the file in his browser.
- *Try animated hover buttons* With FrontPage, you can create image links that change when the user passes the mouse pointer over them. Chapter 20 covers animated hover buttons (also called *rollovers*).

The Least You Need to Know

- You can link to other Web sites, pages on your own Web site, files, and areas within a Web page (FrontPage bookmarks) from the Create Hyperlink dialog box.
- You can see where all your links go by displaying your Web site in the Hyperlinks view. To display your Web site in the Hyperlinks view, click the Hyperlinks icon from the Views list.
- On the Background tab of the Page Properties dialog box, you can make your text links change color when a visitor passes the mouse pointer over them. However, if your Web page has a theme, you cannot change your background properties.
- To view a jump map of your Web site or create a navigation map so you can set up navigation bars, click the Navigation icon from the Views list. In the Navigation view, pages are displayed like a flow chart and designated as parent-level and child-level pages.
- To create a navigation structure for your Web site, go to the Navigation view, select the main page, drag your parent-level pages onto the main page from the Folder List, and then drag your child-level pages onto the parent-level pages from the Folder List.
- You can design your own navigation bar, as explained in Chapters 4 and 14.

Chapter 8

The Picture-Perfect Web Page: Placing and Tweaking Images

In This Chapter

- Putting pictures on your pages
- Importing pictures to your Web
- Using the FrontPage Clip Art Gallery
- Aligning and resizing pictures
- Adding space and borders around pictures
- Specifying alternative text for pictures
- Converting between Web image formats
- Five cool places to get free images

A Web site with no pictures? That's no fun. Naturally, you'll want to liven up your pages with a few graphics. With FrontPage, it only takes a few seconds to place your images and make them look fabulous. You don't even need to be an artist. FrontPage has all the tools you need, and it even comes with a Clip Art Gallery. You can also find lots of free artwork on the Web—see the "Five Cool Web Sites Where You Can Get Free Pictures" section at the end of this chapter.

Placing a Picture on Your Page

Have you ever used pictures in your word processing or desktop publishing documents? If so, you already know how to put a picture on your Web page. If the computer thang is completely new to you, don't worry—FrontPage can help you get those images onto your Web page in a snap.

Now, there's one thing you should know before you start working with images. On the Web, graphics come in only three flavors: GIF, JPEG, and PNG. The GIF format works best for *line art* images and JPEG works best for *photorealistic* images (the following list explains what these terms mean). Both GIFs and JPEGs have much smaller file sizes than other types of images—which makes them perfect for the Web. When you place an image that is formatted as a different image file type, FrontPage automatically converts it to a GIF or a JPEG.

In addition, FrontPage lets you import and convert your GIFs and JPEGs to PNG format, an up-and-coming type of image for the Web. PNGs offer many features that professional graphics people need for creating high-quality graphics. If that's not good enough, PNG images are even smaller (and download faster) than GIFs or JPEGs. See the "Converting Pictures" section later in this chapter for more information.

FrontPage Converts Your Pictures Automatically!

There are many other popular image file formats for Windows, including BMP, PCX, TIFF, and WMF. If you already have pictures that you've scanned, taken with a digital camera, or have on a CD-ROM, they may have been saved to one of those file formats instead of Web-friendly GIFs, JPEGs, or PNGs. That's OK, you can still put your images on your Web page. Just add the image, as covered later in this chapter, and FrontPage will convert it to a GIF or a JPEG for you.

Types of images used in Web pages:

- *Patterned backgrounds* You can use images as patterned backgrounds, as explained in Chapter 3, "Fooling Around with Web Pages."
- *Line art* This term applies to logos, clip art, cartoons, and other drawn images with simple lines and solid colors.

- *Photorealistic images* This term is used for photographs, scans of oil paintings or watercolors, and other graphics with complex textures, shading, and gradations of colors. The graphics pros often refer to these types of images as *continuous tone images.*
- *Text graphics* Typography on the Web has its limitations. When you want to use a special font for a heading, or want a line or two of text to appear just so, you can create it as an image and place it on your Web page.
- *Graphical bullets* These are small images used as accents for bulleted lists, as explained in Chapter 6, "Making a List, Checking It Twice."
- *Horizontal lines* Also referred to as *page dividers* or *horizontal rules*, these graphical page dividers can spice up your page while separating information on it.
- *Navigation buttons* Used to help visitors find their way around your Web site. For more about links and navigation buttons, see Chapter 7, "Think Links: Adding Links to Your Pages."

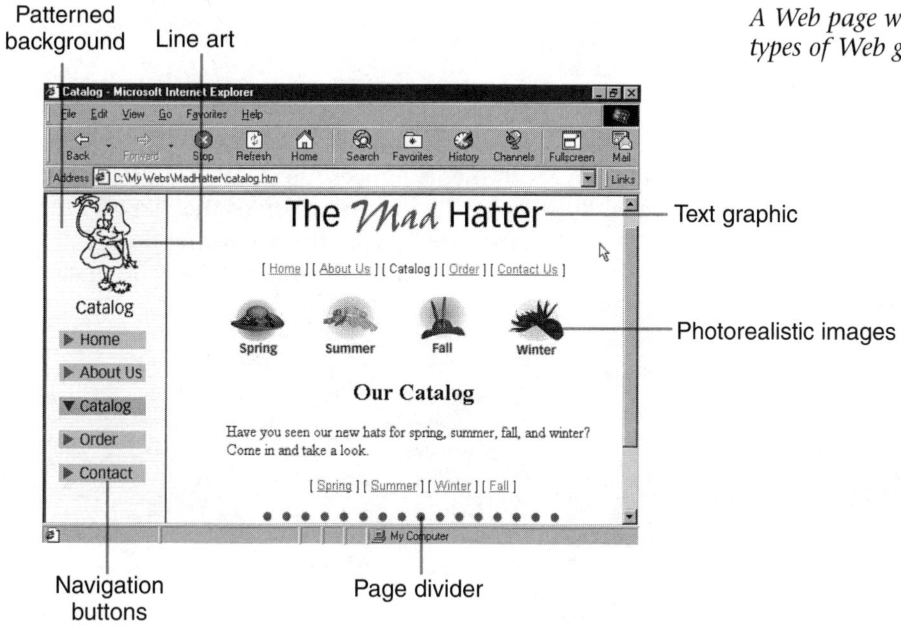

A Web page with different types of Web graphics.

Importing Pictures into Your Web

If you plan to upload your pages to a remote server, you should import pictures into your Web before placing them on your pages. No, FrontPage isn't trying to give you a hard time. It just wants to make sure that your images are displayed correctly when you upload your pages to your server.

To import your pictures into the current Web, go to the Folders view, open your Images folder (which is where FrontPage likes you to put your pictures), and select Import from the File menu. When the Import File dialog box appears, click the Add File button to display the Add File to Import List dialog box. Browse for a file, click the Import button to add the file to your images folder, and return to the Import File to FrontPage Web dialog box. You can then click the Add File button again to import as many pictures as you like. The Import File to FrontPage Web dialog box displays a list of your files, as shown in the following figure.

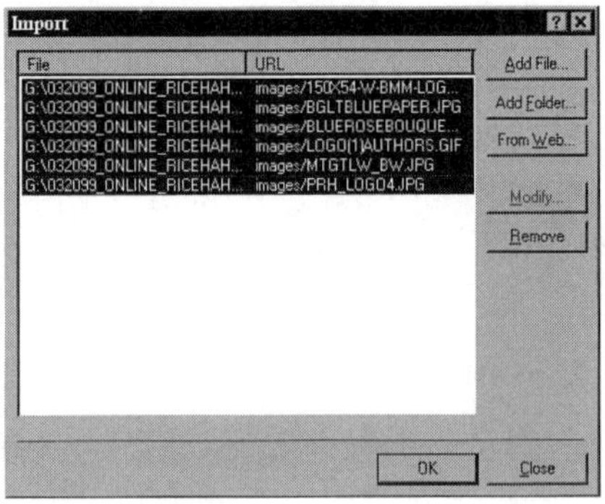

The Import File to FrontPage Web dialog box.

When you finish adding your pictures to the list, make sure that all of the images you want to import are selected by clicking the file at the top of the list, holding down the Shift key, clicking the last file on the list, and then clicking the OK button. You can click the Close button to return to FrontPage without adding the images to your Web.

Save Yourself Some Work

Do you need to import a *lot* of pictures? You can select more than one picture at a time from the Add File to Import List dialog box if they're all located in the same folder. Browse for the folder that contains your images, and open the folder to display the list of image files. To import multiple files that appear consecutively on the list, hold the Shift key down, click the top and bottom items on the list, and then click the Import button. To import multiple files that do not appear consecutively on the list, hold the Ctrl key down while selecting the pictures you want, and then click the Import button.

Inserting a Picture from the Current Web

Let's go back to the Page view and put a picture on your page. Place your cursor where you want to put the picture (don't worry about positioning it yet—we'll get to that) and click the Insert Image button on the Standard toolbar, or select Picture from the Insert menu and then select From File. When the Picture dialog box appears, select a picture from the Images folder and click OK. FrontPage displays the image on your page and also displays the Picture toolbar so you can tweak your image, as explained later in this chapter and in Chapter 9, "Spiffing Up Pictures."

Inserting FrontPage Clip Art Goodies

FrontPage comes with lots of clip art organized into a variety of categories, including Dividers and Decoration, People at Work, Emotions, Seasons, Web Bullets and Buttons, Plants, and Travel. To insert a FrontPage clip art item, click the Insert Image button to display the Picture dialog box. Click the Clip Art button to display the Clip Art Gallery, as shown in the following figure. You can also display the Clip Art Gallery by selecting Picture from the Insert menu, and then Clip Art. If a category catches your fancy, click on it to display pictures from that category. When you pass your mouse pointer over a category or picture, a ToolTip appears with a description.

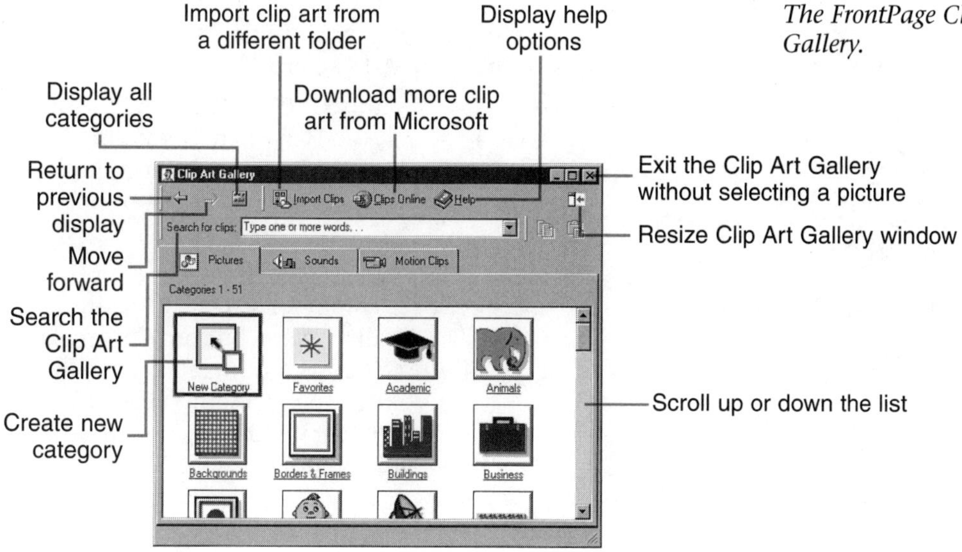

The FrontPage Clip Art Gallery.

When you click on any picture in the Clip Art Gallery, a pop-up menu appears with options. To add the picture to your Web page, click the Insert clip button. To preview the image at actual size, click the Preview button. To add the picture to a different category, click the Add Clip to Favorites or Another Category button. To search for similar pictures in the Clip Art Gallery, click the Search button.

The FrontPage Clip Art Gallery also has some other tricks up its sleeve:

- *Return to the main list from a picture list* After checking out pictures in a category, you can get back to the main list by clicking the All Categories button or using the Alt+Home key combination.
- *Import clip art from a different folder* You can import artwork from any other source, such as a folder on your own computer (or one on your network) or a CD-ROM, by clicking the Import Clips button. When the Add Clip to Clip Gallery dialog box appears, you can browse for your pictures. FrontPage imports the artwork to the currently selected category. If you import an image straight from the main list, the image appears on the main list.
- *Download more clip art from Microsoft's Web site* Microsoft updates their clip art, photographs, and multimedia from time to time. To download the latest files from Microsoft's special Web site, dial up your Internet connection and click the Clips Online button. When the Connect to Web for More dialog box appears, click the OK button. When Internet Explorer launches and displays Microsoft's clip art Web site, you can select the clips that you want to download and FrontPage will automatically update your Clip Art Gallery.
- *Get help!* Confused? Click the Help button. You can search the Help menu by typing in a word that relates to the task you need help with or by looking through the list of help topics.
- *Resize the Clip Art Gallery window* Short on space on your computer screen? Click the Change to Smaller Screen button. This makes the Clip Art Gallery window smaller so you can see any other open windows more easily. To display the larger window again, click the Change to Full Window button.

Search the Clip Art Gallery

To search for a piece of clip art related to a particular topic (such as "birthday" or "office"), type a keyword in the Search for Clips box.

- *Create a new clip art category* Before importing artwork from another source, you may want to create a new category for it. This helps you keep your pictures organized so you can find 'em when you need 'em. To create a new category, display the main list by clicking the All Categories button, then click the New Category icon on the main list. When the New Category dialog box appears, enter a name for the new category in the Enter New Category box and click the OK button.
- *Close the Clip Art Gallery without inserting a picture* Click the Close box in the upper-right corner of the Clip Art Gallery dialog box.

Inserting a Picture from Your Computer or Network

If you're building an intranet Web site for your organization and don't plan to upload it to a remote server, you can insert pictures in your pages from anywhere on your computer or network. From the Picture dialog box, click the Select a File on Your Computer button. When the Select File dialog box appears, browse your folders or drives for the image and click OK once you've found it.

Scanners and Digital Cameras

If you have a scanner or a digital camera hooked up to your computer, you can grab an image from it right now. From the Picture dialog box, click the Scan button to display the Camera/Scanner dialog box. To pick a source (especially important if you have both a digital camera and a scanner attached to your computer), click the Source button to display the Select Source dialog box, select a camera or scanner from the list, and click the Select button. To scan or take a picture and import it straight into your Web page, click the Acquire button. When you finish, click the Close button.

Displaying an Image from Another Web Site

You can also display an image from another Web site. From the Picture dialog box, enter a Web site address (such as `http://www.website.com/images/picture.gif`) instead of selecting a picture. Why would you want to do this? Well, I don't recommend it in most cases. When you display an image from someone else's Web site, it takes longer to load in the browser and your visitors might get cranky. But sometimes you might need to. For example, if you win a Web site award or join a

How Convenient!

When you insert an image or click on one, FrontPage displays the Picture toolbar so you can spiff it up. The next chapter covers the Picture toolbar options in detail.

banner ad exchange program (as explained in Chapter 26, "Don't Just Let It Sit There! Publishing Your Web Site"), you'll be given an image URL and asked to insert it on your Web page.

Changing Your Picture Properties

Once you've placed an image, you may want to fool around with it a little so it looks good with your other page elements. You can determine how the picture appears in relation to the surrounding text by changing the alignment, adding some buffer space, or displaying a border around it. If the picture looks too large or too small, you can also resize it to fit. Finally, if you're worried that an image might take too long to load in a browser, you can set things up so a smaller file is displayed first while the larger image loads.

To change an image's properties, display the Picture Properties dialog box by right-clicking the image and selecting Picture Properties from the shortcut menu. You can also click on the image the normal way and choose Properties from the Format menu. When you finish, click OK to apply your changes. Or, you can click Cancel to return to FrontPage without making any changes. The following sections explain different properties in detail.

Aligning a Picture with Text

Don't like the way your picture lines up with the surrounding text? Take it to the Picture Properties shop for a realignment. Display the Picture Properties dialog box and click the Appearance tab. You can then select an item from the Alignment List drop-down menu. When you finish, click OK to apply your changes. Or, you can click Cancel to return to FrontPage without making any changes. Yikes! What do all these choices mean? Not to worry—the following figure shows the image alignment settings in action.

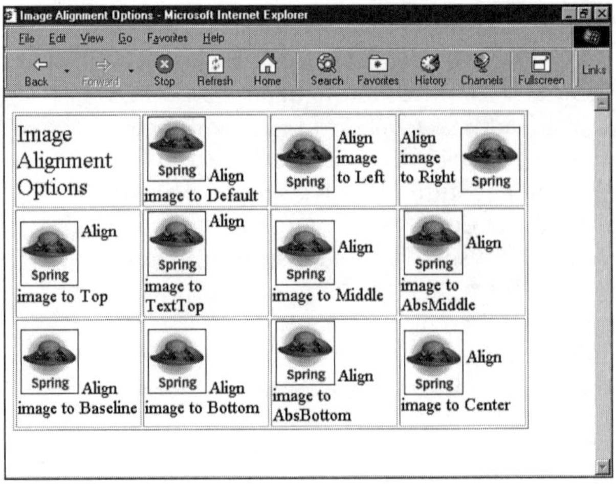

Image alignment options.

These image alignment options are explained in the following list:

- *Default* If you don't pick an alignment setting, the image aligns to the bottom, as explained later in this list.
- *Left* Aligns the top of the image with the highest letter in the first line of text, and wraps the text around the image (with the image on the left).
- *Right* Aligns the top of the image with the highest letter in the first line of text, and wraps the text around the image (with the image on the right).
- *Top* Aligns the top of the image with the highest element in the first line of text (even if there's another graphic on the line that is taller than the rest of the text). The following lines of text fall below the image.
- *TextTop* Aligns the top of the image with the highest letter in the first line of text. The following lines of text fall below the image.
- *Middle* Aligns the middle of the image with the bottom of the first line of text. The following lines of text fall below the image.
- *AbsMiddle* Aligns the middle of the image with the middle of the largest element in the first line of text (even if there's another graphic on the line that is taller than the rest of the text). The following lines of text fall below the image.
- *Baseline* Aligns the bottom of the image with the *baseline* of the first line of text. The baseline is where the bottoms of all the letters that don't have tails (like lowercase p's and q's) line up.
- *Bottom* Also aligns the bottom of the image with the baseline of the first line of text.
- *AbsBottom* Aligns the bottom of the image with the bottom of the lowest letter in the line of text (the tails of p's, q's, g's, and y's).
- *Center* Aligns the middle of the image with the middle of the first line of text. The following lines of text fall below the image.

Giving Pictures Some Elbow Room: Adding Space Around an Image

If you choose to wrap text around the right or left of an image, you can create a buffer to keep the text from butting up against the image. To create some buffer space around your image, go to the Picture Properties dialog box and click the Appearance tab. Pick a number from the Horizontal Spacing box by clicking the up or down arrow (5-10 pixels usually does the trick). This specifies the amount of space between the image and the text to the right or left. Pick a number from the Vertical Spacing box by clicking the up or down arrow. This specifies the amount of space between the image and the text below it. (3-5 pixels generally works fine—you don't need as much vertical space as horizontal space.)

When you finish, click OK to apply your changes. Or, you can click Cancel to return to FrontPage without making any changes.

Resizing an Image

If you think your image looks too big or too small, you can resize it in FrontPage. Select the image, display the Picture Properties dialog box, and click on the Appearance tab, as shown in the following figure. Click the Specify Size check box and leave the Keep Aspect Ratio check box selected so your image resizes proportionally and doesn't wind up looking yucky. You can choose to use pixels or a percentage (such as 75%) as your unit of measurement by clicking the In Pixels or In Percent radio button. Now, enter a number in the Width or Height box (if you change one measurement with the Keep Aspect Ratio check box selected, FrontPage adjusts the other measurement automatically). When you finish resizing your picture, click OK to apply your changes. Or, you can click Cancel to return to FrontPage without making any changes.

The Picture Properties dialog box with the Appearance tab selected.

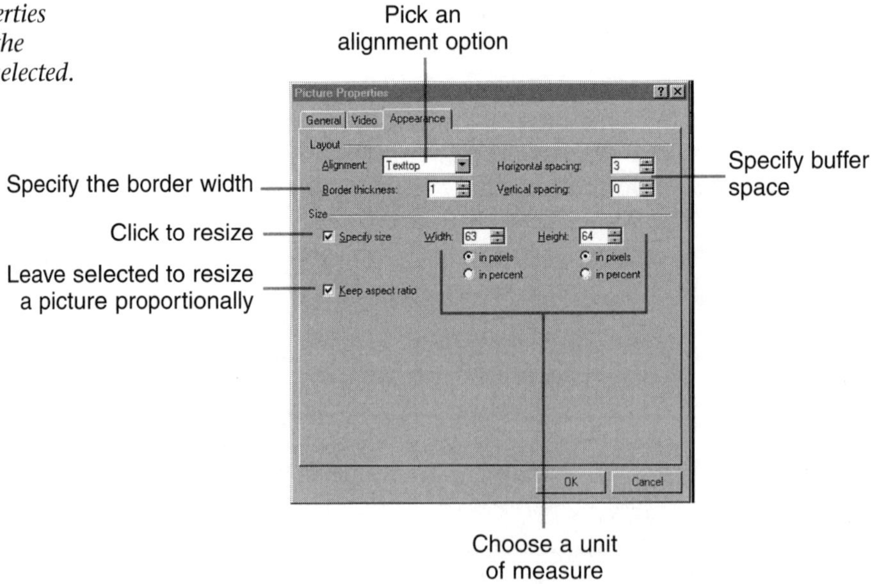

Bait and Switch: Displaying a Smaller Image While a Larger Image Downloads

You've taken one of those once-in-a-lifetime photographs of a gorgeous sunset or your daughter scoring a goal for her hockey team, and now you'd like to show it off on your Web page. Alas, the image file is *huge*! How do you keep your visitors from losing patience while it loads in the browser? Do the old bait-and-switch—black-and-white images take hardly any time to download.

So why not create a black and white copy of your image and display it first? When the *real* picture is ready, it replaces the black and white picture. This technique is called using a *low-res* (low resolution) image. As long as the two pictures have the same dimensions (width and height), this technique works great. Once you've set everything up, you can even click the Preview button on the Standard toolbar to see it in action.

Sounds like magic—try it! Select the bandwidth-hogging critter, display the Picture Properties dialog box and leave the General tab selected, as shown in the following figure. Click the Browse button to the right of the Low-Res box, select the smaller version of your image from the Select Alternate Picture dialog box, and click OK. When you return to the Picture Properties dialog box, the name of the image appears in the Low-Res box. Now you can click OK to return to the FrontPage window.

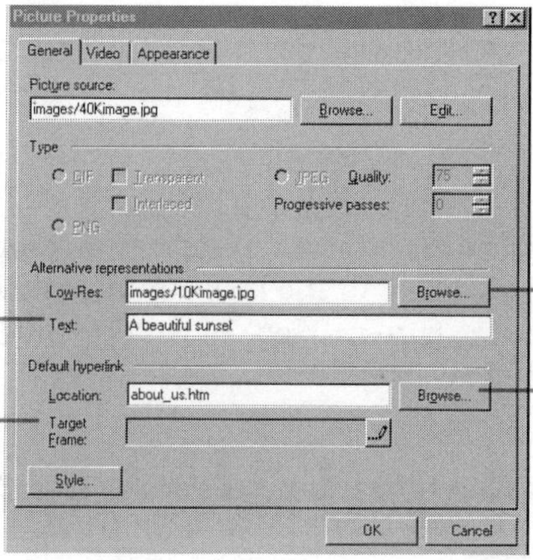

The Picture Properties dialog box with the General tab selected.

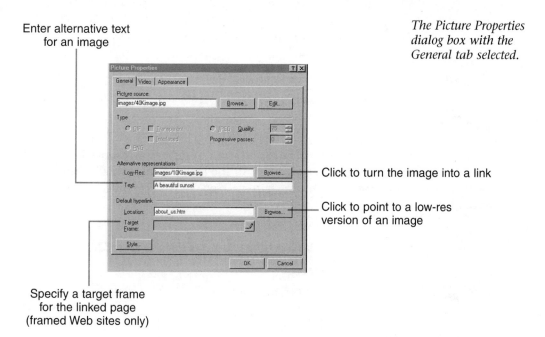

How Do I Get a Black and White Copy of My Picture?

You can make a copy of your picture from the Folders view, place it in your Web page, and use the Picture toolbar to make the picture black and white. The next chapter talks about ways that you can spiff up your pictures with the Picture toolbar, and Chapter 24, "You and Your Web Files," covers working with files in the Folders view. You can also use an image program like PhotoDraw (which comes with Office 2000 and is mentioned in Chapter 18, "A Match Made in Redmond: FrontPage and Microsoft Office 2000") or Paint Shop Pro (`http://www.jasc.com/`) to edit your images.

Linking an Image

Images make great links—in fact, Web surfers often click images to see if they lead anywhere. To link an image, select a picture and launch the Picture Properties dialog box with the General tab selected. Enter a URL in the Location box, or click the Browse button to browse for a page in the current Web. When you finish, click OK to apply your link and return to the FrontPage window.

Images Make Great Navigation Buttons!

You've probably visited snazzy-looking Web sites that use pictures as navigation buttons instead of boring old text links. Chapter 7 tells you more about how links and navigation bars work.

Putting a Border Around an Image

You can also put borders around your images. If you link the image, the border is displayed as the default link color. Otherwise, the border is displayed as the default text color. (For more about color schemes, see Chapter 2, "Instant Web-Site-O-Matic: Spinning FrontPage Webs.")

To add a border to your image, select the image, display the Picture Properties dialog box, and click the Appearance tab. You can then click the up or down arrow next to the Border Thickness box to adjust the border width. If you don't want a border around your image, select 0. When you finish, click OK to apply your changes. Or, you can click Cancel to return to FrontPage without making any changes.

Specifying Alternative Text for a Picture

Pictures can help convey ideas and information—we often can't find our way around the Web without them. But what about visitors who can't see your pictures for some reason? I'm not just talking about the visually challenged. You'd be surprised by how many people turn off their browsers' graphics options for faster Web surfing. Also, those cute little personal digital assistants (PDAs) like the PalmPilot can't display images either.

Pictures and Style Sheets

You may have heard about style sheets on the Web. You can create style sheets that automatically apply borders and other formatting to images throughout your Web site. For more about style sheets, read Chapter 15, "Now You're Stylin'! Using Style Sheets."

That's why you should always enter *alternative text* for your images. If someone can't see your pictures, they can at least read the text or have their computer read it to them. In addition, in newer browsers your alternative text displays as a tooltip when a visitor passes the mouse pointer over the image. Select your image, display the Picture Properties dialog box with the General tab selected, and enter a descriptive word or two for the image or the linked page (such as "Picture of me and my poodle, Tilly" or "Customer Service Page"). Click OK to apply your changes and return to the FrontPage window.

Copying and Pasting a Picture

If you need to use the same image on a page more than once, you can copy and paste it. Right-click on a picture and select Copy from the shortcut menu (you can also select the picture by left-clicking it, clicking the Copy button on the toolbar or using the Ctrl+C key combination). Then place your cursor where you want to insert a copy of your picture and click the Paste toolbar button, or use the Ctrl+V key combination.

Converting Pictures

If you think that your JPEG image would look better as a GIF, or vice versa, try converting it. You can also make your pictures smaller by converting them to PNGs. Select an image and display the Picture Properties dialog box. You can then choose a new image format by selecting the GIF, JPEG, or PNG radio buttons, and then click OK to return to your Web page. FrontPage copies your picture and reformats it, so you don't have to worry about losing the original if you don't like the results.

If you like the new version of your image, save your Web page. When the Save Embedded Files dialog box appears, as shown in the following figure, click the OK button to save the new image and include it on your Web page.

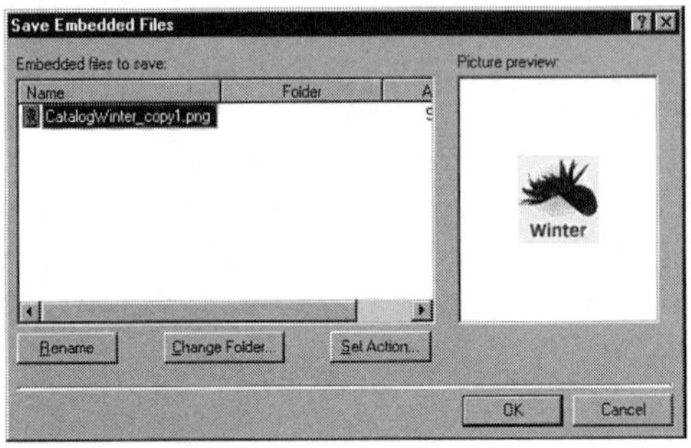

The Save Embedded Files dialog box.

Speed Up Your Web Pages!

Images can sure slow down your Web page. A quick glance at the status bar at the bottom-left corner of the FrontPage application window (covered in Chapter 1, "Get Ready to Rock with FrontPage 2000") tells you how long visitors have to wait to see your page. So what do you do when your pages get too fat? Convert your JPEGs to PNGs to reduce them to a third of their original size! There's just one problem with PNGs: People with pre-4.0 browsers won't be able to see them.

Five Cool Web Sites Where You Can Get Free Pictures

Need some good-looking images for your pages? Grab 'em from the Web. The following list points you to places that offer clip art free for the taking—although you should give them credit somewhere on your Web site.

➤ *Microsoft's Web site* (`http://cgl.microsoft.com/clipgallerylive/cgl23/eula.asp`) You can download brand-spankin'-new clip art goodies from Microsoft's Web site via the Clip Art Gallery, as explained earlier in this chapter.

- *The Icon Bazaar* (`http://www.iconbazaar.com`) Get your backgrounds, buttons, GIF animations, page dividers, bullets, symbols, and other cool stuff here. You can also find helpful information and answers to your image-related questions.
- *Best Free Clip Art On the Net* (`http://www.net-matrix.com/graphx/index.html`) Huge collection of clip art relating to everything from sports to the office.
- *The Animation Factory* (`http://www.eclipsed.com/`) Thousands of GIF animations, along with the usual icons, buttons, and images.
- *The Mining Company* (`http://webclipart.miningco.com`) Lots of free graphics sorted into categories to make it easy to find what you want.

The Least You Need to Know

- Pictures on the Web come in three flavors: GIFs, JPEGs, and PNGs. GIF works well for line art, and JPEG works best for photorealistic images. PNG is a newcomer to the Web and makes images significantly smaller for faster download times.
- If you place an image that was saved to a non-Web-friendly format, such as a BMP or PCX file, FrontPage converts it to a GIF or JPEG for you.
- You can insert pictures on your Web page from the Picture dialog box. You can also import pictures from different folders into the current Web through the Import File dialog box.
- Don't have any images to jazz up your pages? Try the FrontPage Clip Art Gallery. Or, you can download a host of great-looking graphics from the Web.
- You can align, resize, add buffer space, create borders, specify alternative text and low-res preview images for your pictures from the Picture Properties dialog box.
- Want to use pictures as links, instead of boring old text? Select an image, display the Create Hyperlink dialog box, and create your link, as explained in Chapter 7.

Chapter 9

Spiffing Up Pictures

In This Chapter

- Resizing and cropping pictures
- Adding cool special effects to your pictures
- Putting text on an image
- Creating transparent GIFs
- Setting up thumbnails
- Positioning and layering pictures
- Editing pictures with your favorite imaging application
- Five cool image programs that you can download from the Web

If you enjoy working with pictures, you might already have an image program like Photoshop or Paint Shop Pro. Or, if you've got Office 2000, you can fool around with PhotoDraw, a nifty new Office application covered in Chapter 18, "A Match Made in Redmond: FrontPage and Microsoft Office 2000." For the rest of us, FrontPage comes with a helpful Picture toolbar with features that the fledgling Web master can't do without. Even if you already have another image program, the Picture toolbar comes in handy for making quick changes on the fly.

Your Own Photo Lab: About the Picture Toolbar

So what's the Picture toolbar and what does it do, anyway? Click on a picture or insert one and you'll see. The Picture toolbar appears at the bottom of the FrontPage application window when you're working on an image, and then it gracefully exits to save space on your screen when you start doing something else. You can do all sorts of cool stuff to your pictures with the Picture toolbar, as shown in the following figures.

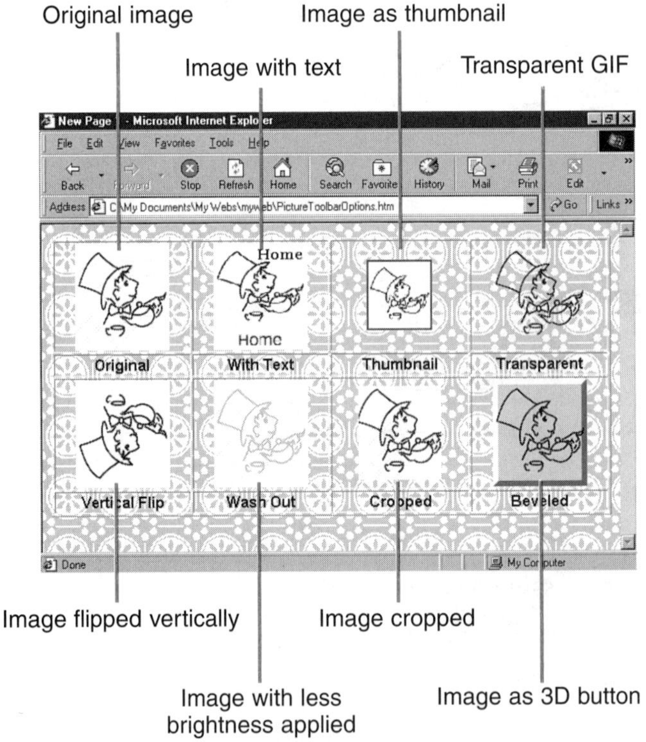

A few image effects that you can apply using the Picture toolbar.

So go ahead and turn a rectangle into a 3D button, and then type a label on it. Crop your ex out of a picture and resize it. Format a graphic as a transparent GIF so it displays well against a Web page background. Fade a picture for a washed-out effect, or make a picture black and white. Rotate or flip a button or text graphic and see how it looks. The sky's the limit. In addition, you can use the Picture toolbar to set up an image map, as explained in Chapter 16, "X Marks the Hot Spot! Making Image Maps." Wow! Not bad for a skinny little toolbar, eh?

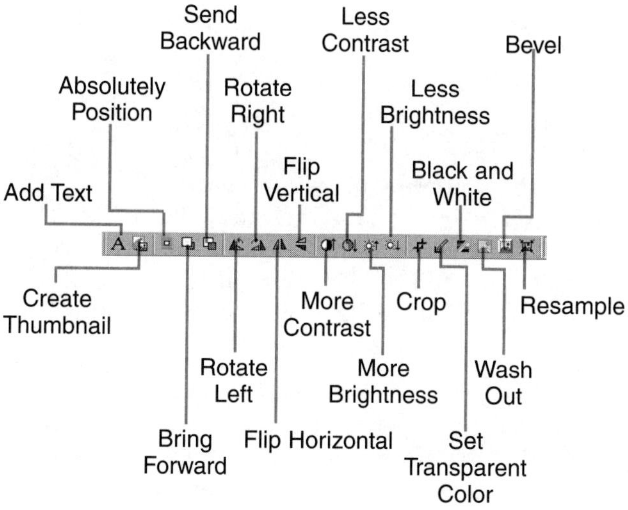

The Picture toolbar.

Sizing It Up: Resampling Pictures

"But you already *told* me how to resize a picture in the last chapter," you're probably thinking. Not to worry, this book was not written by the Federal Department of Redundancy Department. *Resampling* pictures works a little differently than resizing them. When you enter new dimensions for a picture in the Image Properties dialog box, it doesn't change the original image's size—it only changes how Web browsers display the image. When you resample a picture, it changes the dimensions of the actual image. Resampling also helps your pages load faster because the Web browser doesn't recalculate the image's dimensions.

Displaying the Picture Toolbar

If you find it more reassuring to see the Picture toolbar on your screen even if you aren't using it, select Toolbars from the View menu and select Picture from the cascading menu.

To make your image file larger or smaller, select it and resize it in the Image Properties dialog box as you normally would. (See Chapter 8, "The Picture-Perfect Web Page: Placing and Tweaking Images," if you've forgotten how to do this.) You can adjust an image by selecting it and clicking and dragging a boundary marker. When you finish resizing your image, click the Resample button on the Picture toolbar.

The Final Cut: Cropping a Picture

Copy Your Pictures First!

When you apply special effects from the Picture toolbar, FrontPage 2000 changes your image files. Before jazzing up your pictures, go to the Folders view and make a copy or two (as explained in Chapter 24, "You and Your Web Files"). That way, you still have your originals to work with.

You love the picture you took of your poodle, Fifi, but you wish it was a close-up. Or maybe you'd like to put that flattering picture of yourself on your Web resume, but you'd rather not have potential employers see the pool table and neon beer sign behind you. Send the Picture toolbar to the rescue! You can crop out all that unwanted background stuff.

Select a picture and click the Crop tool on the Picture toolbar. A selection box with dashed lines and little square handles appears. Place your cursor over a handle until it turns into a two-way arrow, and then press your mouse button down and drag the handle. Adjust the handles until the selection box surrounds the part of the image you want to keep. When you finish adjusting your cropping area, click the Crop button again.

You can also draw a selection box yourself. Click anywhere on the picture to display the crosshair cursor. Click this cursor on the upper-left corner of the part of the image you want to keep, and drag it diagonally to the right to create a rectangle or square. When you finish drawing your cropping area, click the Crop button again.

Adding Cool Special Effects

Okay, enough of the basics—let's move on to the *fun* stuff. You can jazz up your images with cool special effects just by clicking a button. If you're more of a practical person, don't turn away quite yet. The Picture toolbar can help you solve last-minute Web page layout problems quickly and efficiently.

Making Transparent GIFs

You've gathered your pictures together and found a great-looking background image. Then all of a sudden, horror strikes! No, it isn't the guy with the painted-white Captain Kirk mask who chases Jamie Lee Curtis around every few years. It's the dreaded rectangular background that appears around your line art images and makes your Web page look mighty clunky. Wouldn't it be nice if the picture floated seamlessly over the Web page background pattern or the picture behind it?

With the Picture toolbar, you can remove your image's background color. Images without a background are called *transparent GIFs*. You can remove any image's background color. Select the picture and then click on the Set Transparent Color toolbar button. This turns your cursor into something that looks like a pencil eraser with an arrow sticking out of it. Click the cursor on the color you want to remove. If the original image is not formatted as a GIF, a dialog box appears and tells you that FrontPage needs to convert the image. Click OK.

Back to the Good Old Days: Making a Picture Black and White

Black-and-white photos can add an interesting antique-y effect to your Web pages. Because they take a shorter time to load in browsers than their Technicolor cousins, black-and-white pictures also work great as low-res images. To make a picture black and white select the picture and click the Black and White button.

Adjusting the Brightness and Contrast

Does your picture look too light or too dark? Select the picture and click the Less Brightness or More Brightness button. If the subject of your picture seems to fade into the background, or the picture looks kind of faded or fuzzy, try the contrast controls. To heighten the contrast, select the picture and click the More Contrast button. You can also soften harsh lines and shadows by selecting the picture and clicking the Less Contrast button.

Washing Out a Picture

With FrontPage, you can create impressive-looking text and image overlays just like the pros, as you'll learn later in this chapter. But this technique can backfire if people can't read the text because the picture underneath it is too dark. The Picture toolbar gives you a way to get around this problem—you can *wash out* the image so that it appears faded. Washing out an image can also lend a dreamy look to your page. To wash out a picture, select it and click the Wash Out button.

Making Instant 3D Buttons

3D buttons go great with Web pages because they just *beg* visitors to click on them. You can turn any graphic into a 3D button by clicking the image and then clicking the Bevel tool. *Bevelling* is an imaging technique that creates an edge around an image to make it look three-dimensional.

Typing Text on a Picture

Not only can you create your own 3D buttons, you can label them too. Or you can type a caption or anything else you want on your images. To type text on a graphic, select the picture and click the Text button on the Picture toolbar. A boundary box appears with a blinking line cursor in the middle. You can type your text and select a font, font size, text style, alignment option, and font color from the Formatting toolbar. When you finish, you can click your cursor anywhere else on the page.

Now that you've sampled some of the Picture toolbar's special effects, let's see how they look on a real Web page.

A Web page with a few special effects applied.

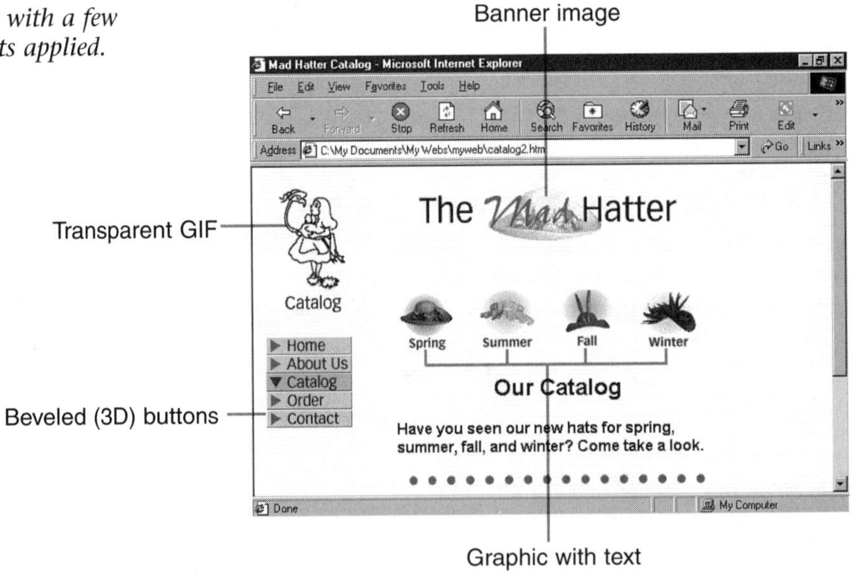

Rotating and Flipping Pictures

You can also rotate pictures to the left or right or flip them horizontally or vertically. This can come in handy if you want to use a text graphic heading as a sidebar graphic or point a bullet or other image in a different direction. To rotate a picture to the left, click the Rotate Left button. To rotate a picture to the right, click the Rotate Right button. To reverse a graphic across its vertical axis, click the Flip Horizontal button. To reverse a graphic across its horizontal axis, click the Flip Vertical button.

Making Thumbnails

A thumbnail is a miniature version of a larger image. If you're an artist or photographer and want to put your portfolio online—or if you want to put those photos of your vacation on your Web site—you'll love the Picture toolbar's thumbnail feature.

At some point you may need or want to share a few large pictures with your visitors. However, even standard 4×5 pictures can take up an awful lot of space on your page—not to mention the long download times. Instead, you can create a thumbnail image and then link it to the original picture. This way, people can preview the thumbnail and decide whether to take the time to view the real thing. To create a thumbnail version of a picture, select the picture and then click the Auto Thumbnail button. FrontPage automatically creates the smaller image and links it to the larger image.

Saving Your Changes

When you change your images, FrontPage needs to make the necessary changes to your Web. (Remember that FrontPage is a Web server too, and that servers need to know everything!) The next time you save your page, the Save Embedded Files dialog box appears with a list of the edited images, as shown in the following figure. FrontPage gives you the option of renaming your enhanced pictures so you can save them as new files instead of changing the originals. It's simpler to make copies of your images before you edit them, as explained earlier in the chapter. But it's nice to know that FrontPage gives you a second chance if you forget.

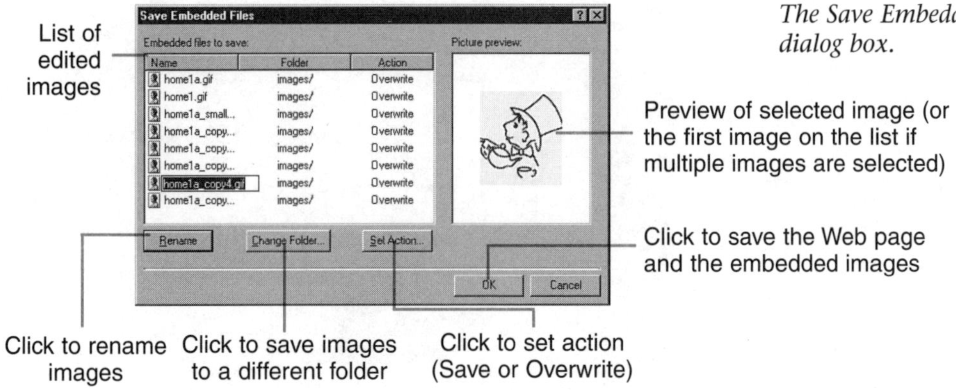

The Save Embedded Files dialog box.

To save your page and replace your original pictures with the changes you've made, click the OK button. To rename your pictures and embed the copies in the current Web page, select an image from the Embedded Files to Save list, click the Rename button, and type a new filename. Repeat for each image, and then click the OK button.

> **Version NEW! 2000**
>
> **Cool Layered Layouts**
>
> FrontPage 2000's Picture toolbar has new buttons for positioning and layering images. FrontPage also makes it easy to create position boxes for text and other page elements so you can position and layer them too.

Positioning Pictures and Text

Web page design used to really frustrate people. The limitations of plain old HTML made it difficult to put things where you wanted them or to ensure that your layouts looked the same in other people's browsers. In addition, you couldn't do really creative layouts with overlapping text and images.

But now, FrontPage and the newer Web browsers support *absolute positioning* and *layering,* which makes working with Web pages more like working with conventional page layout programs like QuarkXPress, Adobe PageMaker, and Microsoft Publisher. These features let you create spiffy page designs that look exactly the same every time someone visits them (as long as they have a 4.0 browser or higher). With absolute positioning, you can grab an image or item in a position box and move it exactly where you want it. Layering enables you to overlap images and text for interesting effects, as shown in the following figure.

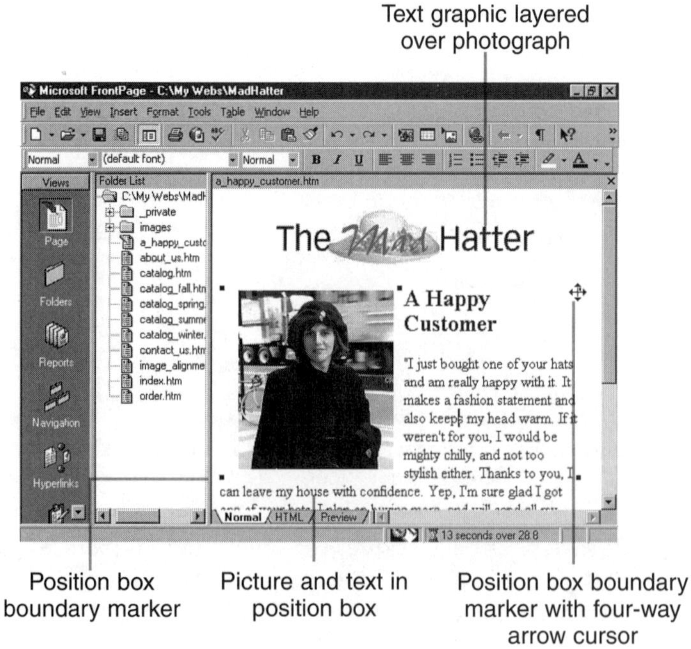

A Web page with absolutely positioned and layered elements.

So What's the Downside?

Having complete control over a Web page's layout makes artsy types jump for joy. Alas, absolute positioning has its downside. Older browsers can't display your pages correctly, and your page layouts might be jumbled and difficult to read and navigate.

Use Transparent GIFs for Layering Text Graphics

How did I get the "The Mad Hatter" text graphic to overlay the picture of the hat without displaying an ugly box and covering up part of the hat? I formatted it as a transparent GIF. You can make your GIF images transparent too—the preceding "Making Transparent GIFs" section tells you how.

Positioning a Picture

Click on a picture on the current Web page. When the Picture toolbar appears at the bottom of the page, click the Position Absolutely button and drag your picture to a new location on the page. Once you've positioned your image, you can move it whenever you want. Simply click the image to display the four-way arrow, and then drag it to another place on your page.

Positioning Text and Other Stuff

If you'd like to position and layer text, tables, or groups of elements, you need to first create a *position box* for them. Positioning text and other page elements works a little differently than with images because you can't activate the positioning feature from the Picture toolbar.

Select the page elements and then choose Position Box from the Format menu to display the Position dialog box, as shown in the following figure. Choose your options, as explained in the following list, and then click OK to create the position box and return to your Web page.

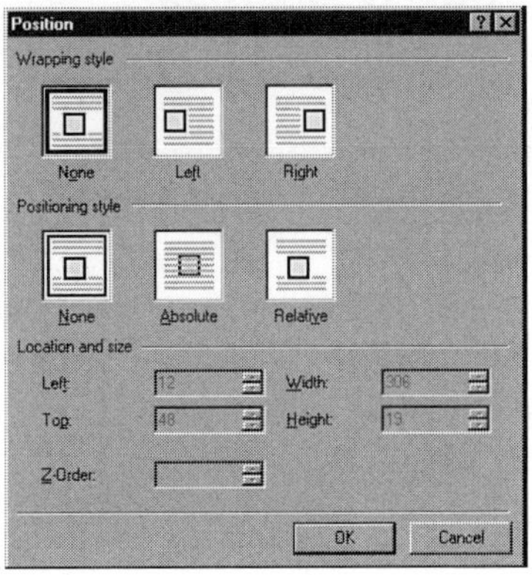

The Position dialog box.

In the Position dialog box, you can choose from the following options:

- *Wrapping style* Determines how text on the page flows in relation to the position box. Choose None to layer your position box (overlap it with another page element) rather than force text to wrap around it. Choose Left to place the position box to the left of the surrounding text and wrap the text around the right side. Or choose Right to place the position box to the right of the surrounding text and wrap the text around the left side.
- *Positioning style* Select Absolute to place and layer the position box. Choose Relative to place the position box and wrap text around it according to the Wrapping style option you've chosen. Don't choose None—that makes your position box behave like a normal page element that can't be positioned or layered! And that's no fun.
- *Location and size* You can also determine the exact location and size of your position box. To place the position box in relation to the top and left side of your Web page, enter the coordinates (in pixels) in the Left and Top boxes. To determine the size of your position box, enter the measurements (in pixels) in the Width and Height boxes. If you don't know a pixel from a pineapple, that's OK. You can also place and adjust the size of your position box from the Page view.

Adjusting a Position Box

To move the position box, pass your mouse pointer over one of the edges until the cursor turns into a four-way arrow. You can then press down your mouse button and drag the position box to a new location. To resize the position box, pass your mouse pointer over one of the boundary markers until the cursor turns into a two-way arrow. You can then press down your mouse button and drag the boundary box up, down, diagonally, or to the right or left, depending on which boundary marker you've selected.

Layering Images and Position Boxes

Thanks to the absolute positioning feature, you can also create interesting overlay effects. Try overlapping text and images for a textured look, or layering some text over a faded photograph for visual impact.

To layer objects, you must first create a *Z-order* for them. This is the third dimension (depth) on a computer screen. By specifying the Z-order of an image or position box, you can determine which objects go on top and which objects go underneath. All you have to do is assign a number to each object—0 puts an object on the bottom layer, 1 moves the object up one level, and so on.

Working with Layered Pictures and Position Boxes

Layered objects can get a little tricky when you need to edit or move them. After all, how do you get at that sneaky little image on the bottom layer? With pictures, you can use the Picture toolbar to move images backward and forward. For position boxes, you'll need to reorder them from the Position dialog box.

To move a picture backward so you can work with it or the position box behind it, select it and click the Send Backward button. To bring a picture to the front so you can edit or move it, select it and click the Bring Forward button.

To move a position box backward or forward, click on the position box and then display the Position dialog box by selecting Position from the Format menu. Enter or select a number in the Z-Order box and click OK. You can also assign Z-order numbers to pictures by following these steps.

Editing a Picture with Another Image Editor

The Picture toolbar works great for basic image editing. If you prefer to use a real image editor like PhotoDraw, FrontPage can launch that program when you need it. But first, you have to tell FrontPage where it is. Once you've configured an image editor, all you have to do is double-click an image and FrontPage launches the program.

Telling FrontPage Where to Find Your Image Program

To configure an image editor, select Options from the Tools menu to display the Options dialog box, and then select the Configure Editors tab. You'll see a list of basic file types and the application that handles those types of files.

Click the Add button to display the Add Editor Association dialog box. Enter a filename extension for the type of file that your editor can edit (such as `.jpeg`, `.jpg`, `.png`, or `.gif`) in the File Type box, and enter the name of your image program in the Editor Name box. Oh, and don't forget that scary-looking box that asks for a command. No worries—it just wants you to tell it where the application is.

Remember to Configure *All* Your Image File Types!

You need to configure your image editor for all of the image file types you generally work with. This includes `.jpeg`, `.jpg`, and `.gif`. You also might want to add other file types to the list, such as `.pcx`, `.bmp`, `.tiff`, and `.wmf`.

(An application is an executable file ending with the `.exe` extension.) Click the Browse button to display the Browse dialog box and locate your program. In most cases, you can find it somewhere in your Programs folder. Select the `.exe` file, and then click the Open button to return to the Add Editor Association dialog box. Click OK to return to the Options dialog box. Now you can repeat these steps for other Web image extensions, or click OK to save your changes and return to the FrontPage window.

Five Cool Image Programs You Can Download

If you get serious about your images, you might want more than you can get from the Picture toolbar. Here are some other programs:

- *Paint Shop Pro by JASC* A $99 shareware program with advanced image editing features. It's available at `http://www.jasc.com/`.
- *LviewPro* A $40 shareware utility for opening and converting different types of images. It also has a few other tools for cropping and applying special effect image filters. It's available at `http://www.lview.com/`.
- *Reptile by Sausage Software* A nifty little freeware gizmo for creating textures and patterned backgrounds for your Web pages. It's available at `http://www.sausage.com/reptile/`.
- *Xara 3D* A $39 program that lets you create cutting-edge 3D text graphics. It's available at `http://www.xara.com/xara3d/`.
- *Ulead Web Razor* A complete suite of Web imaging programs for keeping track of your files, building GIF animations, creating buttons, applying special effects, and compressing your images to small file sizes. It's available at `http://www.ulead.com/`.

The Least You Need to Know

- The Picture toolbar automatically appears when you select a picture or insert an image. The Picture toolbar has options for touching up, layering, positioning, and adding special effects to your pictures.
- You can use the Picture toolbar to position, layer, flip, crop, wash out, bevel, and adjust the brightness and contrast of your pictures. In addition, you can make a GIF transparent by removing the background, and you can automatically create a small thumbnail that links to the original picture.
- When you save a Web page with images that you've just edited, the Embedded Files dialog box appears so you can save copies and leave the originals untouched.
- You can position and layer images from the Picture toolbar, and you can create position boxes for text and other page elements from the Position dialog box. The Position box also allows you to layer pictures and place by assigning a Z-order for each element.

Part 3

You've Got the Look! Designing Pages Like the Pros

First impressions count. And when it comes to your Web site, you want the visitor's first impression to be a good one, don't you? The Web gives you an exciting, inexpensive way to create, communicate, and publish. But this new medium also takes a little getting used to. Visitors expect more from a Web site than readers expect from a printed brochure, report, or magazine article.

For example, if you write Mom and Dad a letter about your trip to France, they'll be happy with decent penmanship and a few photos. If you create a Web page about your trip and email Mom and Dad the URL, that's a whole new ball game! They'll expect lots of pictures and links to related Web sites, and they'll want it fast.

Luckily, FrontPage 2000 makes it easy to create Web sites that keep your visitors happy. The first chapter in this part gives you the lowdown on organizing and designing your Web site so it looks good and is easy for people to navigate. Then you'll learn how to use FrontPage 2000's tools to lay out great-looking pages with frames, tables, online forms, templates, and style sheets.

Elements of Style: Web Design Basics

In This Chapter

- Planning your Web site
- Designing navigation elements
- Laying out your pages
- Choosing colors and graphics
- Five cool Web sites to visit for design help

The media hype about the Web makes it sound like a giant online magazine, catalog, brochure, and TV set all rolled into one. As they say back in New York City, *fuhgeddaboutit*. The Web is in a class of its own. Sure, it has pictures and text, just like printed stuff, and some Web sites broadcast audio and video like TV and radio stations do. But it's important to understand the difference between *linear* and *nonlinear* media.

We're used to linear media like books, movies, plays, and TV programs, which move forward from beginning to end. The Web is nonlinear—Web surfers can follow any number of links to explore a Web site or move to a different site entirely. This means that when you design and organize your Web site, you'll have to think a little differently. Fortunately, FrontPage goes a long way towards helping you get started. This chapter explains basic planning and design concepts and runs through the process of planning a small business Web site called Four Goldens Press (at `http://www.fourgoldenspress.com/`). The company is run by an artist who sells greeting cards and prints.

"The Medium Is the Message"

The famed media critic Marshall McLuhan coined that phrase to explain how different types of media change the way we think. Although McLuhan was talking about television, the same goes for the Web. First, you have to think about links and design your pages accordingly. Web surfers expect more from Web pages than they do from magazines or TV shows. They expect to click a link to easily find what they want, and to be able to skip stuff that doesn't interest them. If you sell products that pique people's interest, they'll want to order a few online *right then*! Likewise, if you recommend another Web site, people expect you to provide a link to it. And when people visit your personal Web site, they expect to find pictures and links to your friends and your favorite Internet hangouts. After all, point-and-click isn't just a concept—it's rapidly becoming a way of life!

Getting Used to the Linking Thang

So how do you design in this exciting new medium? First, start thinking about how links work and how things look on a computer screen. You probably already know more than you think. After all, you've probably done a fair amount of Web surfing. Links enable your visitors to point and click at will, so each of your Web pages should make it easy to get to other pages and sections on your site. In addition, if you mention other Web sites or material on your own site, you should also provide the related links.

Designing for People's Computer Screens

When you lay out your pages and add your pictures, you're designing a presentation for people to view on their computer screens. Many of the old-fashioned print design rules still apply, but what looks good on paper might not work well on a computer screen. First of all, your Web pages might not look the same on other people's computers and monitors. Windows 95/98, Macintosh, UNIX, and Windows 3.*x* all handle colors differently.

You can avoid any potential pitfalls by testing your designs at different monitor settings before you build your entire Web site (as explained in the "Experimenting with Monitor Settings" sidebar later in this chapter) and by sticking with *browser-safe colors* for your text, page backgrounds, and line art graphics. Chapter 3, "Fooling Around with Web Pages," introduced you to the browser-safe color palette.

Keeping Your Colors Browser-Safe

The browser-safe color palette consists of 216 colors that look the same in everyone's Web browser, no matter what kind of computer they use. When you use colors that aren't browser safe, they may *dither* when displayed on someone else's computer system. This means that if a computer can't display a color correctly, it displays the closest approximation instead—which might not look the way you intended! You don't have to worry about your photographs (usually formatted as JPEGs) because the gradations of color are so subtle that people won't notice the difference. However, you should be careful with your line art (hand-drawn or text images with solid colors and bold lines that are formatted as GIFs) and your page color schemes (as explained in Chapter 3).

FrontPage's Colors dialog box displays all of the browser-safe colors so you can pick them for your page background, text, link, and font colors. In addition, you can get ready-made browser-safe graphics from the FrontPage Clip Art Gallery and from the Web (as explained in Chapter 8, "The Picture-Perfect Web Page: Placing and Tweaking Images"). If you want to create your own pictures, today's image programs (including the ones listed in Chapter 9, "Spiffing Up Pictures") all have tools to help you create browser-safe graphics. To learn more about coloring graphics for the Web, you can visit the Web sites listed at the end of this chapter, or pick up Lynda Weinman's excellent book from New Riders called *Designing Web Graphics.*

Getting Organized

Before you start building your Web site in FrontPage, you can plan ahead and save yourself some time down the road. Try writing down everything that you want to include and gathering all your documents and pictures into a folder on your computer. You can then open the folder, select all the files (by choosing Select All from the Edit menu or using the Ctrl+A key combination), and print out a file list by selecting Print from the File menu. Or you can use the Ctrl+P key combination. You can also name the folder something like `Original_Web_Files` so you can later import your files into your FrontPage Web as a separate folder. This lets you work with your files easily without mixing them up with your final Web pages.

Experimenting with Monitor Settings

Want to see how your Web page looks at different monitor settings? First, display your page in the browser. Then right-click anywhere on your desktop and select Properties to fire up the Display Properties control panel. Then select the Settings tab. To see how your Web page looks to a Windows 3.x user (and many Windows 95/98 laptop users too), select 256 Colors from the Colors list, move the Screen Area slider all the way to the left until the text underneath says "640x480 pixels," and then click OK. Yikes! Pretty ugly, huh?

To see how your Web page looks to most users (and to return to your default screen settings), display the Properties control panel and select the Settings tab again, select True Color (24-bit) from the Colors list, and move the Screen area slider to the right until the text underneath says "800x600." Click OK to return to your desktop.

Finally, you'll have to contend with increasing numbers of people who use the *really* high screen area settings. This makes everything on your computer screen teeny-tiny. From the Properties control panel with the Settings tab selected, leave the True Color (24-bit) item selected in the Colors list and move the Screen area slider to the right until the text below the slider says "1280x1024 pixels," and then click the OK button.

Egads! It's tough to create a Web site that pleases everyone. And you don't necessarily have to. As a Web designer, I create Web sites with 640x480 and 800x600 screen areas in mind because most people seem to use those settings. As for the 1280x1024 power users, I figure that they either have superhuman eyesight or enjoy squinting a lot.

Pulling It All Together

Once you've organized the files you want to use, you can start thinking about how everything fits in with your overall plan. You can approach your Web site as you would any other project—write an outline with all your main sections as the headings and your pages as secondary headings under each main heading. Beneath each heading or subheading, try writing down a list of the files you want to include. You should also create a *file naming scheme*—a way of naming your pages and images so you remember what they are and how they fit into your Web site.

The Four Goldens Press Web Site Outline shows how you can create a basic outline with a file naming scheme for your Web site.

Making a Jump Map

A *jump map* (also called a *navigation map*) looks a lot like a flow chart and helps you visualize how the pages on your Web site relate to one another. The Four Goldens Press Web site's jump map is shown in the following figure. Chapter 7, "Think Links: Adding Links to Your Pages," tells you how to create a navigation map in FrontPage in the Navigation view. However, it's a good idea to plan your jump map *before* you start creating a Web site with FrontPage. You can sketch one out with a pen and paper. There, now isn't it nice to get away from your keyboard for a bit? This helps you figure out how to organize your Web site, determine what your main section pages are, and which pages they should link to. You'll also get a better idea of how to design your pages and navigation bars.

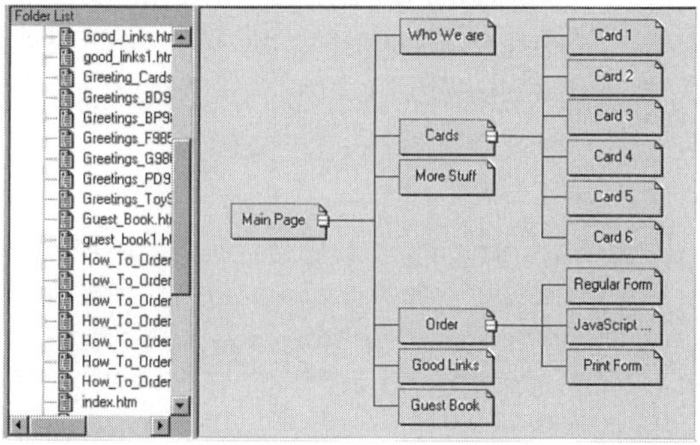

The jump map for the FourGoldens Press Web site.

Guess What?

Did you know that most Web surfers don't bother to scroll down a Web page? Try to limit each page to a screen-and-a-half graphics and text (which means about 150 to 200 words of text per page). If your information extends beyond that, figure out how to divvy things up into separate pages that you can link to. Naturally, there are exceptions to this rule, but you should still keep it in mind.

Designing Your Pages

Once you've figured out the overall structure of your Web site, you can start experimenting with page layouts. If you've never designed anything in your life and have no desire to do so, check out FrontPage's professional themes. Chapter 4, "Poof! You're a Designer with FrontPage Web Themes," tells you how to apply themes to your pages, and Chapter 7 helps you set up a navigation bar for your site. But if the Web gets your creative juices flowing, dive in! The water's fine. You don't need an art school degree to create an attractive Web site—that's what FrontPage is for. The tips in the following section can help keep you on track, and you'll get more confident as time goes on.

Consistency Is Key

Although it's good to vary your pages a little bit throughout your site, you should keep your design somewhat consistent from page to page. This way, visitors will know where to look for your navigation buttons and won't wonder whether they've jumped to someone else's Web site. For example, the color scheme navigation buttons and basic page structure should stay the same throughout your Web site.

Choosing Colors Wisely

Chapter 2, "Instant Web-Site-O-Matic: Spinning FrontPage Webs," already talked a little bit about creating color schemes, so I hope you don't mind my bringing up the topic again. But colors are important. The colors of your background, text, links, and graphics should complement each other and also reflect the purpose of your Web site. For example, a lawyer would probably want to use more conservative color combinations than a comedian would. You should also pay attention to contrast—if your page has a dark background, you need to use light-colored text and graphics so people can see them. The reverse is true for pages with light-colored backgrounds.

Getting Around: Helping Visitors Navigate

You will need to include text or graphical navigation bars on each page so visitors can get to the other pages on your site. If you take a look at a few corporate Web sites, you'll see that the pros usually include one navigation bar for main sections and another navigation bar for pages or topics within each section.

Another good design technique is to provide visual cues that tell people which page they're on. You can do this by titling your pages so the text on the browser's title bar changes (as explained in Chapter 2) or by changing the heading or text graphic for each page. You can also display a different version of the navigation button for the current section on each page. To do this, you need to create a second set of buttons that look different from the originals. You can then replace the navigation button for the current page with the alternate button. FrontPage calls these types of buttons *active graphics*.

Automate Your Active Graphics

Whew! Changing your navigation bar for every Web page to display an alternate button sounds like a lot of work! Not to worry—FrontPage can help. If you use FrontPage themes and turn on the Active Graphics option (as explained in Chapter 4), and then create a navigation bar (as covered in Chapter 7), FrontPage does the grunt work for you. If you'd rather use your own pictures instead of the ones that come with the themes, you can customize themes with your own graphics. Chapter 14, "Don't Like What You See? Designing Your Own Page Template," discusses it in greater detail.

Choosing Your Graphics

And now for the fun part—picking out your pictures. In addition to the photographs you want to include, you can use images for navigation buttons, bullets, page headings, dividers, page backgrounds, and much more. But yikes! Whether you have an image collection on CD-ROM, visit one of the clip art sites on the Web, or use the FrontPage Clip Art Gallery, the choices can seem overwhelming.

When you're choosing your graphics, consider the following:

- *Colors* Pick images that fit in with your overall color scheme so your page doesn't clash or look too busy.
- *Style* Some pictures look casual and friendly, others look businesslike, and some look wild and crazy. Choose graphics that fit in with the tone and purpose of your Web site.
- *Size* Make sure that the images fit in with your overall page layout.
- *Motif* See if you can find images that complement the basic idea behind your Web site. For example, Four Goldens Press sells greeting cards with paintings of golden retrievers and uses dog-related images throughout their Web site, as shown in the following figure. The four dogs in the logo, the dog bone pattern in the background, and the frisbee navigation buttons all contribute to the motif. Designers refer to this technique as creating *metaphors*.

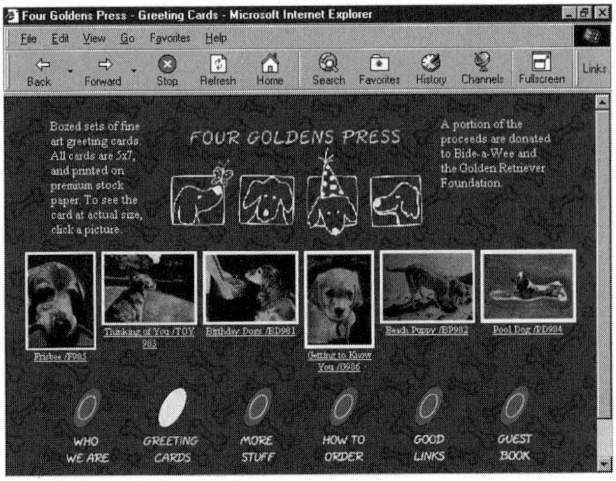

The Four Goldens Press Greeting Cards page (`http://www.fourgoldenspress.com/`*).*

Why Less Is More

Overcrowding doesn't happen just in inner-city schools, you know. The Web abounds with busy-looking pages that make visitors hit the Back button *really* fast. FrontPage's features make it pretty tempting to jam your pages with pictures, animations, scrolling marquees, multimedia, and other gee-whiz stuff. Go ahead with the bells and whistles—Chapters 19, "A Grab Bag of Helpful Doodads: FrontPage Components," and 20, "Gee-Whiz Pages with Animated Special Effects," tell you how—but limit yourself to one moving element per page.

You can also make your Web pages easy on the eyes by leaving plenty of *white space*, or empty space between page elements, in your layout. To break up your text a bit, use plenty of headings and paragraph spaces. To separate and arrange your page elements, use tables (Chapter 12, "Table It! Arranging Text and Images with Tables"), position boxes (Chapter 9), and frames (Chapter 11, "Get Framed! Building a Web Site with Frames").

Five Cool Web Sites to Visit for Design Help

If you've never designed anything before and have no idea how to begin, you can find information and creative inspiration on the Web. In addition to the resources I've recommended in the following list, you can also mark the Web sites you like as favorites or bookmarks with your Web browser. You can then visit them again, think about what makes them look so good, and apply what you learn to your own Web site.

The following Web sites can help you learn more about Web design:

- *Web Page Design Introduction* (`http://www.wpdfd.com/wpdhome.htm`) Editorials, design resources, information about graphics and palettes, design tips, cool Web tricks, and more. You can also use the site search engine to look up topics by a keyword.
- *Microsoft Site Builder Network* (`http://msdn.microsoft.com/default.asp`) Visit Microsoft's helpful Web site for articles, a workshop with how-to's and real life examples, and more.
- *Will Harris House* (`http://www.will-harris.com/`) A fun, great-looking Web site with tips on design, typography, and more.
- *Earthlink - Creating Web Pages* (`http://www.earthlink.net/internet/workshop/`) A list of helpful links organized by category for a variety of Web building topics.
- *Big Weenie's Wurst of the Web* (`http://www.bigweenie.com/`) Learn from other people's mistakes! This site gives awards to the ugliest and most ridiculous places on the Web.

The Least You Need to Know

- When you're planning your Web site, always think in terms of links. Web surfers expect to easily find what they want when they click a link, and to be able to skip stuff that doesn't interest them.
- Remember that people will view your pages on a computer screen and that all computer screens don't look the same. To make sure that your pages always look good, preview your pages at different monitor settings and use browser-safe colors.
- You can start off on the right foot by planning ahead. Try writing out an outline of your Web site, creating a file-naming scheme so you can keep track of your pages and images, and sketching out a jump map.
- You don't need an art school degree to build a great-looking Web site. Just keep your layout consistent from page to page, choose colors that look good together and make your Web pages easy to read, use well-placed navigation bars to help visitors get around, and choose your pictures wisely.
- Remember that less is more! Even pages with well-organized, easy-to-read text and no images at all look better than cluttered pages!

Chapter 11

Get Framed! Building a Web Site with Frames

In This Chapter

- How frames work
- Building a frameset
- Putting pages in a frameset
- Editing pages in frames
- Adjusting margins, borders, and scrollbars
- Making links within framed pages
- Five cool uses for frames

You've probably seen framed Web pages—they divide into different parts and sometimes have separate scrollbars for each section. Not only do frames look kind of neat, but they can also save you some work. Why keep adding a logo or a table of contents for each page when you can keep them in one frame and link them to the rest? Are frames hard to set up? No way. With FrontPage, you can frame your Web site in a matter of minutes.

What Are Frames?

Frames look pretty mysterious and complicated on the Web, but they're actually very simple. First, you create a *frameset document*, a Web page that divides into different window panes and displays content from different Web pages in each pane. Then you choose which pages to display in each pane. A frameset document is sort of like a window. It provides a framework but holds no content of its own.

Creating a Frameset Document

FrontPage comes with templates for popular frames layouts to help you get started with building your frameset. If you don't find exactly what you want, you can pick the closest thing and tweak it later. Select New from the File menu. When the New dialog box appears, click the Frames Pages tab, as shown in the following figure. Click on a template icon. See? On the right is a brief explanation of the type of frameset document you're about to create and a preview of what your pages will look like. When you find a frameset that looks like what you had in mind, click the OK button.

The New dialog box with the Frames Pages tab selected.

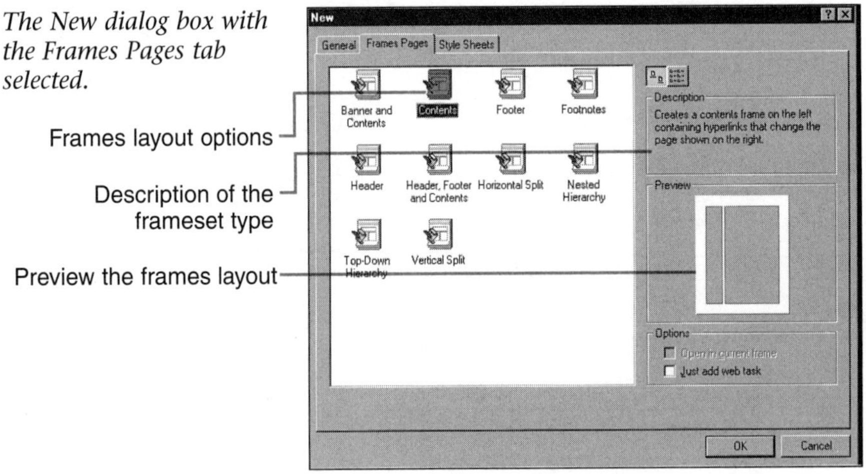

Putting Pages in Your Frameset

When you pick a frameset layout and return to the FrontPage window, you might say, "What the heck *is* this, anyway?" Yep, frames without any Web pages in them look mighty strange, as shown in the following figure. Better get some stuff in there fast! Each empty frame has a set of buttons. If you've already created the pages for your frameset, click the Set Initial Page button. When the Create Hyperlink dialog box appears, select a page to place in the frame and click OK. You can also display someone else's Web page in a frame. From the Create Hyperlink dialog box, type a Web page address in the URL box and click OK. Repeat these steps for the rest of your frames until you've put your pages in them.

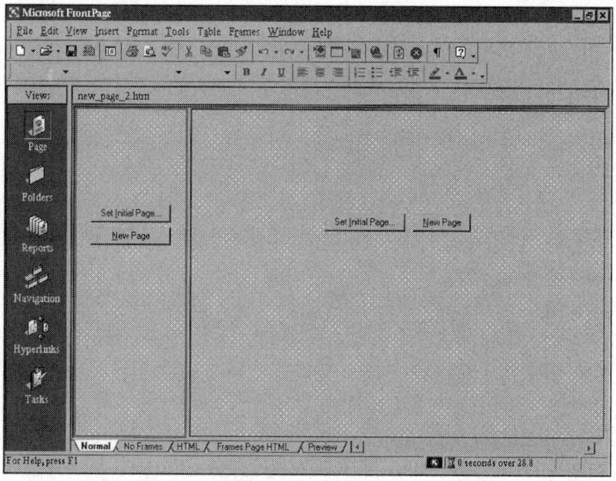

A brand spankin' new frameset waiting for your Web pages.

Creating a New Page for a Frameset

If you aren't the planning type, you might not have pages for your frames yet. That's okay. You can create them now. Click the New Page button and a brand new page appears in the frame. You can type text, create color schemes, and place images the same way you would with normal pages.

Setting Up a Frames Alternative

Frames look cool, but older Web browsers can't display them and neither can those increasingly ubiquitous handheld computers. Frames also make it difficult for the search engine spiders to gather information about your pages and add you to their listings, as explained in Chapter 26, "Don't Just Let It Sit There! Publishing Your Web Site." Why put up with these inconveniences when FrontPage gives you a simple solution?

Look below your frameset. See how the page view tabs have suddenly multiplied? Click the No Frames tab to display a blank page (it's actually a special area in the frameset document). Now you can type a message like "This Web site looks better with frames, but you can click here if you want to visit." And make

Creating a Table of Contents for Non-Frames Users

You can create a table of contents for your entire Web site and link back to it from your pages so that visitors whose browsers don't support frames can still find their way around your Web site. Sound like too much extra work? Let FrontPage generate a table of contents for you. Chapter 19, "A Grab Bag of Helpful Doodads: FrontPage Components," tells you how.

sure to provide a link to another page on your Web site. If some poor hapless soul whose browser cannot display frames visits your Web site, the frameset document displays this message as a Web page instead of showing your beautiful frames.

Saving a Frameset

When you click the Save button to save your frameset, the Save As dialog box appears, just as it does when you save any other kind of Web page. A preview of the frameset also appears on the left. Enter a name for your frameset document in the File Name box and click the Save button. If you created new pages for your frameset, the Save As dialog box appears for each of those pages so you can save them too.

Editing Pages in Frames

You can edit framed pages from within the frameset document so you can view your changes on the fly. Or you can open them separately the way you normally open files and make your changes. If you need to change the HTML source code for a Web page within a frameset document, click the HTML tab. You can also edit the frameset page's source code by clicking the Frames Page HTML tab.

Adjusting Your Frames

Once you've created your frameset, you may want to fool around with your frames a bit until they look exactly the way you want them to. You can make a frame larger or smaller, set up a margin between the frame border and the text, and determine whether or not to display a border around the frame or not. To change the settings for a frame, display the Frame Properties dialog box (as shown in the following figure) by right-clicking a frame and selecting Frame Properties from the shortcut menu.

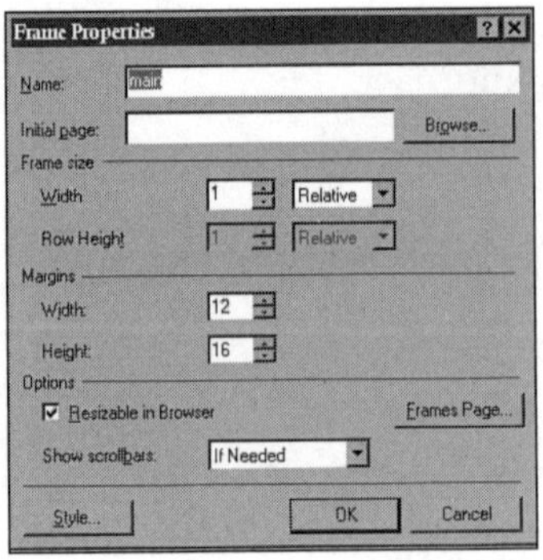

The Frame Properties dialog box.

Resizing a Frame

You don't need the Frame Properties dialog box this time. To resize a frame, click on a border (if you choose to display scrollbars, the border is next to the scrollbar), hold your mouse button down, and drag the mouse up, down, to the left, or to the right. If you prefer to enter pixel or percentage measurements, you can do so through the Frame Properties dialog box.

To specify a pixel or percentage height or width value, display the Frame Properties dialog box, enter a measurement in the Width or Row Height box, and select a unit of measurement from the list on the left. You can choose Relative (sizes the frame based on the size of the other frames), Percent (sizes the frame based on a percentage of the entire browser window), or Pixels (an absolute measurement).

Adding Margins to a Frame

You can create space between the edge of a frame and the contents of the frame. To add margins, display the Frame Properties dialog box and enter values in the Width and Height boxes.

Changing a Page in a Frame

You can change the default page that appears in a frame when it loads. For example, you may want to show this month's bulletin instead of last month's. Launch the Frame Properties dialog box and enter a new document name in the Initial Page box, or click the Browse button to search for a file.

To Scroll or Not to Scroll: Displaying Scrollbars

Scrollbars come in handy if you have a lot of material in your frames. But they also look kind of ugly, and sometimes you don't need them. For example, if a frame contains nothing but your logo or a single line of text, you can probably remove the scrollbar without cutting anything out. Be careful, though—without a scrollbar, users won't be able to view anything on your page that goes beyond the frame's border. Scrollbars can get tricky because you never know what size your visitor's monitor is or how they've sized their browser window.

To remove the scrollbar from a frame, display the Frame Properties dialog box and select Never from the Show Scrollbars list. Or you can choose Always from the Show Scrollbars list if you want the scrollbar to appear whether the user needs it or not. I recommend choosing the default If Needed option. That way, the scrollbar appears when needed and disappears otherwise.

Allowing Visitors to Resize Your Frames (or Not)

By default, FrontPage sets up your frames so your visitors can resize them if they want. This works well in most situations because it's hard to tell exactly how your layout looks to others. In some cases, however, you may not want visitors to mess around with certain frames. For example, you wouldn't want someone to resize your logo or a banner advertisement.

To keep people from resizing a frame, fire up the old Frame Properties dialog box and deselect the Resizable in Browser check box. If you change your mind, you can always select the check box again.

Frame Spacing and Borders

If you would like more space between your frames or don't want to display the borders between them, FrontPage gives you additional options. When you choose not to display scrollbars and borders, it gives your frames a smooth, seamless look, as though everything was on a single Web page. From the Frame Properties dialog box, click the Frames Page button. This displays the Page Properties dialog box with the Frames tab selected. To remove your borders, deselect the Show Borders check box. To increase or decrease the amount of space between frames, enter a number in the Frame Spacing box. FrontPage applies your new frame spacing and border settings to the entire frameset, not just a single frame.

Making Links on a Framed Web Site

Making links on framed Web pages works the same way as making links with regular Web pages. The difference is that you can do much more interesting stuff, like setting up a link in one frame that loads a new page in a different frame. When you last looked at the Page Properties dialog box, you may have noticed that each frame in your frameset has its own name. FrontPage names each frame automatically, but you can change the name to anything you want. These names allow you to *target* your links to a specific frame. To make a link on a framed Web site, select the text or image you want to link and click the Hyperlink button on the toolbar to display the Create Hyperlink dialog box. You can also select Hyperlink from the Insert menu, or use the Ctrl+K key combination. Select a page or enter a URL to link to, and then select a target frame from the list by clicking the Change Target Frame button, choosing a target from the list, and then clicking OK.

The Target Frame list offers the following options:

- *Page Default* If you set up a default target frame for the current page, all links on the page will load the new page in the same target frame unless you specify otherwise. To select a default target for the current page, click the Change Target Frame button to display the Target Frame dialog box. Select an item from the target list, select the Make Default for Hyperlinks on the Page check box, and click OK.

- *Same Frame* Loads the new page in the current frame and replaces the current page in the frame.
- *Whole Page* Replaces the entire frameset with a new page. This type of target lets visitors break out of your frameset.
- *New Window* Launches a second browser window and loads the new page in the window. This type of target comes in handy when you want to show your visitors a page outside of your frameset without losing them entirely (the browser window with your frameset remains open).
- *Parent Frame* Loads the new page in the frame that contains the current frame.

The names you chose for the frames in your frameset also appear on the Target Frame list so you can select them as frame targets.

When Targeting Pages from the Outside World

Be careful about linking to other people's pages and targeting them to load in your frameset. Some people *really* don't like for their pages to appear as part of someone else's frameset. Perhaps they're very particular about how their page looks, or maybe they don't want people to think *you* created their pages. When linking to pages in the outside world, you should either ask for permission or use the New Window option from the Target Frame list.

Five Cool Uses for Frames

Some people like frames, and some people don't. But when they're used well, they can save you a lot of work and help visitors find information on your Web site easily.

Here are some good reasons to use frames:

- *Table of contents* Frames give you a great way to keep your site map always in view. Just use the Contents template and put your list in the left frame.
- *Headers and footers* If you have special page information that you always want to keep in view, like a logo or copyright notice, you can use the Header or Footer template.
- *Keep visitors from getting lost* If you have lots of links to other sites but want to make it easy for visitors to get back to your Web site, you can load pages in a separate window or in one of your frames.
- *More layout options* Sure, you can use tables (as discussed in Chapter 12, "Table It! Arranging Text and Images with Tables"), but frames are much easier to create. Plus, you get more flexibility with background images and colors because you can use different color schemes for different pages in your frameset.

- *Less work* Create a page with a table of contents and one with header and footer information by using the Header, Footer, and Contents frame template, and boom, you're almost done with your Web site. Now you're free to develop the pages with your main content.

The Least You Need to Know

- A frameset document appears as a set of window panes with a different Web page in each pane. To frame your Web site, choose a FrontPage frameset template, adjust your layout, and then insert a page in each frame.
- Need to edit a page that's displayed in a frameset? No problem. With FrontPage, you can edit individual pages that are displayed in a frameset document.
- Don't quite like the way your frames look? In the Frame Properties dialog box you can adjust the size, margins, and borders and choose whether or not to display a scrollbar.
- You can make a link in one frame load a page in a different frame—or in a separate window—by choosing a target from the Hyperlink dialog box.

Chapter 12

Table It! Arranging Text and Images with Tables

In This Chapter

- Creating tables and putting objects in table cells
- Aligning and adjusting tables and objects in table cells
- Creating background colors and borders for your tables and table cells
- Adding and removing rows and columns
- Merging and splitting table cells
- Five cool table tricks

When you think of tables (assuming you think of them at all), boring statistics and sales figures may come to mind. Well, sure, you can publish those kinds of tables on your Web pages if you'd like. But if you use desktop publishing applications or even an advanced word processing program like Microsoft Word, you've probably already noticed that the Web still has its limitations when it comes to page layout.

That's where tables come in. With tables, you can create sophisticated page layouts and arrange your pictures and text with a fair amount of precision. Just about every browser supports tables, so you don't have to worry about whether your pages will display correctly for visitors who haven't upgraded recently.

What Tables Are Made Of

If you've created tables with office productivity programs like Microsoft Word or Excel, you probably already know a fair amount about them. Tables on the Web work pretty much the same way, as shown in the following figure. Tables are composed of rows, columns, and cells. Table cells appear where the rows and columns intersect and contain *data*—text, images, or placeholders for files that launch with browser plug-ins, as explained in Chapter 17, "Strut Your Stuff: Sound, Video, and More." You can adjust the size of your tables, rows, and columns, add colored backgrounds to tables and cells, create borders and color them in, and merge or split table cells, as explained in this chapter.

A table displayed in FrontPage.

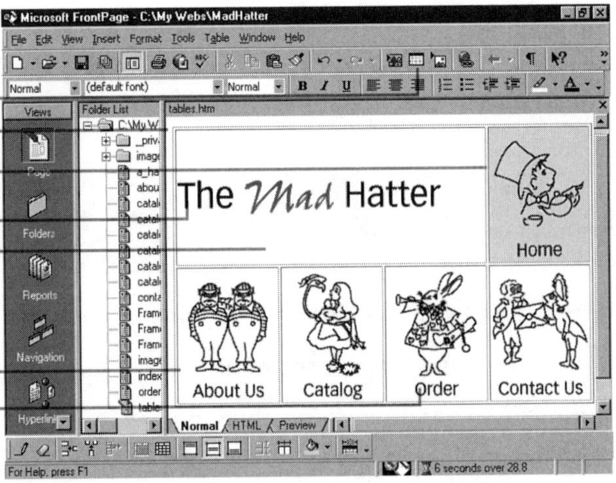

Displaying the Tables Toolbar

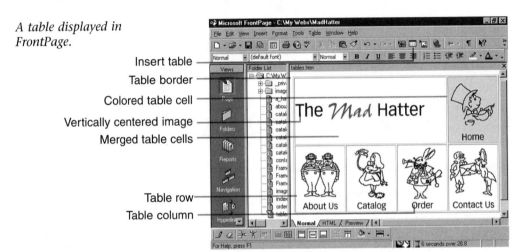

Before you start creating tables, try displaying the Tables toolbar. Although you can adjust tables and table cells through the Table menu, the Table Properties dialog box, and the Cell Properties dialog box, it's easier to do most things with the toolbar. To display the Tables toolbar, select Toolbars from the View menu and then select Table. Or, click your right mouse button anywhere on any toolbar and then select Table from the shortcut menu (shortcut menus can save a lot of wear and tear on your mouse trigger finger).

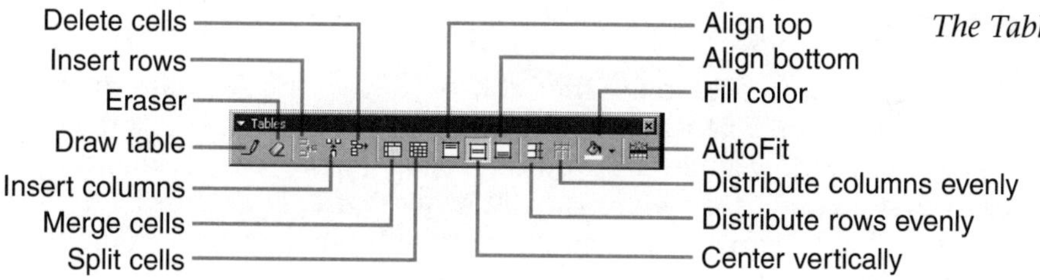

The Tables toolbar.

Customizing Your Toolbars

We all work differently, and our computer screens come in all different sizes. If your toolbars get in your way, or you find that you don't use certain toolbar buttons and would rather not have them cluttering up your screen, you can customize your toolbars.

Want to move a toolbar so it's displayed vertically on the right or left side of the application window? You can put your toolbars anywhere you want. Pass your cursor over a toolbar's *selection bar* (the little ridge on the left or top of the toolbar, depending on whether your toolbar is displayed horizontally or vertically). When the cursor turns into a four-way arrow, press down your mouse key and drag your toolbar to another location.

Want to get rid of a few superfluous toolbar buttons? Click on the More Buttons arrow on the far right or bottom of your toolbar, select Add or Remove buttons, and then pick a button from the cascading menu.

Docking the Tables Toolbar

Ack! What the heck is that Tables toolbar doing smack dab in the middle of the computer screen? No problem—you can *dock* (or attach) it by dragging it toward one of the edges of your application window. To dock your toolbar, click on the toolbar's title bar (it's navy blue and says Tables), hold down the mouse button, and drag it to the top, bottom, left, or right side of the application window. When it's docked, the title bar disappears and you can release the mouse button.

FrontPage also comes with advanced options for customizing your toolbars. Click your right mouse button on a toolbar's selection bar and then select Customize from the handy dandy shortcut menu. When the Customize dialog box appears, you can click the Toolbars tab to choose which toolbars to display, select the Commands tab to rearrange your menu items, or click the Options tab for other nifty stuff like forcing the Standard and Formatting toolbars to share one row.

Creating a Table

The simplest way to create a table is to use the Table button on the Standard toolbar. Place your cursor where you want the table to appear on your page and click the Table button. A pop-up window appears so you can create a basic table by dragging your cursor across the squares, as shown in the following figure. The status bar underneath tells you the number of rows and columns your table will have. For example, a 2-by-4 table has two rows and four columns.

If you need more columns or rows, hold your mouse button down and keep dragging your mouse downward or to the right. The extra columns and/or rows will appear. When you've selected the number of rows and columns you want, click your mouse button to add the table to your page. If you don't quite like the way the table looks, not to worry—this chapter tells you how to tweak your tables in a variety of ways.

Creating a table with the Table pop-up box.

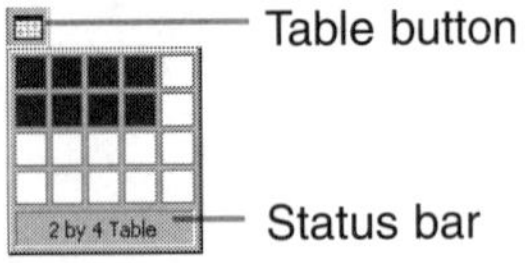

"Whoops—never mind!" If you change your mind and decide not to make a table, move your cursor to the Table pop-up box's status bar. When the text on the status bar at the bottom of the pop-up box says Cancel, click the status bar to return to your page without adding a table.

Drawing a Table

If you plan on creating a table with irregular rows or columns, you might find it easier to draw your table. This can save you a bit of time and work because you won't have to merge or split your cells and rows later. Click the Draw Table button on the Tables toolbar. When your cursor turns into a pencil, you can start drawing your table. The table-drawing tool works similarly to other drawing tools.

First, create the outer border for your table (one big table cell) by clicking the upper-left corner of where you want your table to begin and dragging your mouse diagonally down and to the right. A dashed-line selection box shows you where the table border will appear. When you finish, release the mouse button.

Now you can create your rows and columns by drawing them as lines. To set up your rows, click anywhere on the left edge of the table and drag your mouse to the right. To set up your columns, click anywhere on the top edge of the table and drag your mouse downward to the bottom. To split a cell, click on one of the cell's edges and drag your mouse across or downwards. Or you can split the cell by right-clicking on the cell and selecting Split Cells from the shortcut menu. For more on splitting cells, see the "Merging and Splitting Table Cells" section later in this chapter. When you finish drawing your table, click the Draw Table button again to get your normal cursor back.

Setting the Table: Putting Text and Images in Table Cells

Once you've created your table, you can start putting stuff in your cells. To move existing page elements into table cells, select an image or some text. When your cursor turns into an arrow, click on the image or text and drag it into a table cell. If you find the click-and-drag thing a total, well, drag, use the Cut and Paste toolbar buttons instead.

If you want to type new text, click on a table cell and start typing. To insert an image, click on a table cell, click the Insert Picture toolbar button, and place your image the way you normally do. By default, FrontPage sizes your tables so all the columns fit in the current screen. When you type text or place an object in a table cell, FrontPage changes the column width and row height to fit the largest element in the column or row.

What Else Can I Serve at My Table?

You can put just about anything in a table cell, including placeholders for multimedia and other files that launch with plug-ins (Chapter 17), special programs or scripts (Chapter 21, "Rev Up Your Web Site with Programs and Scripts"), FrontPage components (Chapter 19, "A Grab Bag of Helpful Doodads: FrontPage Components"), and animations (Chapter 20, "Gee-Whiz Pages with Animated Special Effects"). So go ahead, put your movie, GIF animation, or sound file in a table cell.

Adjusting Your Table

Now that you've got your table set up, you can fool around with it until you get it to look the way you want. You can align your table in relation to the rest of your Web page, change the borders, create more space between table cells and the objects inside, and change the table's background color.

To adjust your table settings (no pun intended), right-click anywhere on the table and then select Table Properties from the shortcut menu. You can also select Table Properties from the Table menu. When the Table Properties dialog box appears, as shown in the following figure, you can change the settings for your table.

The Table Properties dialog box.

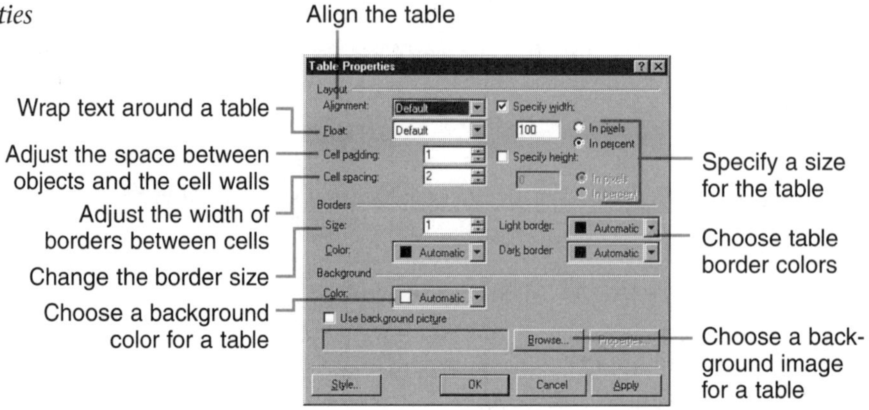

Aligning a Table

To align your table to the left, right, or center of your Web page, select an option from the Alignment menu in the Table Properties dialog box. If you don't change this setting, FrontPage automatically aligns your table to the left.

Padding Your Table Cells

If your text and pictures look a bit crowded, give them some elbow room. You can adjust the amount of space between the objects in your table cells and the table cell walls. To adjust the padding in the cells, go to the Table Properties dialog box and enter the number of pixels you want in the Cell Padding box.

Try a Borderless Table!

Borderless tables do not have borders around the table cells and give your page layouts a seamless look. To create a borderless table, enter the number 0 in the Border Size box.

Changing the Table Border Width

You can widen the border of your table, or remove it entirely, from the Table Properties dialog box. The border is the large square that encloses the table or its cells, you can also specify a different width for the borders between the table cells. To change the border size, enter a value in the Border Size box.

Coloring Your Table Border

If you put a border around your table, why not go whole hog and add a dash of color? Select your colors from the Border Colors list boxes in the Table Properties dialog box. You can even choose complementary border, highlight, and shading colors. To color in the border, use the Border menu. To choose the border highlight color, use the Light Border list. To pick a color for the shadow, use the Dark Border list. Set all three border options to the same color if you want a solid-colored border.

Adjusting the Width of Table Cell Borders

Table cells have borders too, and you can make them narrower or wider than the border around the table. To adjust the width of the table cell walls, go to the Table Properties dialog box and enter the number of pixels you want in the Cell Spacing box.

Adjusting the Table Width and Height

If you'd like to make your table fit in better with your page layout, try adjusting the table width or height. By default, FrontPage spreads out your table cells to fit in the browser window. If you need to place table elements more closely together or want to leave more space between the edges of the browser window and your table, change the Minimum Size settings.

A Table Height Caveat

If you specify a table height that is shorter than the combined heights of the objects in your table, FrontPage and your browser will ignore it.

To constrain the width of your table, display the Table Properties dialog box, select the Specify Width check box, and enter a value in the Specify Width box. You can also click a radio button to specify the width in pixels or as a percentage. To constrain the height of your table, click the Specify Height check box, enter a number in the Specify Height box, and click a radio button to specify the height in pixels or as a percentage.

Adding a Background Color to Your Table

Tables can have their own background colors or patterns just like Web pages have. This lets you create an interesting contrast between your Web page and the table. To add a background color to your table, select an item from the Background Color menu. To add a patterned background to your table, click the Use Background Picture check box and then click the Browse button to display the Browse for File dialog box so you can find your image.

Wrap Text Around Your Table!

Would you like to wrap text from the rest of your Web page around your table so it flows to the right or left? Try the Float options. To flow text along the right side of your table, select Left from the Float box. To flow text along the left side of your table, select Right from the Float box.

Adding a Background Color to a Table Cell

The easiest way to color in a table cell is to click on it and then click on the little arrow next to the Fill Color button on the Table toolbar. Then you can choose a color from the palette. You can also add a background image for the selected table cell through the Cell Properties dialog box. Right-click on the cell to display the shortcut menu, and then choose Cell Properties. When the Cell Properties dialog box appears, click the Use Background Picture check box, and then click the Browse button to display the Browse for File dialog box so you can find your image.

Working with Rows, Columns, and Table Cells

Well, creating table and table cell backgrounds and padding cells makes for hours of amusement. But if you want to do some serious layouts, you need to learn how to work with rows, columns, and individual table cells. In the following sections, you'll finally take the Table toolbar for a spin. In addition, you can change some table cell settings in the Cell Properties dialog box, which you can launch by right-clicking a table cell and selecting Cell Properties from the shortcut menu. The Cell Properties dialog box is very similar to the Table Properties dialog box.

Selecting Cells, Columns, and Rows

Before you can adjust objects in your table cells, columns, and rows, you'll first need to select them. To select items in your table, place your cursor in a table cell, choose Select from the Table menu, and then select the Table, Column, Row, or Cell option from the pop-up menu. You can also select adjacent cells by clicking your mouse on a cell. When the cursor changes to an I-beam, drag it across the rows you want to select.

Aligning Text and Images in Table Cells Horizontally

To align the text, images, or other objects in your table cells, select the objects and click the Center button on the Format toolbar. You can also place your cursor anywhere in the table cell, fire up the Cell Properties dialog box and select Left, Right, or Center from the Horizontal Alignment box. This automatically aligns all the elements in the table cell.

Aligning Text and Images in Table Cells Vertically

To change the vertical alignment of objects in a table cell, click anywhere in the table cell and then click the Align Top, Center Vertically, or Align Bottom buttons on the Tables toolbar. If all of the items in the table row are pretty much the same height, you may not notice any difference. But it can cause dramatic results when the text and graphics vary in height.

Evening Out Your Rows and Columns

If you've been fiddling around with your tables a bit, you might find that your columns or rows are starting to look a bit uneven. Perhaps you've created irregular columns or rows on purpose ("I *meant* to do that!"). But if not, you can make them even again. To make your rows even, select an entire column and then click the Distribute Rows Evenly button on the Table toolbar. To make your columns even, select an entire table row and then click the Distribute Columns Evenly button on the Tables toolbar.

Adjusting the Width of a Table Column

Cells in a column automatically size themselves to the widest object in the column. But if you just have text in a column, you can resize the column. The simplest way is to click on the column border, hold the mouse button down, and drag it to the left or right when the cursor turns into a two-way arrow. If you'd like to enter a precise column width, you can enter a number of pixels or a percentage of the entire table width in the Cell Properties dialog box.

Adjusting the Height of a Table Row

Adjusting the height of a table row works a lot like changing the width of a column. Place your cursor on a row border, hold the mouse button down, and drag the cursor up or down when it turns into a two-way arrow. You can also enter an exact row height by displaying the Cell Properties dialog box and entering a number of pixels or a percentage in the Specify Height box.

Adding Rows and Columns

Face it, you can't always plan ahead. Sometimes, you might need to add a row or a column to a table. To add a column to a table, click a cell in the column to the right of where you want the new column to appear and then click on the Insert Columns button.

To add a new row, click a cell in the row below where you want the new row to appear and click the Insert Rows button on the Tables toolbar. FrontPage puts the new row above the selected row. Well, gee, that's a fine kettle of fish—what if you need to add a row to the *bottom* of a table? Click on the last table cell in the bottom row and far-left column, and press the Tab key. FrontPage adds the row to the bottom of the table.

Removing Rows and Columns

If you wind up with a couple of extra rows or columns, no problem. Select the entire row or column and then click the Delete Cells button on the Tables toolbar. Because you cannot delete a single table cell without deleting the row or column that goes with it, the Delete Cells button is disabled unless you select a whole row or column.

Take Control of Your Table Layout!

FrontPage resizes table cells to fit the tallest object in a row and the widest object in a column. You can merge and split cells to control the size of your table layouts and to accommodate larger objects.

Merging and Splitting Table Cells

Depending on your table layout, some of your text and graphics may only need one table cell each, while others might take up two or three table cells. In addition, you might sometimes need to divide a table cell in half. *Merging* table cells means combining two or more adjacent cells together, and *splitting* a table cell means dividing it into two or more cells.

To merge table cells, grab the Eraser from the Tables toolbar and drag it across the cell borders you want to remove. Or you can select adjacent cells and click the Merge Cells button on the Tables toolbar.

To split a table cell, select the Draw Table tool from the Tables toolbar and draw lines across the cell. You can also click the Split Cells toolbar button. When the Split Cells dialog box appears, select the Split into Columns or Split into Rows radio button, enter a number of rows or columns in the number box, and click OK.

Five Cool Table Tricks

Once you get used to tables, you can do lots of interesting things with them. You can try the following table tricks, for starters:

- *Faux Frames* If you like the look of frames but don't want those ugly scrollbars, use a table to create a frames-like layout.
- *Pixel Shims* If your layout requires an empty column and you want to make sure the column always stays the same width even if a visitor resizes the browser window, try a *pixel shim*. That's a funny term for a tiny, blank GIF that acts as a placeholder and is invisible. Once you've inserted a pixel shim as an image, you can resize it to the number of pixels you need.

Creating a Pixel Shim

To create your own pixel shim, grab a solid-colored little square from the Clip Art Gallery, insert it on your page, and click the Set Transparent Color tool on the Picture toolbar. To jog your memory about the Clip Art Gallery and inserting images, see Chapter 8, "The Picture-Perfect Web Page: Placing and Tweaking Images." For more on transparent GIFs and the Picture toolbar, see Chapter 9, "Spiffing Up Pictures."

- *Instant Button Bars* If you like 3-D buttons but don't like fiddling with graphics, try creating a table, creating a text link in each table cell, and then adjusting the Cell Space width and Border Colors in the Table Properties dialog box.
- *Excel Tables and Back* You can also import tables that you've created with other applications, like Microsoft Excel and Word. Chapter 18, "A Match Made in Redmond: FrontPage and Microsoft Office 2000," tells you more about working with FrontPage and Microsoft Office.
- *Fake Image Maps* You can take individual images and arrange them in a borderless table so they look like an image map. You can learn more about image maps in Chapter 16, "X Marks the Hot Spot! Making Image Maps."

The Least You Need to Know

- Tables give you an easy way to create page layouts and arrange pictures and text. Even older Web browsers display tables correctly.
- The Table toolbar helps you create and edit your tables. To display it, select Toolbars from the View menu and then choose Table.
- You can create a table by using the Table button on the Standard toolbar or the Draw Table button on the Table toolbar.
- To enter text or insert an image in a table cell, place your cursor in the table cell and then type your text or insert your image. You can also copy objects from other pages or areas on the current Web page and paste them into a table cell.
- You can adjust the alignment, float, cell padding, cell spacing, width, height, borders, and background colors for a table from the Table Properties dialog box.
- You can adjust the horizontal and vertical alignment for table cells through the Cell Properties dialog box. In addition, you can change the colors of a table cell's borders and background from the Cell Properties dialog box.

Chapter 13

Form and Function: Building Online Forms

In This Chapter

- Forms and form fields
- Building forms with templates and wizards, or from scratch
- Inserting and editing form fields
- Validating your forms
- Telling FrontPage what to do with your forms
- Five cool ways to use forms

You can yell at TV commercials that bug you until you turn blue in the face, but nobody can hear you. The Web, on the other hand, is a two-way street. Have you ever filled out an online form to order a product, tell someone you like their Web site, or tell a Webmaster that one of their links doesn't work? Email links (as explained in Chapter 7, "Think Links: Adding Links to Your Pages") and online forms enable us to respond to a Web site instantly. But in many cases, online forms work even better than email links because they let you prompt people for specific information. FrontPage makes it simple to set up online forms of your own to get feedback, gather data, or enable visitors to order products or request information.

How Forms Work

Online forms are Web pages that you set up to get input from your visitors. When visitors fill out and submit a form, the results are sent to you as an email message or saved to a text file on your server. Forms include text boxes, radio buttons, lists, and other types of form fields that allow visitors to enter information, choose options, and then click a button to send the form to you.

Form Fields 101: An Introduction

Whether you're subscribing to a magazine, paying taxes, buying a house, or applying to a school, you probably spend a fair amount of time (maybe more than you'd like!) filling out forms. Web forms work a lot like the paper kind, minus the envelopes and postage stamps. They have lines for short items of information like names and addresses, lists of items or check boxes that people can select, and comment areas for longer answers. On the Web, these blank spaces, check boxes, and other items that wait for people to fill them in are called *form fields*.

With FrontPage, you can include the following types of form fields in your forms:

- *One-line text box* Displays a text field so visitors can enter shorter lines of information, such as a first name, last name, email address, or telephone number. Non-FrontPage-usin' Web developers call these *text boxes*.
- *Scrolling text box* Allows visitors to provide information that requires multiple lines of text—such as comments or a detailed description. Non-FrontPagers call these *text areas*.
- *Check box* For prompting visitors for a yes or no answer, such as a Subscribe me to your email newsletter check box. If the visitor clicks the check box, that means yes, while an unselected check box means no.
- *Radio button* For prompting a visitor to choose one option from a list of items.
- *Drop-down menu* Allows visitors to choose one option from a list of items. Or you can set up a drop-down menu that allows visitors to select more than one option from the list.
- *Push button* Looks similar to a toolbar button and prompts visitors to send (submit) the form. You *have* to put a Submit button on your form or people won't have a way to send it to you. You can also create a Cancel button that lets people clear their data if they decide not to fill out your form.

You can see all of these form fields in the following figure.

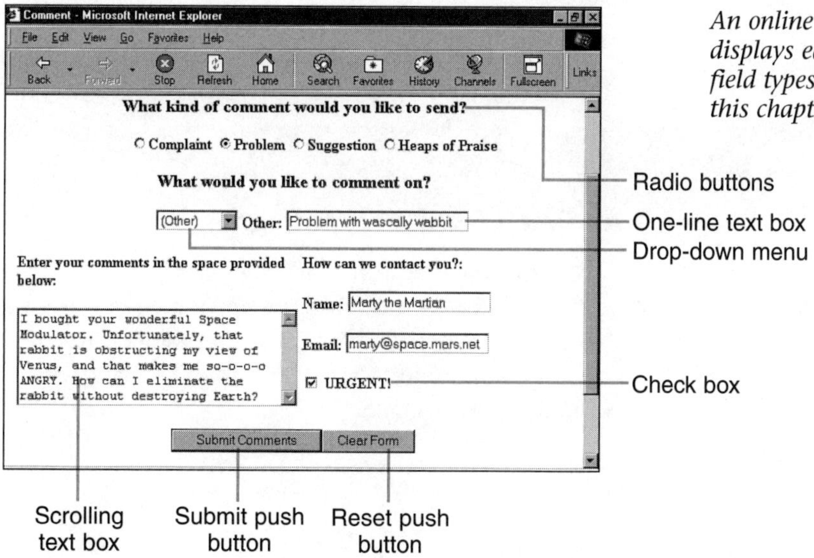

An online form that displays each of the form field types described in this chapter.

About Names and Values

Form data is stored or emailed to you as lists of name and value pairs, as shown in the "An Email from a Form Page" sidebar. You (or the template or FormPage Wizard) define a *name* for each of your form fields, as explained in the "Setting Up Your Forms" and "Editing Form Field Information" sections later in this chapter. Form field *values* are entered or selected by visitors when they fill out and submit the form.

Setting Up Your Forms

FrontPage gives you plenty of ways to set up your forms. Some of the FrontPage Web Wizards discussed in Chapter 2, "Instant Web-Site-O-Matic: Spinning FrontPage Webs," automatically set up form pages for you when they generate the rest of your Web site. You can also pick a form template or launch the Form Page Wizard from the New dialog box that appears when you create a new Web page, or you can build a form from scratch.

An Email from a Form Page

When Marty the Martian filled out my Web form (as shown in the figure above) and clicked the Submit button, I received the following email message. The names I created for the form fields are in bold text, followed by the values entered or selected by the visitor. Whether you choose to store your form's data in a text file or Web page, the results should still look similar:

FeedbackType: Problem

Subject: (Other)

SubjectOther: Problem with wascally wabbit

Comments: I bought your wonderful Space Modulator. Unfortunately, that rabbit is obstructing my view of Venus, and that makes me so-o-o-o ANGRY. How can I eliminate the rabbit without destroying Earth?

Name: Marty the Martian

Email: marty@space.mars.com

Urgent: Yes

Submit: Submit_Comments

Instant Forms! FrontPage Templates

Don't wanna fiddle around with forms too much? Try a FrontPage template on for size. FrontPage comes with ready-made pages for popular types of forms, including a guest book and a feedback form. To create a form from a template, select New and Page from the File menu or use the Ctrl+N key combination to launch the New dialog box with the General tab selected. You can then pick a form template and click the OK button.

Another Reason to Like FrontPage

Before FrontPage came along, setting up a form handler meant programming a special *CGI script* and installing it on your server. Yuck. CGI stands for *common gateway interface*—a scripting language that runs on most types of servers. Scripting languages are easier to learn than programming languages—but they still require programming! So let's thank our lucky stars that FrontPage spares us these traumas. For more about CGI scripts and other types of Web programming, see Chapter 21, "Rev Up Your Web Site with Programs and Scripts."

Building a Form with the Form Page Wizard

If none of the templates quite seems like the right fit, let the Form Page Wizard guide you through the steps of building a form of your very own. (No lions, tigers, or bears, I promise!) First, display the New dialog box with the General tab selected (just like the last time, select New Page from the File menu), and then click on the Form Page Wizard and click OK. This launches the Form Page Wizard dialog box.

The wizard asks a few questions to help you build the form. You can click the Next button to move through the steps, click the Back button to go back to previous steps and make changes, click the Cancel button to return to FrontPage without creating a form, or click the Finish button to return to FrontPage and display your new Web form.

The Form Page Wizard takes you through the following steps:

1. *Begin building your Web form* The Form Page Wizard displays a dialog box with some helpful introductory text. When you finish reading the message, click the Next button to display the question list dialog box, as shown in the following figure.

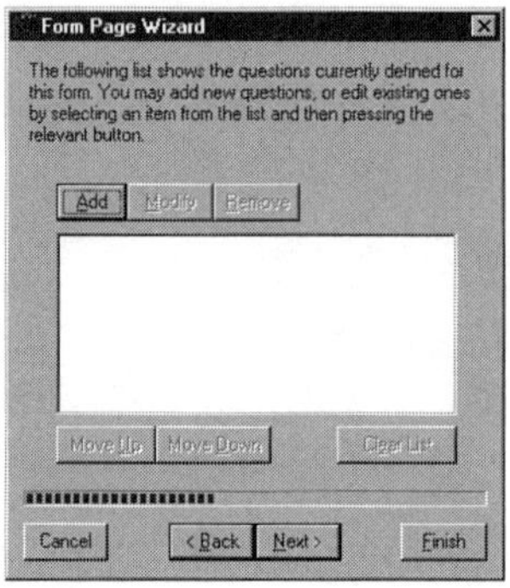

Form Page Wizard dialog box with blank question list.

2. *Create a question list* The question list dialog box asks you to create a list of questions for your form. Questions appear as text on your form page, followed by form input fields, like check boxes and text boxes with text prompts. To begin setting up the questions on your form, click the Add button to display the dialog box with the input type list, as shown in the following figure.

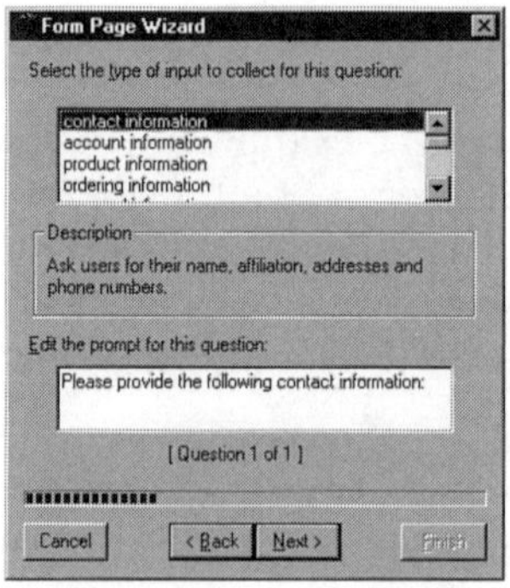

Form Page Wizard dialog box with input type list displayed.

3. *Choose a question for your first set of form fields* Choose the list item that best matches the type of information you want to gather. For example, you can prompt for contact or account information. A description of the selected item appears below in the Description box, and a question (the text that appears on your Web page) displays in the Edit the prompt for this question box. You can replace this text by typing in your own words. Click the Next button to move on to the input type items dialog box.

   This dialog box displays different options, depending on which type of question you choose from the previous input selection dialog box. When you choose the Contact Information option, the input item types dialog box appears, as shown in the following figure.

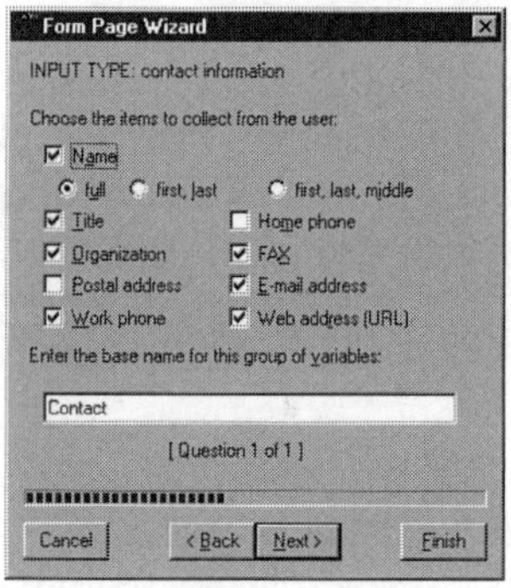

Form Page Wizard dialog box with input type items for contact information.

4. *Choose input type items* Select check boxes and radio buttons for the items that you want to include on your Web form, and then click the Next button. This brings you back to the question list dialog box.
5. *Create additional sets of form fields by adding another question* To add more form questions to the list, repeat these steps. Once you've created a list of questions, the question list dialog box will look similar to the one shown in the following figure.

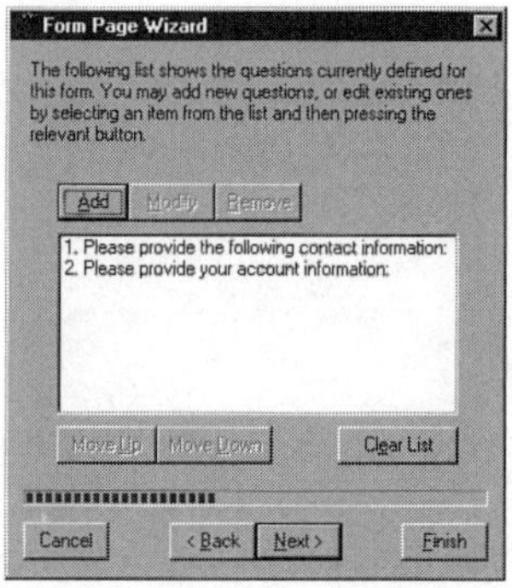

Form Page Wizard with question list displayed.

6. *Check and edit your list of questions* To edit an item on your list (remember, each item represents a collection of questions or input options), select the item and click the Modify button. When the list of available questions and descriptions appears, click the Next button to display the list of input options for that question. You can then change your input option selections and click the Next button to return to your question list.

   To remove an item, select the item and click the Remove button. To move an item up or down on the list (the Form Wizard arranges items on your Web page in the order that they appear on the list), select the item and click the Move Up or Move Down button.

   When you finish creating your list of items, click the Next button to choose your presentation options.

Copy and Paste Is Your Friend

You can place a form that you've created with a template or the Form Wizard into an existing Web document with the ol' copy and paste trick. From the new form document, choose Select All from the Edit menu (or use the Ctrl+A key combination) to select the entire form, and then click the Copy button (or use the Ctrl+C key combination). Close the new form without saving it, open a document, place your cursor where you would like to insert the form, and click the Paste button (or use the Ctrl+V key combination).

7. *Lay out your form* Once you've finished creating and editing a list of questions and form input fields, the wizard displays your presentation options so you can make your form look the way you want. For example, you can display your questions in paragraph or list form or lay out your text prompts and form fields in a table. When you finish, click the Next button to choose your output options.
8. *Tell FrontPage how to handle form data* You can tell FrontPage what you want the server to do with forms after visitors have filled them out and sent them to you. You can save the result to a Web page so you can view it in your browser, save the result in a text file, or process the form with a custom CGI script. The "Handle with Care! Setting Up Form Handlers" section of this chapter tells you more about options for handling form data.
9. *Run for the finish line!* Click the Finish button to exit the wizard and check out your new form page. FrontPage opens your new form in the Page view.

Creating Forms from Scratch

If you've created Web forms before, you can build your form from scratch instead of using a template or the Form Page Wizard. To create a form, select Form from the Insert menu and then choose Form from the cascading list. FrontPage places a dashed-line bounding box on your page with two push buttons labeled Submit and Reset. All forms need these buttons so people can send their information or cancel. Now you can type your text prompts and insert your form fields within the dashed-line bounding box. If you create a Web form from scratch, you'll also need to edit your form field properties, as explained in the "Editing Form Field Information" section later in this chapter.

Inserting and Removing Form Fields

No matter how you created the form, if you realize that you forgot an item or two, you don't need to launch the Form Page Wizard and start all over again. To insert a new form field, type your text prompt (such as "Your Name"), choose Form from the Insert menu, and pick an element from the cascading list. As for removing form fields, you can get rid of them the same way you get rid of other unwanted stuff on your Web pages. Drag your mouse across the form field to select it, and press the Delete key.

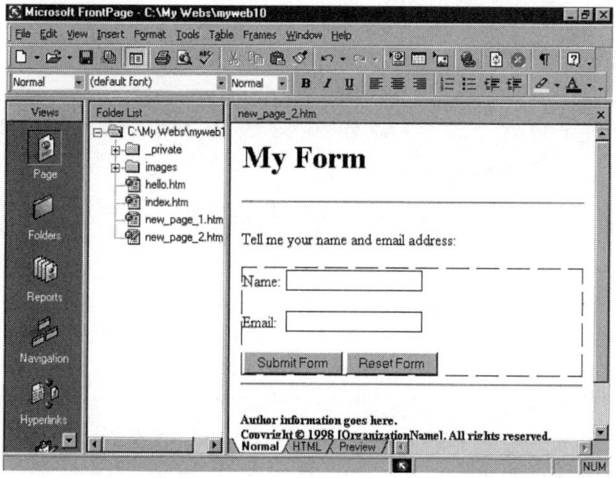

Web form with bounding box displayed in FrontPage.

Do you want to create a special mystery form that lets visitors enter and select items at random? Probably not. You should include explanatory text for each form field by placing your cursor near each one and typing your text—that's all there is to it.

Editing Form Field Information

There's more to form fields than meets the eye. Each form field has information or properties that determine how it looks and how it returns your data to you. You can tweak your form fields so your form looks and behaves exactly the way you want.

The following sections talk about properties for different types of form fields in detail. However, you can edit form field information by displaying the form field's properties, making your changes, and clicking the OK button to return to your form. To display a form field's properties, right-click on the form field and select Form Field Properties from the shortcut menu. Or you can click on the form field and choose Properties from the Format menu. For more about form field properties, see the "About Names and Values" section, earlier in this chapter.

What's the Tab Order?

You might have noticed that all the Form Field Properties dialog boxes have a Tab Order option. When savvy Web surfers fill out online forms, they move from field to field by pressing the Tab key (try it next time you fill out an online form). You can number your form fields by entering a value in the Tab Order box, determining the order of tab stops. Here's a trick: Wait until you're sure that you've created all of the fields you're going to need, and then go back and enter the tab order in the Form Field Properties dialog box.

Editing a One-Line Text Box

You can use the Text Box Properties dialog box to change the form field's name, display text inside the text box, and resize the text field to fit better in your page layout. To display the One-Line Text Box Properties dialog box, right-click the text box and select Form Field Properties from the shortcut menu. To rename the text box, type a new name in the Name box. If you would like to display default text inside the text box, enter it in the Initial Value box. To make the text field longer or shorter, change the number in the Width in Characters text field.

Editing a Scrolling Text Box

Want to rename the form field, display some text inside the scrolling text box, or resize it? Display the Scrolling Text Box Properties dialog box and go for broke. To display the Scrolling Text Box Properties dialog box, right-click the scrolling text box and select Form Field Properties from the shortcut menu. To change the form field name, enter a new name in the Name box. You can also enter some default text to display inside the scrolling text box in the Initial Value box. To determine the width of your text box, type a number in the Width in Characters box. To determine the height of your text box, enter a number in the Number of Lines box.

Validating Form Fields

If you *really* need a particular bit of information, you can require people to fill in certain one-line text boxes. For example, you may want to remind visitors to give you their email address. When a visitor forgets to fill in a validated text box form field and then tries to submit the form, an error message asks them to enter that information.

To validate a text field, display the Text Box Properties dialog box and click the Validate button. When the Text Box Validation dialog box appears, select an item from the Data Type list (choose Text for email addresses or names, Integer for a quantity or dollar amount, or Number for a telephone number or ZIP code) and click OK.

If you plan to use your form results with a database, you probably need visitors to submit information in a format that works with your database. The Text Box Validation dialog box provides additional options so you can exclude those pesky commas and white spaces, require a minimum or maximum number of characters, and more. The topic of Web forms and databases is too broad to cover in this book, but if they spark your interest, see Chapter 22, "If You've Got It, Flaunt It: Putting Your Access Databases on the Web."

Editing a Check Box

Check boxes may look simple, but that doesn't mean you don't have options. You can use the Checkbox Properties dialog box to change the form field's name or choose to have the check box checked automatically. To display the Checkbox Properties dialog box, right-click the check box and select Form Field Properties from the shortcut menu. To rename the check box, enter a name in the Name box.

Want to encourage visitors to say "yes"? Maybe you'd like visitors to enter a contest or sign up for a free email newsletter subscription. Choose the Checked option to have your check box checked automatically. Don't worry, you aren't being a control freak—visitors can still deselect the check box if they want.

Editing Groups of Radio Buttons

You need to assign radio buttons to a group and give each of them a value by entering text in the Group Name and Value boxes in the Radio Button Properties dialog box. To display the Radio Button Properties dialog box, right-click the radio button and select Form Field Properties from the shortcut menu. For example, the group name for all of the radio buttons shown in the first figure in this chapter is FeedbackType, and the values for the radio buttons are Complaint, Problem, Suggestion, and Heaps of Praise. You can also automatically select one radio button in the group by clicking the Selected option in the Initial State list. As with check boxes, visitors are free to deselect the default radio button and choose another option.

Editing a Drop-Down Menu

It's easy to put a drop-down menu on a page, but it won't do much good until you create a list of items for visitors to choose from. To display the Drop Down Menu Properties dialog box, right-click the drop-down menu and select Form Field Properties from the shortcut menu. To create your drop-down menu list, display the Drop Down Menu Properties dialog box and enter a name in the Name box. To add an item to your list, click the Add button to launch the Add Choice dialog box. Enter a name for your menu choice in the Choice box. If you want an item to be selected automatically, click the Selected radio button. When you finish, click OK to add the item and return to the Drop Down Menu Properties dialog box.

To change the text of the items on your list, click the Modify button. To remove an item from your list, select it and click the Remove button. You can also move items up or down on the list by selecting them and clicking the Move Up or Move Down button. And one of the coolest things about drop-down menus is that you can allow people to select more than one item from the list by clicking the Yes button from the Allow Multiple Selections option.

Try an Image Push Button!

If you think those gray Submit and Cancel buttons look ugly, you can use pictures for your push buttons instead. Image push buttons work exactly like regular push buttons—only they look a lot better!

Editing a Push Button

When it comes to Web forms, a push button can do one of two things: submit a form or reset the form (clear all the data and cancel submitting the form). To display the Push Button Properties dialog box, right-click the push button and select Form Field Properties from the shortcut menu. In the Push Button Properties dialog box, enter a name in the Name field and enter a label for the button in the Value/Label box. Make it short and snappy because this text has to fit on the actual button. You also need to choose a button type by selecting either the Submit or the Reset option.

Handle with Care! Setting Up Form Handlers

Okay, you've just created a fabulous form. How does the form data get back to you? FrontPage helps you set up something called *form handlers*, which tell FrontPage how to handle the forms that you create.

Form handlers can do some pretty cool stuff, and Web forms are useless without them. They can send forms to you as email messages, store them in a text file that you can import into other applications, save the results directly to a database, or all of the above. Form handlers can even display a page that thanks people for sending the form. It's too bad that form handlers can't take out the garbage and straighten out those messy piles on your desk, too.

To set up your form handlers, right-click anywhere on your form and select Form Properties from the shortcut menu. Or place your cursor anywhere inside of the form's bounding box and select Form from the Insert menu. Then, when the Form Properties dialog box appears, choose your options and click OK. You can create as many form handlers as you want. For example, you may want one form handler for sending form data to you via email and another form handler to display a Web page that says "Thank you" when a visitor submits a form from your Web page.

Special Delivery: Getting Forms by Email

Getting form results as email messages is easy, convenient, and fun, and most people like to handle their forms this way. To set up a simple email form handler, display the Form Properties dialog box, click the Send To radio button, and then enter your email address in the E-mail Address box. But wait—FrontPage has a couple more tricks up its sleeve. Click the Options button to display the Options dialog box, and click the E-mail Results tab.

Want to make your form data easier to read? Pick a text format from the E-mail format list, and make sure to click the Include field names check box too. If you'd like text from a certain form field to appear in the subject line of your email messages, enter a form field name in the Subject Line box and select the Form Field Name check box. You can also tell the form handler to put email addresses in the reply-to line of your email messages. Type the name of

About Email Format Options

If you want to include form results in the body of your email messages, choose one of the options for HTML (if your email program supports HTML) or formatted text (if your email program does not support HTML). If you want to receive form results as attached text files that you can import into a database, you can choose one of the text database options. For more on forms and databases, see Chapter 22.

the form field that gathers email addresses in the Reply-to line box and select the Form Field Name check box. This lets you reply to form messages the way you reply to normal email messages—by clicking the Reply button.

Forms and Databases

If you dig databases—or at least don't mind learning a bit about them—you can do some pretty amazing stuff with them and with Web forms. For example, visitors can search your database and generate Web pages on-the-fly by clicking a button. You can even set up a form that lets people add information directly to a database. For more on Web forms and databases, see Chapter 22.

Saving Form Results to a Text File

Email form handlers give you a convenient way to receive form results. But what if your fabulous Web site suddenly becomes popular and hundreds of fans bombard you with forms every day? When you get your 15 minutes of fame, you can set up a form handler that saves form results to a text file on the server. You can then download the file periodically, import it into a database, word processor, or spreadsheet program, and reply to all your fan mail.

To send forms data to a text file, go to the Form Properties dialog box and select the Send To radio button. FrontPage automatically creates a file and puts it in the `_private` folder in your Web so nosy people can't peek at it.

Processing Forms with Scripts

If you know how to work with scripting languages like Perl or active server pages (ASP), you can use your own form handlers instead of FrontPage's. This gives you a lot more flexibility with your forms. You don't even have to be a programmer. Chapter 21 tells you where to download free, ready-made scripts. If you choose to go this route, go to the Form Properties dialog box, select the Send to Other radio button, and click the Options button. When the Options for Custom Form Handler dialog box appears, enter a command line (usually the folder and filename for the script, as in `cgi-bin/mail.cgi`) in the Action box and select a method (usually Post) from the Method box. When you finish, click OK to return to the Form Properties dialog box.

Mind Your Ps & Qs: Thanking Visitors for Sending a Form

When we were kids, the grownups always told us to say "please" and "thank you." (I never figured out what the "q's" in "p's and q's" stood for.) So why not thank visitors when they take time to fill out our forms? This isn't just a snooty etiquette thang—it also reassures people that their forms went through successfully. And best of all, setting up a confirmation page only takes a few minutes.

First, create a new Web page and type your message. (You should also include links to other parts of your Web site so people don't have to click their browser's Back button.) Then go back to your form, display the Form Properties dialog box, and click the Options button. From Options for Saving Results of Form, click on the Confirmation Page tab. You can then enter the filename for your confirmation page in the URL of the Confirmation Page box. Or you can click the Browse button to look for the Web page. When you finish, click OK.

Five Cool Ways to Use Forms

- *Web site search form* Chapter 19, "A Grab Bag of Helpful Doodads: FrontPage Components," tells you how to set up a simple search form so visitors can search your Web site. When they enter a keyword in the text box and click the Search button, a page with a list of related Web pages loads in the browser.
- *Opinion poll* If you're into current events or want to do some informal research for business or school, you can set up a form and invite people to participate.
- *Forms and scripts* If you don't mind learning a little programming (or can get a geeky friend to help you), you can make your forms do cool things like add up customer's totals when they order products. Chapter 21 tells you a little about Web programming.
- *Web discussion groups* You can create an online community and provide a form where your guests post messages to a Web page. Sound like a lot of work? Relax. The Discussion Group Wizard, as covered in Chapter 23, "Switchboard Central: Setting Up a Discussion Web," sets up the form and pages for you.
- *A guestbook* You don't need to run a business to use Web forms. Lots of people put guestbook forms on their Web sites. You can ask visitors about their favorite Web pages (you might find some interesting places to visit), what they think of your Web site, and more. Just don't get *too* nosy, okay?

The Least You Need to Know

- Web forms can help you gather feedback and information from people who visit your Web site. You can set up form fields to gather different types of information.
- FrontPage templates and the Form Page Wizard can help you build forms, or you can set up a form from scratch.
- All form fields have names. When you receive forms from visitors, the form field names appear with the values that visitors have selected or entered.
- Once you've set up your form page, you can edit form field properties to specify form field names and default values or change their appearance. You can also validate text box form fields.
- You can set up form handlers that send form results to you by email, save the results to a text file that you can bring into a database, word processor, or spreadsheet application, and display a confirmation page that thanks people for sending the form.
- FrontPage also gives you lots of ways to work with Web forms and databases. If this interests you, Chapter 22 can help you get started.

Chapter 14

Don't Like What You See? Designing Your Own Page Template

In This Chapter

- About templates
- Saving and opening new pages as templates
- Planning and designing your template
- Setting up shared borders and FrontPage navigation bars
- Using Include Page components for repeating page elements
- Applying a style sheet to your template
- Five cool tips for templates

All this talk about themes, wizards, and templates might give you the wrong idea about FrontPage. Sure, these tools can lend a helping hand to people without a lot of artistic talent. But that doesn't mean you can't get creative. If you're an artist or graphic designer, or just want to experiment, by all means go for it. With FrontPage, you can have the best of both worlds: a unique look for your Web site *and* full access to timesaving tools like shared borders, FrontPage navigation bars, Include Page components, and style sheets.

What's a "Repeating Page Element"?

You'll see the phrase "repeating page element" several times in this book, and it's quite a mouthful. But if I said "graphics, text, and groups of links or navigation bars that appear throughout a Web site or sections of a Web site" instead, this book would be way too long!

What's a Template?

Templates are special types of Web pages that you can open from the New dialog box to create new pages. As explained in Chapter 2, "Instant Web-Site-O-Matic: Spinning FrontPage Webs," FrontPage comes with a variety of templates with ready-made page layouts to help you lay out pages in a snap. You can also create your own templates that contain all of your basic page elements, like color schemes, pictures, headers, footers, and navigation bars. Once you build a template, it works sort of like a plaster mold. Pour in your text, add a new image or two, and voilà! An instant Web page.

Saving a Web Page as a Template

Saving a page as a template works a lot like saving a regular Web page—with just a few more steps. Once you've created your template, select Save As from the File menu. When the Save As dialog box appears, enter a name for your file in the File Name box. Now take a look at the page title suggested by FrontPage. It will either be the page title of the existing file or something really exciting like New Page 1. If it's not the title you want for your page, click the Change button to type a new title. Select FrontPage Template from the Save as Type list, and click the Save button.

The Save As Template dialog box will appear. Type a brief description of the template file in the Description box (this text is displayed when you select the template from the New dialog box), click the Save Template in Current Web check box if you plan to use the template for the current Web only, and click the OK button. If your template includes images, the Save Embedded Files dialog box will appear then. You *need* to embed your files in order for the template to work, so click the OK button.

Opening Your Template as a New Document

After creating your template, go ahead and try it out. You can create a new document from your template the same way you would create a new document from a FrontPage template. Select New from the File menu (or use the Ctrl+N key combination), make sure the General tab is selected, and click on your template. If you didn't find your template on the first try, take another look—the New dialog box lists templates by document title, not filename.

Planning the Work, Working the Plan: What to Put in Your Template

Creating a template means planning ahead. After all, the rest of your Web pages will be based on this document. Although the template should include all of your basic page elements, you should also allow yourself some flexibility. The Web page shown in the following figure provides an example of a template design.

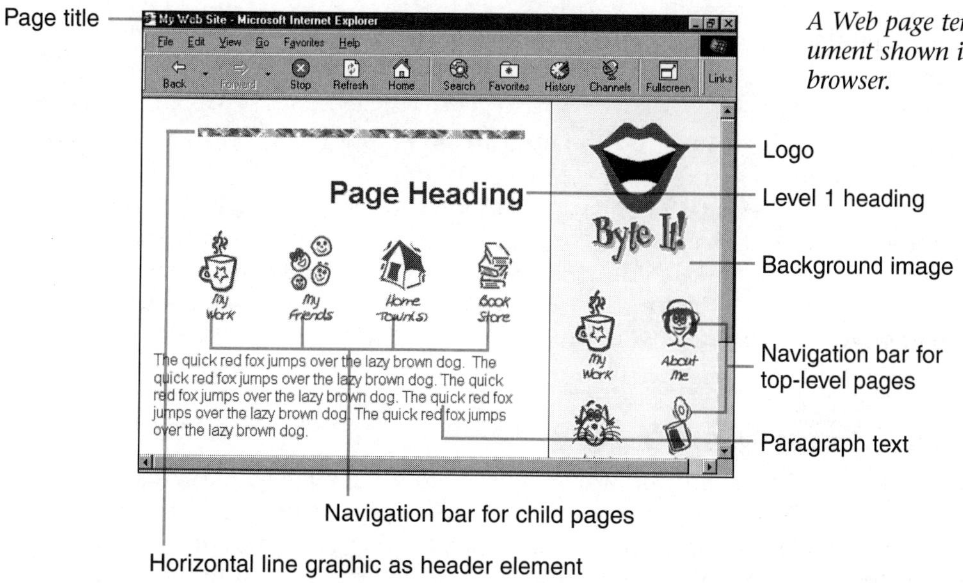

A Web page template document shown in a Web browser.

When you plan your template, consider the following page elements:

- *Color scheme* Choose background, text, and link colors that work well for your Web site. Chapter 3, "Fooling Around with Web Pages," talks more about color schemes and background images.
- *Page title* Give the template a basic title, like your company name or the name of your Web site, so you can easily pick it out from the rest of the page templates.
- *Text* You can add what graphic designers call *greeked text* to your template so you can pick text styles and formats and use them consistently throughout your Web site. If you look at some of the existing FrontPage templates, you'll see that greeked text is total nonsense that exists only to hold the place for your real text. You can either copy and paste greeked text from an existing FrontPage template or type whatever text you want. You can also apply style sheets to format the text on your template, as explained later in this chapter and in Chapter 15, "Now You're Stylin'! Using Style Sheets." At the very least, you should include sample text for paragraphs, bulleted lists, numbered lists, and different heading levels.

- *Header and footer information* Think about whether you have certain graphics or text that you want to appear consistently at the top and bottom of your pages. For example, the page shown in the preceding figure displays a horizontal line graphic at the top of every page (and the bottom too, although you can't see it). Most Web sites also include copyright and contact information at the bottom of each page.
- *Graphics* Images make Web pages look more interesting, and you don't have to be Michelangelo to put a few pictures on your Web site. You can add visual interest to your pages by using graphics for bullets, horizontal lines, text, navigation buttons, page backgrounds, and a special logo. Chapter 8, "The Picture-Perfect Web Page: Placing and Tweaking Images," tells you how to use the FrontPage Clip Art Gallery and where to get free images on the Web.
- *Navigation elements* Whether you want to use button graphics or plain ol' text links, you need to figure out how to help visitors find their way around your Web site. Most Web sites provide a row of links to top-level (parent) pages and another row of links to child (second-level or lower) pages, as explained in Chapter 7, "Think Links: Adding Links to Your Pages." You can either use FrontPage navigation bars or the Include Page component (covered later in this chapter) to help automate your links.

Laying Out Your Template

Once you've figured out what you want to put in your template, you can start laying it out. When designing your page, you should make sure that important information—like your site links, page topic (heading), logo, and first paragraph—appear at the top of the screen because some Web surfers are too lazy to scroll to the bottom. Tables sure come in handy for putting your page elements exactly where you want them. (See Chapter 12, "Table It! Arranging Text and Images with Tables.") For more on page design and resources, check out Chapter 10, "Elements of Style: Web Design Basics." *Creative Web Design* by Lynda Weinman and *Que Special Edition: Using HTML 4* by Molly Holschlag offer useful information and creative inspiration for experienced and novice designers alike.

Let FrontPage Help! Handy Tools for Managing Your Pages

A Web site is kind of like that pile of paper sitting in your In tray. It keeps getting bigger and bigger, and before you know it, you barely have time to manage the thing. Well, FrontPage can't sort out your papers for you, but it can definitely help you manage your Web pages. The following sections explain how features like shared borders, navigation bars, Include Page components, and style sheets can save you lots of time and effort down the road. When you're creating your Web page template, keep these tools in mind.

Setting Up Shared Borders

Planning Makes Perfect

Chapter 10 gives some guidelines for planning your Web site before you begin creating pages. Knowing how your pages work together will make it easy to identify which borders to place on your Web pages.

Templates are great, but they do have their limitations. For example, different sets of pages may require separate sets of graphics, navigation bars, and header and footer information. Sure, you can create separate templates for each of your sections, but you might want to try out the shared borders feature first. You can create a template that contains basic page elements, and then apply a different shared border for the information that changes on different pages on your Web site.

Shared borders are areas along the top, left, right, and bottom of pages that contain information shared by more than one Web page. When you apply shared borders to pages and place text, links, or graphics in the border areas, FrontPage displays them on all the pages that share the same borders. When you revamp your Web site, you only need to edit one page and FrontPage changes the rest of your pages for you.

To use shared borders on your Web site, do the following:

1. Set up a template that does *not* include navigation bars or other header or footer information that changes throughout your Web site, and then create your pages.
2. Switch to the Folders view, hold down the Ctrl key, and click on your pages. (Holding down the Ctrl key allows you to select several non-consecutive files at once—you can try this in the Windows Explorer, too!) If you want to apply shared borders to your entire Web site, you can skip this step.
3. Select Shared Borders from the Format menu to display the Shared Borders dialog box, as shown in the following figure.

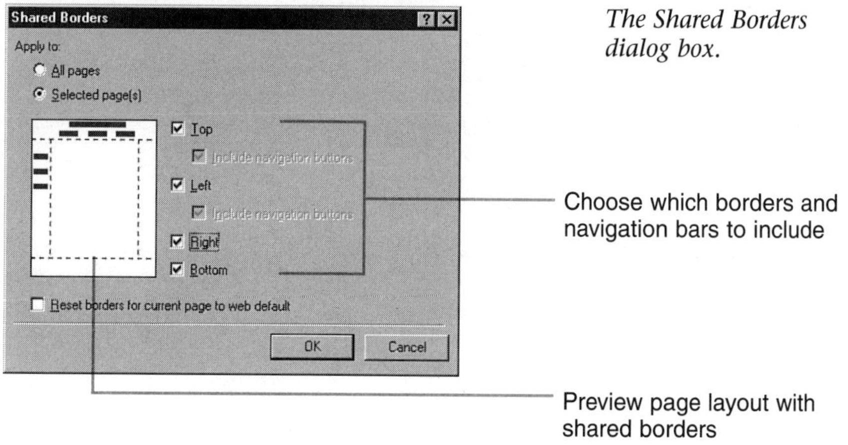

The Shared Borders dialog box.

Shared Border Options

To apply your borders to all the pages on your Web site, click the All Pages radio button.

Choose which types of borders you want to include by clicking the Top, Left, Right, and Bottom buttons. You can add as few or as many borders as you want.

To add a horizontal FrontPage navigation bar to the top border or a vertical FrontPage navigation bar to the left border, click the Include navigation buttons check box for the selected borders.

4. The preview on the left shows you what your borders will look like. When you finish, click OK to return to FrontPage.
5. Open one of the pages that you just applied a shared border to and add your shared information to the border areas (FrontPage displays a bounding box with comments to let you know where the border areas are). When you save the page, FrontPage applies your changes to all pages that share the same border.

Adding FrontPage Navigation Bars with Shared Borders

Shared borders are great for adding navigation bars to documents. If you want to use the same FrontPage navigation bar throughout your entire Web site, you can apply it from the Shared Borders dialog box. However, this method doesn't allow you much flexibility. Instead, you can create shared borders for groups of pages, and then use a separate FrontPage navigation bar for each group, as shown in the following figure.

A Web page with shared borders and navigation bars, displayed in FrontPage.

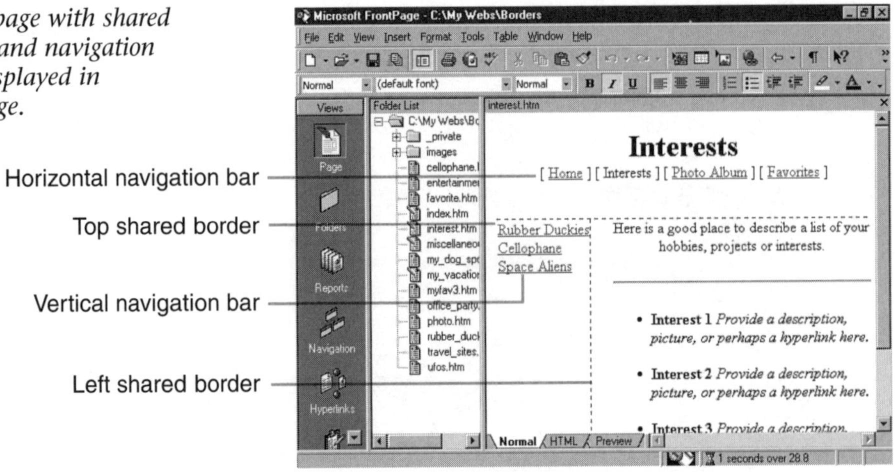

Add a Shared Border to a New Page

Now that you've applied the shared borders to all of your existing pages, what are you going to do when you want to create a new one? Not to worry; FrontPage has you covered. You can apply the shared borders from the Page view too. Just open a new page and select Shared Borders from the Style section of the Format menu.

First, open a page with shared borders, place your cursor in a border area, and select Navigation Bar from the Insert menu. When the Navigation Bar Properties dialog box appears, you can select options for page levels, additional pages, and the navigation bar's appearance. The dialog box displays previews to help you make the right choices, and Chapter 7 explains navigation and hyperlink levels in greater detail. When you finish, click OK to add the navigation bar to your shared border pages.

Navigation Bar Tips

Before you can set up navigation bars, you need to go into the Navigation view and create a navigation structure for your Web site, as explained in Chapter 7.

When you're choosing the orientation for your buttons, pick Horizontal for a top or bottom border and Vertical for a left or right border. Otherwise, your page layout may look a little screwy.

To make changes to a navigation bar, click it with your right mouse button and select Navigation Bar Properties from the shortcut menu to display the Navigation Bar Properties dialog box.

You can also add navigation bars to individual pages. Place your cursor in a non-border area of your Web page and follow the steps from the "Adding FrontPage Navigation Bars with Shared Borders" section.

If you change the structure of your Web site in the Navigation view of your Web site, FrontPage changes all of the related navigation bars on your Web pages.

Inserting Include Page Components

If you want the convenience of shared borders but need more flexibility with your page layouts, try FrontPage's Include Page component. Here's how it works: First you create a Web page with a single repeating page element, such as an image, some text, or a group of links or navigation buttons, and save it to your `_private` folder. You can then place the contents of that page element anywhere in your template, not just in the border area. If you later need to change something, open the Web page that you inserted as an Include Page component and make your changes. FrontPage then applies your changes to any pages that contain the Include Page component. Pretty nifty, huh? Chapter 19, "A Grab Bag of Helpful Doodads: FrontPage Components," tells you how to create Include Page components and more about how they work.

Love That Style

If you're fussy about your text, you can create a style sheet and attach it to your template. Style sheets are special documents that contain formatting for different types of text styles, like headings, paragraphs, bulleted lists, and numbered lists. This way, you don't have to keep fooling around with font properties, text colors, and styles. For more about creating style sheets, see Chapter 15.

Five Cool Template Tips

- *Let FrontPage help* FrontPage has lots of nifty tools to make managing a Web site easier. Consider how these tools can help you in the future while designing your template.
- *Test your template page at different screen resolutions* You can't completely control how your pages will look on other computers. However, you can avoid serious problems by testing the page you plan to use as your template at different screen resolutions. Chapter 10 has a sidebar on changing your computer's display settings so you can do this.
- *Resize the browser window while testing your template page* You can't count on everyone to size their browser to the full screen while they surf the Web. And funny things can happen to pages when you make the browser window smaller. Experiment with resizing your browser window and make sure that your graphics and text don't shift too much. It's okay if some elements don't appear unless you scroll or the paragraph gets narrower. But if you have a row of images and some of them shift down to the next line, your page might look yucky. Tables can help you control your layout, as explained in Chapter 12.
- *Use more than one version of your template for larger sites* If you have a large Web site, you may need to create a few variations of your template so you can create different sets of shared borders and other page elements.

- *Create a mockup with a graphics program* If you have an image program like PhotoShop or Paint Shop Pro, try creating a mockup of your layout before setting up your template. To set up your page to display about a screen and a half of information on a browser, size the image to 640×480 pixels and use 72 dpi resolution.
- *Look around* You can explore the Web and read books for great design ideas. For more design tips and resources, see Chapter 10.

The Least You Need to Know

- Templates are ready-made Web pages that save you the work of setting up all of your pages individually. FrontPage comes with templates, but you can create your own templates, too.
- When you create a Web page that you want to save as a template, select Save As from the File menu and choose FrontPage Template from the Save As menu. You can open a template from the New dialog box.
- Before setting up your template, plan ahead. Consider which graphics, links, text, headers, and footers you want to display on every page and which text styles you want to use. You can also figure out how you can take advantage of FrontPage tools like shared borders, navigation bars, Include Page components, and style sheets.
- Shared borders come in handy when you want to stick with a basic page design, but you also need to display different information (such as navigation bars) on different groups of pages. You can apply shared borders to selected pages or an entire Web site.
- Shared borders are ideal for displaying different FrontPage navigation bars for different sections of a Web site. To place a navigation bar in a shared border, select Navigation Bar from the Insert menu. Chapter 7 tells you how to create a site structure in the Navigation view and gives you the basic lowdown on navigation bars.
- Include Page components give you a more flexible way to add repeating page elements to your template. Chapter 19 talks about them in greater detail.
- You can also attach style sheets to your template to shave off some of the time you spend fiddling with text. Chapter 15 talks about creating and applying style sheets in greater detail.

Chapter 15

Now You're Stylin'! Using Style Sheets

In This Chapter

- Introduction to style sheets
- Applying styles to Web pages
- Creating and editing style sheets
- Creating custom styles
- Five cool style sheet resources

Typography on the Web? An awful lot of graphic designers think of that phrase as an oxymoron, like "user-friendly computers." If you've gotten used to fiddling around with text in your desktop publishing program or fancy word processor, working with text on your Web pages can get a little frustrating.

Send style sheets to the rescue! Whether you're a designer who wants to do fancy stuff with text or a novice who wants to save a little time when formatting it, style sheets can help. With style sheets, you can create formats for different types of text and apply those formats to a single document, several documents, or your entire Web site.

New Style Sheet Support!

FrontPage 2000 fully supports style sheets, offers user-friendly dialog boxes to help you create them, and provides lots of useful style sheet templates.

What Are Style Sheets?

Style sheets (also called *cascading style sheets*, or *CSS* for short) are lists of descriptions of different types of text styles, such as headings, paragraphs, and bulleted lists. When you create style sheets in FrontPage's Page view, these descriptions are invisible unless you look at your source code by clicking the HTML tab.

You can either place a style sheet directly in a Web page or create a style sheet document and link it to your Web pages, as explained in the "Applying Style Sheets to Your Web Pages " section later in this chapter. With style sheets, you can assign fonts, borders, and backgrounds to different types of text, and also control the indents, margins, line spacing (space between lines in a paragraph), character spacing (space between letters), and more.

It is also worth mentioning that style sheets aren't only for text. You can also use them to position and display other objects, like tables, forms, embedded files that launch with plug-ins, and components of JavaScript, Java, and ActiveX. However, that topic is a little more advanced and goes beyond the scope of this book. You can learn more about style sheets by exploring some of the resources listed at the end of this chapter.

Text Styles vs. Style Sheet Styles

All this stylin' can get a bit confusing. First we have *text styles*, which refers to a whole range of text formats, such as bold, italic, font, and font size, as well as headings, lists, and so on. Then we have *style sheet styles*, which are descriptions that you assign to all these text styles. Whew! Of course, more precise terms exist. But technical jargon isn't very much fun, and you don't need much of it to learn FrontPage.

What Are Tags?

HTML *tags* are the codes used to format the text and layout for Web pages. Think of tags as *containers* that enclose Web page elements and tell Web browsers how to display them, just like a mold determines the shape of its contents.

All Web page elements—such as headings, paragraphs, images, and tables—have corresponding opening (and usually closing) tags as well. For example, the `<P>` opening tag begins a paragraph, and the `</P>` closing tag ends a paragraph. Many tags also contain *attributes*—additional characteristics for the enclosed page elements. For example, `<P Align=Center>` begins a paragraph that is centered on the page.

Pick a Tag, Any Tag: Creating Styles for Different Types of Text

You don't have to be an HTML expert to use style sheets, but you do need to know which HTML tags go with which types of text. Also, if you *really* know your HTML, you can format just about anything with style sheets—including tables and all the elements inside of them. The "Five Cool Style Sheet Resources" section at the end of this chapter points you to some Web sites where you can learn more. Chapter 1, "Get Ready to Rock with FrontPage 2000," also tells you a bit about how HTML and Web pages work.

The following list explains some basic HTML tags so you know which ones to pick:

- *Body* Text on your page that has no paragraphs or other formatting applied. FrontPage also applies Body text styles to all text elements that have no other styles assigned to them.
- *P* For paragraphs.
- *Address* Applies to text that you've formatted by selecting Address from the Style menu on the Formatting toolbar. People generally use this style for the copyright and contact information that appears at the bottom of a Web page.
- *H1, H2, H3, H4, H5, H6* Different levels of headings that you can apply from the Style menu on the Formatting toolbar. H1 is the largest heading and H6 is the smallest.
- *A* Stands for *anchor* and applies formatting to your linked text. By default, links are formatted in the same font as the surrounding text, and are set apart with an underline and a different color. With style sheets, you can use different types of text formatting to make your links stand out. (A quick warning: If you try this, make sure your visitors can still figure out where your links are. If the links look different enough from the surrounding text, people will probably be able to figure it out.)
- *UL* Stands for *unordered list* and applies to bulleted lists, as explained in Chapter 6, "Making a List, Checking It Twice."
- *OL* Stands for *ordered list* and applies to numbered lists, as explained in Chapter 6.
- *DT* Stands for *defined term* and applies to the non-indented lines in definition lists, as explained in Chapter 6.
- *DD* Stands for *definition description* and applies to the indented lines in definition lists, as explained in Chapter 6.
- *B* For bold text. For more about bold and italic text, see Chapter 5, "Entering Text and Fiddling with Fonts."

- *I* For text with italics.
- *HR* Stands for *horizontal rule* (called *horizontal line* in FrontPage). For more about horizontal lines, see Chapter 5.
- *Img* Short for *image*. This is the tag used for placing images on a Web page, as covered in Chapter 8, "The Picture-Perfect Web Page: Placing and Tweaking Images."
- *Embed* For embedding a file on a Web page, as covered in Chapter 17, "Strut Your Stuff: Sound, Video, and More."
- *Table* Applies formatting to a table. For more about tables, see Chapter 12, "Table It! Arranging Text and Images with Tables."
- *TD* Stands for *table description* and applies formatting to table cells.
- *TR* Stands for *table row* and applies formatting to table rows.

Style Sheets and HTML Tags

When you create style sheets, you specify special attributes for different HTML tags. For example, you can choose to display all of your level one headings (<H1>) as 24-point red text. You can then apply the style sheet to pages on your Web site so you don't have to select each level one heading individually and format it as 24-point red text. This can save you an awful lot of time and work, even if you only have a small Web site!

The Cheese Stands Alone

And so do some types of HTML tags. Tags that designate individual objects don't have closing tags. Common examples are the <Img Src> tag (for inserting images, as covered in Chapter 8) and the <Embed> tag (for embedding files, as covered in Chapter 17).

Creating a New Style Sheet Document

Style sheets work best when you create them as separate documents (with the `.css` file name extension) and then link your Web pages to them. When you work with an individual style sheet document, FrontPage displays your style list in the Normal view of your Web page so you can see what you're doing. You can also apply your style sheet document to documents throughout your Web site.

FrontPage comes with special style sheet templates that you can open by selecting New and Page from the File menu and then clicking the Style Sheets tab from the New dialog box. From here, you can build a style sheet from scratch by selecting Normal Style Sheet from the list and clicking the OK button. This template not only helps you get started on the right foot, it also shows you how style sheets tick.

A Few Style Sheet Terms

If you want to learn more about style sheets and explore the Web sites listed at the end of this chapter, you might run into a few unfamiliar terms:

Selector An HTML tag with a style assigned to it (or one to which you plan to assign a style).

Class A document language. For example, HTML is a language used for Web pages, and CSS is a language used to create style sheets.

ID A name that you can give to a style that you've created for an HTML tag.

Declarations, properties, and values Declarations are pairs of *properties* and *values* assigned to an HTML tag (selector). For example, if you decide to make your Level 1 headings blue, H1 is the selector, Color is the property, and Blue is the value.

Inheritance With HTML and style sheets, some page elements can *inherit* properties and values from other page elements. This can save you a little time when you're creating styles for tags that fall within the same group. For example, you can create a style for a Level 1 heading (H1), and you can set up lower-level headings (H2-H6) to inherit the same font style, colors, and other characteristics.

Formatting a New Style Sheet

Now let's get down to brass tacks. To begin building a style sheet, create a new style sheet document or open a Web page, and then choose Style from the Format menu. The Style dialog box appears, as shown in the following figure, to help you create your list of style descriptions. You can create as few or as many styles as you like. If you're starting from scratch, select All HTML Tags from the List box, choose a tag from the Styles list, and click the New button.

The Style dialog box.

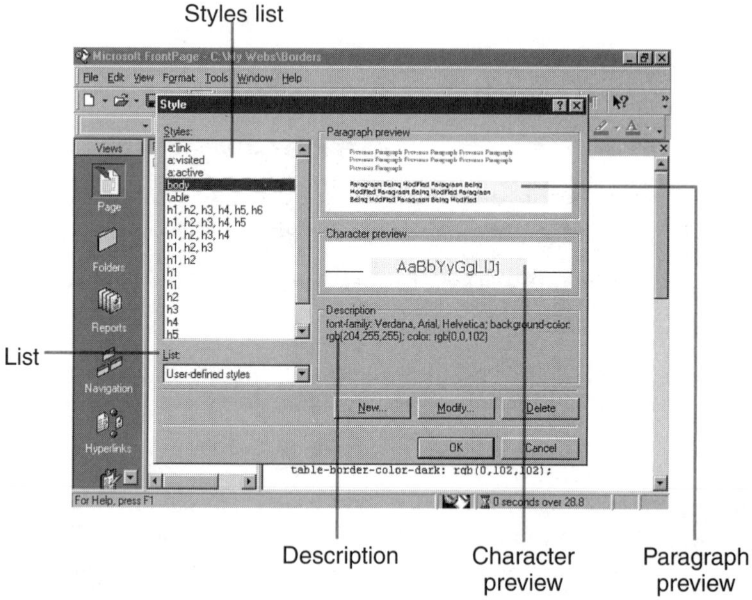

If you're working with an existing style sheet, you can select User-Defined Styles from the list to see which tags have already been formatted. The "Editing Style Sheets" section later in this chapter tells you how to change (or take a peek at) existing styles.

When the New Style dialog box displays, you can create a style with the following steps:

1. Type a name (any name you want) for your new style in the Name (selector) box. When you're working with style sheets, HTML tags are referred to as *selectors* because you select them.
2. To apply different types of formats to your style, click the Format button to display the pop-up list, and then choose Font, Paragraph, Border, Numbering, or Position. The following sections explain these options in greater detail.
3. When you finish creating your style, click the OK button to return to the Style dialog box. You can apply styles to as many tags as you want.
4. Your styles appear when you select User-Defined Styles from the List box. Click OK to save your changes and return to your style sheet document or Web page.

Style Sheets and Numbers

When you set up your style sheets, you can enter numbers for font sizes, border widths, character widths, and other attributes. Font sizes are specified in points, as in 10 pt. Other values can be entered as pixels, percentages, inches, or centimeters, as in 10 px for 10 pixels, 5 % for 5 percent, 1 cm for 1 centimeter, and .5 in for half an inch. You can also select values from the number lists.

Picking Font Styles

Sure, you can apply different fonts and formats to your text by selecting the text and using the Formatting toolbar options or the Font dialog box. But style sheets can spare you the grunt work of having to format the same type of text over and over again. Apply a font to an HTML style once, apply the style sheet to your Web pages, and you're all set. In the Style dialog box, select a style from the list and click the New button to display the New Style dialog box. Click the Format button and select Font from the pop-up menu to display the Font dialog box, as shown in the following figure. This dialog box includes a Preview area so you can see how your text will look on your Web pages. When you finish applying font styles, click OK.

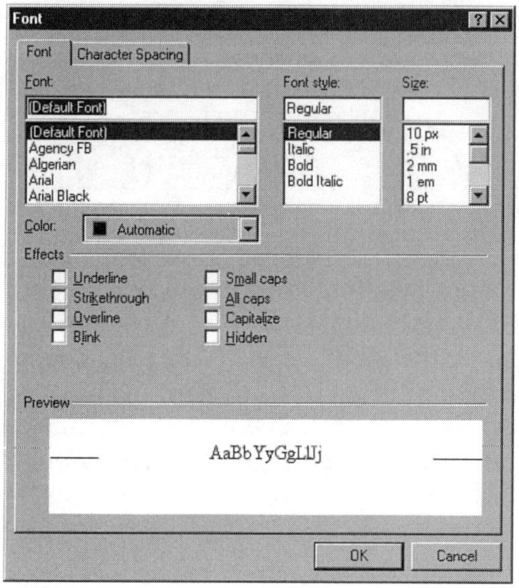

The Font dialog box with the Font tab selected.

With the Font tab selected, you can choose fonts from the Font list, font styles (such as bold and italic text) from the Font Style list, colors from the Color list, font sizes from the Font Size list, and character effects from the list of options. With the Character Spacing tab selected, you can space letters further apart by selecting Expanded from the Spacing list, or tighten up the spacing between letters by selecting Condensed from the Spacing list. To set the distance between letters, enter a value in the By box. You can also raise or lower your letters in relation to the line height by choosing Raised or Lowered from the Position list and entering a value in the By box. For more about formatting fonts, see Chapter 5.

Choosing Paragraph Styles

The right paragraph styles can make a page more attractive and easier to read. You can specify alignment, indentation, line spacing, and the space between words by setting your Paragraph options. From the Style box, select a tag from the Styles list, and click the New button to display the New Style dialog box. Then click the Format button and select Paragraph from the pop-up menu. The Paragraph dialog box displays a Preview area so you can see how your text looks before applying the style, as shown in the following figure.

The Paragraph dialog box.

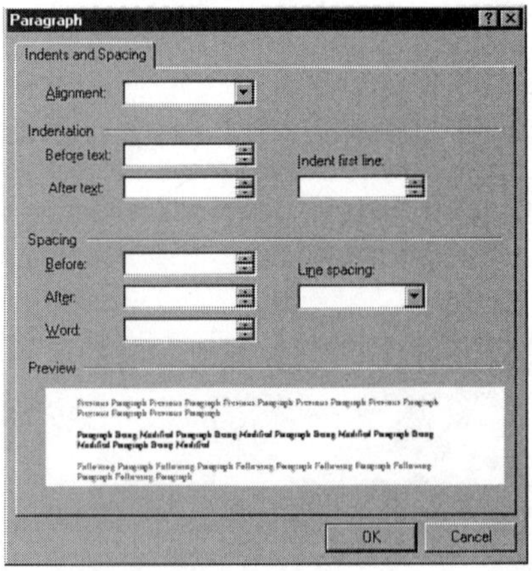

To automatically align text to the left, right, or center of the page, pick an option from the Alignment list. Or you can create left indents (Before Text), right indents (After Text), and first-line indents (Indent first line) by selecting or entering a number in the appropriate boxes. To determine the space before or after a paragraph, enter or select a value in the Before or After box. You can also make paragraphs single- or double-spaced by choosing a value from the Line Spacing box—or you can enter a value in pixels, percentages, inches, or centimeters. Finally, you can space words further apart or closer together by entering or selecting a value in the Word box. For more about formatting fonts, see Chapter 5.

Specifying Borders and Shading Styles

Want to jazz up your headings or other text elements to set them apart from the rest of your text? Try creating styles with borders and shading. From the Style dialog box, select a tag from the styles list, and click the New button to display the New Style dialog box. Then click the Format button and select Borders from the pop-up menu. When the Borders and Shading dialog box appears, as shown in the following figure, you can click the Borders tab to create a border around your text or click the Shading tab to create a background. To see what your border or shading will look like, take a peek at the Preview area.

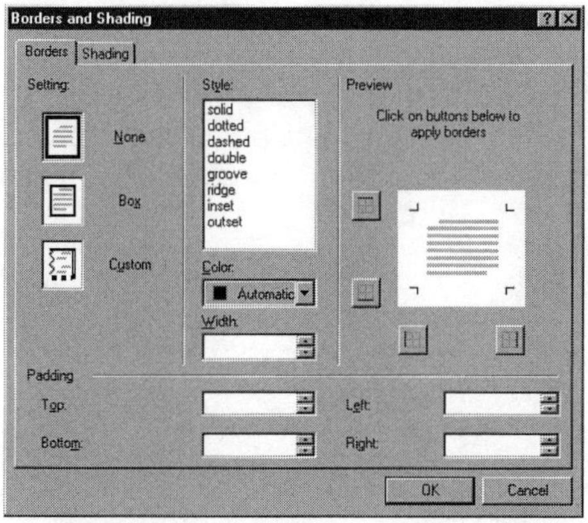

The Borders and Shading dialog box, with the Borders tab selected.

With the Borders tab selected, you can choose Box to create a four-sided, rectangular border, Custom to display borders on some sides and not others, or None. To choose a border style, select an item from the Styles list, click the New button, choose a color from the Color box, and enter or choose a width in the Width box. You should also put a little space between the border and the text by entering or selecting numbers in the Padding boxes.

And what about custom borders? Adding a border to only one or two sides of a box can give your pages a more elegant look. To create a custom border, click the Custom button and then click the border buttons in the Preview area to add or remove lines from different sides.

Psst! Try the Blockquote Tag

Blockquote text looks great with borders and shading. In HTML, the blockquote tag indents text on the left and right to set it apart from the rest of the page.

Choosing Styles for Bulleted and Numbered Lists

Chapter 6 told you how to set up bulleted and numbered lists with different bullet and number styles. But why format all your lists from scratch when one style sheet can do it all for you? First, go to the Style dialog box and select UL (for bulleted lists) or OL (for numbered lists) from the Styles list, and then click the New button to display the New Style dialog box. Click the Format button and select Numbering from the pop-up menu. When the Numbering dialog box appears, click the Image Bullets tab to use graphics for your bullets, click the Plain Bullets tab to apply regular bullet styles, or click the Numbers tab to choose number styles.

Applying Position Styles

With FrontPage, you can place pictures, text, tables, and other page elements from the Picture toolbar, as covered in Chapter 9, "Spiffing Up Pictures." If you want certain page elements to always appear on a certain part of a Web page, you can apply absolute position files.

From the Style dialog box, select a tag from the Styles list, and then click the New button to display the New Style dialog box. Click the Format button and select Position from the pop-up menu. When the Position dialog box appears, as shown in the following figure, you can choose a wrapping style, positioning style, location and size options, and layering (Z-order) options, as explained in Chapter 9.

The Position dialog box.

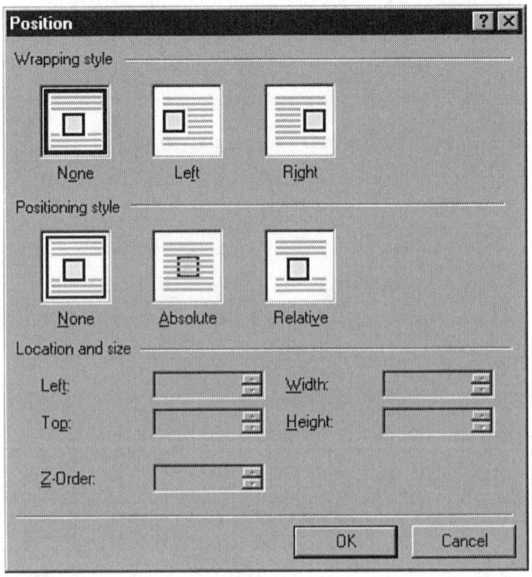

Creating a Style Sheet for a Single Web Page

You can also set up a style sheet for an individual Web page. This approach is ideal when you want to format a single page in a particular way, but you don't want to use the same formatting for your other pages. To create a style sheet for a single Web page, open the Web page and then format your style sheet as described earlier.

Applying Style Sheets to Your Web Pages

If you created your style sheet in a Web page, you're all finished. FrontPage applies the style sheet to the current page as soon as you finish creating your styles. But if you set up your styles in a separate document, you'll need to apply them to your Web pages. To attach a style sheet to your entire Web site, select Style Sheet Links from the Format menu. When the Link Style Sheet dialog box appears, select the All Pages radio button and click OK.

To attach a style sheet to a single page or a group of pages, go to the Folders view, select your pages (you can hold down the Ctrl key to select nonconsecutive pages), and choose Style Sheet Links from the Format menu. When the Link Style Sheet dialog box appears, choose the Selected Pages radio button and click OK.

Editing Style Sheets

Time for a change? You can edit your style sheets at any time. Open the style sheet document, and then select Style from the Format menu to display the Style dialog box. You can then choose User-defined styles from the List box to display the styles you've created.

To edit a style, select it from the list and click the Modify button. To remove a style, select it and click the Delete button. To add more styles to your list, select All HTML Tags from the List box, click on a tag, and then click the Modify button.

Applying Your Styles to Text

Once you've created a style sheet and attached it to a Web page, you can apply it by placing, entering, and formatting your page elements as you normally do. For example, if you've set up a style for a link and you create a link, FrontPage applies the style to it. And what about style elements that don't appear on your toolbars? You can pull them down from the Style menu on the Formatting toolbar.

Five Cool Style Sheet Resources

Wanna do more stylin'? Once you get a little HTML under your belt, you can learn more about style sheets from the Web. The following sites provide all sorts of useful information to get you started.

- *Guides to HTML* If you want to do serious stuff with style sheets, you need to learn some HTML basics. This Web site offers everything from tutorials to design tips (`http://www.hypernews.org/HyperNews/get/www/html/guides.html`).
- *Microsoft SiteBuilder Network - DHTML, HTML, & CSS* A treasure trove of resources for Web people (especially ones who use Microsoft products), and plenty of information about style sheets, along with some cool examples (`http://msdn.microsoft.com/workshop/author/default.asp`).
- *Guide to Cascading Style Sheets* The Web Design Group provides an introduction, a quick tutorial, and more (`http://www.htmlhelp.com/reference/css/`).
- *Writing Cascading Style Sheets* Tips, resources, examples, and simple explanations (`http://www.canit.se/~griffon/web/writing_stylesheets.html`).
- *Effective Use of Style Sheets* Article by Jakob Nielsen with lots of good advice (`http://www.useit.com/alertbox/9707a.html`).

The Least You Need to Know

- Style sheets are lists that describe formats for different HTML tags. When you format text with an HTML tag that has a style assigned to it, and the current Web page has a style sheet attached to it, FrontPage applies the style sheet formatting to the text.
- Everything on your Web page is formatted with HTML tags. But you won't see that unless you view your source code.
- You can place a style sheet on a single Web page, or you can create a separate style sheet document (with the `.css` file name extension) and link it to several Web pages or all the Web pages on your site.
- You can create a style sheet for the current document by selecting Style from the Format menu to display the Style dialog box. From there, you can assign styles to different tags or edit existing styles.
- You can use style sheets to format fonts, paragraphs, borders, shading, and lists.
- If you want to create a style for a tag that doesn't appear on the list in the Style dialog box, you can click the New button to add the new tag to the list and create styles for it.
- Once you create style sheets, you can edit them at any time by opening the style sheet document and selecting Style from the Format menu to display the Style dialog box.
- Many style sheet topics go beyond the scope of this book, but you can learn more about them on the Web.

Part 4

Wow! Amaze Your Friends with Web Page Wizardry

You've probably visited Web sites with cool bells and whistles like animated special effects, QuickTime movies, search forms, hit counters, online databases, and background sounds. But only programmers and other technical folks can create advanced Web pages, right? Right… unless you happen to use FrontPage 2000.

So get ready to strut your stuff! FrontPage 2000 turns you into an instant Web wizard with features that let you build exciting, interactive Web pages without any programming or coding. If you do your own programming and scripting or know how to work with scripts and programs that you've downloaded from the Web, FrontPage makes it easy to integrate this into your pages. You can also prepare files created with other Microsoft Office 2000 programs for the Web in a matter of minutes.

This part tells you how to use FrontPage's advanced features to spiff up your pages, save time, and make your Web site more useful for your visitors.

Chapter 16

X Marks the Hot Spot! Making Image Maps

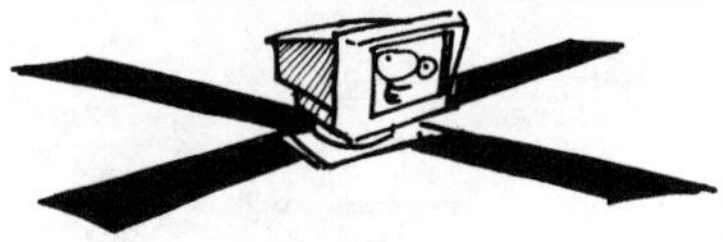

In This Chapter

- About image maps
- Creating hot spots
- Setting up a default link for the image
- Editing hot spots
- Highlighting hot spots
- Five cool image map ideas

Image maps are plain old pictures with links. When you click on different parts of an image map, you go to different parts of the Web site. Image maps are fun, and they give your visitors an interesting way to explore your Web site. For example, if you saw a Web page that had nothing but a map of the United States, wouldn't you click on each state to see what happened? You can create image maps by scanning a suitable photograph or by combining different pictures into a single image and arranging them.

What's an Image Map?

An image map consists of two parts: the image itself and the *hot spots*, which are shapes that you draw on a picture to define the hyperlinked areas of the picture, as shown in the following figure. When you draw a shape, the Hyperlink dialog box appears so you can enter a page or URL for the link.

Creating an image map in FrontPage.

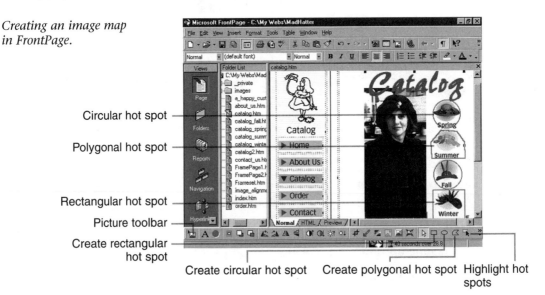

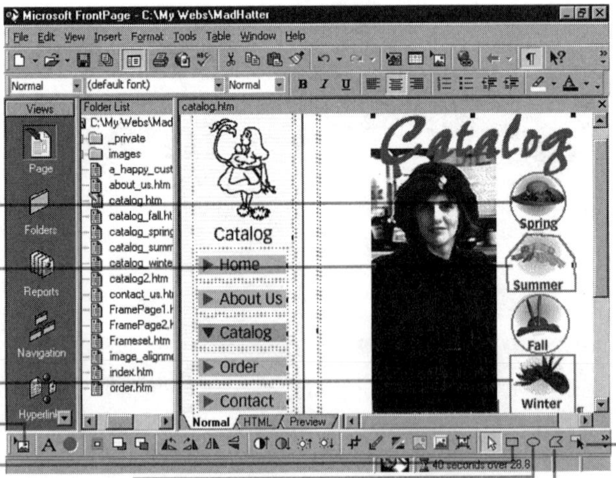

Creating Image Hot Spot Links

Can you draw some simple shapes? Oh good, then you're ready to define some hot spots for your image. When you select an image, the Picture toolbar appears at the bottom of the FrontPage window, with the image map tools on the far right. Don't worry if you don't like how the shapes look on your image—they do not appear when you view your page in a Web browser.

Drawing the Shapes

Drawing rectangles and circles is easy. With the picture selected, just click on the Rectangular or Circular button. When the cursor turns into a pencil, click anywhere on the picture, hold down the mouse button, drag upwards or downwards diagonally, and then release the mouse button. You can also create irregular shapes with the Polygonal tool. Select it to make your cursor turn into a pencil, and then play "connect the dots." Click your cursor on the picture, and then drag your mouse (you don't need to hold it down) to the next point in your shape and click the mouse again. Continue to create new points until you've enclosed an area, and then double-click at the point where you want to close the shape.

Making the Links

When you finish drawing a shape, the Create Hyperlink dialog box pops up. Enter a URL or select a page from your Web and click the OK button. Congratulations, you've created your first hot spot!

Highlighting Hot Spots

You can also choose to highlight hot spots. This means that when a visitor clicks on a hot spot, the shape flashes on for a moment. Many people think that highlighted image map hot spots look horrible, but to each their own. To highlight a hot spot, select it and then click on the Highlight Hot Spots button.

Editing Hot Spots

Once you've created your hot spots, you can move, resize, or change the link anytime you want. To move a hot spot, click on a shape and drag it to its new location. To resize a hot spot, click on it to display the bounding box with the square resize handles and then pass your cursor over a handle. When your cursor changes to a two-way arrow, hold down your mouse button and drag your mouse inwards or outwards.

Missed! When Visitors Click on the Wrong Spot

What if someone clicked on the wrong part of your image, and nothing happened? Boy, would you feel silly. (Then again, maybe you wouldn't.) You can specify a *default link* for your entire image that loads a page if a visitor clicks an area outside of all the hot spots.

To set up a default link, click the image with your right mouse button and select Picture Properties. When the Picture Properties dialog box appears, you can enter a URL in the Default hyperlink section's Location box near the bottom of the screen. When you finish, click OK.

How About Creating a Special Default Hyperlink Page?

You can create a new Web page as the default hyperlink page for your image map. The page can say something like, "Whoops! You missed the hot spot on my image map! The image map links to the following pages," and then provide a list of links.

Five Cool Image Map Ideas

- *Group photo* Take a picture of your family, friends, or coworkers, draw a hot spot around each person, and make links to their Web pages or email address.
- *A real map* Get a map of your hometown or a favorite vacation spot. (You can find maps on the Web; just make sure to ask for permission before you use one.) Draw hot spots around places on the map and make links to pages that tell people about them. Or you can tell your own stories about these places.
- *A multimedia image map* Show a photograph or drawing of a room in your house or your office. When the user clicks on different objects in the room, it plays a sound file or movie that relates to the object. Learn more about using multimedia with FrontPage 2000 in Chapter 17, "Strut Your Stuff: Sound, Video, and More."
- *For artists and designers* If you're used to creating more sophisticated layouts for printed materials, image maps can help you get around some of the Web's limitations. (Just don't make your pictures too large or they might take too long to download!) Chapter 8, "The Picture-Perfect Web Page: Placing and Tweaking Images," contains tips for keeping the file size small.
- *Image map rollovers* You can create image maps that change when the user passes the mouse cursor over different hot spots. But you need to learn a little JavaScript in order to do this. For more on exploring JavaScript and other types of scripting, see Chapter 21, "Rev Up Your Web Site with Programs and Scripts."

The Least You Need to Know

- An image map is a picture with clickable hot spots that function as links. To create an image map, draw your hot spots and then link them to your Web pages.
- To draw a hot spot, select the image to display on the Picture toolbar, click the Rectangular Hotspot, Circular Hotspot, or Polygonal Hotspot toolbar buttons, and then draw a shape on the part of the image that you want to link.
- When you finish drawing a hot spot and release the mouse button, the Create Hyperlink dialog box appears so you can make your link. For more about creating links, see Chapter 7, "Think Links: Adding Links to Your Pages."
- You can also create a default link for your picture. When someone clicks on a part of your image that doesn't have a hot spot defined for it, the Web page for the default link appears. To specify a default link, display the Picture Properties dialog box and type a URL in the Default Hyperlink Location box.

Chapter 17

Strut Your Stuff: Sound, Video, and More

In This Chapter

- Embedding sounds, movies, and other types of files
- Creating a background sound
- Placing and tweaking a picture movie
- File types and plug-ins
- Linking to files
- Ten cool places to visit for free multimedia goodies

The Web isn't just for text anymore. Whether you want to create an online portfolio, share documents with coworkers, or have fun with multimedia, you can publish just about anything on your Web page. Even though browsers only support Web pages, images, and some sound files, plug-in applications exist for just about every kind of file. In addition, FrontPage and Internet Explorer make it easy to add movies and background sounds to make your Web site more interesting and fun.

Linking or Embedding? Deciding How to Strut Your Stuff

If you want to publish movies, sounds, PowerPoint presentations, and other types of files on your Web site, go ahead. Most companies offer free plug-ins so you can put the files you create with their applications on the Web. Now, you need to decide whether to create links to the files or embed the files. You can also display AVI-formatted videos as movies, as explained earlier in this chapter. The following figure compares different methods of strutting your stuff. The following sections explain linking and embedding in greater detail.

Different ways to include files on a Web site.

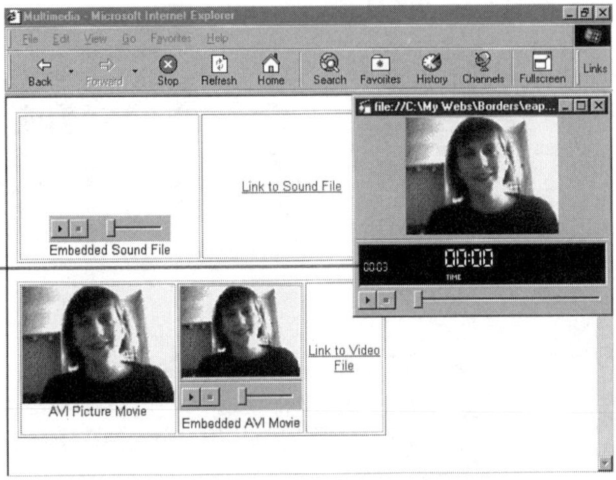

Multimedia Player application launched after clicking link to video file

A Little Mood Music: Adding a Background Sound

Television shows have theme songs—why shouldn't your Web page? With FrontPage, you can set your page up to play a sound when it loads. It doesn't *have* to be a song—you can use a sound effect or some other type of noise. A background sound can play over and over again (*very* annoying), or play once or twice and then stop.

If you already have a sound file to include on your Web page, right-click on your page and choose Page Properties from the shortcut menu or select Properties from the File menu. When the Page Properties dialog box appears with the General tab selected, click the Browse button in the Background Sound area and select your file. When the filename appears in the Location box, you can set the Loop options to determine how many times your audio file will play. To loop it indefinitely, leave the Forever check box selected. To play your background sound only a certain number of times, deselect the Forever check box by clicking it and enter a number in the Loop box. When you finish placing your background sound, click OK to return to your Web page.

Don't know where to find a sound file? Check out the list of resources at the end of this chapter for some cool sounds.

Everything and the Kitchen Sink: Linking to Files

When you make a link to a file, the browser launches the plug-in in a new window—or in some cases, an application starts up and launches the file. Linking to files gives you the most flexibility because you don't have to worry about whether your visitors have the plug-in or not. If they don't have the plug-in, they can either get it or choose not to click the link. In addition, some types of files may require too much space on your page to be displayed well if embedded in a Web page.

To make a link to a file, select the text or image you want to link from, select Hyperlink from the Insert menu, and then browse for the file as you normally do when you create a link. If you've forgotten how to make links, Chapter 7, "Think Links: Adding Links to Your Pages," can refresh your memory.

Help Visitors Get the Right Plug-In

If you offer files that require plug-ins, give your visitors a link so they can get those plug-ins. Most plug-ins are free, although some companies also sell more robust versions of their freeware plug-ins for users who want more features. When you link to a page or file that requires a plug-in, you should also include some text that tells visitors the file type and required plug-in so they can decide whether or not to click the link.

Straight from Your Web Page: Embedding Files

When you embed a file, the file and plug-in application (complete with toolbar buttons) are displayed on your Web page as images. This looks much slicker… but only if visitors have the plug-in. Otherwise, a broken plug-in icon is displayed in the browser window and your page looks yucky.

To embed a file, place your cursor where you want to insert the file, select Advanced from the Insert menu, and choose Plug-In from the cascading menu. When the Plug-In Properties dialog box appears, click the Browse button to search for the file, and then click OK to insert the plug-in and return to your Web page.

Boy, does that thing look ugly! Not to worry. FrontPage can't display embedded files in the Normal view, so it creates a placeholder instead. If you click the Preview tab or preview your page in your browser by clicking the Preview in Browser button, you can see how your embedded file *really* looks.

Editing Plug-In Properties

Once you've embedded your, file, you can fool around with the plug-in properties to make it look the way you want. To display the Plug-In Properties dialog box for your embedded file, right-click the plug-in placeholder and select Plug-In Properties from the shortcut menu. Or you can click the placeholder and select Properties from the Format menu.

You can set the following options:

- *Data Source* Click the Browse button to replace the current file with a different file.
- *Message for browsers without Plug-In support* Most browsers support plug-ins, but you might as well stay on the safe side and type some text like "You need a browser that supports plug-ins to view this file."
- *Size* FrontPage usually figures out the correct height and width for your file. But hey, nobody's perfect. If your file looks distorted, you can enter the correct dimensions (in pixels) in the Height and Width boxes.

Check Out the Clip Art Gallery

Remember the FrontPage Clip Art Gallery from Chapter 8, "The Picture-Perfect Web Page: Placing and Tweaking Images"? It offers cool sound and video clips, as well as images. To display the Clip Art Gallery, choose Picture from the Insert menu, and then select Clip Art. When the Clip Art Gallery dialog box appears, use the left and right arrow buttons to select the type of file you want. You can select Sounds or Motion Clips.

The Ex(ternal) Files

You can put pictures, movies, and other files in your Web pages, right? Well, not exactly. When you insert a picture or movie in a normal Word document, the file becomes part of your document. HTML documents, on the other hand, only have text and HTML markup tags in them. Pictures, movies, and other objects are stored *externally* as separate files. When you insert an object, FrontPage generates source code that tells browsers where the file is located and how to display it. This means that when you publish your Web pages to a server (as explained in Chapter 26, "Don't Just Let It Sit There! Publishing Your Web Site"), you also have to upload all the external files.

Before FrontPage came along, moving files around meant changing a lot of source code. You also had to make sure that the Web site folders and files on your computer exactly mirrored the folders and files on your server. This made managing Web sites a lot of work. Now FrontPage does all that work for you.

- *Hide Plug-In* Most plug-ins come with toolbar buttons and other application window elements. You can hide these elements by clicking the Hide Plug-In check box. Choosing this option doesn't generally work out well because in most cases, your visitors need their toolbar buttons and other options.
- *Layout* You can align your embedded file in relation to surrounding page elements by selecting an option from the Alignment box. To display a border around your embedded file, enter a number in the Border Thickness box. You can also add some buffer space between the embedded file and surrounding page elements by entering numbers (in pixels) in the Horizontal Spacing and Vertical Spacing boxes. These options are a lot like image layout options, as covered in Chapter 8.

Roll 'Em! Inserting a Movie as a Picture

With FrontPage, you can insert an AVI-formatted movie so it displays the first frame as an image—a picture movie. Movie files take a while to download, so this feature gives visitors something to look at while waiting for the rest of the movie to load. To insert an AVI movie that first appears as a picture, select Picture from the Insert menu, and then select Video from the cascading list. When the Video dialog box appears, you can browse for your movie file and select it.

Editing Your Picture Movie's Properties

When you place a picture movie on your page, FrontPage assumes that you want the movie to play as soon as your page loads in the browser. However, you may want to set up your picture movie so that it only plays when visitors click on it or pass their mouse pointers over it. To display the Properties dialog box for your picture movie, right-click on it and select Picture Properties from the shortcut menu, then choose the Video tab. You can also select the picture movie and select Properties from the Format menu. When you finish entering and selecting settings, click OK to apply your settings and return to FrontPage.

Browser Compatibility Alert!

Not all background sounds and movies inserted as pictures work with all browsers. If you add a background sound to your Web page and a Netscape Navigator user visits, that's okay. Although they can't hear your background sound, your page will load normally and they won't even know they've missed anything. However, inserting a movie as a picture is a different matter because incompatible browsers will display a broken image icon instead of your picture movie. If you want everyone to be able to view your movie, consider inserting it as a plug-in instead, as explained in the "Straight from Your Web Page: Embedding Files" section. For more on dealing with browser compatibility issues so everyone can use your Web site, see Chapter 26.

Want to Sound Like a Web Pro?

Web-savvy people call picture movies *dynamic source images.* That's because the picture comes from the first frame of a movie rather than a regular image file. On the Web, movies are *dynamic* because they've got motion and sound, and images are *static* because they just sit around the Web site like couch potatoes.

When the Picture Properties dialog box appears with the Video tab selected, you can set the following options:

- *Show Controls in Browser* Displays video player control buttons with the picture movie so visitors can play it by clicking the Play button.
- *Repeat* Here you can determine how many times the movie plays. To loop the movie over and over again, click the Forever button. To play the movie one or more times (I recommend only playing it once), enter a number in the Loop box. You can also specify the number of *milliseconds* (1,000 milliseconds equals one second) that elapse between loops by entering a number in the Loop Delay box.
- *Start* You can set your picture movie to start playing when your page loads in the browser by clicking the On File Open check box. Or you can have it begin playing only when a visitor passes their cursor over the image by clicking the On Mouse Over check box.

About File Types, Plug-Ins, and ActiveX Controls

Have you ever wondered why you have to bother with those filename extensions like `.gif`, `.jpg`, and `.htm`? A filename extension tells FrontPage, Web browsers, your computer's operating system, and other applications what *kind* of file it is. The file type determines how an application should handle the file, or if it can do anything with the file at all.

On the Web, a filename extension tells the browser whether to load the file on the page, open the file with a plug-in or ActiveX control, or save the file to your computer so you can open it with a different application. Plug-ins and ActiveX controls are separate applications that work with the browser so you can view files that browsers don't support by themselves.

Both Netscape Navigator and Internet Explorer support plug-ins. If you put a file on your page that requires a plug-in, the user has to have the plug-in installed on their system in order to launch your file. If they do not have the necessary plug-in, the browser displays an error message that says you need to download a plug-in.

You can also place ActiveX controls on your Web page, as explained in Chapter 21, "Rev Up Your Web Site with Programs and Scripts." ActiveX controls are mini-applications that, among other things, automatically load whichever program a visitor needs to view your file. However, Netscape Navigator does not support ActiveX.

Plug-Ins, ActiveX... What's the Diff?

Plug-ins are programs that you need to download and install separately, like Apple QuickTime and Macromedia Shockwave. Plug-ins work with both Internet Explorer and Netscape Navigator, and they launch automatically when needed.

ActiveX is a technology invented by Microsoft that allows experienced Web-users to create software programs that run from a Web page. Among other things, ActiveX controls can function as plug-ins that download automatically when you need them without having to be downloaded and installed separately. Remember, though, that ActiveX controls only work with Internet Explorer.

File Types 101

Whether you're surfing the Web or creating Web pages, knowing a little bit about popular file types can't hurt:

- *Audio* Popular audio file formats on the Web include AU, AIFF, WAV, and MIDI (or MID). Just about every browser supports AU and AIFF files. Current browsers also have built-in support for MIDI files. WAV files are also extremely popular. All Windows-based computer systems support WAV sound files, and Macintosh users can download free player applications for them. If you're a true audiophile, you can also get the Crescendo MIDI file plug-in from `http://www.crescendo.com/`.
- *Video* Most movies on the Web are formatted as AVI, QuickTime, or MPEG files. All Windows systems come with a built-in AVI video player. In addition, Apple's free QuickTime plug-in supports QuickTime (naturally), AVI, and MPEG. You can get it at `http://quicktime.apple.com/`.
- *Portable documents* Lots of companies and individuals use Adobe Acrobat to distribute *portable document files (PDF)* on the Web. To view manuals, brochures, and other PDF files, you can download the free Acrobat Reader plug-in from Adobe's Web site at `http://www.adobe.com/`.
- *Shockwave movies* The Web abounds with Shockwave movies, created with Macromedia's multimedia and image applications. You can get the free Shockwave plug-in from `http://www.macromedia.com/`. Shockwave movies have a DCR filename extension.
- *RealPlayer files* You should also grab RealNetworks' free RealPlayer plug-in for audio and video broadcasts from `http://www.realplayer.com/`. RealPlayer files have a RAM filename extension.

- *Microsoft Office files* You can put your Word (DOC), Excel (XLS), and PowerPoint (PPT) files on the Web, as explained in Chapter 18, "A Match Made in Redmond: FrontPage and Microsoft Office 2000." Visitors who don't have these applications can download Word, Excel, and PowerPoint viewers from Microsoft's Web site at `http://www.microsoft.com/msdownload/`.

Before You Put Something on Your Web Page...

Make sure the audio or video clip you've picked is free for the taking! You can grab anything you want on the Web for your own enjoyment. But putting someone else's work on your Web site is another matter. If you see something you like and the Web page doesn't *say* that other people can use the file, click the email link and ask the Web site owner for permission before you slap it on your Web page. In many cases, the person finds it flattering and gives the go-ahead in exchange for credit and a link to their Web site.

Most of the Web sites in this section encourage you to use their clips however you want. The Web site owners have either gotten permission to use the files or the files are in the *public domain* (which, in short, means that nobody owns the copyright). In some cases, *fair use* laws also apply for review and educational purposes. For example, if you review CDs and movies on your Web site, you can generally use related sounds and movies.

Ten Cool Places to Visit for Free Multimedia Goodies

Oh, you don't have any sound clips or movies, or equipment for creating your own? Don't let a trivial matter like *that* keep you from jazzing up your pages with audio and video. The Web abounds with sites that offer free goodies that you can download. In fact, it was impossible to keep this list down to the usual five items.

- *Multimedia Stuff* Lists of Web sites and links where you can get sound clips, video, and more (`http://www.olg.com/driko/mmedia.html`).
- *Sun Site's Sound Archive* A collection of sounds organized by category. Don't let the lack of explanatory text throw you off. Most of the files only take a few seconds to download and play, so you can check them out for yourself (`http://sunsite.unc.edu/pub/multimedia/sun-sounds/`).
- *The Internet Video Oasis* Hundreds of music and supermodel videos (`http://www.geocities.com/SunsetStrip/1737/`).
- *Jesse's Movies* Clips from movies and television shows, and links to other movie sites (`http://www.uslink.net/~edgerton/index.html`).
- *Web Corp's Historical Archives* "Hysterical archives" is more like it—visit for satirical sound clips, including "Nixon's Greatest Hits" (`http://www.webcorp.com/realaudio/`).

- *Sound America* Sounds from cartoons, movies, TV, comedians, and more. You need to first download the Mpeg Layer 3 Codec (software that can handle the new Mpeg3 file format) before you can play sounds from this Web site. Don't worry—it's free and Sound America tells you how to get it (`http://soundamerica.com/`).
- *Partners in Rhyme Music and Sound Design* Free background music and sound effects that you can use on your pages (`http://www.partnersinrhyme.com/`).
- *Video Links* QuickTime clips with movie trailers, music videos, scenes from TV shows, and more (`http://video-links.com/`).
- *The MIDI Farm* Everything about MIDI, including freebies for your Web pages (`http://www.midifarm.com/`).
- *Macromedia Shockwave Gallery* An impressive and frequently updated gathering of the coolest interactive animations, presentations, and games. Actually, these Shockwave movies are copyrighted works and you can't use them on your Web pages. But you can still enjoy them and get a glimpse of what's happening on the cutting edge of multimedia (`http://www.macromedia.com/shockwave/gallery/`).

The Least You Need to Know

- Background sounds play when your page loads in the browser. You can add a background sound to your Web page from the Page Properties dialog box with the General tab selected.
- Picture movies (also called dynamic source images) are AVI-formatted videos that display the first frame as an image when your page loads in the browser. To insert a picture movie, choose Picture from the Insert menu, and then select Video from the cascading list to display the Video dialog box.
- Plug-ins are separate applications that enable browsers to handle a variety of file types. Browsers, FrontPage, and other applications can figure out what a file's type is and how to handle it based on the file's three- or four-letter filename extension (like `.htm`, `.jpeg`, or `.avi`).
- You can publish different types of files on your Web page by making links to them or embedding them in your Web page.
- To determine how a file appears and behaves, you need to edit the file's properties. To display those properties, click on the file and select Properties from the Format menu.
- If you want to experiment with multimedia but don't have any files, you can find lots of audio and video freebies on the Web and in the FrontPage Clip Art Gallery.

Chapter 18

A Match Made in Redmond: FrontPage and Microsoft Office 2000

In This Chapter

- What comes with Microsoft Office 2000
- Putting Office files on the Web
- Collaborating on files with NetMeeting
- Displaying Office files on a Web page
- Word, Excel, PowerPoint, Access, Publisher, PhotoDraw, and Outlook
- Five cool ways to use FrontPage and Microsoft Office

So, kids… Whatcha gonna put on your Web site? Hobbyists can type text, add pictures, and have fun with FrontPage as they go along. It's too bad that people who create and manage Web site content as part of their job don't have that luxury. If you're creating a Web site for a business, you probably have lots of documents, brochures, spreadsheets, charts, and other existing files that need to go online.

Back when the Web began, formatting files for it involved days—possibly even weeks or months—of tedious grunt work. Now, FrontPage and Microsoft Office 2000 are tightly integrated so you can send files back and forth with ease. So go ahead—save a Word document or Excel chart as an HTML file. With Microsoft Office, you won't lose any of your fancy formatting or information. When you need to edit your file again, you can open it in the original application. The people at Microsoft call this *round-trip HTML*. I call it a heck of a lot less work!

Welcome to Microsoft Office 2000

Microsoft Office 2000 is a suite of business applications that work smoothly together. For example, you can import a table from an Access database into Excel to create a spiffy chart, and then import that chart into Microsoft Word for your monthly report. And what happens if your boss loves your report and asks you to do a presentation for the marketing division? Generate an outline of your report and then import the text and your charts into PowerPoint, of course. And naturally, you can use FrontPage to put all this great stuff on the Web, too.

Chances are that you're already familiar with Microsoft Office, even if you don't have the entire suite. Most of us use the hugely popular Word and Excel applications on a daily basis. Office 2000 comes with FrontPage, a desktop publishing program, and an image editing application, too. Although this chapter can't cover all these applications in detail, it will introduce you to Office 2000 and get you started with sharing files over networks and putting them onto your Web site.

Microsoft Office 2000 includes the following applications (which can also be purchased and used separately):

- *FrontPage* Well, you're already familiar with FrontPage, right?
- *Word* For word processing.
- *Excel* For spreadsheets and charts.
- *PowerPoint* For multimedia presentations.
- *Access* For databases.
- *Publisher* For desktop publishing.
- *PhotoDraw* For creating and editing images.
- *Outlook* For sending and receiving email and keeping track of appointments and contacts.

Need a Little Help?

Launching Microsoft Office Applications

You can launch Microsoft Office programs by clicking the Start button, selecting Programs, and then choosing an application from the cascading menu as you do when starting up your other applications.

Yikes! You'd have to be awfully dedicated to learn how to use eight entire applications. If you're like most people, you might need a helping hand every now and then. Fortunately, Microsoft Office applications provide help when you need it. If you forget what a particular toolbar button does, pass your cursor over it to display a ToolTip with a reminder.

And of course, there's the ever-present Mr. Paper Clip, the Office Assistant, as shown in the following figure. When you click on him, a word balloon appears and asks what you want to do. Type a question in the text field and click the Search button for an answer. He also chimes in with suggestions and tips as you go about your daily business. If he starts to annoy you, get rid of him by selecting Hide the Office Assistant from the Help menu. You can always show the Office Assistant when you need him by selecting Help from the application's Help menu.

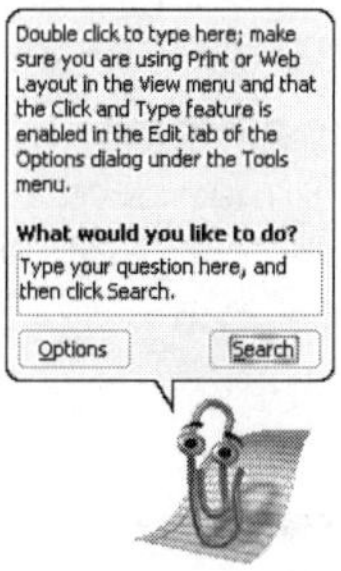

The Office Assistant.

Speaking of the Help menu, it offers lots of ways to get help. If you forget what something in the application window does, select What's This? and click on the unfamiliar object to display some explanatory text. Or connect to the Internet and choose the Office on the Web option to launch your browser and get the latest tips, news, and application updates from the Microsoft Office Web site. If you're migrating to Office from a similar program, some applications also provide assistance in this area. For example, WordPerfect users can select WordPerfect Help from the Help menu in Microsoft Word.

Collaboration Tools

Microsoft Office can also help your department head or network administrator set things up so you and your co-workers can work together more productively via an intranet. FrontPage comes with all the administration tools you need to manage files on your Web.

And what if *you* happen to be the administrator of a small office network or a FrontPage Web? Chapter 29, "It Doesn't Take a Village to Build an Intranet: Publishing, Sharing, and Updating Files," tells you how to add these intranet collaboration features to files in your FrontPage Webs.

Other Microsoft Office and FrontPage collaboration tools include the following:

- *Project management* With the FrontPage server, you can assign files to different workgroups so you and your co-workers can share files over the network and keep track of what everyone else is doing.
- *File subscriptions* If you or your co-workers update a file on an ongoing basis and send it to a FrontPage Web, you can subscribe the network file to the file on your hard drive. When someone changes the file on her computer, the network file is automatically updated and an email message is sent to other people in your workgroup to notify them.
- *Automatically generated links* If you have a Web page with a list of links to files, you can set up a page that adds links when new files arrive on the server.
- *File access settings* You can also determine who gets to view and work on which files on a FrontPage Web. For example, you may decide that Bob and Sue can edit a file, the whole purchasing department can look at it, and people from other departments can neither edit nor look at it.

Microsoft Office 2000 File Properties

If you save Office files to a FrontPage Web on your computer, a network, or a Web site, it's a good idea to enter properties for your Web pages and other files. This makes it easier for you, your co-workers, and your Web site visitors to find the information they need. When you or a co-worker creates a site search engine so others can enter keywords to retrieve Web pages and other files (as covered in Chapter 19, "A Grab Bag of Helpful Doodads: FrontPage Components"), the file property information helps the search engine locate relevant files more quickly and accurately.

To enter properties for an Office file, open the file in the appropriate application and select Properties from the File menu. When the Properties dialog box appears with the Summary tab selected, as shown in the following figure, enter your summary information. In the Keywords box, type a few words that you think someone would be likely to enter if they were searching for the file through a Web site search engine. When you finish entering your summary information, click OK to return to your application.

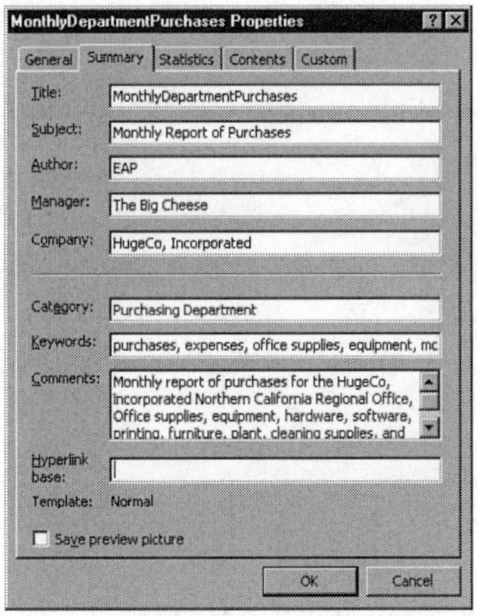

The Properties dialog box.

You can display or enter the following types of information by clicking the other tabs in the Properties dialog box:

- *General* Tells you the file's type (such as a Word document or Excel workbook), location, size, and name, along with the date and time that the file was created, last modified, and last accessed (viewed).
- *Statistics* Provides a history of the file, including who last worked on the document, how many times it was revised, how much time has been spent editing it, and the number of pages.
- *Contents* Displays the title and an overview of the file (for example, a list of all the headings in a Word document).
- *Custom* For entering or viewing workgroup and tracking information, such as the department, the person in charge of the file, the status of the file, and the date of completion. For more about file and project management, see Chapter 29.

File Properties and FrontPage

FrontPage handles Web page file properties a little differently than other Office applications. When the Page Properties dialog box from the Page view appears (as shown in the following figure), you can enter Web page-specific properties, such as the background, text, and link colors. To display the file properties, go to the Folders view, double-click on a document and, when the page opens, select Page Properties from the shortcut menu.

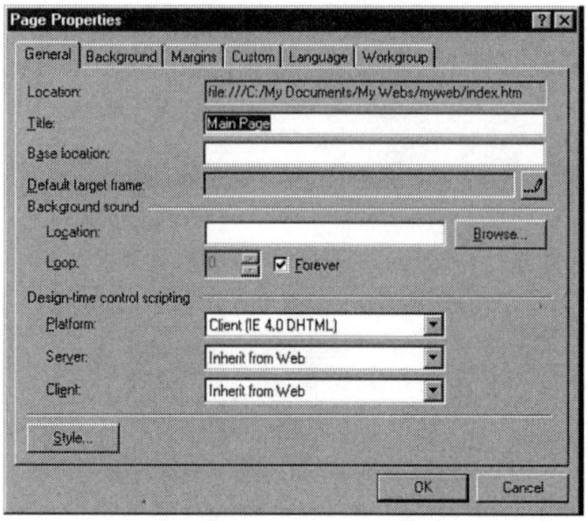

The Page Properties dialog box shown in FrontPage.

In FrontPage, you can view and adjust Page Properties by clicking the following tabs:

- *General* As with the Properties dialog box for other types of Office files, this tab tells you the file's location and name. In addition, you can add a background sound (as covered in Chapter 17, "Strut Your Stuff: Sound, Video, and More") and choose which platform, server, and browsers you want to target your pages for (as covered in Chapter 26, "Don't Just Let It Sit There! Publishing Your Web Site").
- *Background* For creating a color scheme, as covered in Chapter 3, "Fooling Around with Web Pages."
- *Margins* You can adjust the size of the top and left margins for the current page. This determines the amount of space that appears between the contents of the page and the Web browser window. To change your margins, click the Specify Top Margin and Specify Left Margin check boxes, and then enter or select a number of pixels from the Pixels boxes.
- *Custom* Other Office applications display workgroup information when you click the Custom tab. With FrontPage, you can display the Custom tab in order to add meta-information that helps visitors find your Web site. Compare these meta options with the meta tags described in Chapter 26. They both do the same thing—help your visitors find the right page quickly.
- *Language* If you create pages in a foreign language, you can choose options to ensure that visitors' Web browsers display the page correctly. To change the language for your document, select the desired language from the Mark Current Document As, Save the Document As, and Reload the Current Document As lists.
- *Workgroup* For entering or viewing workgroup and tracking information, as you would in the Custom dialog box for files created in other Office applications. For more about file and project management, see Chapter 29.

What's the Word? Web Pages and Word Documents

Word 2000 is a versatile word processing program, and over 80% of people who own a word processor own Word. If you've used previous versions of the program, you may have saved your documents as Web pages before. When you save a file as a Web page and view it in FrontPage or an Internet Explorer or Netscape Navigator version 5.0 Web browser, your document looks exactly as it does in Word. You can edit the file with FrontPage or open it in Word again. And as with Word 97, you can create all of your links straight from Word.

Before You Go Wild with Office and FrontPage...

You need a server that supports FrontPage 2000 and a version 5.0 browser, like Netscape Navigator or Internet Explorer, to take advantage of the full range of Microsoft Office 2000's features. Not to worry—Navigator and Explorer are free and most people already own them. But there are plenty of features that work with older browsers.

To save a Word document as a Web page, select Save As Web Page from the File menu. When the Save As dialog box appears, make sure Web Page is selected from the Save As Type menu and browse for a folder on your FrontPage Web or on a server. If the file is more than a couple of pages long, you should also create bookmarks and make a list of links to them for easier navigation, as covered in Chapter 7, "Think Links: Adding Links to Your Pages." You can do this in either Word or FrontPage. To learn more about Word, pick up a copy of *The Complete Idiot's Guide to Microsoft Word 2000* at your local book store.

Totally Excel-lent! Working with Excel Tables and Charts

Excel 2000 makes it easy to organize data into spreadsheets, generate graphical charts, and build interactive pivot tables that allow users to sort data in different ways and generate charts. With Excel 2000, you can save spreadsheets, charts, and entire Excel workbooks as HTML documents. In addition, you can create active Web pages with components that allow people to enter information in a spreadsheet or use pivot tables to analyze data.

To put your Excel files on the Web, open your file, click on the tab for the worksheet you want to save (unless you plan to publish the entire workbook), and choose Save as Web Page from the File menu. When the Save As dialog box appears, as shown in the following figure, select options for your table, browse for a file, and click the Save button. If you'd like to learn more about Excel, grab *The Complete Idiot's Guide to Microsoft Excel 2000* and you'll be up and running in no time.

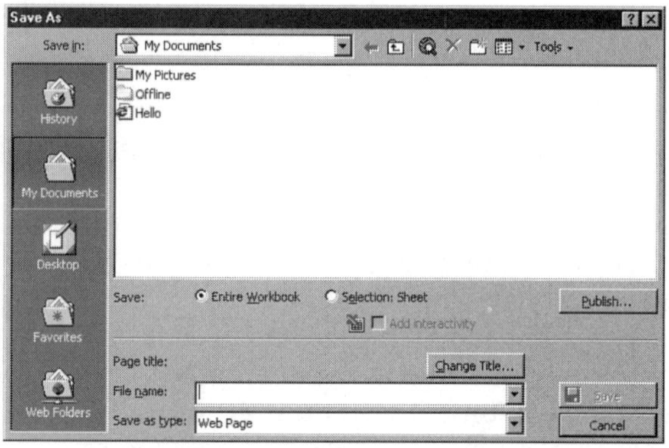

The Save As dialog box for Excel.

The Save As dialog box provides the following options for saving your table:

➤ *Entire Workbook as a static Web page* Click the Entire Workbook radio button to save your Excel workbook file as a plain old (static) Web page.

➤ *Current sheet as a static Web page with embedded spreadsheet* Click the Selection: Sheet radio button to save the current worksheet as a static Web page with a copy of the worksheet inserted as an embedded file. Static embedded files appear on the page but cannot be changed. For more about embedded files and Web pages, see Chapter 17.

➤ *Current sheet as a dynamic Web page with embedded interactive spreadsheet* Click the Selection: Sheet radio button and the Add Interactivity check box to save the current worksheet as a dynamic Web page. Instead of embedding a copy of a file, the embedded sheet is linked to the real file so users can change the data.

➤ *Current sheet as a dynamic Web page with an interactive Spreadsheet component* Gives users full spreadsheet functionality, such as entering, editing, and calculating data. It's like having a mini-version of Excel running from your Web page. As with embedded interactive spreadsheets, the original file is updated when users make changes. To publish an interactive spreadsheet, click the Publish button to display the Publish as Web Page dialog box. Then click the Add Interactivity With check box, select Spreadsheet functionality from the list, and click the Publish button.

➤ *Current sheet as a dynamic Web page with an interactive PivotTable component* Gives users full PivotTable functionality so they can display and analyze different data and charts. To publish an interactive spreadsheet, click the Publish button to display the Publish as Web Page dialog box. Then click the Add Interactivity With check box, select PivotTable functionality from the list, and click the Publish button.

Static and Dynamic Web Pages

All Web pages are interactive, in a way. After all, when you click links, the browser responds to you by displaying a different page. But in the world of Web publishing, some pages are considered more interactive than others. Static pages are normal Web pages with text, pictures, links, and maybe a simple form or an embedded file or two. Dynamic Web pages provide more sophisticated levels of interaction and involve some sort of programming. For example, Spreadsheet and PivotTable components are ActiveX controls. For an introduction to Web programming, see Chapter 21, "Rev Up Your Web Site with Programs and Scripts."

The Power of PowerPoint: Putting Your Presentations on the Web

PowerPoint 2000 is a sophisticated multimedia presentation program that lets you save your presentations as Web pages. Because PowerPoint files are designed for viewing on a computer screen instead of as printed pages, they look as good on the Web as they did at your meeting. FrontPage and Explorer support a variety of animated transitions and special effects, so you don't even have to worry about your flying logos and other bells and whistles. For more about animation on the Web, see Chapter 20, "Gee-Whiz Pages with Animated Special Effects."

To save a PowerPoint presentation as a Web page, open a file and select Save as Web Page from the File menu to display the Save As dialog box. You can either browse for a folder and click the Save button or click the Publish button for additional options. Want to learn more? *The Complete Idiot's Guide to Microsoft PowerPoint 2000* can get you started.

When you display the Publish as Web Page dialog box, as shown in the following figure, you can do the following:

- *Include a range of slides* To publish a part of your presentation instead of the entire thing, click the Slide Number radio button and enter the starting and ending slide numbers in the number boxes. To publish the entire presentation, leave the Complete Presentation radio button selected.

- *Customize the slide show* You can also create a custom slide show by including slides from presentations that you've already created. Click the Custom Show radio button to display a list of your other files and select an item from the list.
- *Display speaker notes* If you included speaker notes with your slides, you can display them on your Web pages. This can help visitors get the gist of what you said during your presentation.
- *Choose which browser version you want to support* You can publish your slide show for the latest browsers for a richer multimedia experience, or publish a less fancy version for people with older browsers. Recent browsers with higher version numbers (such as 4.0 or 5.0) have much better support for your slide layouts, fonts, and animation. Because older browsers don't support many of these features, you may want to reformat your pages so people won't have trouble viewing them. For more about browser compatibility issues, see Chapter 20.

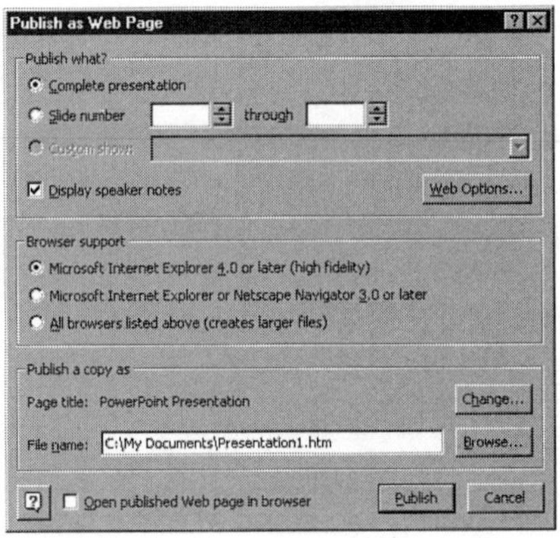

The Publish as Web Page dialog box for PowerPoint.

When you finish choosing options, click the Publish button.

Webtop Publishing with Publisher

Publisher 2000 is a spiffy little desktop publishing program with plenty of features and wizards to help you design professional-looking printed materials. Now you can put your brochures, annual reports, and newsletters on the Web, too. As with PowerPoint presentations, you can save individual pages as Web pages or publish an entire file as a set of Web pages. To save an individual page as a Web page, go to the page and select Save As Web Page. When the Save As dialog box appears, browse for a folder, enter a filename in the File Name box, and click Save.

To save your publication as a set of Web pages, choose Create Web Site from Current Publication from the File menu. When the Convert to Web Site dialog box appears, select an option—Publisher can either format the pages for you and create links for your table of contents and pages, or it can let you create your own Web layout. (I recommend letting Publisher do everything for you until you get the hang of things.) When you're done, click OK. When the Save As dialog box appears, enter a name in the File Name box to create a folder for your Web pages. Publisher then sets up the folder and builds your Web site.

Making Data Access-ible with Access Databases

Access is a powerful database program that lets you publish databases to a Web page or create databases that run on your Web site. Because databases are complex and Access gives you many ways to use them on your Web site, this topic is covered separately in Chapter 22, "If You've Got It, Flaunt It: Putting Your Access Databases on the Web."

Saving Outlook Files as Web Pages

Think of Outlook 2000 as your personal assistant. It handles your email, manages your appointment calendar, stores people's contact information, and more. Want to give co-workers access to your calendar so they know when you're available to meet with them? Publish it as a Web page. And if someone emails you a message with valuable information that you want to share with your department, it's easy to save it as a Web page. If you aren't familiar with Outlook, try *The Complete Idiot's Guide to Microsoft Outlook 2000*.

Publishing Your Calendar

To save your appointment calendar as a Web page, go to the Calendar and select Save As Web Page from the File menu. When the Save as Web Page dialog box appears, as shown in the following figure, select your starting and ending dates from the lists and click the Browse button to display the Browse dialog box so you can locate a folder. If you have an existing Web page with your schedule, select the file. Or you can type a new filename in the File Name box. When you finish browsing, click the Select button to return to the Save as Web Page dialog box and then click the Save button.

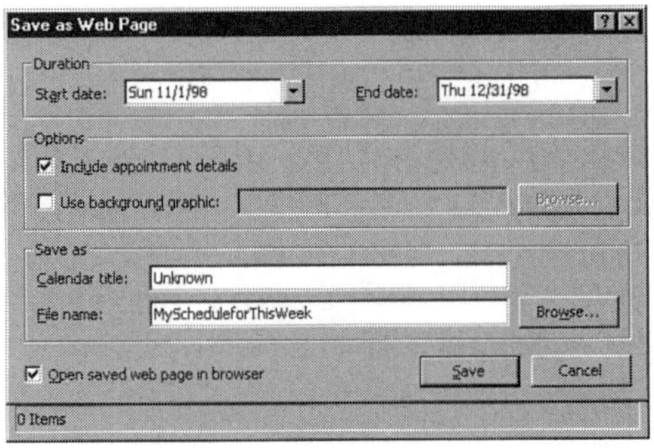

The Save as Web Page dialog box for saving Outlook Calendar entries.

Publishing an Email Message to the Web

Every now and then something great lands in your inbox, like a hilarious joke, an invitation to an event, or some useful tidbits of information that everyone in your office should know about. Luckily, Outlook 2000 and many other email programs support HTML and let you save messages as Web pages.

To save an email message as a Web page, select the message from your message list and select Save as Web Page from the File menu. When the Save as Web Page dialog box appears, browse for a Web folder, enter a filename in the File Name box, and click Save.

GIF or JPEG?

Flat-color line art, like logos, clip art, and charts, looks best in the GIF format. Photographs and complex illustrations with shading or blends of color look better as JPEGs.

Working with Web Images and PhotoDraw

PhotoDraw 2000 is a feature-packed imaging program that makes creating, editing, and applying special effects to pictures easy and fun. You can also configure it as your image editor in FrontPage (as covered in Chapter 9, "Spiffing Up Pictures"). You can then launch PhotoDraw and work on a picture straight from FrontPage by double-clicking the picture. Although FrontPage's Picture toolbar helps with your basic imaging needs, PhotoDraw 2000 lets you get truly creative.

You can also use PhotoDraw to save images as GIFs and JPEGs, two common image types for the Web. Although FrontPage automatically converts images from other file formats, PhotoDraw does a better job. To save an image as a GIF or JPEG with PhotoDraw, choose Save As from the File menu, browse for a folder, enter a name for your picture in the File Name box, and select JPEG File Interchange Format (for JPEG) or Graphics Interchange Format (for GIF) from the Save As Type box.

Office Files and Office Viewers

In some situations, you may decide that it's better to embed or link to Microsoft Office files on a Web page than it is to publish the actual files as Web pages. For example, you may want people with older browsers to see your PowerPoint presentations or Word documents in their full glory. If so, go ahead. Chapter 7 tells you how to link to files, and Chapter 17 tells you about embedding files.

You don't even have to worry about whether your visitors have Microsoft Office. They can download the free Word, Excel, and PowerPoint viewers from Microsoft's Web site at `http://www.microsoft.com/msdownload`. Just make sure you mention the viewers on your Web page!

Publishing Office Files Straight to the Web

You don't have to settle for merely saving an Office file to a Web folder on your computer or network. You can also save it straight to a folder on your Web site.

First, you need to create a Web site as a Web folder. You can then save files to the folder from an Office application the way you normally would, with a slight twist. When the Save As dialog box appears, click the Web Folders icon, choose a Web folder, type a name for your file in the File Name box, and click Save. If you aren't connected to the Internet, your dialer appears so you can call up your server. Depending on how the server is set up, a dialog box may appear and ask you for your password.

To create a Web folder with a Web site address so you can publish Office files straight to a Web site, do the following:

1. Connect to the Internet.
2. Click the My Computer icon on your desktop to open the My Computer window.
3. Double-click the Web Folders icon.
4. When the Web Folders window appears, double-click the Add Web Folder icon to display the Add Web Folder dialog box.
5. Type a URL (such as `http://www.mywebsite.com/myfolder/`) and click the Next button.

Wait for a minute so the Add Web Folder Wizard can connect to the Web site and find your folder. When it finishes, the new Web site appears in the Add Web Folder window.

Five Cool FrontPage and Office Tips

Before you go, here are a few helpful tips for working with FrontPage and Microsoft Office:

- *Use PowerPoint or Publisher for page layout* If you're a PowerPoint or Publisher whiz and you're just getting used to the Web, try laying out pages in those programs and saving them as Web files. With your basic layout in place, you can finish your Web site in FrontPage.
- *Use Word for longer documents* Although FrontPage has great tools, it's easier to create and work with longer documents in Word. You can then save the file as a Web page. Remember to add bookmarks and some additional hyperlinks to them for easier navigation, as covered in Chapter 7.
- *You can import files into existing Web pages, too* As explained in Chapter 5, "Entering Text and Fiddling with Fonts," FrontPage can import other Web pages, Word documents, and Excel spreadsheets. This trick also comes in handy if you don't have Microsoft Office 2000 and someone gives you a file without converting it first!
- *Check the Microsoft Office Web site* You'll find plenty of news, helpful tips, tricks, and hints for making the most of Microsoft Office applications. You can fire up your browser and jump to the Office Web site at `http://www.microsoft.com/office/`, or you can select Microsoft Office on the Web from an Office 2000 application's Help menu.
- *Keep your Office CDs handy!* The Microsoft Office setup programs don't install all of the available features, templates, clip art, and themes because they might take up too much space on your hard drive. This means that when you try to do something in Office, a dialog box may appear and ask you for a CD. When you put the CD in your CD-ROM drive, Office automatically installs what you need. Make sure to save your work first because you may need to restart your computer!

The Least You Need to Know

- You can purchase FrontPage alone or as part of Microsoft Office 2000, a suite of business programs. Office includes Word for documents, Excel for spreadsheets and charts, Access for databases, Outlook for messaging, scheduling, and contacts, PowerPoint for multimedia presentations, Publisher for desktop publishing, and PhotoDraw for image editing.
- Office applications come with helpful features, including the Office Assistant, ToolTips, and information that you can access from the Help menu.
- Office 2000 and FrontPage also provide tools that help you and your co-workers work with files via an intranet (see Chapter 29).
- With Office 2000, you can enter properties for your files so people can search for them more easily on a Web site. Find out more about how this works in Chapter 26.
- You can save files created with Office applications as Web pages that you can work with in FrontPage and view in a Web browser. When you need to edit the files, you can open them in FrontPage or the original application.
- You can make Office files available on your Web site through embedding or linking, rather than converting them to Web pages. Visitors can then open the files in the appropriate application or download and use the free Word, Excel, and PowerPoint viewers from Microsoft's Web site. Find out more in Chapter 17.
- You can also save Office files straight to the Web.

Chapter 19

A Grab Bag of Helpful Doodads: FrontPage Components

In This Chapter

- Setting up an Include Page
- An instant table of contents
- Time-stamping your pages
- Adding page information
- Building a search form
- Creating a hit counter
- Creating automatic links to pages by category
- Five cool tips for FrontPage components

You've set up your Web site. Now, how can you make the site easier for you to manage and more useful to your visitors or co-workers? Try some FrontPage components. They do lots of cool things that used to take hours—or even days—of programming. Ick. You wouldn't want to do *that*, now, would you?

With FrontPage components, you can create a search form, generate a table of contents for your site, schedule information to appear on a page during certain dates, and more. All in a matter of seconds! Before you try FrontPage components, however, make sure your ISP or Web host supports FrontPage. Components only work when FrontPage extensions are installed on the server.

Don't Type That *Again*! Try the Include Page Component

Tired of typing and formatting the same stuff over and over again? Stop doing it! If you've got information that you want to put on more than one page, FrontPage has two ways to help—shared borders (see Chapter 14, "Don't Like What You See? Designing Your Own Page Template") and the Include Page component. You can place the Include Page component anywhere you want in your page layout, not just on the top, bottom, and sides of your page.

So how does it work? With the Include Page component, you create a separate Web page with your text, graphics, and links and save it in your _private folder. You can then use the Include Page component to place this content on as many pages as you want. When you need to make changes, you only need to edit the included page and FrontPage automatically changes all the pages for you.

Don't Sweat the Include Page Color Schemes

When you place an Include Page component in a Web page, the included page adopts the Web page's color scheme. So don't worry about the included page's color scheme or other page properties.

Creating a Page to Include

Before you insert an Include Page component, you've gotta create it, right? Open a new Web page and save it to the _private folder. (All FrontPage Webs have a _private folder for stuff that you don't want visitors to see. After all, if a visitor stumbles on the page by accident, she might get confused.) Enter your text, insert images, create links, and arrange the information on the page as you would with a regular Web page.

Adding an Include Page Component to a Web Page

And now for the easy part. To place an Include Page component, put your cursor where you want the included information to appear on your page. Then select Component from the Insert menu and choose Include Page from the list. When the Include Page Component Properties dialog box appears, click the Browse button and find your page in your _private folder, and then click OK to select the included page. The included page embeds itself in the current Web page. When you pass your mouse pointer over the Include Page component, a FrontPage Component icon appears. This icon tells you when a page element is a FrontPage Component. You cannot edit an Include Page component from within a Web page that contains the component. However, you can make changes to the included page itself by opening it from the _private folder and editing it as you would a normal Web page.

It's a Date! Updating Text and Images Automatically

We all need change now and then, and some changes are more predictable than others. If you're an accountant, you might want to display a reminder on your page when tax filings and estimated quarterlies are due. Or maybe you'd like to greet the seasons and holidays with special artwork. With the Scheduled Include Page and Scheduled Picture components, you can tell FrontPage when to display an included page or image and when to stop displaying it.

Updating Text with the Scheduled Include Page Component

The Scheduled Include Page component works a lot like the regular old Include Page component (with just a *few* more settings). Create your Scheduled Include Page the same way you would create a regular Include Page. Remember to save it in the _private folder of your Web. Then, place your cursor where you want the Include Page to appear, select Component from the Insert menu, and then choose Scheduled Include Page from the list.

When the Scheduled Include Page Properties dialog box appears, as shown in the following figure, do the following:

1. Click the Browse button next to the During the Scheduled Time box to locate and insert your Include Page.
2. Do you have information that you normally want to display in that spot? Tell FrontPage where that page is by clicking the Browse button next to the Before and After the Scheduled Time (Optional) Page Link button. The page you select is displayed as the default Include Page when the Scheduled Include Page is inactive.
3. Choose a year, month, date, and time from the Starting Date and Time lists. This tells FrontPage when to start displaying the page.
4. Choose a year, month, date, and time from the Ending Date and Time lists. This tells FrontPage when to stop displaying the page.
5. Click OK to apply your settings and return to your Web page.

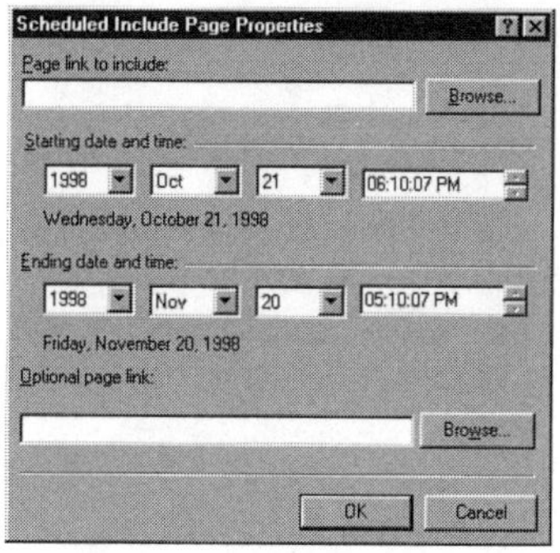

The Scheduled Include Page Properties dialog box.

Updating a Picture with the Scheduled Picture Component

If you leave your winter holiday decorations up until the summer, you'll like the Scheduled Picture component. You can schedule an image pretty much the same way as you would schedule an Include Page. Place your cursor where you want the image to appear, choose Component from the Insert menu, and select Scheduled Picture from the list. When the Scheduled Picture Properties dialog box appears, you can choose your picture, pick your starting and ending times, and pick a default image that appears when the included image is inactive.

Generating a Table of Contents Page

You've probably flipped through the table of contents for this book, and your visitors would surely appreciate a similar roadmap of your site. But that sounds like a lot of work! No problem. The Table of Contents component can do it for you in no time. To create a table of contents for your Web site, open a Web page (or create one), place your cursor where you want the table to appear, select Components from the Insert menu, and then select Table of Contents.

When the Table of Contents Properties dialog box appears, as shown in the following figure, do the following:

1. Enter a Web page filename in the Page URL for Starting Point of Table box, or click the Browse button to locate a page. The table of contents will start with this page.
2. Choose a size for the table of contents headings from the Heading Font Size list.
3. Click Show Each Page Only Once to only show pages once, even if more than one page links to them.
4. Click Show Pages with No Incoming Hyperlinks to make sure FrontPage gets pages that you may not have made links to yet. FrontPage is even smart enough to ignore the files stored in your _private folder.
5. Click Recompute Table of Contents when Any Other Page Is Edited to make sure that FrontPage updates the table of contents when you make changes.
6. Click OK to return to your Web page.

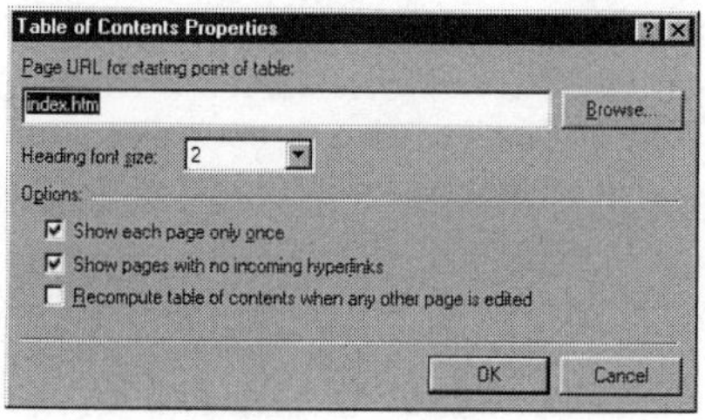

Table of Contents Properties dialog box.

What's Wrong with My Table of Contents?

Don't worry. Nothing's wrong. When you insert the Table of Contents component, a generic heading appears with three list items below it in the FrontPage window, no matter what the table of contents *really* says. Click the Preview in Browser button on the Standard toolbar to view your new Table of Contents page in a browser. That looks better, doesn't it?

This Page Was Updated *When*? Time-Stamping Your Pages

Do you update your pages frequently? Whether you publish company announcements, reports, or the latest installments of your online novel, you don't want your regular visitors to miss out. With FrontPage, you can put a time stamp on a page. When you update the page, the time stamp automatically changes.

To place a time stamp on your page, place your cursor where you want the time stamp to appear and then select Date and Time from the Insert menu. When the Date and Time Properties dialog box appears, do the following:

1. Click one of the Display radio buttons. You can tell FrontPage to change the date when you edit a page or when FrontPage automatically updates a page with a Scheduled Include Page component.
2. Select an option from the Date Format list—such as 1/1/2000 or January 1, 2000.

3. If you want, you can also choose a time format, as in 09:08:36 AM or 09:08 AM, from the Time Format list. Or you can leave None selected if you prefer not to display a time.
4. Click OK to return to your Web page.

Keeping Track of Stuff with the Substitutions Component

Do you and your co-workers publish Web pages on an intranet? The Substitutions component can help you all keep track of who's doing what and which project or department each page originates from. The Substitutions component works best when you place it in small print at the top or bottom of the page, as you would a header or footer for a word processing document. If this sounds a bit confusing, not to worry. You'll have a better understanding shortly.

To add automatic substitutions, select Components from the Insert menu and then choose Substitution. When the Substitution Component Properties dialog box appears, select an option from the Substitute With list and click OK. To add other substitutions, repeat these steps.

Options include the following:

- *Author* The person who originally created the document (or sometimes a job title, such as Administrator).
- *Modified By* The person who updates the document (or sometimes a job title or department name, such as Sales).
- *Description* A brief summary of what the page contains, such as Monthly Sales Report.
- *Page URL* The location of the page on the local or remote server, depending on how your network is set up.

When you finish inserting your substitutions, they'll look like the following:

```
Betty Jones Tom Smith Monthly Sales Figures
http://janes_server/marketing/reports/monthly.htm
```

In order to make your substitutions more readable, you may want to first type the following identifiers on your Web page, before inserting the substitutions:

```
Author: Modified by: Description: URL:
```

You can then insert each substitution following the appropriate text.

Where Does the Substitution Information Come From?

FrontPage gathers this information from the Workgroup settings and puts it on your Web page. You can choose and enter Workgroup settings by going to the Folders view, selecting a file, and displaying the Properties dialog box with the Workgroup tab selected. For more about Workgroup settings, see Chapter 18, "A Match Made in Redmond: FrontPage and Microsoft Office 2000" and Chapter 29, "It Doesn't Take a Village to Build an Intranet: Publishing, Sharing, and Updating Files."

The Searchable Web Site: Adding a Search Form

As your Web site grows, it can get *awfully* hard to find stuff. With FrontPage, you can create your very own search engine so visitors can search your Web site, as shown in the following figure. It works just like the big search engines such as Yahoo! and Excite, but only for the pages on your own Web site. When visitors enter their keywords in the search form's text box and click the Start Search button, a new page appears with page titles and links.

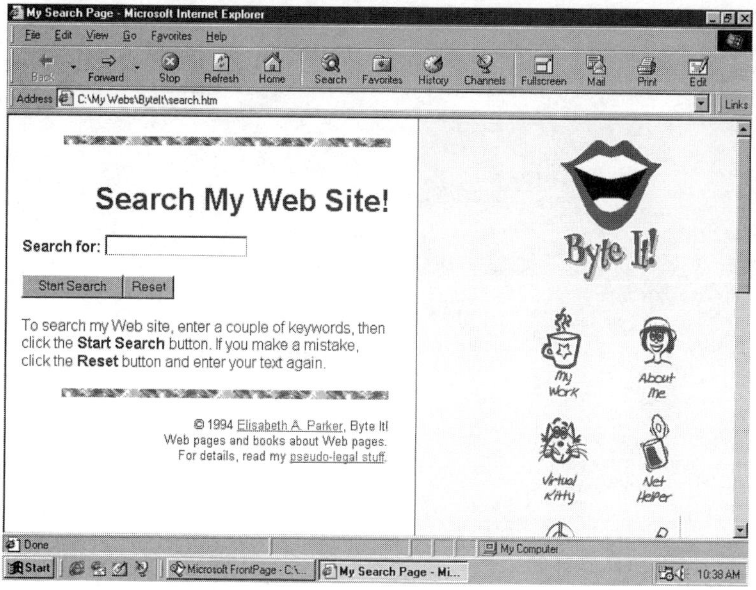

A Web page with a search form.

To create your site search engine, select Component from the Insert menu and then select Search Form. When the Search Form Properties dialog box appears, do the following:

1. With the Search Form Properties tab selected, enter a label in the Label for Input box. (FrontPage automatically enters Search For, but you can change this to something like Enter a Keyword.) This text will appear before the one-line text box in the search form.
2. In the Width in Characters box, enter a width (measured in text characters, not pixels) for the one-line text box.
3. You can also enter text for the Submit and Reset buttons by typing it in the Label for "Start Search" Button and Label for "Clear" Button boxes.
4. Click the Search Results tab. These options determine how the search results page lists your pages.
5. Leave All entered in the Word List to Search box. This ensures that the Search component will search all of the words for the documents on your Web site.
6. If you choose to display the dates when pages were created or updated, you can choose date and time formats from the Date Format and Time Format lists.
7. You can also choose to display page information along with search results by clicking the check boxes from the Display Options list.
8. Click OK to return to your Web page.

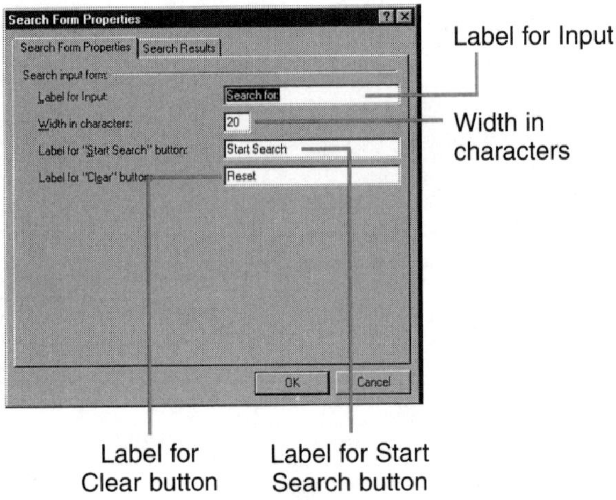

Search Form Properties dialog box with Search Form Properties tab selected.

Countin' Up the Hits

Want to show off how many visitors you've had? Put a hit counter on your Web page. To insert a hit counter, select Component from the Insert menu and then choose Hit Counter. When the Hit Counter Properties dialog box appears, as shown in the following figure, choose how you want your numbers to look by selecting a Counter Style and clicking OK. If you want to reset your counter and start over again, right-click your counter and select FrontPage Component Properties from the shortcut menu. When the Hit Counter Properties dialog box appears, click the Reset Counter To check box and enter a number.

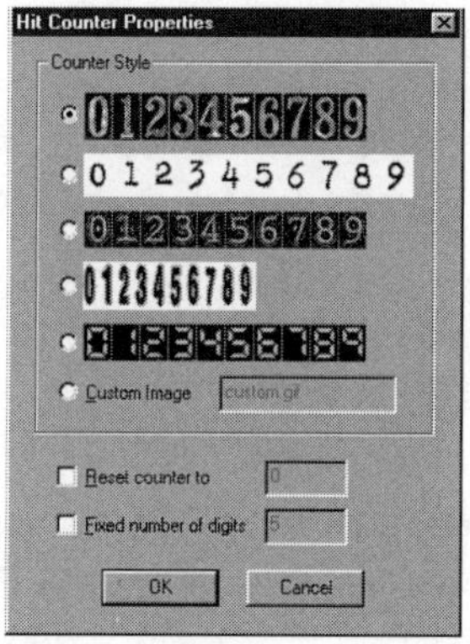

The Hit Counter Properties dialog box.

Creating Automatic Category Links

If you or your FrontPage administrator has assigned categories to the files on your Web site, such as Expense Report, Ideas, or Goals/Objectives, you can use the Categories component to automatically create links to all of the pages that fall within these categories. For more about assigning categories, see Chapter 18 and Chapter 29.

To create automatic links to pages by category, select Component from the Insert menu and then choose Categories from the shortcut menu. When the Categories dialog box appears, as shown in the following figure, click check boxes on the Choose Categories to List Pages By list and click OK to return to your Web page.

You can also choose to sort pages alphabetically by title or modification date by selecting an option from the Sort Pages By list, and you can include modification dates and page comments by clicking on check boxes from the Include the Following Information list.

The Categories Properties dialog box.

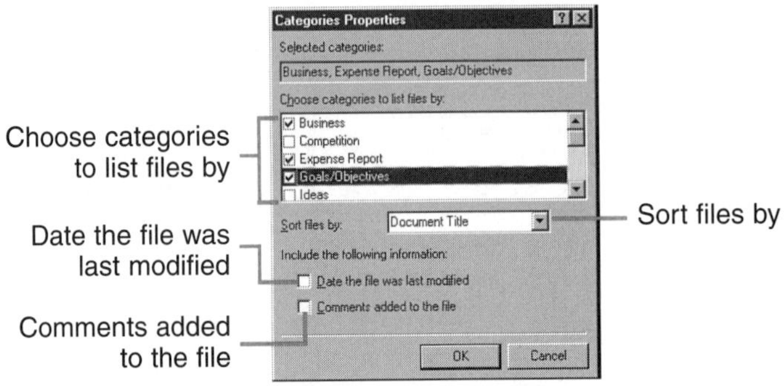

Five Cool Tips for FrontPage Components

FrontPage components are so easy to use that you probably don't need any tips to figure them out. But here are a few anyway.

Editing FrontPage Components

You might want to change the settings for your components down the road. That's easy. Simply right-click a component and select Component Properties from the shortcut menu. This displays the appropriate dialog box for your component so you can enter new settings.

- *Size can matter* Do you plan to use the Scheduled Picture component to schedule more than one image to appear in the same spot? It helps to use images that are about the same size. That way your layout always looks the same, even when different pictures appear.
- *Add some thoughtful touches* Got some downtime? Use the Scheduled Include Page or Scheduled Picture component to wish co-workers a happy birthday, display festive holiday artwork, or announce upcoming events that are important to your visitors. People will appreciate your thoughtfulness, and you'll only have to change things once a year from now on!
- *Make your own hit counter numbers* Don't like FrontPage's hit counter number styles? The Hit Counter Properties dialog box enables you to choose a custom image. To make your own set of numbers, use an image program to create a GIF file with a row of numbers from 0-9 (make sure you space them evenly apart), and then save it to your Web. Or, you can find numbers that you like at one of the free clip art Web sites listed at the end of Chapter 8, "The Picture-Perfect Web Page: Placing and Tweaking Images."

- *Tweak your time stamp and substitution text* Once you insert a time stamp or substitution text, you can select the text as you would normal Web page text and reformat it to your liking.
- *Be aware of the hit counter's limitations* Hit counters are fun and they look really cool. But if you hope to attract paid advertising with your huge number of hits, think again. Hits don't always mean human visitors. Search engine robots (explained in Chapter 26, "Don't Just Let It Sit There! Publishing Your Web Site") and server programs can also "visit" your Web site. Also, hit counters can't tell you where your visitors come from or what links they follow. For this information, you need server statistics—which most ISPs and Web hosts provide on a monthly basis with your account (though sometimes you have to ask).

The Least You Need to Know

- FrontPage components let you add cool and useful features to your Web site that would normally require programming. For example, you can create an instant table of contents, a hit counter, a time stamp, and a search form.
- You can create separate Web pages with information that you use on multiple pages—such as copyright text, contact stuff, and links—and add them as Include Page components to other Web pages. If you edit the included Web page, FrontPage applies your changes to all of the Web pages that contain the Include Page. You can also add Scheduled Include Page and Scheduled Picture components to your pages. This displays the included pages or images between dates that you specify.
- The Categories and Substitution components make it easier for you and your co-workers to keep track of different pages and projects. The AutoLinks and Substitutions components only work when the FrontPage Administrator defines Workgroup settings for the files on your Web site. For more about Workgroup settings, see Chapter 18 and Chapter 29.
- You can edit your components by right-clicking the components and selecting Component Properties to display the appropriate dialog box.
- Remember to check your changes in the browser. Some FrontPage components aren't displayed correctly in the Page view but are displayed correctly when viewed in a Web browser.

Chapter 20

Gee-Whiz Pages with Animated Special Effects

In This Chapter

- Setting up animated hover buttons
- Creating buttons that play sounds when people click on them
- Animating text and images, and turning your Web site into a slide show with animated page transitions
- Building GIF animations and banner ads
- Making a scrolling text marquee
- Five cool places to visit for animation ideas

Have you ever visited a Web site with spiffy animations and wondered, "Gee, how did they do that?" In the past I would have answered, "First you learn JavaScript and DHTML…" Yawn. That kind of talk sure wouldn't make anyone the life of the party! Especially since FrontPage makes it easy for techies and newbies alike to liven up a Web page.

So get ready to create hover buttons that change shape or play sounds when visitors navigate your pages, set up pages with text and pictures that move into place when the page loads, build transitions that appear when visitors follow a link to a new page, and more. If you want to learn more about scripting, DHTML, and Web programming, see Chapter 21, "Rev Up Your Web Site with Programs and Scripts." In the meantime, have fun and let FrontPage take care of the yucky technical stuff.

Setting Up Animated Hover Buttons

Hover buttons are image links that change when a visitor passes (or *hovers*) their mouse pointer over them. Web designers also call these buttons *rollovers* or *mouse overs*. Hover buttons look cool and also help visitors figure out which page elements work as links. If you like rectangular buttons with text labels, you can use the FrontPage Hover Button component. Or you can create hover buttons from your own graphics.

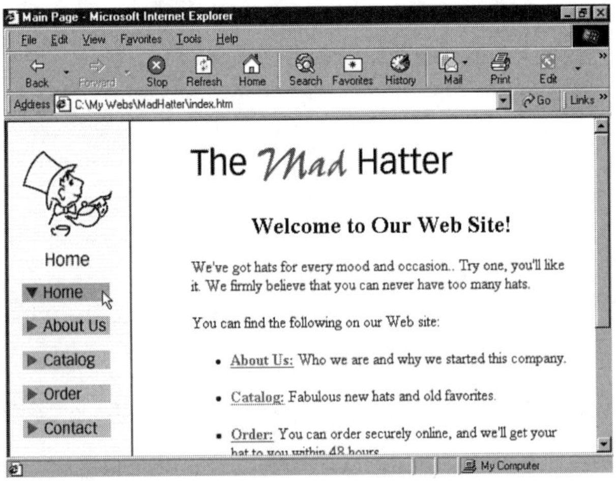

Hover buttons used as a navigation bar in a Web page.

Creating Instant FrontPage Hover Buttons

FrontPage hover buttons are colored rectangles with text labels that change color when a visitor hovers the mouse pointer over them. You can create a whole row or column of hover buttons and use them as a navigation bar. The Hover Button Properties dialog box makes it easy to create your buttons.

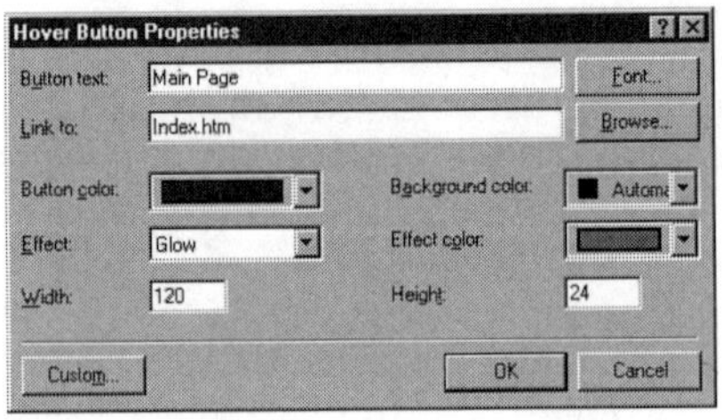

The Hover Button Properties dialog box.

To create a hover button, place your cursor where you want the hover button to appear, select Component from the Insert menu, and then choose Hover Button from the cascading menu. When the Hover Button Properties dialog box appears, use the following list to set your options. When you finish creating your hover button, click OK to insert the button and return to your Web page.

The Hover Button Properties dialog box gives you the following options:

- *Button text* Type in text to create a label for your button. You should limit your label to one or two short words so you don't have to make the button too large.
- *Font* Click the Font button to display the Font dialog box. Then select a font, font style, size, and color from the lists. The font color should contrast with the button so people can read the label. For example, you should put light-colored text on a dark-colored button. When you finish, click OK to return to the Hover Button Properties dialog box.
- *Link* Link the button to a Web page by typing in the filename. If you don't remember the name of the file, you can also click the Browse button to locate and select your file from your Web folders. When you finish browsing, click OK to return to the Hover Button Properties dialog box.
- *Button color* Displays a color menu so you can choose a color for your button. If you've forgotten how to select colors from FrontPage's color menus, see Chapter 3, "Fooling Around with Web Pages."
- *Background color* Select a color to keep your special effects within a certain color range. For example, if you choose the Glow effect, the hover button displays color gradients ranging from the selected Background color to the selected Effect color. If you only want the button to change to shades of blue, you could select navy blue for the Background color and light blue for the Effect color. You can experiment if you want. Or, if you're too busy to fiddle around, select Automatic from the color menu.

Try Some Effect Options!

The Color Fill option changes your button to a solid color (which you can select from the Effect Color menu). The Color Average option automatically selects a contrasting color for you. The Glow, Reverse Glow, and Light Glow options change your button to color gradients that look iridescent. The Bevel out and Bevel in options turn your hover buttons into 3-D buttons that look pushed down or popped up when the button changes.

Try the Include Page Component

FrontPage makes it easy to put rows or columns of hover buttons on all of your Web pages, but it still can take an awfully long time. Save yourself a few hours of work! Instead, create an Include Page with your hover buttons and insert it in all your pages. For more about the Include Page component, see Chapter 19, "A Grab Bag of Helpful Doodads: FrontPage Components."

- *Effect* Choose an option to determine what happens when the hover button changes.
- *Effect color* Select an option from the color menu to determine the color—or range of colors—that the hover button should change to.
- *Width and Height* You can enter measurements in pixels to determine the width and height of your hover buttons, or you can resize the buttons after you put them on your Web page. Click on a button. When the handles appear, move your mouse pointer over them until a two-way arrow appears and then drag the handle. Be aware that if you use your own graphics for buttons, changing the dimensions can distort them.
- *Custom* You can set up your hover button to play a sound when it changes, or you can use an image as your button. Both of these options are explained further in the following sections.

Previewing and Editing FrontPage Hover Buttons

"Yikes!," you may exclaim when you try to test a hover button in FrontPage. "Why doesn't it work?" FrontPage doesn't run scripts because they slow things down too much while you're working. To see your hover buttons in action, save your page and click the Preview in Browser toolbar button, or select Preview in Browser from the File menu. See? Your hover buttons work just fine in your Web browser.

Want to change your hover buttons? It's easy to edit them. Right-click a button and select Hover Button Properties from the shortcut menu to display the dialog box again. Or, you can select a button and choose Properties from the Format menu. Don't forget to save the file before you view it.

Playing Sounds with Your FrontPage Hover Buttons

Wanna have some fun? How about creating hover buttons that play sounds? Imagine a button that barks when a visitor hovers the mouse pointer over the link to Fido's Web page. To make some noise, display the Hover Button Properties dialog box and click the Custom button.

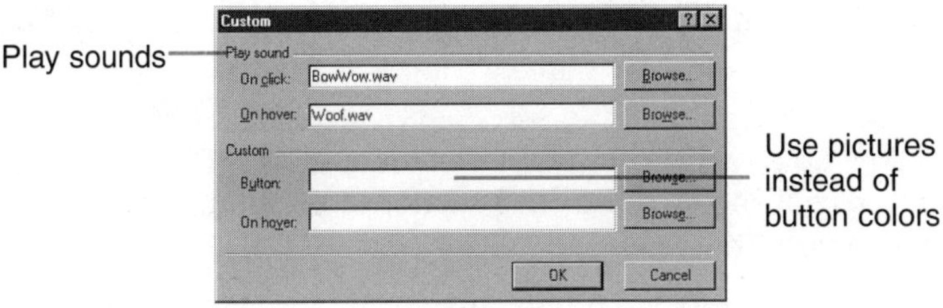

The Custom dialog box with sound filenames entered.

Type the name of the sound file (as in `sound.wav`) in the On Click box. To play a sound when a visitor passes his mouse pointer over your hover button, type the name of the sound file in the On Hover box. You can also display the Select Sound dialog box and look for sound files by clicking the Browse buttons next to the On Hover and On Click boxes. When you finish, click OK to return to the Hover Button Properties dialog box.

Using Your Own Images as Hover Buttons

Do plain old rectangular hover buttons squelch the artist in you? Feel free to use any graphics you want for your buttons. You'll need two sets of images: The original picture appears when your page loads, and the second picture appears when a visitor hovers his mouse pointer over the button. Web designers call this *swapping images*. If your graphics don't need labels, you can leave the Button text box blank.

To turn images into hover buttons, display the Hover Button Properties dialog box and do the following:

1. Type a URL or page name in the Link To box.
2. If you want to label your button, type your text in the Button text box.
3. Display the Custom dialog box by clicking the Custom button.
4. Type a filename for the original image in the Button box, and type a filename for the swap image in the On Hover box.

   If you don't know the filename for the image you want to add, you can click the Browse button to display the Select Picture dialog box so you can find and select your images.
5. Click the OK button to return to the Hover Button Properties dialog box.
6. Click OK to insert the button and return to your Web page.

Read This Before You Create Image Hover Buttons!

If you create hover buttons from your own graphics, make sure the original image and swap image are the same height and width. Otherwise, your buttons won't be displayed properly. This rule applies to both replacing FrontPage hover button colors with images and creating hover buttons with your own images.

Pages in Motion: Creating Dynamic HTML Special Effects

Impress your friends and co-workers with your spiffy Dynamic HTML (DHTML) pages. FrontPage helps you whip up cool special effects in a matter of minutes. But—shhhhh! That's our little secret, right?

To create a Dynamic HTML special effect, do the following:

1. Click a picture or select some text.
2. Display the DHTML toolbar by selecting Dynamic HTML Effects from the Format menu.

The DHTML toolbar.

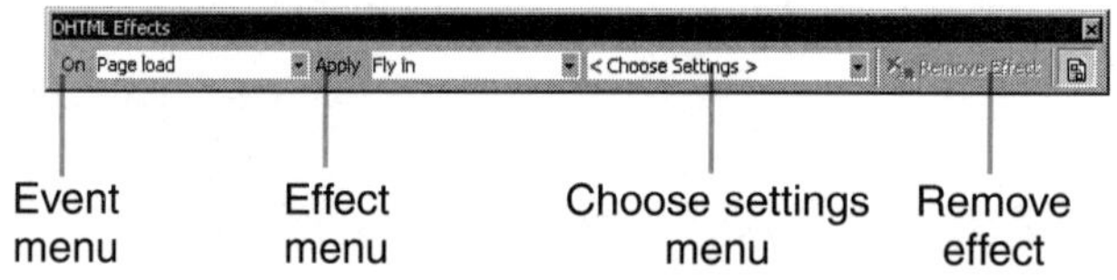

3. Select an event from the Choose an Event menu.
4. Select a special effect from the Choose an Effect menu.
5. Select settings for your special effect from the Choose Settings menu.

If you don't know what events, special effects, or special effect settings are, not to worry. The following sections tell you what you need to know.

Selecting DHTML Events

Events? No, I'm not talking about big earthquakes or your crazy uncle's annual New Year's Eve bash. With FrontPage, *events* are things that happen to Web pages or objects in a Web page. When an event occurs, the text or graphic does something. Web designers call this *triggering an action.*

You can select the following types of events from the Choose an event menu on the DHTML Effects toolbar:

- *Click* Triggers an action when a visitor clicks on the text or graphic. You can use this to swap a linked image or change the appearance of linked text before the new page loads.
- *Double click* Triggers an action when the visitor double-clicks the text or graphic. I don't recommend using this event because people usually only click once on text and images on a Web page.

- *Mouse over* Triggers an action when the visitor passes their mouse pointer over the text or graphic. If your server doesn't support FrontPage, you can use this event to create hover buttons instead of using the FrontPage Hover Button component.
- *Page load* Triggers an action when the page appears in a visitor's browser. You can use the Page load event to create animated page layouts with text and graphics that move into place as the page is displayed.

Choosing DHTML Effects

Effects are the actions that are triggered by events. For example, when a visitor hovers the mouse pointer over a text link (a Mouse over event), the font color changes (a Formatting effect). The Choose an effect menu items will change, depending on the type of object and event you select.

You can select the following types of effects from the Choose an effect menu on the DHTML Effects toolbar:

- *Fly out* The text or image moves away when an event occurs. You can use this effect for text or pictures with the Click and Double click events.
- *Formatting* The text changes to a different font, font style, or font color when an event occurs. You can use this effect for text with the Click, Double click, and Mouse over events.
- *Swap picture* A new image appears and replaces the original image. This works very much like FrontPage hover buttons. You can use this effect for pictures with the Click and Mouse over events.

The following effects only work with the Page load event:

- *Drop in by word* The selected pictures and graphics appear on the page one by one. This effect only works when you select more than one object on a page.
- *Elastic* The image or text moves onto the page from the top, right, left, or bottom, and then it bounces gently before settling into place.
- *Fly in* The image or text slides into its place from the top, right, left, or bottom of the page.
- *Hop* The image or text appears in its place and bounces once.
- *Spiral* The image or text spirals across the page before it moves into place.
- *Wave* The image or text moves across the page in a wave-like motion and then moves into place.
- *Wipe* The image or text fades into view from top to bottom, right to left, or from the middle radiating outwards.

Selecting DHTML Settings

Once you've selected an event and an effect for your text or image, you can fine-tune your special effects by choosing settings for them. For example, if you apply the Fly out effect, you need to tell FrontPage the direction in which the text or image will move. As with the effects menu, the Choose Settings menu changes depending on your other selections.

The Choose Settings menu on the DHTML Effects toolbar offers the following options:

- *Choose font* Changes the selected text's appearance when an event occurs. This option is only available when you apply the Formatting effect to text (which is only available for the Click, Double Click, and Mouse Over events). When you select Choose Font, the Font dialog box appears so you can apply font settings to determine how the text will change. For more about the Font dialog box, see Chapter 5, "Entering Text and Fiddling with Fonts."
- *Choose border* Displays a border and/or a shaded area around the selected text when an event occurs. This option is only available when you apply the Formatting effect to text. When you select the Choose Border dialog box, the Borders and Shading dialog box appears so you can apply options to the text. With FrontPage, you can apply both Font and Border settings to the same text. For more about borders and shading, see Chapter 15, "Now You're Stylin'! Using Style Sheets."
- *Direction (To left, To top, and more)* When you apply the Fly out effect to pictures and text, you can decide the direction in which you want your object to fly. The Choose Settings menu allows you to fly your text and pictures out to the left, top, bottom-left, bottom-right, top-right, and top-left of the page. If you've applied the Fly out effect to more than one object, you can also select To Top-right by word to move them out of the browser window one by one.
- *Choose picture* This option is only available when you apply the Swap Picture effect to an image. When you select Swap Picture, the Picture dialog box appears so you can browse for your swap image. Swap images are similar to hover buttons.
- *From right, From bottom, and more* When you apply effects to pictures for Page load events (such as Fly in or Drop in by word), you can choose the direction you want the objects to come from. The Choose Settings menu allows you to move text and pictures in from the right, bottom, left, top, bottom-left, bottom-right, and top-right of the page. Some of these options may not be available for all the effects.

Previewing DHTML Effects

As with hover buttons and many FrontPage components, DHTML special effects do not run in the FrontPage Normal view. To take an animated page for a spin, save the page and click the Preview in Browser button (or select Preview in Browser from the File menu) so you can see the page in your Web browser. When you finish, click the Close box for the DHTML Effects toolbar to return to your work.

Editing and Removing DHTML Effects

Not quite happy with your DHTML effects? Try, try again! It's fun to experiment. To edit an effect, click on the text or image to display the selected object's settings on the DHTML Effects toolbar. If you've closed the DHTML Effects toolbar, you can display it again by selecting Dynamic HTML Effects from the Format menu.

You can edit your special effects in the following ways:

- *Change a DHTML effect* You can apply different events, effects, and settings to the picture or text by selecting different items from the menus.
- *Remove highlighting from a DHTML effect* In the Normal view, FrontPage displays DHTML effects in a highlighted area so you can see the amount of space used to create the effect. If a highlighted area distracts you, you can remove it by clicking the Highlight button on the DHTML Effects toolbar. The highlighted areas are not displayed in Web browsers.
- *Remove a DHTML effect* To remove a DHTML effect entirely, click the Remove Effect button on the DHTML Effects toolbar.

Creating Slide Show Effects with Page Transitions

What's a transition? If you've ever watched a movie, television show, or slide show presentation, you've seen transitions. They're simple animations that move things along from one scene to the next you know, like *fade to black*. They look pretty neat and now you can add transitions to your Web pages so that one page shifts nicely into another when a visitor follows your links. For example, the Circle Out transition reveals the new Web page in a circle that gradually gets wider.

Creating slide show transitions for your Web pages is easy:

1. Open a Web page.
2. Select Page Transitions from the Format menu to display the Page Transitions dialog box.

Revealing a new Web page with the Circle Out transition.

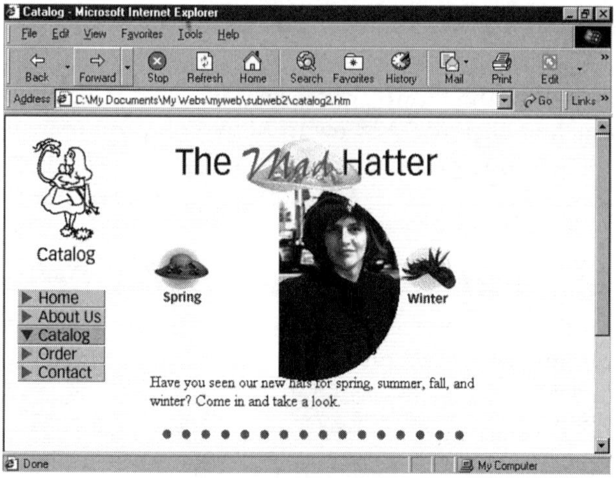

The Page Transitions dialog box.

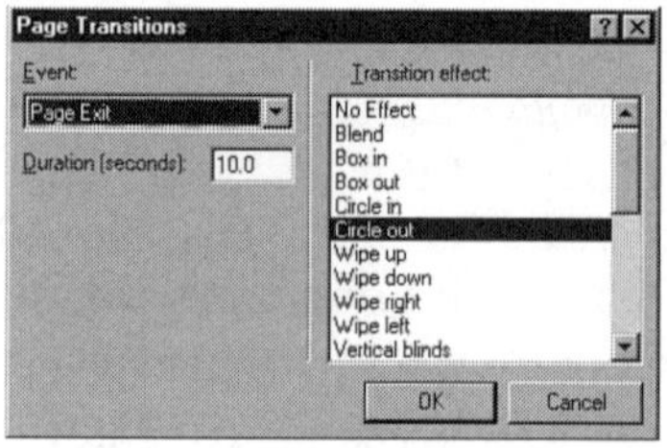

Transition Events

Page Enter displays the transition when a visitor goes to (enters) your page. Page Exit displays the transition when a visitor exits your page. Site Enter and Site Exit only display the transition when a visitor enters and leaves your Web site.

3. Choose an event from the Event menu. You can apply transitions to as many of the listed events as you like, but don't overdo it!
4. Enter a number of seconds in the Duration (seconds) box. Choose a number between 5 and 10 to give visitors enough time to admire your artistry without making them impatient.
5. Select an effect from the Transitions effect menu. FrontPage comes with over 20 transitions—feel free to experiment and try 'em all!

Editing and Removing Transitions

You can change a Web page's transitions at any time by displaying the Page Transitions dialog box and editing your settings. To remove a transition, select the event from the Event list and choose No Effect from the Transition effect menu.

Designing GIF Animations with the Banner Ad Manager

Many businesses run banner ads on the Web these days. They're those pesky animated advertisements that you see on popular Web sites. If you run your own business, you might want to try online advertising too. (Chapter 26, "Don't Just Let It Sit There! Publishing Your Web Site," tells how to get started.) The Banner Ad Manager can help you quickly create your own animated banner ads.

If you hate banner ads and don't ever plan to run an online promotional campaign, you can still have fun with the Banner Ad Manager. Despite its name, it's really a tool for creating *GIF animations*. GIF animations are a series of pictures that appear in sequence on a Web page. They're sort of like those little flipbooks with a drawing on each page. When you flip the pages with your thumb, a miniature cartoon unfolds.

GIF Animation Ingredients

To create a GIF animation, you need a series of two to 10 pictures formatted as GIF files (more than 10 pictures takes too long to load in people's browsers). Your images should all be the same height and width in order for the animation to run properly. If you're artistically inclined, try drawing some graphics yourself. Or you can use any pictures you want—even favorite photographs that you've taken with a digital camera or had someone scan into your computer.

Free Animated *GIFs*!

Don't have any pictures to put in your GIF animation? Don't let a silly detail like that ruin your fun. The First Internet Gallery of GIF Animation (`http://www.netm.com/animations/`) has lots of cool, free animations that you can download and use on your pages. Once you've downloaded a GIF animation, you can put it on your Web

Putting Your Animation Together

Once you've gathered your images together and put them into a folder, you'll need to import them into your Web. Chapter 2, "Instant Web-Site-O-Matic: Spinning FrontPage Webs," tells you how to import files into FrontPage Webs. To build your GIF animation, you first need to display the Banner Ad Manager Properties dialog box. You can do this by selecting Component from the Insert menu and then choosing the Banner Ad Manager from the cascading menu.

Banner Ads

If you decide to create a banner ad, most online advertising companies want your animation to be 468 pixels wide and 60 pixels high.

When the Banner Ad Manager Properties dialog box appears, you can cook up a GIF animation with the following steps:

1. Enter the width and height for your animation (in pixels) in the Width and Height boxes.
2. Choose a transition from the Transition effect menu, or choose None if you prefer to keep things simple.
3. Determine how long each picture should appear by entering a number of seconds in the Show each picture for (seconds) box. Two to five seconds should do the trick.
4. If you want your GIF animation to also work as a link, enter a URL or filename in the Link to box. You can also click the Browse button to locate and select a page from your Web.
5. Add your pictures to the animation by clicking the Add button. When the Add Picture for Banner Ad dialog box appears, you can browse for your image and click the OK button to continue.
6. Click the Add button again for each picture you want to add to the animation.
7. When you finish, click OK to add the animation to your Web page.

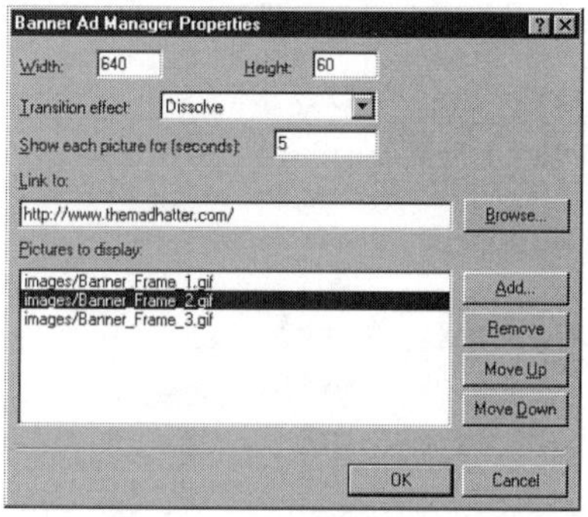

Banner Ad Manager Properties dialog box.

Previewing and Editing a GIF Animation

To see how your animation looks, click the Preview in Browser button to launch your Web page in a browser. Or you can click the Preview tab to preview it. You also can change or rearrange the pictures in your animation anytime you want. To edit your GIF animation, right-click it and select Banner Ad Manager Properties from the shortcut menu. Or you can select the ad and select Properties from the Format menu.

When the Banner Ad Manager Properties dialog box appears, you can change your settings and rearrange your picture list in the following ways:

- *Add more pictures* To add more pictures, click the Add button.
- *Remove pictures* To take a picture out of your animation, select the image from the Pictures to display list and click the Remove button.
- *Change the display order* The animation displays your pictures in the order that they appear on the Pictures to display list. You can move a picture towards the top of the list by selecting it and clicking the Move Up button, or move it towards the bottom of the list by selecting it and clicking the Move Down button.

Making a Scrolling Text Marquee

Scrolling text marquees display text messages that scroll across your Web page. They're great for grabbing people's attention when you want them to see your joke of the day or an important announcement. To create a scrolling text marquee, select Component from the Insert menu and then select Marquee. When the Marquee Properties dialog box appears, type your message in the Text box (you can make it as long as you want), choose your settings (described below), and click OK to insert the marquee and return to your Web page.

The Marquee Properties dialog box provides the following options:

- *Direction* Click the Left radio button to scroll your message from right to left, or click the Right radio button to scroll your message from left to right.
- *Speed* Enter a number (in milliseconds) in the Delay box to determine how quickly the text scrolls, and enter a number in the Amount box to determine the number of characters to scroll between delays. One thousand milliseconds equals one second. If you enter 90 for the delay and 6 for the amount, your marquee will scroll quite nicely.
- *Behavior* Click a radio button to determine how you want your text to scroll. Scroll loops your text continuously across the screen. Slide scrolls your message once and then stops. Alternate scrolls your message in one direction and then switches directions when it reaches the end of your text.
- *Align with text* Select Top, Middle, or Bottom to determine where you want your text to align in relation to the marquee box.
- *Size* Enter measurements for the width and height of your marquee. You can enter measurements either in pixels or as a percentage of the height and width of your Web page.
- *Repeat* Leave the Continuously check box selected to scroll your text over and over again. Or deselect the check box by clicking it, and then enter a number in the Times box to specify a number of times to repeat the text.

- *Background color* You can leave Automatic selected if you want the marquee box's background color to be the same as your Web page's. Or you can choose a different color.
- *Style* Don't like the boring old default font and font color? Click the Style button to display the Style dialog box so you can apply font styles, borders and shading, and other styles to your marquee. For more on working with styles, read Chapter 15.

The Marquee Properties dialog box.

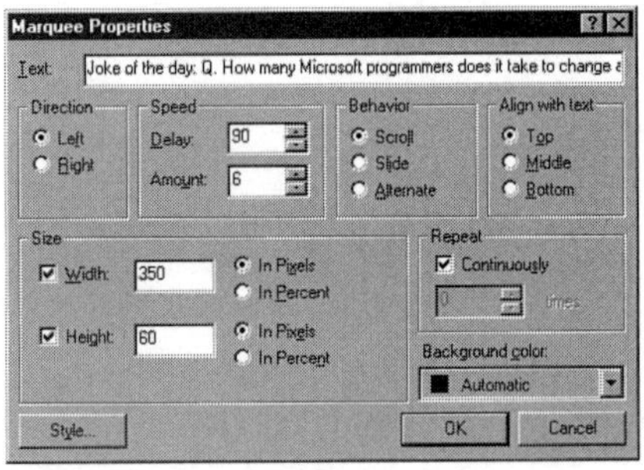

Five Cool Places to Visit for DHTML and Animation Ideas

Now that you've fooled around with DHTML a little bit, let's take a quick tour and see what the techno-hipsters are doing with it. Sure, they use advanced techniques, but you'd be surprised at what you can accomplish with FrontPage. Also, don't forget—DHTML does more than animate Web pages. It's also the technology behind those space-saving collapsible lists (see Chapter 6, "Making a List, Checking It Twice"), style sheets (see Chapter 15), and more.

- *Jeff Rule's Dynamic HTML Demos* Here you'll find elegant examples of all the things talked about in this chapter—including hover buttons with sound and slide show transitions (`http://www.ruleweb.com/dhtml/`).
- *Dynamic HTML Resource* Visit the Dynamic HTML Gurus Web page for beautiful animations, creative examples, and tutorials (`http://www.htmlguru.com/`).
- *Microsoft Site Builder Network's Dynamic HTML Page* Helpful examples, a gallery, technical explanations, and more (`www.microsoft.com/workshop/author/default.asp`).
- *The Dynamic HTML Zone* Macromedia, the maker of new media software programs like Director and Shockwave, takes you on a tour of the cutting edge. They spotlight a new DHTML site every week and provide links to other Web sites with interesting DHTML examples and information (`http://www.dhtml-zone.com/index.html`).

- *Dynamic HTML Invaders* Remember the old video arcade game Space Invaders? (Yikes! I'm giving away my age!) Now you can play Sitewerks' Dynamic HTML version of the game in full color. It takes a while to load the game, but it's worth the wait (`http://www.sitewerks.com/~erikw/`).

The Least You Need to Know

- Hover buttons are images that change when a visitor passes their mouse pointer over them. The FrontPage Hover Button component can create hover buttons from scratch, or you can use your own images. Web designers also call these buttons *rollovers* and *mouse overs*.
- You can create hover buttons that play sounds when a visitor hovers the mouse pointer over them or clicks them.
- The DHTML Effects toolbar makes it easy to add sophisticated special effects and animations to your pages. DHTML, which stands for Dynamic HTML, is an advanced Web feature that only works on version 4.0 browsers and higher. DHTML is explained in more detail in Chapter 21.
- If you want to do something really cool, try adding transitions to your Web pages. Transitions are simple animations that appear when visitors move from one page to the next. Thanks to the Page Transitions dialog box, you can set up transitions in a few seconds.
- The Banner Ad Manager helps you assemble GIF images into animations in a jiffy. Use the Banner Ad Manager to create ads for an online advertising campaign (as explained in Chapter 26), or just for fun.
- The FrontPage Marquee component helps you generate animated text messages that scroll across your Web page.

Chapter 21

Rev Up Your Web Site with Programs and Scripts

In This Chapter

- The difference between programs and scripts
- What's a client and what's a server?
- DHTML and XML
- Java applets
- ActiveX
- JavaScript and VBScript
- Active server pages
- CGI scripts
- XML
- Ten cool places to get free programs and scripts

"Give me a break!," you might say. "I'm just getting the hang of FrontPage and now you want to talk about *programming*?!?" It does take a while to learn programming and scripting. But you might find it helpful to know what all these technologies do, how they can make Web sites more exciting or useful, and how they work with FrontPage. Otherwise, when someone hears that you create Web pages and starts chattering about CGI, ASP, DHTML, and XML, it'll sound like alphabet soup to you.

Wanna Learn Scripting?

Dive in! Even non-technical folks can get the hang of a scripting language like JavaScript or Perl fairly quickly, if they're determined enough. Scripting languages aren't nearly as complex as full-fledged programming languages. You'll even find some helpful Internet resources at the end of this chapter.

Programs and Scripts: What's the Diff?

You've probably heard about Web programming and Web scripting. What are they, and how do they differ from each other? *Programs* are complex applications written in a programming language such as Java, C++, or Visual Basic. Fancy Web site features, such as online games and shopping carts that keep track of Web store purchases, require Web programming.

Although Web *scripts* don't offer a programming language's robustness, you can still do a lot with them. In fact, FrontPage forms, components, and discussion Webs (as covered in Chapters 13, "Form and Function: Building Online Forms," 19, "A Grab Bag of Helpful Doodads: FrontPage Components," and 23, "Switchboard Central: Setting Up a Discussion Web") all run with scripts that FrontPage generates for you. So how do scripts stay so simple and do so much? They make other programs do the work. For example, JavaScript scripts send commands to a Web browser, while FrontPage component scripts rely on FrontPage's server software.

Client Versus Server and What It Means to You

You may have never given this a thought, but PCs and servers have a relationship. Because the PC is always asking the server for things like Web pages and email messages, it's called a *client*. Internet programs that get data from servers, including Web browsers, are called *client applications*. As for programs that run on a server, such as FrontPage server extensions, you can call them *server applications*.

So why should you care? All Web programs and scripts depend on the browser or server's capabilities—or sometimes both. For example, many of FrontPage's nifty Web site features rely on *server-side* programs, so they work only on FrontPage-friendly servers. And remember those cool Web page animations covered in Chapter 20, "Gee-Whiz Pages with Animated Special Effects"? FrontPage uses Dynamic HTML (DHTML) and JavaScript to generate those. JavaScript and all versions of HTML are *client-side* technologies that work only with browsers that support them. Recent browsers always support more JavaScript and HTML features than their predecessors.

Table 21.1 Web Languages

Web Language	Where Accessed
HTML	Client-side
DHTML	Client-side
XML	Client-side
Java	Client-side
ActiveX	Client-side(works only in Internet Explorer for Windows)
JavaScript	Client-side; also has extended server-side capabilities with LiveWire, a Netscape server product
VBScript	Client-side for Internet Explorer only; server-side when used with ASP
JScript	Client-side for Explorer only; server-side when used with ASP
ASP	Server-side
CGI	Server-side

DHTML: HTML with More Zip!

Dynamic HTML (DHTML) sounds a little intimidating, but it simply refers to HTML extras that let you position and animate text and pictures. As you may recall from Chapter 3, "Fooling Around with Web Pages," HTML is the language used to format Web pages. Thanks to DHTML, you can put your text and images exactly where you want them to go, as covered in Chapter 9, "Spiffing Up Pictures," or create animated special effects, as discussed in Chapter 20. Only Internet Explorer 4.0 and Netscape Navigator 4.0 and higher browser versions support DHTML. FrontPage generates all these HTML and DHTML codes for you, of course, but you can always take a peek at the code behind your fabulous-looking Web pages by opening a Web page in FrontPage and clicking the HTML tab.

X'd for Success: What's XML?

XML stands for Extensible Markup Language, a recent technology that is still under development. Only version 5.0 browsers and higher provide support for XML. XML makes HTML more powerful because it allows you to create your own tags so you can work with files more easily. XML certainly isn't for beginners or the faint of heart, but FrontPage and Microsoft Office 2000 use it behind the scenes to preserve the formatting of your Office files when you save them as Web pages. For more information about XML, visit XMLU.com at `http://www.xmlu.com/`.

Jumpin' Java! What Are Java Applets?

Why is everyone jumping for Java? It's Sun Microsystems' powerful language for writing client-side programs—called *applets*—that run in a Web browser. With Java, you can add all kinds of intelligent features to a Web site, no matter what's on the server. No wonder programmers love Java!

A downside to Java applets is that they take a long time to load in the browser the first time around. After the first download, they run more quickly.

Want to see what Java can do? Visit Talk City, an online chat community, at `http://www.talkcity.com/`. Their Java chat program runs in a Web browser and works great.

Getting Java Applets

If you want to learn Java, you'll have to take some programming courses or buy a couple of big books. But don't let that stop you from using Java applets on your Web pages! You can download programs that create applets for you from Tucows' Java Web Development section at `http://tucows.tierranet.com/java/webdeveljava.html`. Or you can grab a readymade applet from the Web. These applets usually come with detailed instructions for the novice on how to use them on your Web page. For a list of Web sites that serve up Java applets, read "Ten Cool Places to Get Programs and Scripts" at the end of this chapter.

Inserting a Java Applet in a Web Page

To insert an applet on a Web page, place your cursor where you want the applet to appear. Choose Advanced from the Insert menu and then select Java Applet from the cascading menu to display the Java Applet Properties dialog box. When you finish entering all of the properties and parameters, click OK to insert your applet and return to your Web page. As with embedded files (see Chapter 17, "Strut Your Stuff: Sound, Video, and More"), an ugly placeholder appears in FrontPage instead of the applet itself. But you can see how your applet looks by previewing your page in the Web browser or by clicking the Preview tab.

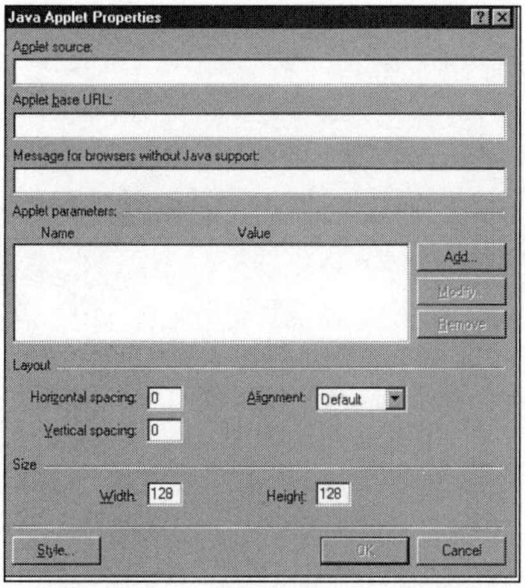

The Java Applet Properties dialog box.

The Java Applet Properties dialog box asks you for the following information (don't worry if you don't know what any of this means—the instructions that come with your applet software or the downloaded applet will tell you what the applet properties and parameters should be):

- *Applet source* Enter the directory path to your applet (Java applet files end with the `.class` filename extension, as in `applets/myapplet.class`).
- *Applet base URL* In most situations, you should leave this box blank. A *base URL* assigns a location to a file once you publish it to your server (such as `http://www.mywebsite.com/`). If you fill in this information, the applet won't work when you test it on your computer because your Web page will look for it on your server instead.
- *Message for browsers without Java support* The Java programming language is over three years old, and most current browsers support it. But to be on the safe side, you can type something like, "Sorry, you need a current version of Explorer or Netscape in order to see my Java applet."
- *Applet parameters* Many applets are set up so that you can customize them by entering a few *parameters*—settings that tell the applet how to run. If this is the case, the instructions that come with the applet should tell you how. Parameters (also called *attributes*) come in pairs of names and values. To add a parameter, click the Add button to display the Set Attribute Value dialog box, type the name in the Name field and the value in the Value field, and then click OK to return to the Java Applet Properties dialog box.
- *Horizontal and Vertical spacing* Enter a number (in pixels) in the Horizontal spacing and Vertical spacing boxes to create some buffer space between your applet and other page elements.
- *Alignment* You can also select an alignment option from the list to determine how your applet aligns with the surrounding text on your Web page.

- *Width and Height* You also need to enter height and width measurements (in pixels) to create a placeholder on your Web page for the applet.

Before You Get Fired Up About ActiveX...

There's a catch. Only Internet Explorer for Windows supports ActiveX. This means that Netscape Navigator, Macintosh, and UNIX users can't enjoy ActiveX pages.

ActiveX—It Ain't the Latest Schwarzenegger Flick

Microsoft developed ActiveX—snippets of Visual Basic programming code—to help even non-programmers add cool features to their Web pages. For example, ActiveX makes it possible to add a completely functional Excel chart or pivot table to your page, as covered in Chapter 18, "A Match Made in Redmond: FrontPage and Microsoft Office 2000." FrontPage even comes with a few ActiveX controls that you can use. To learn more about ActiveX controls and how to use them, visit Microsoft's site.

Inserting ActiveX Controls into a Web Page

To insert an ActiveX Control into your Web page, place your cursor where you want to place the control, choose Advanced from the Insert menu, and select ActiveX Control. When the Insert ActiveX Control dialog box appears, pick a control from the list and click OK.

Next, right-click your control and select ActiveX Control Properties from the shortcut menu. When the ActiveX Control Properties dialog box appears with the Object Tag tab selected, you can enter options as you would for an embedded object (see Chapter 17) or Java applet (see the section on Java applets in this chapter). ActiveX controls can have parameters just like Java applets. Click the Parameters tab (as explained in the section on Java applets) to set your parameters. When you finish, click OK to return to your Web page.

Client-Side Scripting with JavaScript, VBScript, and JScript

JavaScript was originally developed by Netscape for the Navigator browser, but it has become standard on the Web and is supported by Internet Explorer as well. In addition, Microsoft has created its own scripting languages, VBScript and JScript. VBScript and JScript work only in Internet Explorer—unless your server supports active server page (ASP) scripting, in which case VBScript and JScript work in both Explorer and Netscape.

How Client-Side Scripts Work

JavaScript, VBScript, and JScript scripts run in Web browsers. Client-side scripts consist of lines of code that you type straight into a Web page's source code. The main ingredients for a client-side script are objects, events, and actions. Take hover buttons (also called rollovers), for example. As covered in Chapter 20 a hover button is a piece of text or a graphic that changes when a visitor clicks on it or passes the mouse pointer over it. The text or graphic is the *object*. When an *event* occurs (a visitor clicks on the object), an *action* follows (the object changes). Scripting languages give you a way to define those objects, events, and actions.

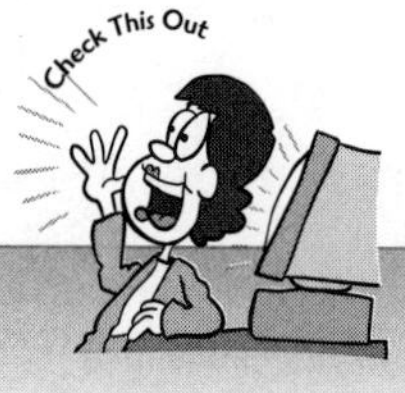

Which Scripting Language Should You Use?

If your server supports FrontPage, it supports ASP too. You'll find it easier to stick with VBScript or JScript because FrontPage comes with a Scripting Wizard that helps you generate scripts with these languages. If your server doesn't provide FrontPage extensions, you should use JavaScript to ensure that your scripts work properly in all Web browsers.

Writing Client-Side Scripts

With FrontPage, you can work directly with HTML source code by opening a Web page and clicking the HTML tab. This means that if you want to write your own scripts or work with other people's scripts, you'll need to learn HTML and a scripting language. The Web sites listed at the end of this chapter provide free scripts as well as links to tutorials and recommended reading.

Introducing the Script Wizard

If you already know VBScript or JScript, the FrontPage Script Wizard can help you generate scripts. The Toolbox contains a list of objects that commonly appear on Web pages. You can also click the Script button to view a script outline and select objects and events, or the HTML button to see an outline of your Web page's content. The work area provides Source, Design, and QuickView tabs so that you can view your source code, display a graphical view of the script (similar to the Normal FrontPage Web page view) so you can see what the scripted elements will look like on your Web page, and see your script in action so that you can test it. The Project Explorer displays your files and folders, and the Properties list provides a list of properties that you can apply to objects.

The Script Wizard.

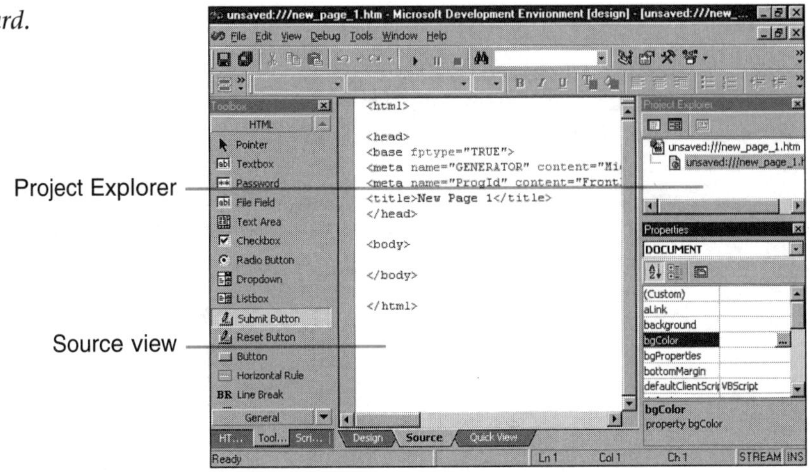

Serving Up Active Server Pages

Active server pages (ASP) are a powerful combination of client-side scripts (VBScript or JScript) that work with ASP server software. FrontPage 2000 uses ASP scripting to help you create the bells and whistles on your Web site. You can also save database applications as active server pages, as covered in Chapter 23. Since FrontPage 2000 and FrontPage servers support ASP, you may want to learn VBScript or JScript and ASP scripting down the road. Although creating your own active server pages requires a fairly high level of technical skill, it enables you to do a lot with your Web site without hardcore programming.

Before You Fool Around with CGI Scripts…

Call your ISP or Web hosting company first! They can help you set up your script so it works on their server. Some companies can even provide you with readymade scripts that can save you a lot of time and hassle. You should also make sure that your Web provider supports CGI scripting—some companies don't.

Working with CGI Scripts

If your server doesn't support FrontPage, you can get some of the same effects using CGI scripts. *CGI* stands for *common gateway interface*—a method of programming that works on most servers. FrontPage components help you do things like processing forms and setting up discussion groups that are normally done with CGI scripts. Although CGI scripts can be written with a variety of programming languages, the most popular is *Perl*.

You don't have to know any programming to use CGI scripts on your Web site, but you *will* have to tweak your HTML code and the script file a bit. You can download CGI scripts from the Web and follow the instructions. First, upload the script (which usually has a `.pl` or `.cgi` filename extension) to a folder called `cgi-bin` or `cgi-win`. Then you need to put HTML code in your Web page that tells the script to launch.

Making Web Pages Compatible with Browsers and Servers

Sure, you can build cool Web pages with FrontPage, but can everyone read them? Older Web browsers can't display cutting-edge stuff like animated special effects and collapsible lists. This means that visitors who haven't downloaded the latest and greatest browsers may not be able to read or navigate your Web site. To make things even more complicated, some programming and scripting languages and HTML enhancements work only in newer browsers or with FrontPage server extensions. Be sure to test your programming.

To change your Web page compatibility settings, select Page Options from the Tools menu. When the Page Options dialog box appears, click the Compatibility tab. Select your options and click OK when you've finished.

Take a Walk on the Safe Side!

If you still aren't sure about which features different browsers and servers support, stay on the safe side. Keep FrontPage's default compatibility settings, stick with a FrontPage-friendly server, and put some text or a graphic on your Web pages that says "This Web site works best with the latest version of Internet Explorer or Netscape Navigator."

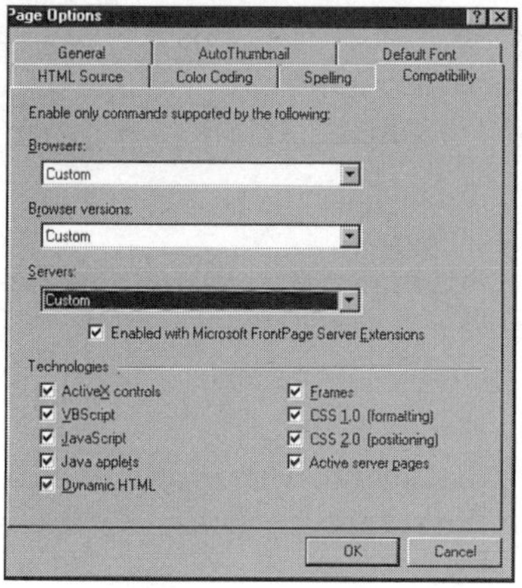

The Page Options dialog box with the Compatibility tab selected.

You can choose options from the following lists:

- *Browsers* To target a particular Web browser, such as Internet Explorer, Netscape Navigator, or WebTV, select an item from the pull-down list.
- *Browser versions* To ensure that your Web pages are compatible with older browsers, choose a browser version from the pull-down list.
- *Servers* If your Web host or ISP uses a server other than FrontPage, deselect the Enabled with Microsoft FrontPage Server Extensions check box and select a type of server from the Servers list.
- *Technologies* To exclude a particular Web enhancement from your Web pages, deselect the check box for the item. Frames and CSS (cascading style sheets) are covered in Chapters 11, "Get Framed! Building a Web Site with Frames," and 15, "Now You're Stylin'! Using Style Sheets."

Ten Cool Places to Get Free Programs and Scripts

So, you want to use programs or scripts in your Web pages? You can download many of them free from the Web. Many Web sites with free programs and scripts also offer tutorials and point you to helpful books and resources on the Web.

- *A Better Home Page's Java Applets page* Free Java applets, recommended books, and links to other applet collections (`http://www.better-homepage.com/java/index.html`).
- *Java Applets Rating Service (JARS)* Reviews of Java applets and links (`http://www.jars.com/`).
- *The JavaScript Source* Hundreds of free scripts that you can copy and paste (`http://javascript.internet.com/`).
- *Microsoft Site Builder and Development Network Sites* The Site Builder network, at `http://msdn.microsoft.com/`, introduces you to tools and technologies you can try, including resources and examples for VBScripting, ActiveX, and Active Server Pages.
- *JavaScript World* Scripts, tutorials, and more (`http://www.jsworld.com/`).
- *Free Scripts* Lots of JavaScript and CGI scripts (`http://www.freeweb.nu/scripts.htm`).
- *Active Server Pages.Com* Tutorials, examples, scripts, and reviews of helpful books (`http://www.activeserverpages.com/`).
- *ActiveX.Com* Free components, articles, and links to other ActiveX resources (`http://www.active-x.com/`).
- *Matt's Script Archive* Tons of free CGI scripts with instructions on how to use them (`http://www.worldwidemart.com/scripts/`).

- *Poor Richard's Web Site* This Web site doesn't actually offer free scripts, but it does offer lots of useful information on how beginners and FrontPage users can use the latest Web technologies without programming (`http://www.poor-richard.com/`).

The Least You Need to Know

- With FrontPage, scripting languages like JavaScript, VBScript, ASP, and Perl aren't too hard for non-programmers to master, and they allow you to add exciting features to your Web page.
- Client-side programs and scripts, like Java applets and JavaScript scripts, run in Web browsers. Server-side programs and scripts, like the ones that FrontPage creates, require special software on the server in order to run.
- FrontPage 2000 and recent versions of Internet Explorer and Netscape Navigator support DHTML and XML, new technologies that let you do more with your Web pages.
- Java is a programming language for creating applications, like games and online chat rooms, that run in a Web browser. You don't need to install any special software on your server to use Java applets on your Web pages. Versions 3.0 and higher of Internet Explorer and Netscape Navigator support Java.
- ActiveX controls are Microsoft's answer to Java applets. Non-programmers can take these bits and pieces of Visual Basic code and run them in a Web browser. Unfortunately, ActiveX works only with Internet Explorer and Windows.
- JavaScript is a scripting language that runs in Internet Explorer and Netscape Navigator. VBScript and JScript work only in Internet Explorer or when your server supports active server pages. FrontPage 2000 servers also support ASP. Many of FrontPage's bells and whistles, including components, forms, and discussion groups, are generated with VBScript and ASP.
- If you already know a fair amount about scripting, FrontPage's Scripting Wizard can make scripting easier.
- Active server pages (ASP) combines scripting with server software so non-programmers can add powerful features to their Web pages. Although ASP requires a fair amount of technical skill, it's easier than creating Web programs from scratch.

- If your server doesn't support FrontPage, CGI scripts can fill in the gaps. You can use them to process forms, set up discussion groups, and more. CGI scripts are stored on your server and use applications that are available on most Web servers to do their work.
- You don't need to be a programmer to use programs and scripts on your Web pages. But if you don't mind tweaking your HTML code, you can download free Java applets, ActiveX controls, and scripts from the Web. These goodies also come with instructions so you can put them on your Web page.

Chapter 22

If You've Got It, Flaunt It: Putting Your Access Databases on the Web

In This Chapter

- Introduction to Access databases
- Static and dynamic databases
- Saving databases as Web pages from Access
- Forms and databases
- Saving form results to databases
- Five cool things you can do with Web databases

Want to put a database on your Web site? You don't *have* to use Access, the popular database program that ships with Microsoft Office 2000. FrontPage supports most popular types of databases. But using Access sure makes things a heck of a lot easier. With Access, even beginners can set up cool databases and put them on the Web.

Access Database Crash Course

To get started with an Access database, you can let the Office Assistant guide you through the steps of setting up a database. You can also install the Northwind sample databases from the Microsoft Office CD-ROM. Northwind is a fictitious company with lots of different types of tables, forms, queries, and reports that you can explore (as explained in the following sections).

Rev Up Your Database Engine!

Before you get all excited about Web pages and databases, make sure that your server supports FrontPage and has a *database engine*. The database engine is a program that tells Web pages and databases how to talk to each other.

Remember Queries!

When you make your database available on the Web, most of the time you'll probably use queries instead of publishing the entire database. Some of the information stored in databases is confidential or unnecessary. You can create a query that prevents that information from showing up on your Web page.

Databases consist of the following basic components:

- *Records* Individual entries in a database.
- *Fields* Types of information for data records, such as a first name or street address.
- *Data files* These contain all of the database records and associated files.

Tables, Forms, Queries, and Reports

With Access, and most other popular databases, you can create tables, forms, queries, and reports for viewing your data. Every database starts out with a table, which looks like an Excel spreadsheet and contains rows and columns. Each row contains information for a data record, and each column contains a data field.

But looking at tables too long is hard on the eyes. That's why you can also view your database by creating forms, queries, and reports:

- *Forms* Database forms look an awful lot like Web forms. They look pretty, and they display information for individual records in the form fields.
- *Queries* With queries, you can create offshoots from the main database that display information for certain fields. For example, a human resources department with a huge employee database can make names, email addresses, and office phone numbers available to everyone (while keeping the other stuff confidential) by generating and publishing a query.
- *Reports* Reports are ideal for printing out mailing labels or information that you need to pass around at the next meeting. As with queries, you can include information from some fields and not others for your records.

Static and Dynamic Databases

With FrontPage, you can put either static or dynamic databases on your Web site. But first, you probably want to know what static and dynamic databases *are*. A static database is a set of Web pages that contain information from a database. Static databases are not automatically updated when the original database changes. Dynamic databases run live on the Web server and are updated constantly.

Saving Databases as Web Pages

To save information from a database as a set of Web pages from Microsoft Access, use the Reports Wizard to create a report. When you finish, Select Export from the File menu. When the Export dialog box appears, choose a folder from the Save in list, select HTML Documents from the Save as type list, type a name for your Web page in the File name box, and click the Save button.

Publishing Database Information to the Web

Once you create a database table, form, or query, you can export that information as a set of active server pages that you can put on your Web site (as explained in Chapter 21, "Rev Up Your Web Site with Programs and Scripts"). The Web pages will look similar to their appearance in Access. For example, if you save data from the Form view, Web site visitors will be able to search for data by form field.

To save a database table, form, or query as a set of active server pages, select Export from the File menu. When the Export dialog box appears, choose a folder from the Save in list, select Active Server Pages from the Save as type list, type a name for your Web page in the File name box, and click the Save button.

When the Microsoft Active Server Pages Output Options dialog appears, type in the information and click the OK button. If you get stuck on something, get in touch with your network administrator.

Forms and Databases

How do visitors interact with databases on the Web? Through Web forms, mostly. On the Web, databases can go both ways. You can invite visitors to fill out a form and send their information to a database, or you can set up a page with a search form so visitors can search for records on a database.

Using a Database to Gather Form Results

Web forms are a great way to gather feedback and all sorts of other useful information from visitors. But after a while, all those email messages that come from the forms can become hard to keep track of. Try saving the messages to a database instead.

To gather form results and save them to a database, open a Web page with a form (for more about forms, see Chapter 13, "Form and Function: Building Online Forms"). Then display the Form Properties dialog box by right-clicking the form and selecting Form Properties from the shortcut menu. When the Form Properties dialog box appears, as shown in the following figure, click the Send to database radio button and select an available database file from the list.

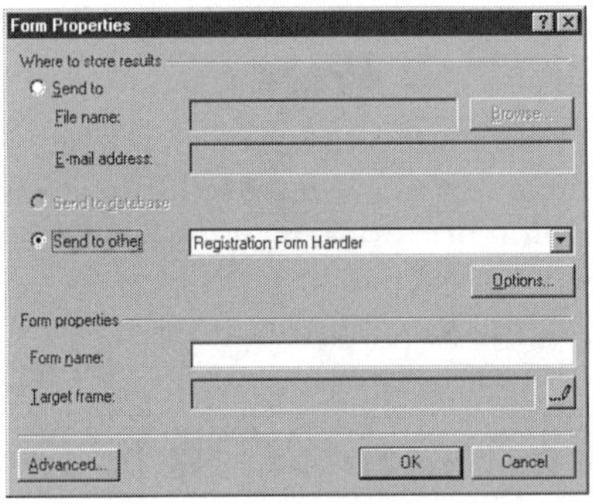

The Form Properties dialog box.

What Are Tab, Comma, and Space Separators?

Database text files separate information into different fields and records with tabs, commas, or spaces. When you open your text file in Access or Excel, a dialog box will appear and prompt you for the type of *delimiters* (another word for separators) used in your file so that Access or Excel can separate the data correctly.

Saving Form Data to a Database Text File

If you don't have hundreds of people sending you messages every day, you can set up your form to post data to a text file. This works great in many situations because you don't need a full database engine on the server to save your form data. You can simply download the text file and import it into Access or Excel to display your data.

Display the Form Properties dialog box, select the Send to other radio button, and click the Options button. When the Options for Registration Form Handler dialog box appears, click the File Results tab. Type a new name for the text file in the File name box, select one of the Text database options from the File Format list, and click the Include field names check box. When you finish, click OK to return to the Form Properties dialog box, and then click OK to return to your form.

Five Cool Things You Can Do with Web Databases

- *The guestbook database* If you're just doing your Web site for fun, try a guestbook database. Save your form results to a text database, import the database into Excel or Access, and then publish your growing list of visitors as a Web page.
- *Keep track of schedules and projects* Sure, the Project Web can help you and your co-workers keep on top of projects (as mentioned in Chapter 29, "It Doesn't Take a Village to Build an Intranet: Publishing, Sharing, and Updating Files"), but you can include much more detailed information in a database.
- *Easy Web publishing* How on earth do all those online magazines keep track of all those articles? In many cases, they store write-ups—along with pictures and links—in a database. When a visitor follows a link to an article, the Web page requests the information from the database.
- *Start the Next Yahoo!* Yahoo!, the famous online search engine (`http://www.yahoo.com/`), started out as two guys and a huge database of Web sites. You too can use a database to keep track of your favorite books, Web sites, movies, and just about anything else (with links, of course). Plus, you can create a search form so visitors can look for stuff.
- *Share information* If you or some of your co-workers go on the road a lot or work from a home office, you can set up your Web site so they can access the database anytime, anywhere.

The Least You Need to Know

- FrontPage Webs and Access databases work great together. You can also integrate other types of databases with FrontPage.
- Databases consist of fields, records, and data files. With Access and many other database programs, you can view a record as a table, from within a form, or as a report. In addition, you can generate queries that contain only selected fields from records.
- A static Web database is a set of Web pages generated from a database report. Dynamic Web databases contain live data that is updated when changes are made to the database. You can save a database to a FrontPage Web as either static or dynamic pages.
- You can set up your Web page forms to gather information and send it to a database, or to allow others to search a database for information.

Chapter 23

Switchboard Central: Setting Up a Discussion Web

In This Chapter

- Setting up a discussion Web with the Discussion Web Wizard
- Choosing features for your discussion Web
- Maintaining your discussion Web
- Five cool ways to use a discussion Web

Get people talking! Start a discussion Web. If you run a business, discussion Webs can help you communicate better with customers and co-workers. Or you can launch a forum for people with common interests such as books, celebrities, music, health, personal finance, hobbies, or community issues. With FrontPage, you can get a discussion Web up and running in a matter of minutes.

You may have come across discussion Webs (also called *newsgroups* or *Web bulletin boards*) during your Net surfing expeditions. Here's how they work: You can view a table of contents and click the links to read *articles* (messages). To participate in the conversation, you fill out a special submission form to reply to an article, ask a question, or begin a conversation on a different topic. When you go back to the table of contents and click your browser's Reload (or Refresh) button, the Subject line of your message appears on the list.

Setting Up a Discussion Web with the Wizard

To begin building your discussion Web, select New from the File menu and then choose Web from the cascading menu. When the New dialog box appears, click the Discussion Web Wizard icon and enter a path to your Web in the Specify the location of the new Web box. Click OK. To add the discussion Web to an existing Web, enter the path to the Web along with the new folder name (as in `C:\My Webs\myweb\discussion_group`) and click the Add to current Web check box.

When the Discussion Web Wizard launches, follow the instructions, choose your options, enter information, and click the Next button to move forward. If you need to make changes, you can return to previous dialog boxes by clicking the Back button. When you've added all the options you want, you can click the Finish button to create your discussion Web and return to FrontPage. The following sections explain the Discussion Web Wizard options in greater detail.

Discussion Web Terms

Articles Messages posted to the Web to start or respond to topics.

Submission form The Web form that visitors use to post articles.

Threads A series of articles posted in response to a particular message.

Moderator The person who runs a discussion Web.

Newsgroup Before the Web came along, discussion groups were hosted on special text-only news servers. These types of newsgroups are still around—they're called *Usenet newsgroups*. Both Internet Explorer and Netscape Communicator come with newsreaders for participating in these types of newsgroups.

Flame An angry message.

Spam A message that has no relation to the discussion Web's community, topics, or current conversations, such as advertisements or promotional announcements.

Selecting Features for Your Discussion Web

First, you need to choose a topic of interest to your audience, and then you need to choose which features you want to include in your discussion Web. When the Discussion Web Wizard launches, click the Next button to display a list of features you can select or deselect by clicking the check boxes. When you finish, click the Next button.

Discussion Web features include the following:

- *Submission Form* FrontPage doesn't give you a choice for this option. You *need* a submission form—otherwise, users have no way to post their articles.
- *Table of Contents* I strongly recommend leaving this option selected. When people post articles, the subject lines appear on the table of contents page with links so other people can follow the discussions and read the articles.
- *Search Form* This works like the Search Form component (explained in Chapter 19, "A Grab Bag of Helpful Doodads: FrontPage Components") and allows users to search discussions by keyword.
- *Threaded Replies* Web discussions can digress just like conversations in the real world. When these digressions revolve around particular topics, FrontPage starts a new conversational *thread*. When you look at the list of articles in the table of contents, threaded articles are indented beneath the article that started the thread.
- *Confirmation Page* When a user posts an article through the submission form, this displays a page to let him know that the article has gone through. Users get a little nervous when nothing happens.

Read This *Before* You Click That No Button!

FrontPage automatically names main Web pages `Index.htm`. If you're creating your discussion Web in the same folder as an existing Web, the Discussion Web Wizard will replace your current main page with a new index page. And you don't want that to happen. If you've created your discussion group in a new folder, you don't need to worry about this.

Naming Your Discussion Web

Once you finish selecting features for your discussion Web and click the Next button, the third dialog box asks for a couple of names. You can give your discussion Web a name—such as "The Newt Gingrich Fan Club Page"—by typing text in the Enter a descriptive title for this discussion box. You can also name your discussion folder in which FrontPage stores all the articles by typing it in the Enter the name for the discussion folder box. (If you don't rename the folder, FrontPage automatically calls it `_disc1`.) Then click the Next button.

Is Your Discussion Web Public or Private?

Before you name your discussion folder, think about whether you want to open discussions to the public or keep them private. When folder names are preceded by an underscore, as in `_disc1`, FrontPage hides everything in the folder so only people in the know can find it. If you *want* people to drop in on your chats, don't put an underscore before your discussion folder's name.

Choosing Form Fields for Posting Articles

The fourth Discussion Web Wizard dialog box helps you create basic fields for your discussion Web's submission form. Select a radio button for the form fields you want to include. You can add more form fields later, just as you would with a regular Web form.

The submission form, as shown in the following figure, works similarly to the Web forms covered in Chapter 13, "Form and Function: Building Online Forms." Visitors can type a brief description of the article in the Subject line, just as you do when sending an email message. The Subject line appears as a linked item on the Contents page. They can then type their article in the Comments area and click the Submit button to send the form. For more complex discussion Webs, you can also have visitors select a category or product. When you've selected an option, click the Next button.

Discussion Web submission form.

Subject that will appear on Contents page

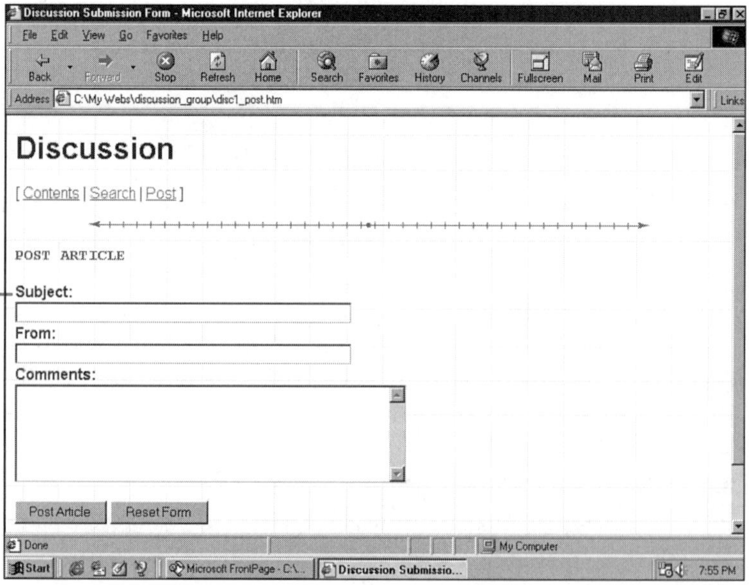

Members Only or Free for All?

The fifth Discussion Web Wizard dialog box asks, "Will the discussion take place in a protected Web?" Here you can choose to limit access to registered users by clicking the Yes, only registered users are allowed radio button. Or you can open your discussion Web to the public by clicking the No, anyone can post articles radio button. For example, you may not want outsiders to read articles about the latest Human Resources department meeting, but you certainly do want your customers to be able to post questions about your products. When you've chosen an option, click the Next button.

Giving People Access to Private Discussions

If you choose to create a protected discussion Web, you need to give access to your users. Chapter 27, "You're the Boss! Becoming a Web Site Administrator," talks about assigning access privileges and other FrontPage server administration stuff.

Sorting Articles

When FrontPage lists articles on the table of contents page, the articles appear in a certain order. Most discussion groups list the oldest articles first and the newest ones last so that visitors can follow the conversations in chronological order. However, discussion groups that focus on frequently updated topics sometimes list the most recent articles first. When the sixth Discussion Web Wizard dialog box appears, select either the Oldest to newest or Newest to oldest radio button and then click the Next button. This dialog box appears only if you choose to have a table of contents in the second Discussion Web Wizard dialog box.

Assigning a Main Page for the Discussion Web

Every Web site has a main page that introduces the site and links visitors to other parts of it. The seventh Discussion Web Wizard dialog box asks you to create yours. FrontPage assumes that you want to use your table of contents page as your main page, but most people don't, because long lists of articles look mighty ugly and take more time to download. If you want to use your table of contents as the main page, leave the Yes radio button selected. Otherwise, click the No button. When you choose an option, click Next. This dialog box appears only if you choose to include a table of contents. Otherwise, FrontPage automatically creates a main page for you.

Making the Discussion Web Searchable

The eighth dialog box asks how you want to display search form results. When users search the discussion group Web site for a keyword, FrontPage displays a page with a list of matches and links. You can have the search results display just the article's subject line, the subject line and file size (in kilobytes), the subject line, file size, and date when the article was submitted, or the subject, file size, date, and score (how closely a article matches the search compared with other articles). Click a radio button to choose an option and then click the Next button. This dialog box appears only if you choose to include a search form in your discussion Web.

Picking a Web Theme

The ninth dialog box lets you apply a FrontPage theme to your discussion Web. To apply a theme, click the Choose Web Theme button to display the Choose Theme dialog box. For more on FrontPage Web Themes, see Chapter 4, "Poof! You're a Designer with FrontPage Web Themes." When you've picked a theme (or chosen not to), click the Next button.

To Frame or Not to Frame

Frames are ideal for discussion Webs because you can display the table of contents in one frame and the articles in another. On the other hand, some people hate frames. The tenth dialog box lets you choose a frames layout for your page or choose the No Frames radio button to avoid framing your site. When you click a radio button, a preview of your frame layout appears on the left. You can also choose the Dual Interface option, which works even if the user's browser doesn't support frames. Click the Next button when you finish choosing your Frames options. For more about how frames work, see Chapter 11, "Get Framed! Building a Web Site with Frames."

Confirming Your Selections

The final dialog box displays a list of the pages that you've chosen, such as a table of contents, a main page with frames, and a search page. Click the Finish button to create your discussion Web and return to FrontPage.

Maintaining Your Discussion Web

Running a discussion group is sort of like hosting a party or taking charge of a meeting. Once you've created your discussion Web, you need to keep it running properly. This involves *moderating* the discussions—looking through messages, posting articles to keep conversations on track, and even deleting messages. You'll also need to do some spring cleaning every now and then. When too many messages are posted, the table of contents takes forever to download and people can't find what they're looking for.

You can also *archive* articles by creating a new folder and moving the articles to it instead of deleting them. If you've already created a private discussion group, the discussion folder is located in the `_private` folder so that only authorized users can find it.

Editing Pages on Your Discussion Web

Once you've created your discussion Web, you can add form fields to the submission form, change text on the search form, and edit your main page as you would do with regular Web pages.

Five Cool Uses for Discussion Web

So why would you start a discussion Web? Because you can. Technical know-how? Phooey. All you need is a good concept, commitment, and FrontPage 2000. The following list can get you started with a few ideas. For links to good discussion group examples and resources, check out Chapter 30, "Building a Web Site That Fits Your Ego."

- *Customer support* Discussion groups are ideal for offering technical support to customers and answering their questions. FrontPage even has a Customer Support Web Wizard to help you set up other resources that your company's customers might need. Chapter 2, "Instant Web-Site-O-Matic: Spinning FrontPage Webs," tells you how to set up a Web.
- *Local happenings* Bring your community together with a discussion Web for your local school or place of worship, or for things happening around town.
- *Special topics* Nobody you know shares your interest in collecting bars of soap from hotels around the world? You can probably find people who share your interests on the Web. Start a fan club or a conversation about current issues, swap home improvement tips, or whatever else catches your fancy.
- *Keeping in touch* Start a discussion group for you and your relatives, old school buddies, or former co-workers, and invite everyone to participate.
- *School or Clubs* If you're taking a class or have joined a club, you can set up a discussion group so people can talk about issues and ask questions between classes or meetings.

The Least You Need to Know

- The Discussion Web Wizard takes you through all the steps of creating a discussion Web.
- Discussion Webs must have a submission form so people can post articles. You can also add a table of contents, a search form, and frames.
- Once you've created your discussion Web, you need to maintain it to keep content fresh and to ensure that it doesn't get bogged down with messages.

Part 5

In the Driver's Seat: Managing Your Web Site

Now that you've created Web pages with exciting and useful content, how do you keep track of it all? Webmasters used to spend a lot of time testing pages, making corrections, and checking for outdated materials. Thanks to FrontPage 2000's helpful site management tools, you can spend less time on the administrative grunt work and more time being creative.

FrontPage's Folders, Tasks, and Reports views make it easy to spot potential problems, fix your pages, and stay on top of Web projects. In addition, FrontPage gives you everything you need to create and maintain a corporate intranet Web site and to publish your pages to the World Wide Web.

This part tells you how to manage files, test your Web site, publish your files to a server, manage and maintain your Webs, use the Reports and Task List features, help visitors find and use your Web site, and build your own intranet. Poof! You're a Web administrator!

Chapter 24

You and Your Web Files

In This Chapter

- Viewing folders and files in the Folders view
- Understanding what all those file details and filename extensions mean
- Creating, renaming, moving, copying, importing, exporting, and deleting files
- Giving your pages titles and summaries
- Closing a Web and exiting FrontPage
- Five cool tips to help you manage Web files

Web files are kind of like bunny rabbits. You've got to keep an eye on them because they multiply mighty fast! So how do you keep track of your Web pages, pictures, and other stuff? Take a peek at your Web site in the Folders view and show your files who's boss.

Peeking at Files and Folders in the Folders View

Psst! Wanna see what's on your Web site? Take a peek at your files and folders by clicking Folders on the Views list. FrontPage displays a Folder List and a File list so you can view all of your folders and files.

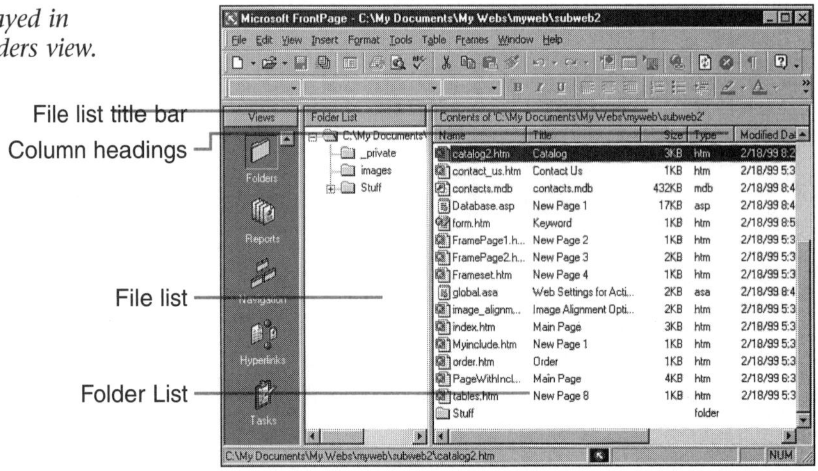

Web files displayed in FrontPage's Folders view.

Folders and Subfolders

Depending on how you've set up your Web site, you also may have folders that contain other folders. When a folder contains other folders, a + sign appears next to it. You can expand the Folder List to display a folder's subfolders by clicking the + sign. The + sign then changes to a - sign. To collapse a Folder List so the subfolders no longer appear, click the - sign.

Viewing Folders on Your Folder List

The Folder List on the left displays the main folder (root directory) for the current Web, along with your other Web folders. FrontPage automatically generates an `images` folder for your pictures and a `_private` folder for your FrontPage components, as covered in Chapter 19, "A Grab Bag of Helpful Doodads: FrontPage Components."

What the Heck Is It? Understanding Your File List

The File list contains a list of files and folders with helpful file details organized under column headings. The Title bar displays the directory path (location) for the current Web. You can use this information to keep your Web site running smoothly and to get rid of files you don't need.

Of course, the file details are pretty useless unless you know what they mean. In the Folders view, file details are organized into columns. They tell you things like the file size, file type, and the last time someone made changes to the file.

- *Name* Displays the names of your Web files.
- *Title* Displays titles for your Web files. Web page titles are displayed in the Web browser's title bar, as covered in Chapter 3, "Fooling Around with Web Pages." You can also give titles to other types of files to help you remember what those files contain.

- *Size* Displays the file size in kilobytes (KB). It's a good idea to do a little weight-watching when it comes to your Web files. Heftier files take longer for your visitors to download. Remember, the status bar in the Page view will estimate the download time.
- *Type* Displays filename extensions for each file so you'll know what kind of files you've got on your Web site. The following section gives you a crash course in filename extensions.
- *Modified Date* Displays the last time a file on your Web site was edited or updated. This helps you keep track of pages that need to be updated or removed altogether.
- *Modified by* Displays the username of the person who last worked on a file. If you share your FrontPage Web with co-workers, roommates, or family members, you can see who's done what in an instant. For more about server administration and generating reports to keep track of stuff, see Chapters 27, "You're the Boss! Becoming a Web Site Administrator," and 28, "Keeping Track of It All with the Task List."
- *Comments* Displays a preview of summary information for each file. Summaries tell you what each file contains and help search engines work more effectively. (Chapter 19 tells you how to set up a search engine.) Chapter 18, "A Match Made in Redmond: FrontPage and Microsoft Office 2000," talks about creating summaries from within a file. You can also create file summaries from the Folders view, as covered later in this chapter.

Filename Extensions 101

On Windows computers and on the Web, all filenames are followed by a period and a filename extension, as in `MyWebPage.htm` or `MyPicture.jpeg`. When you open a file or a file loads in your Web browser, the filename extension tells your computer which program it should use to handle the file. For example, if you click a link to an AVI movie, Windows opens the built-in multimedia player.

When you work with files in Windows 95 or Windows 98, you don't always see the filename extensions. Windows normally hides them from you. However, since filename extensions are so important on the Web, FrontPage always shows them to you.

Show Your Filename Extensions!

Windows doesn't always show you the filename extensions for the files on your computer, but you can tell Windows to do so. Open a folder and select Folder Options from the View menu to display the Folder Options dialog box. Click the View tab and deselect the Hide file extensions for known file types check box, click the Reset All Folders button, and then click OK to apply your changes and return to your desktop.

When you view your Web files, you may see the following Web filename extensions:

- `.HTM` *or* `.HTML` *for Web pages* HTML stands for Hypertext Markup Language, the set of codes used to format Web pages. For more about HTML, see Chapter 3.
- `.ASP` *for Active Server Pages* An active server page is a type of Web page that contains special scripts. FrontPage and FrontPage servers support ASP. For more about ASP and other programmed Web pages, see Chapter 21, "Rev Up Your Web Site with Programs and Scripts."
- `.JS` *for JScript scripts* JScript is Microsoft and Internet Explorer's answer to Netscape Navigator's JavaScript—a Web page scripting language. When you create animated special effects for your pages, as covered in Chapter 20, "Gee-Whiz Pages with Animated Special Effects," FrontPage automatically generates JScript files for you. For more about Web page scripting, see Chapter 21.
- `.CLASS` *for Java applets* Java applets are programs that run in a Web browser. When you create hover buttons and other special components, FrontPage creates the Java applets for you.
- `.CGI` *and* `.PL` *for server scripts* Before FrontPage came along, people who wanted to process Web forms, create hit counters, and do other cool stuff had to write Common Gateway Interface (`.CGI`) scripts that run on a server. *Perl* (`.PL`) is a popular language for writing CGI scripts. If your Web site existed before you or your company installed FrontPage, you may find a script or two in your Web. In most cases, CGI scripts are stored in a folder called `CGI_Bin` or `CGI_Win`.
- `.DOC`, `.XLS`, `.PPT`, `.Pub`, *and* `.MDB` *for Office files* If you've imported Word documents (`.DOC`), Excel workbooks (`.XLS`), PowerPoint presentations (`.PPT`), Publisher publications (`.PUB`), or Access databases (`.MDB`) into your Web, you'll find some or all of these filename extensions floating around your Web. You can also format your Office files as Web pages, as covered in Chapter 18.

- `.GIF` *or* `.JPEG` These are Web-friendly image formats, as covered in Chapters 8, "The Picture-Perfect Web Page: Placing and Tweaking Images," and 9, "Spiffing Up Pictures." FrontPage normally stores pictures in the `images` folder in your Web.
- `.TXT` *for text files* When you create a Web form (Chapter 13, "Form and Function: Building Online Forms") or set up a discussion group (Chapter 23, "Switchboard Central: Setting Up a Discussion Web"), FrontPage gives you options for saving your visitors' information to a plain text file. FrontPage generally stores text files to the `_private` folder.
- `.AU`, `.WAV`, `.AIFF`, `.MIDI`, `.MP2` *for audio files* If you use sound files on your Web site that you've recorded yourself, downloaded from the Web, or grabbed from the Clip Art Gallery (covered in Chapter 8), they'll have one of these filename extensions. For more about multimedia, see Chapter 17, "Strut Your Stuff: Sound, Video, and More."
- `.AVI`, `.VFW`, `.MOV`, `.MPEG` *for video files* If you've put movies on your Web site, they'll have one of these filename extensions. For more about multimedia, see Chapter 17.
- `.EXE` *for executable files* An executable file is a program, such as the many commercial or shareware applications you already have on your computer. If you distribute any shareware programs, games, or ActiveX controls through your Web site, these files will have the `.EXE` filename extension. For more about ActiveX controls, see Chapter 21.
- `.CSS` *for cascading style sheets* Style sheet documents contain information that helps format text and other page elements on a Web site. For more about cascading style sheets, see Chapter 15, "Now You're Stylin'! Using Style Sheets."

Displaying Files Within a Folder

When you display your Web site in the Folders view, FrontPage automatically displays the files contained in the main Web folder. So how do you find out what's in your other folders? Click a folder and the File list for that folder appears. To return to the main folder for your Web, click the folder icon at the top of the Folder List.

Information, Please? Adjusting File Detail Column Widths

The FrontPage Folders view organizes file details under column headings. But unless you have a huge monitor, some of the file information gets cut off, such as titles, modification dates, or columns. You can fix this by adjusting the width for that column. Click a column divider to display the two-way arrow cursor, and then drag it to the right or left until all of the column information is displayed in the list of files below.

Sorting Your File List

The Folders view automatically displays your files alphabetically by filename. Want to view your File list by page title, file type, modification date, or file size instead? It's as easy as clicking a column heading. When you click a column heading once, FrontPage sorts your File list in *ascending order* (from A-Z, least recent to most recent, or lesser to greater). When you click a column heading again, FrontPage sorts your File list in *descending order.*

Fooling Around with Files

Want to rename a file, give it a new title, add a summary, or move it to a different folder? You can do all those things instantly from the Folders view. When you change a file's name or location, FrontPage automatically adjusts any pages that link to that file so your Web site will continue to work properly. If you've ever used the Windows Explorer to manage the files on your computer, FrontPage's Folders view will look familiar to you. If you haven't, not to worry. This chapter shows you how to take charge of your files.

Renaming Files

Whoops! That filename doesn't make any sense! Whether you're reorganizing your Web site or didn't type the filename correctly the first time, you can change the filenames for your pages, pictures, and other files anytime.

To rename a file, right-click it from the list to display the shortcut menu, and then select Rename. When FrontPage highlights the filename, type a new filename for it. (Make sure to include the correct filename extension!) When the Rename dialog box appears and asks if you want to update other pages on your site so the hyperlinks will not be broken, click Yes.

Creating a New Page

If you want to add a new page to your Web site but don't plan to work on it right away, you can do it from the Folders view. This comes in handy when you're building a new Web site from scratch and want to set up a FrontPage navigation bar, as covered in Chapters 7, "Think Links: Adding Links to Your Pages," and 14, "Don't Like What You See? Designing Your Own Page Template."

To create your brand-spanking-new Web page, select New from the File menu and then select Page from the cascading menu. Or you can skip those two steps and use the Ctrl+N key combination instead. FrontPage adds a new Web page to your list and names it `new_page_1.htm`. You can then rename the page, as explained in the previous section.

Creating a New Folder

As your Web site grows—and they almost always do—you may want to create folders for different sections or types of content. For example, if your company has pages for each employee and it suddenly expands from five to 25 employees, you may want to create a special `People` folder for everyone's Web pages.

To create a new folder, select New from the File menu and select Folder from the cascading menu. When FrontPage creates the new folder and adds it to your list as `New_Folder`, you can rename it the same way you would rename a file.

Moving Files to Another Folder

As your Web site grows, you may need to shuffle things around a bit and move your Web pages, pictures, and other files around. To move a file into another folder, select the file from the File list and drag it into a folder on the Folder List. The Rename dialog box appears to tell you that FrontPage is changing the pages that link to the file so they'll continue to work properly.

You can also move a file to another folder with the cut-and-paste method. Select a file, choose Cut from the Edit menu (or use the Ctrl+X key combination), open a folder by selecting it from the Folder List, and select Paste from the Edit menu (or use the Ctrl+V key combination).

Copying and Pasting Files

Why create all your new pages from scratch? Sometimes it's easier to copy an existing page and paste it into your Web as a new page instead. You can then rename the new page and start working on it. The old copy-and-paste trick also works great for pictures and other types of files too.

First, copy your file by selecting it from the File list and choosing Copy from the Edit menu (or use the Ctrl+C key combination). Then, paste the new file by selecting Paste from the Edit menu (or use the Ctrl+V key combination). FrontPage adds the new file to the File list and gives it the same name as the original file followed by the word `Copy` and a number in parentheses, as in `MyFile_Copy(1).htm`. You can then rename the file, as explained earlier in this chapter.

Remember Your Key Combinations!

Dragging down menus can sure be a drag sometimes. That's why I've been giving you key combinations throughout the book. When you're managing your Web files, the following key combinations can save a little wear and tear on your mouse hand:

Ctrl+C Copies the selected file, text, or object.

Ctrl+X Cuts the selected file, text, or object so you can paste it to another location.

Ctrl+V Pastes a file, block of text, or object that has been copied or cut.

Ctrl+A Selects all of the files in a folder or all of the text and objects in a file.

Ctrl+O Opens the selected file.

Ctrl+F4 Closes a file (available only from the Page view).

You can also use key combinations to find and replace words and phrases or check the spelling throughout your Web site, as covered in Chapter 25, "Testing, Testing, One, Two, Three: Checking Your Web Site":

Ctrl+F Displays the Find dialog box.

Ctrl+H Displays the Find and Replace dialog box.

Ctrl+Z Cancels the previous action.

Ctrl+Y Redoes a canceled action.

F7 Displays the Spelling dialog box.

Importing Files into Your Web

Chances are you've got some Web pages, pictures, and other stuff on your computer that you'd like to add to your Web site. If so, go ahead and import them. Did you already have a Web site up and running before you picked up FrontPage 2000? Then you may have used the Import Web wizard to bring your files into your FrontPage Web. You can also import individual files whenever you need to—with fewer steps!

To import files from your computer or a computer on a network, select Import from the File menu to display the Import dialog box. Click the Add File button to display the Add File to Import List dialog box, browse for a file, select the file, and click the Open button to return to the Import dialog box. When the file appears on the File list, you can click OK to import the file, or you can choose additional options.

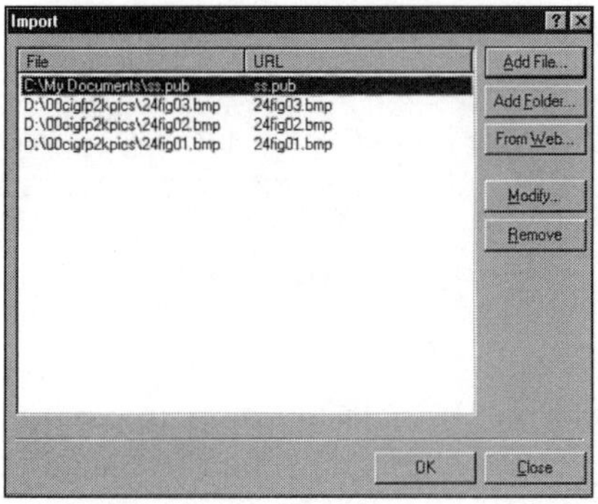

The Import dialog box.

The Import dialog box provides the following choices:

- *Add File* Add a new file to the Import File list.
- *Add Folder* Add an entire folder full of files to the Import File list.
- *From Web* Add files from another FrontPage Web to the Import File list.
- *Modify* Display the Edit URL dialog box so you can type a directory path (such as `myfolder/filename.htm`) to import the selected file into a particular folder.
- *Remove* Removes the selected file from the Import File list so FrontPage does not import it to your Web.
- *Close* Closes the Import dialog box without importing any files.
- *OK* Imports the files into your Web from your File List.

Opening a Web Page from the Folders View

With FrontPage, you can easily open a Web page from the Folders view and start working on it. Just select a page from the list and choose Open from the File menu (or use the Ctrl+O key combination). You can also try double-clicking a page.

Exporting Files from Your Web

Back in kindergarten our teachers always told us to share, right? If you want to share a Web page with a coworker, you can export pages to another FrontPage Web. To save a Web page to a different location, open the file in the Page view and select Save As from the File menu. When the Save As dialog box appears, browse for a folder and click the Save button. If your Web page contains any images or other embedded files, the Save Embedded Files dialog box appears with a list of files. Click OK to make sure those files get sent over with your page!

Removing Files and Folders from Your Web

Need to clean out some of your tired old files? Select a file or folder and press the Delete key. When the Confirm Delete dialog box appears and asks if you're sure you want to remove the file, click the Yes button. If you've selected more than one file, click the Yes to All button.

Displaying File Properties

To view more details about a file, including the file summary and who created it, you can display the file's Properties dialog box by right-clicking the file and selecting Properties from the shortcut menu. Or you can click the file and select Properties from the File menu. When the Properties dialog box appears, you can view information by clicking a tab:

- *General* Shows the filename, title, file type, where the file is located, and file size (in kilobytes (KB) if the file is 1KB or more, or in bytes otherwise).
- *Summary* Displays the file's summary (Comments), the creation date (Created), who created the file (Created by), when the file was last edited (Modified), and who last edited the file (Modified by).
- *Workgroup* Shows the category and status of a file, and shows the person in charge of it. For more about collaborating with coworkers on files, see Chapter 29, "It Doesn't Take a Village to Build an Intranet: Publishing, Sharing, and Updating Files."

Changing Page Titles

As you may remember from earlier chapters, you can title your Web pages when you first save them, or you can do so from the Page Properties dialog box. When a page is viewed in a Web browser, the page title appears in the browser's title bar. Titles also come in handy when you look over your Web site in the Folders view. You can use them to provide brief descriptions for each page.

To change a page title from the Folders view, right-click the filename and select Properties from the shortcut menu. When the Properties dialog box appears with the General tab selected, type a title in the Title box and click OK. When you return to the Folders view, the new page title appears.

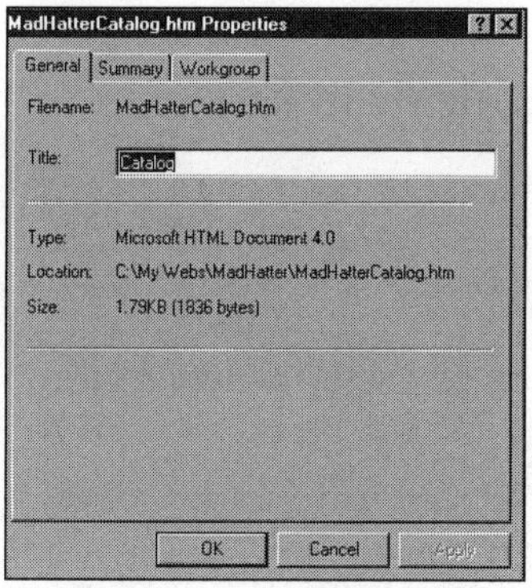

The Properties dialog box.

Creating Page Summaries

If you work on a Web site with your co-workers, or your Web site is starting to get large, you can also create summaries for your pages. A summary is a brief description or list of keywords associated with the page. If you add a Search component to your Web site, as covered in Chapter 19, your summaries help your on-site search engine find files more quickly for your visitors. The first few words of the file summaries appear in the Comments column on the file list.

To create a page summary, right-click a file and choose Properties from the shortcut menu. When the Properties dialog box is displayed, click the Summary tab, type a summary in the scrolling Comments box, and click OK to return to the Folders view. As with titles, you can also create summaries for pictures and other types of files. If you use other Microsoft Office programs, you can also create summaries for Word, Excel, Publisher, PowerPoint, and Access files before you import them into FrontPage, as covered in Chapter 18.

Jog Your Memory!

You can also create titles for pictures and other files to help you remember what they are and what they go with. By default, FrontPage titles non-Web page files with the directory path and filename, as in `images/MyPicture.jpeg`.

Closing FrontPage

Need to take a break? You can close FrontPage by selecting Exit from the File menu or clicking the X in the upper-right corner of the application window.

Closing a Web

You can also close your Web without exiting FrontPage by selecting Close Web from the File menu.

Five Cool Tips to Help You Manage Web Files

Managing a Web site and keeping track of all your files can be big job, but you can try out the following tips to make the job easier:

- *Try nested sub-Webs* Nested sub-Webs come in handy when you have different departments, family members, or groups of coworkers working on different parts of a Web site. Nested sub-Webs are Web folders in a FrontPage Web that also function as FrontPage Webs. You can publish them independently of the rest of your FrontPage Web, assign them to workgroups, and more. For more about nested sub-Webs, read Chapter 27.
- *Select multiple files* When you need to move files around or delete them, you can select more than one file at a time. To select a group of consecutive files, hold down the Shift key and click on the files at the top and bottom of the list. This also selects the files in-between. To select a group of non-consecutive files, hold down the Ctrl key and click on each of the files.
- *Group files by name* By default, FrontPage sorts files in alphabetical order. You can group files together on the file list by naming them with the same first letters or numbers, as in `Catalog_Fall.htm`, `Catalog_Spring.htm`, `Catalog_Summer.htm`, and `Catalog_Winter.htm`.
- *Create folders* If you have a particularly large and complex Web site with many types of files, you can also create folders for different sections and file types.
- *Use the Task list* If you get interrupted a lot or tend to forget things, Task lists and reports can help you remember the different things you need to do. For more information, see Chapter 28.

The Least You Need to Know

- You can display all of your folders and files in the Folders view. When you click a folder on the Folder List, the contents appear on the File list.
- The File list shows the files in the current folder, along with details such as the filename, title, file size, file type, last editing date, last user to edit the file, and comments (a summary).
- You can sort items on the File list by clicking column headings. You can also adjust the widths of different column headings to better see your file details.
- All filenames are followed with a period and a filename extension, as in `.HTM` or `.JPEG`. The filename extension tells computers and Web browsers the type of file and which application should be launched to handle the file.
- You can create, move, copy, rename, import, and delete files from the Folders view. You can also open a Web page straight from the File list.
- For additional information about a file, select the file and display the Properties dialog box. You can also change a page title, type a summary, or assign categories and people to files. (Chapter 29 tells you more about collaborating with others on your Web site.)

Chapter 25

Testing, Testing, One, Two, Three: Checking Your Web Site

In This Chapter

- Displaying Web site reports to check for problem pages—and fix them too!
- Browsing your Web pages
- Ten totally uncool Web site bloopers to avoid

Do you have a fussy relative whose visits put you in a tizzy? We all have one who just loves to point out all the dust bunnies, unwashed dishes, full wastebaskets, and other examples of your crummy housekeeping skills. Sadly, many Web site visitors act that way too. And they especially enjoy sending you email messages that list all of the errors they find on your Web pages!

If you do all of the things described in this chapter, they won't find a single thing to complain about. FrontPage makes it easy to check your spelling, search and replace text throughout your Web site, make sure all your links work, and generate helpful reports about the files on your site. You should also view all of your pages individually and make sure they work right.

What's the Scoop? Displaying Web Site Reports

With FrontPage, you can display reports that help you check for problems with your Web site. To view reports for your Web, click the Reports icon from the Views list. The Reports toolbar should also appear (if it doesn't, choose Toolbars from the View menu and select Reports from the cascading list). You can then select Site Summary from the Reports list for an overview of your Web site, as shown in the following figure.

The FrontPage Reports view with the Site Summary and Reports toolbar displayed.

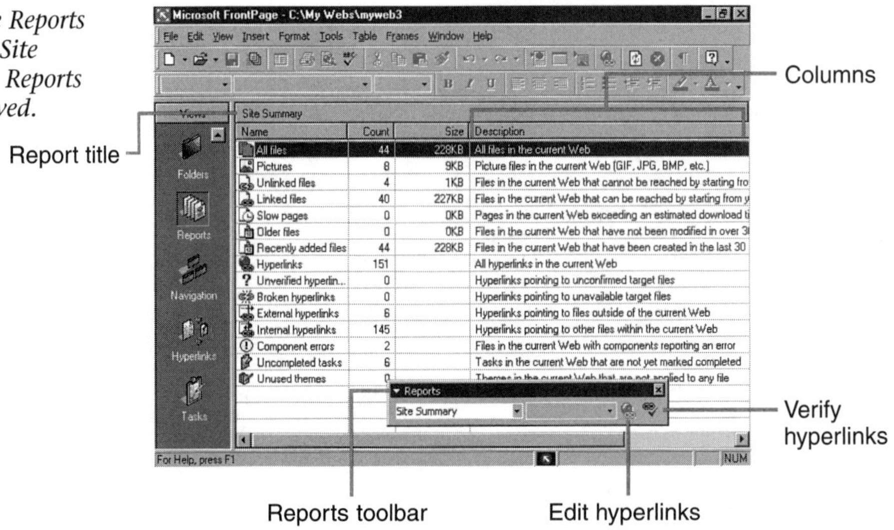

The Site Summary lists different categories, such as broken hyperlinks, the number of times each element occurs on your Web site, the total file size (when relevant), and a description of each category. To view the details for a category, double-click the list item or select the category from the Reports list.

A complete list of report categories follows, and the following sections tell you how to use those reports to keep your Web site running properly.

- *Site Summary* Provides general information about your Web site, such as the number of unverified hyperlinks and the number of uncompleted tasks.
- *All Files* Displays a list of all the files on your Web site, with details about each file.
- *Recently Added Files* Lists all files that you've added within a certain number of days, along with file details. You can change the number of days by selecting an item from the list on the Reports toolbar.
- *Recently Changed Files* Shows a list of files that you've edited within a certain number of days, along with file details. You can change the number of days by selecting an item from the list on the Reports toolbar.
- *Older Files* Lists all files that are older than a certain number of days, along with file details. You can change the number of days by selecting an item from the list on the Reports toolbar.
- *Unlinked Files* Displays a list of files that are not associated with or linked to any pages in your Web. This comes in handy when you want to remove unneeded files from your Web site.
- *Slow Pages* Shows a list of Web sites that may take too long to download.
- *Broken Hyperlinks* Lists any links on your Web site that don't work.

- *Component Errors* Warns you if your Web site has any components that don't work, and suggests ways to fix them. Sometimes fixing a component is as easy as reinserting it. For more information, see Chapter 19, "A Grab Bag of Helpful Doodads: FrontPage Components."
- *Review Status* Displays a list of files, along with status information so you can track projects more easily. For more on tracking projects, see Chapter 29, "It Doesn't Take a Village to Build an Intranet: Publishing, Sharing, and Updating Files."
- *Assigned to* Lists all of your files and who they've been assigned to. For more on assigning files to people, see Chapter 29.
- *Categories* Shows a list of your Web files, along with the category, title, file type, and folder. For more on assigning categories to files, see Chapter 29.
- *Publish Status* Tells you whether or not pages have been published. Chapter 29 tells you how to keep FrontPage from publishing pages that still need work. Also see Chapter 26, "Don't Just Let It Sit There! Publishing Your Web Site."

About the Reports Toolbar

As with many of FrontPage's toolbars, menus, and dialog boxes, the Reports toolbar is *adaptive*. It changes depending on the type of report you select.

Checking Your Links

Testing links on a Web site used to take a lot of time because you had to click on every single one of them. Now you can relax because FrontPage can check your links for you. When you select Broken Hyperlinks from the Reports menu, a list of problem links appears with the URL, the pages that contain the link, and the titles of those pages.

If a link just doesn't work, a broken chain link icon appears next to the word "Broken" in the Status column. If you have a link to an external Web page (a page on someone else's Web site), FrontPage may not have verified the link yet. If so, a question mark icon appears next to the word "Unknown" in the Status column.

Verifying External Links

To check unknown links to other Web sites, display the Broken Links report and click the Verify Hyperlinks button on the Reports toolbar. When the Verify Hyperlinks dialog box appears, select the Verify all hyperlinks radio button and then click the Start button. If you haven't connected to the Internet yet, the Dial-up Connection dialog box appears so you can dial up your account. When the Verify Hyperlinks dialog box appears, select the Verify all hyperlinks radio button, and click the Start button. If a link works, FrontPage displays a check mark followed by the word "OK" in the Status column. If the link doesn't work, FrontPage marks it as "Broken" in the Status column.

You don't have to check all of your links at once. You can select particular items from the Broken Hyperlinks report (click on each item while holding down the Ctrl key), and then click the Verify Hyperlinks button. When the Verify Hyperlinks dialog box appears, select the Verify selected hyperlink(s) button and click the Start button.

What If I Get Disconnected?

Getting disconnected from the Internet sure is annoying when you're checking your links! Luckily, FrontPage has got you covered. Reconnect, go back to the Broken Hyperlinks report, and display the Verify Hyperlinks dialog box again. You can then select the Resume verification radio button, click Start, and pick up where you left off.

Correcting Your Links

Want to correct your broken links? Select an item from the Broken Hyperlinks report list and click the Edit Hyperlinks button on the Reports toolbar to display the Edit Hyperlink dialog box, as shown in the following figure. Type the correct URL (as in `http://www.yourwebsite.com/page.htm`) in the Replace hyperlink with box, click the Change in all pages radio button to apply your change to any pages on your Web site that contains the broken link, and click the Replace button. You can also automatically correct your internal links by selecting Recalculate Hyperlinks from the Tools menu.

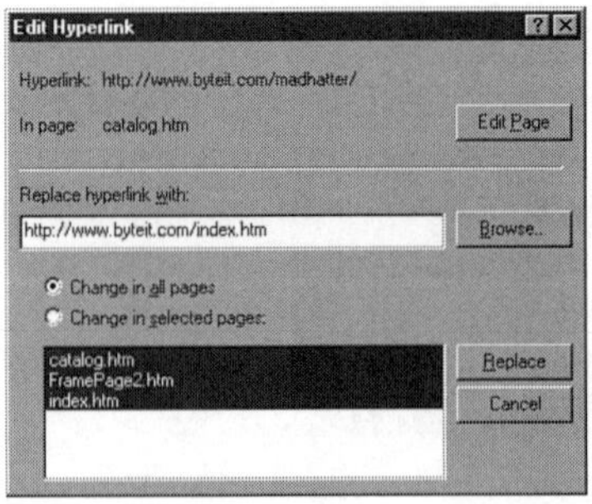

The Edit Hyperlink dialog box.

Keeping Your Content Fresh

Even the coolest Web pages can get stale after a while. Some companies update all of their Web pages every single day. Whew! That's a lot of work. In most situations, you probably only need to update your Web pages every week, month, or even six months. Regardless of how often you plan to change the material on your pages, it's a good idea to check for older files so you can decide whether or not to freshen them up.

To display a list of pages that haven't been updated in a while, select Older Files from the Reports list and select a number of days from the Report Setting list. For example, if you want to update your pages once every month, you should select 30 days to find documents that haven't been updated within the last 30 days. When a list of pages is displayed, you can double-click list items to edit the pages.

Finding Slow Pages

As a rule of thumb, anyone who uses a 28.8Kbps modem shouldn't have to wait more than 15 or 20 seconds for your page to download. Some pages can't help being slow, of course, and your visitors will expect that. For example, when people follow a link to your embedded multimedia presentation, a 50-page report, or an 8×10 inch picture, they're expecting to wait a while.

To see if your pages are up to speed, select Slow Pages from the Reports list and a number of seconds from the Report Setting list. The Slow Pages report lists the filenames, page titles, download times, sizes, and document types. To view and edit a page in the normal page view, select the page from the Slow Pages report list and then click the Page icon from the Views list.

Speeding Up Slow Pages

So how can you speed up pages that take too long to download? In most cases, graphics are the culprit. You may have to edit your slow pages and remove some of the images. Getting rid of fancy stuff, like background sounds and animated special effects, can also speed up pages. You can also visit the GIF Wizard home page at `http://www.gifwizard.com/`. It will make your GIF image files smaller—and they'll still look great. You can find more tips in Chapter 8, "The Picture-Perfect Web Page: Placing and Tweaking Images."

Fixing Component Errors

FrontPage components (covered in Chapter 19) help you add cool things to your Web site, like a site search engine. Although FrontPage makes components seem simple and easy, they're actually quite complicated. And once in a while they don't run properly. This sometimes happens when you move a page or file that the component needs in order to work.

To check for problems with your FrontPage components, select Component Errors from the Reports list. The Components Errors report displays a list of files with the page name and title, a description of the error, and the file type. To open the page and fix the component error (or delete the component and re-create it), select the page from the list and then either double-click the filename or click the Page icon from the Views menu.

Don't Forget the Task List!

Before you publish your Web site, you should also check your task list and make sure you haven't forgotten anything. The task list reminds you about things you need to do on your Web site, such as fixing misspelled words or adding information to pages that were generated with wizards. To display your task list, click the Task icon on the View list. For more on working with your task list, see Chapter 28, "Keeping Track of It All with the Task List."

Browsing Your Web Site

Sure, FrontPage has lots of helpful tools that help you find and correct problems. But it's still a good idea to test all of the pages on your Web site with your browser. You can do this by opening your pages in FrontPage and clicking the Preview in Browser toolbar button. Or you can launch your browser, type in the local URL for the home page of your Web site (such as `http://mycomputer/mywebsite/index.htm`), and then follow all of your links.

PDAs, Too!

No, I'm not referring to public displays of affection. I'm talking about all the people who use personal digital assistants (PDAs), like the popular Palm Pilot. Nowadays, lots of people use PDAs to surf the Web, even though PDA browsers have limited capabilities and can only display text. The Accessibility Wizard also helps PDA users navigate your Web site.

Remember Everyone

When you're creating a Web site, you should also remember to take the handicapped into consideration. For example, if you add alternative text to your pictures, as covered in Chapter 8, people with vision problems can hear a description of your images when their voice software reads your pages aloud. If you use graphics for links, these people may need descriptions of your pictures so they can get around your Web site.

Aren't you glad that FrontPage comes with an Accessibility Add-In to help make your Web site a friendlier place? Put your FrontPage CD in your CD-ROM drive, select Add-Ins from the Tools menu, and then select Accessibility to launch the Accessibility Wizard. The wizard checks your Web pages for accessibility issues, points out problems, and suggests ways to fix them.

Ten Totally Uncool Web Site Bloopers to Avoid

- *Spelling mistakes* Spelling mistakes look unprofessional, and they annoy people! FrontPage's spell checker gives you an edge over everyone else.
- *Broken links* FrontPage makes it easy to check for and correct broken links. Also, the Web changes all the time, so you'll need to check your links to other Web sites occasionally to make sure the pages still exist.
- *Unlinked pages* Don't leave your visitors stranded! When you put pages on the Web, remember to add links to the other pages on your Web site. To display a list of unlinked pages, go to the Reports view and select Unlinked Pages from the Reports list.
- *Bandwidth behemoths* People don't like waiting more than 15 or 20 seconds for a page to download. Too many images, sounds, or pages of text can weigh a page down. FrontPage lets you check for slow pages so you can decide whether or not to slim them down.
- *Permanent construction zones* Sure, you can put an "under construction" sign on a page when you don't have time to finish it today. But if you leave the page unfinished for weeks or months, visitors will stop coming back.
- *Pages that just don't work* Make sure to test all your pages in your own Web browser and make sure your FrontPage components, plug-ins, and animated special effects work correctly. You can also generate a report that tells you if there are problems with your FrontPage components.
- *Endlessly scrolling pages* If you publish reports and other long documents to your Web site, don't make your visitors scroll too much. It's a good idea to create bookmarks and provide links throughout the document so visitors won't have to scroll for more than a page and a half or so. Chapter 7, "Think Links: Adding Links to Your Pages," tells you how to create bookmarks and links.
- *Frameset orphans* If you use frames on your Web site, be nice to visitors who may accidentally stumble onto a page that belongs in a frameset. This may confuse people because framed pages often don't make any sense without the rest of the frames. You can create links on all your pages that people can click to view the pages as you intended. Chapter 11, "Get Framed! Building a Web Site with Frames," tells you how to work with frames.
- *Web page circuses* Special effects, FrontPage components, animations, text marquees, background sounds, and multimedia are way cool. But gaudy pages with too many dancing and singing elements can make people dizzy! Limit your fun stuff to one or two elements per page.
- *Unreadable pages* Tiny fonts, insufficient contrast between the background and text colors, cluttered layouts, and other factors can make Web pages impossible to read. Ask some of your coworkers or friends to take a look at your pages before publishing them to the whole wide world.

The Least You Need to Know

- Before you publish your Web site, you should check every page and make sure you haven't made any embarrassing mistakes. Luckily, FrontPage comes with lots of features that can help you tune up your Web site.
- You can use FrontPage's built-in spell checker to search your entire Web site for misspelled words. When it displays a list of pages with spelling errors, you can open the pages and make the corrections.
- You can find and replace text throughout all of the pages on your Web site. This will come in handy if you make the same mistake on more than one Web page.
- You can display reports with lists of broken links, older Web pages that may need updating, slow pages that take too long to download, component errors, and unfinished tasks from the Reports view.
- FrontPage also makes it easy to correct broken links and edit pages from the Reports view.
- You should also preview your Web pages with a browser, follow your links, and test all your components to make sure your Web site looks and behaves the way you want it to.

Chapter 26

Don't Just Let It *Sit* There! Publishing Your Web Site

In This Chapter

- The difference between local and remote Web servers
- Publishing your Web site to a server
- Special publishing options
- Search engines and how you can help them find and catalog your pages
- Registering your Web site with search engines
- Creating content ratings for your Web site
- Ten cool tips for bringing visitors to your Web site

Now that you've built your Web site, you probably just want to let it sit on your computer so you can admire it... *Not!* You'll want to publish your fabulous creation for everyone to see, of course. Publishing a Web site means *uploading* all your stuff to an Internet server. Servers are computers that other people can connect to so they can view your pages, and uploading is the opposite of downloading. You download stuff from servers every time you surf the Web. When you enter a URL or click a link, you're asking a server to give you text, pictures, or other files, which then appear in your browser.

Uploading files isn't quite as simple as downloading them, and that's a darned good thing. Imagine a world where anyone could put their stuff on other people's servers whenever they wanted! On second thought, let's not. FrontPage's Publish tool makes uploading files as easy as possible, while still making sure that only people with the correct password can put stuff on your Web site.

And once you get your Web site up and running, you'd like people to visit, right? Whether you're building a Web site for business or fun, this chapter tells you about some simple things you can do to attract visitors to your site. You'll also learn how to make sure visitors can read what's on your pages once they get there.

Remote and Local Servers—What's the Diff?

No, the term *remote server* doesn't mean a computer located in Afghanistan. It refers to a computer that you can access through your Internet service provider (ISP) or Web host. A *local server* is located somewhere in your office (or your house—in which case you probably already know the difference between local and remote servers). You don't have to dial up your Internet account to access a local server because you're connected to it all the time. Whether you publish your pages to a remote server or a local one, the FrontPage Publisher asks you for a URL and may request a username and password as well.

Publishing Your Web Site

Are you ready? Okay, let's go. First, you'll need to connect to the Internet if you plan to upload your Web site to a remote server. Then open your Web in FrontPage and select Publish Web from the File menu. When the Publish Web dialog box appears (as shown in the following figure), enter the URL for your Web site in the Specify Location to publish your FrontPage Web to: box and then click the Publish button. The next time you publish, your URL will appear as a list item so that you won't have to type it in again. This feature comes in especially handy if you publish Webs to more than one location; you can just pick the correct URL from the list and away you go.

FrontPage's Publish Web dialog box.

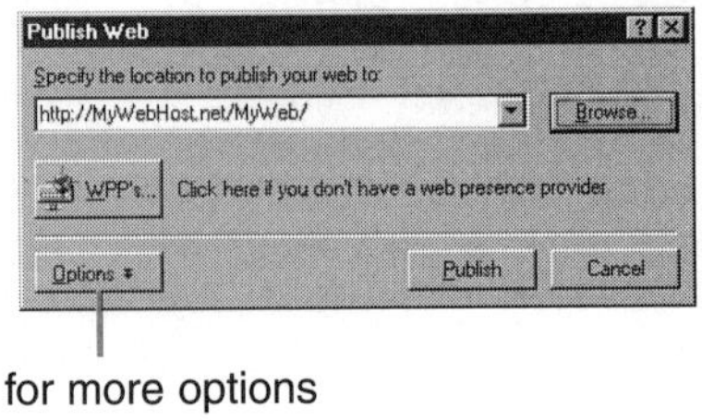

Depending on your Web host's setup, FrontPage may also ask for your username and password. A dialog box then appears to show you how the upload is progressing. Depending on your connection speed and how much stuff you've got on your Web site, publishing might take a while. Go ahead and take a coffee break.

If you aren't sure of the location of your Web site, click the Browse button. The Connection dialog box appears so you can connect to the Internet and find the Web site through your Web browser. When you close the Connection dialog box, the Open Web dialog box appears so you can browse for a folder on your network.

A FrontPage Publisher Info Checklist

Before you begin publishing your Web site, you'll need the following information. If you don't have it, ask your ISP, Web host, or network administrator.

Web location With FrontPage, you always enter a URL beginning with `http://` to publish your pages—even if you're publishing to a local server. For example, a remote URL looks something like `http://www.YourWebsite.com` (or `http://www.YourISP.com/YourWebSite/`), and a local URL looks something like `http://LocalServer/YourWeb/`.

Directory path Sometimes you may need to upload a Web page to a folder within an existing Web site. This happens when one server hosts more than one Web. In this case, you would enter a URL that points to a server or domain, along with the directory path, such as `http://www.YourWebsite.com/MainWeb/YourWeb/` for a remote server, or `http://LocalServer/MainWeb/YourWeb/` for a local server.

Username and password In most situations, a dialog box will appear and ask for your username and password. So make sure you've got them handy.

More Publishing Options

Need more options? You've got 'em. From the Publish FrontPage Web dialog box, click the Options button to display the options (see the following figure). To publish only new files and pages that you've changed so you don't have to upload your entire Web site, click the Publish changed pages only check box. To include your nested sub-Webs with your uploads, click the Include subwebs check box. (For more on nested sub-Webs, see Chapter 27, "You're the Boss! Becoming a Web Site Administrator.") If your Web host requires a secure connection (most do not), click the Secure connection required (SSL) check box.

The Expanded Publish Web dialog box.

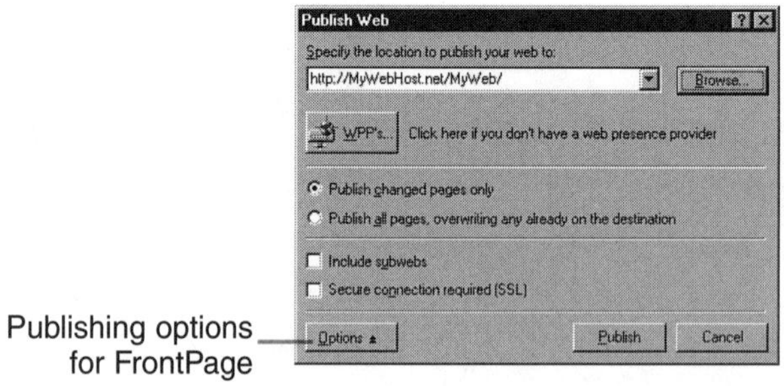

Signing Up with a FrontPage-Friendly Web Host

If you haven't yet signed on with a Web host that supports FrontPage, now's your chance. Click the WPPs (Web Presence Providers) button in the Publish Web dialog box. FrontPage launches your browser and jumps you to a list of ISPs and Web hosting companies that provide FrontPage server extensions. You also might want to flip through your phone book or look through ads in local newspapers to find a FrontPage-friendly Web host or ISP near you. After all, Microsoft can't list them all.

How People Find Web Sites

How do people find Web sites? There are lots of ways. Most of the time, Web site visitors come from cyberspace. They follow a link from someone else's Web site or their ISP's site, locate a site through a search engine like Yahoo!, or click a banner ad (those advertisements that you see everywhere on the Web).

People also find Web sites through more old-fashioned methods: word of mouth, print advertisements, business cards, brochures, or reviews or write-ups in publications. And of course, there's always email—if someone likes your Web site, they might email your URL to a friend.

You don't need a huge advertising budget to get the word out. You can start out on the right foot by registering with search engines (I'll tell you how later in this chapter) and announcing your Web site by email to all your friends, family, and business associates. You can also send press releases to newspapers and publications. Finally, you'll find a list of ten useful tips for attracting visitors at the end of this chapter.

Don't Forget Your ISP or Web Host!

Many ISPs and Web hosting companies provide links to their customers' Web sites. They offer Web forms where you can submit information about your Web site (usually its name and a brief description) and be added to the company's list or database. Smaller companies often list customer Web sites by category or alphabetically by username. Larger companies generally add your Web site to a database so that others can find it through their search sites.

About Search Sites

You've probably used a search site before. Go to a search site, enter a word or two that describes what you're looking for, click a button, and voilà! In a few seconds, you'll see a list of Web pages with names, brief descriptions, and links. Some search sites help you find information all over the Web, while others let you search for pages on a particular Web site.

So how do the big search sites like Yahoo!, AltaVista, Lycos, Excite, HotBot, Snap, and Infoseek keep track of all the information on the Web? That depends. Although most people refer to all search sites as *search engines*, there are actually two types of search sites: *search engines* and *directories*.

Search engines, like AltaVista and Lycos, send out *robots* (also called *spiders* or *search bots*) that roam all over the Internet looking for Web pages. When they find a new or updated Web page, they catalog the URL, page title, and other page information and send it to the search engine's giant database. Directories, like Yahoo! and Snap, use humans instead of robots and let you browse for information by topic as well as by using the search form to locate listings by keywords. When someone sends information about a new Web page to Yahoo!, a human being visits the Web site, looks things over, and decides whether or not to add the page to the search engine's database.

Many of the search sites these days, like Excite, are *hybrids*. They use a combination of robots and humans to catalog Web sites. Robots automatically gather information about Web sites, and humans also visit sites and review them. When you visit a hybrid Web site, you can browse through different categories to look for Web pages or you can use the search form.

No matter how a particular search service works, you can improve your chances of being listed by registering your Web site, as explained later in this chapter.

What the Heck Is Meta-Information?

With FrontPage, you can add *meta-information* to your Web pages. That's a highfalutin term meaning "information *about* information." For our purposes, meta-information means information about your Web pages.

Why should you care about meta-information? Search engine robots catalog your pages by reading your URL, page title, and the text on your pages. You may believe the old adage that "a picture is worth a thousand words" and have designed your Web site accordingly. Alas, the search engine robots stubbornly refuse to agree!

When you use pictures and other non-text page elements instead of text, the search engine robots can't gather your page information correctly. Let's say you own an online widget shop. Your interactive, picture-filled catalog is your pride and joy. Too bad those search engine robots don't know that you sell widgets! When a potential customer searches for widgets, your competitors' Web sites are listed instead. Yikes!

Are you ready to trade in your cool graphics for boring old text? Relax, you don't have to compromise. Search engines do pick up the alternative text for your images—another reason why you should create alternative text for each picture, as covered in Chapter 8, "The Picture-Perfect Web Page: Placing and Tweaking Images." And FrontPage can help you include meta-information (also referred to as *meta tags*) with your pages. Since most search engines speak meta, a combination of alternative text and meta-information will make those design-challenged robots behave themselves from now on.

Adding Meta-Information to Your Web Pages

You can add all sorts of meta-information to your Web pages. Let's stick with the basics: giving those search engine robots a brief page description, some keywords, and the name of the page's author or company. First, this section goes through the general process for including meta-information on your Web page. The following three sections give you the details so you can add information for each category (description, keywords, and author).

To add meta-information to a Web page, do the following:

1. Open the Web page in the Page view.
2. Select Properties from the File menu to display the Page Properties dialog box, and then click the Custom tab.

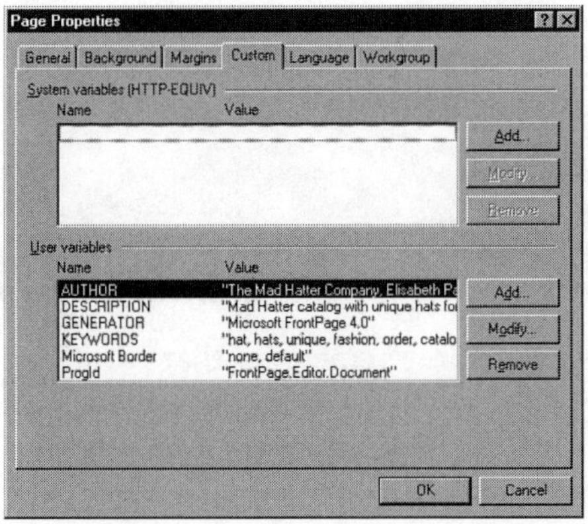

The Page Properties dialog box with the Custom tab selected.

3. Click the Add button next to the User Variables list to display the User Meta Variable dialog box. (Don't worry about the System Variables list—that's for more advanced stuff.) *User variable* is a fancy term for a type of meta-information.

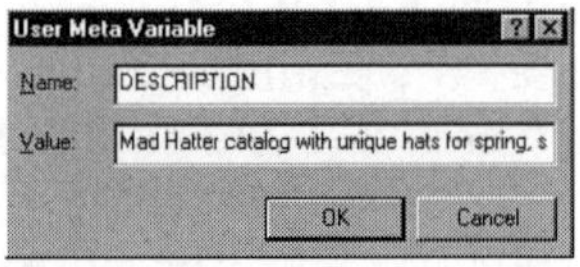

The User Meta Variable dialog box.

4. Enter the name of the type of information (description, keywords, author, and so on) in the Name box and a value (the information itself) in the Value box, and then click OK. If you don't quite follow this, not to worry. The following three sections will tell you what names to enter and how to type in values.
5. Click OK to add your meta-information to the User Variables list, and then return to the Page Properties dialog box.
6. Click the Add button again to create each new information type. Click OK to add the meta-information to your Web page or click Cancel to return to your Web page without adding the meta-information.

The Page Properties dialog box also lets you edit items on your User Variables list. To edit the information for a list item, select the list item and click the Modify button to display the User Meta Variable dialog box so you can make changes. To delete an item from the list, select the list item and click the Remove button.

Think Before You Edit or Delete Meta-Information!

When you're working with meta-information, remember that FrontPage sometimes works in strange and mysterious ways. If you find a few strange items on your User Variables or System Variables list, don't delete or edit them. FrontPage might *need* those list items. So go ahead and delete or change list items that you or a co-worker have added—but don't change anything that FrontPage has created for you.

Describing Your Web Page

Can you describe your Web page in 25 words or less? If you create a brief summary for your Web page, search engines will display the summary beneath the title and a link to your page. As a rule of thumb, search engines only display the first 25 words of a Web page summary. To include a description with your Web page's meta-information, display the Page Properties dialog box with the Custom tab selected and then click the Add button next to the User Variables list.

When the User Meta Variable dialog box appears, type

```
DESCRIPTION
```

in the Name box and type your text in the Value box. (It's okay if your description is longer than the box—just remember to stay under 25 words.) When you finish, click OK to return to the Page Properties dialog box.

Entering Keywords to Search Your Web Page

Just for a moment, try to think like one of the people you hope will visit your Web site. If you were looking for a Web page like the one you're working on now, what words would you type into a search engine's Search box? You'll need to come up with about 10 keywords that are relevant to your page to help people find it.

To include keywords with your meta-information, display the Page Properties dialog box with the Custom tab selected and then click the Add button next to the User Variables list. When the User Meta Variable dialog box appears, type

```
KEYWORDS
```

in the Name box and type your keywords in the Value box. Make sure to separate each word with a comma, as in "animal, vegetable, mineral."

And put yourself in your potential visitors' shoes. Think about which words *you* would enter if you were searching for the kind of information you're offering on your Web page. For particularly important keywords, you should also include synonyms and the singular, plural, gerund, and other forms of the words. For example, if you publish a Web site to promote your housecleaning business, you should include keywords like "house, houses, home, homes, clean, cleaning, cleaner, cleaners." When you finish, click OK to return to the Page Properties dialog box.

Some People Don't Spell Well

Face it, English isn't the easiest language to master when it comes to spelling! Even the best-educated and most intelligent people spell and type poorly on occasion. You can increase the chances that people will find your Web site by including misspelled versions of keywords that people might enter into a Web search form. Keep frequent misspellings like "occassion," "recieve," "infromation," "reccommendation," and "ettiquette" in mind.

Telling People Who Created Your Web Page (That's You!)

Sometimes people search for Web sites by name or company name. You can include your name or the name of your organization with your meta-information. To tell the search engine robots who created your page, display the Page Properties dialog box with the Custom tab selected and click the Add button next to the User Variables list. When the User Meta Variable dialog box appears, type

```
AUTHOR
```

in the Name box and then type your name or the name of your organization in the Value box. When you finish, click OK to return to the Page Properties dialog box.

Techno Talk

Create a Web Page Splash Screen!

Want to try a cool trick with meta-information? You can put up a page that appears in the Web browser for a few seconds and then switches to another page. This is sort of like the splash screens that appear when you start up a program. Web pros call this technique *meta-refresh* or *document redirection.*

To turn a Web page into a splash screen, go to the Page Properties dialog box and click the Custom tab. Click the Add button next to the System variables (HTTP-EQUIV) list. (Yep, this is one of those advanced meta-information techniques I mentioned earlier in this chapter.) When the System Meta Variable (HTTP-EQUIV) dialog box appears, type "Refresh" in the Name box and type `10;URL=YourNextPage.htm` in the Value box.

10 is the number of seconds the page is displayed before changing. You can enter any number you want. Where I entered `YourNextPage.htm`, you should type the filename for the new Web page.

Registering Your Site with Search Engines

Once you've added meta-information to your Web pages and published them to your server, send in the search bots. But how do you summon them? Sure, you can wait for them to find your Web site, but that could take forever.

If you look carefully at the search engine Web sites, you'll find a link that invites you to submit your URL. These links usually say something like Suggest a Site, Add URL, or Register URL. Sometimes you have to look carefully. Click the link, follow the directions, and fill out the convenient Web form. Some search sites add your Web pages within a few hours, while others may take several weeks.

You should also keep in mind that directory search sites, like Yahoo! and Snap, require you to first go to a page that lists Web pages for the category and subcategory that you want your Web site to be listed under (such as `Businesses/California/San Francisco/Photographers`). Then you must click a link to go to a Web form that allows you to register your URL. This ensures that you put your listing in the correct category. Yahoo! and Snap allow you to list your Web site with two categories.

Where to register your Web site:

- *Yahoo!* `http://www.yahoo.com/`
- *AltaVista* `http://www.altavista.com/`
- *Lycos* `http://www.lycos.com/`
- *HotBot* `http://www.hotbot.com/`
- *Excite* `http://www.excite.com/`
- *Snap* `http://www.snap.com/`
- *WebCrawler* `http://www.webcrawler.com/`
- *MSN Web Search* `http://search.msn.com`
- *Infoseek* `http://www.infoseek.com/`
- *Nerd World* `http://www.nerdworld.com/`
- *Planet Search* `http://www.planetsearch.com/`

Paying a Service to Register Your Web Site

You can also pay a service to register your Web site with search engines. This generally costs anywhere between $30 and $250, depending on which plan you choose. But why pay someone when you can register with those search engines yourself? It depends on just how much you want to promote your Web site. There are thousands of search engines on the Web—how can anyone even *find* them all, let alone find the time to fill out all those Web forms?

If you publish Web pages just for fun or for a business that doesn't sell anything online, you can probably stick with the search engines listed in the previous section. However, if you're opening an online shop, you should definitely have your Web site listed with as many search engines as possible—especially if you want to reach potential customers in foreign countries, where people may not use the same search engines that we use. For starters, visit Web Promote (`http://www.webpromote.com/`) and Submit It! (`http://www.submit-it.com/`) and see if you like their offerings.

Rating Your Web Site for Concerned Parents and Others

Many parents (and some companies) use special programs to keep kids and others out of trouble when they surf the Web. These Net baby sitters allow Mom and Dad to block access to Web pages with offensive material. They do this by looking for the ratings data for each Web page and rejecting pages with no ratings or the wrong ratings.

Want to pass muster with the Net baby sitters or keep kids away from your Web site? Get a Web site rating from the Recreational Software Advisory Council (RSAC), a non-profit organization located at `http://www.rsac.org/`. You get an email message with instructions and ratings meta-information that you can paste into your Web pages from the HTML view.

The FrontPage RSAC Ratings Add-In makes it easy to get a Web site rating. Put your FrontPage CD into your CD-ROM drive, select Add-Ins from the Tools menu, and then select RSAC Ratings to launch the Ratings Wizard. The wizard guides you through the process and generates an email message that will be sent to RSAC the next time you check your email.

Ten Cool Tips for Bringing Visitors to Your Web Site

Want to attract more visitors to your Web site? The following list offers a few easy ways to tell the world about your Web site and provide attractions that keep people coming back:

- *Offer free goodies* You can offer screen savers, documents, software, artwork, sound clips, multimedia, fonts, and other stuff to promote your company or assist your customers, or just for fun.
- *Add some bells and whistles* Well-chosen frills can keep visitors coming back and help promote your business. For example, a real estate agent can set up a JavaScript mortgage calculator. (Chapter 21, "Rev Up Your Web Site with Programs and Scripts," tells you where to get free applets and scripts.) Or you can set up your own Web cam—it's easier than you think. (For more information, see `http://www.byteit.com/Cam/`.)
- *Publish a newsletter* An interesting, frequently updated newsletter focused on a favorite topic can attract regular visitors. Heck, some people may even offer to write articles. You should also include a prominent link to a Web form that invites your readers to subscribe to your mailing list. You can then send email to your readers with notifications of updates and provide links to pages with new material. Most email programs, like Outlook Express and Netscape Mail, provide address book features that allow you to do this.
- *Host a discussion Web* Web discussion groups can build communities, support customers, assist brainstorming, promote events, or all of the above. For more on setting up a discussion Web, see Chapter 23, "Switchboard Central: Setting Up a Discussion Web."
- *Run a banner ad campaign* You don't necessarily need deep pockets! The Link Exchange offers a free banner ad exchange program and lots of helpful tips for creating successful banner ads. Drop by the Link Exchange Web site at `http://www.linkexchange.com/`. Chapter 20, "Gee-Whiz Pages with Animated Special Effects," tells you how to create banner ads with FrontPage 2000.

- *Host online chats* Become the next Oprah Winfrey or Jay Leno! You can sign up with Talk City at `http://www.talkcity.com/` and get your own free chat room so you can host exciting online events with special guests. Other services, like Undernet (`http://www.undernet.org/`), also offer free chat rooms. (In fact, you can chat with your favorite Macmillan computer book authors, ask questions, and get feedback by visiting `http://www.blueroses.com/authors/`.)
- *Start an online postcard shop* Turn your favorite photographs and artwork into online postcards that visitors can email to friends. If you're an artist or photographer, online postcards are an ideal way to promote your work. To find out how to get started, visit `http://mypostcards.com/`.
- *Trade links* Email friends, associates, and Webmasters of sites that cover related topics and ask them to create links to your Web site. Be polite, and link back to them!
- *Add your Web site address to your email signature* Most email programs have a signature feature that automatically attaches text—such as your name, email address, Web site, and a favorite saying (or a snippet of self-promoting text)—to your outgoing email messages. Make sure to include your URL in the signature.
- *Schmooze* It's fun to do things online, but don't forget about old-fashioned face-to-face schmoozing. You can still go a long way by sending out printed announcements about your new Web site and handing out business cards with your URL.

The Least You Need to Know

- The FrontPage Publisher makes it easy to get your Web site onto your server. Before you begin, ask your ISP, Web host, or server administrator for your Web site address (URL), username, and password.
- If your Web site is located on a remote server, you need to connect to the Internet before you publish your pages. If your Web site is located on a local server, you're already connected and can go straight to the Publisher.
- Meta-information is a fancy term for information about your Web site, including a description, keywords, and author. To help people find your Web site, you should register with popular directories and search engines like Yahoo! and HotBot.
- Search engines send out special programs called robots that roam the Internet and catalog Web pages. You can include meta-information with your Web pages to help these robots.
- The RSAC Ratings Add-In helps you rate your Web site for programs that block access to sites with potentially offensive material. These programs often block out sites that are not rated, too.

Chapter 27

You're the Boss! Becoming a Web Site Administrator

In This Chapter

- Deleting FrontPage Webs
- Root Webs
- Creating nested sub-Webs
- Giving individuals access to Webs and Web pages
- Giving groups of computers access to Webs

If you create your Web pages at home and live by yourself, you probably won't need to worry about Web site administration. But if you share responsibility for your Web site with your co-workers or have other people in your household who want to build Web pages too, you'll need to become a Web site administrator. After all, you may want your co-workers to enjoy the experience of Web publishing, but you don't want them messing up *your* pages! Luckily, FrontPage makes it easy to create Webs, give people their own passwords, and decide who can change pages on which Webs.

Spring Cleaning: Removing a Web

You learned how to create FrontPage Webs in Chapter 1, "Get Ready to Rock with FrontPage 2000," and you've probably even created a couple of Webs that you never use. Perhaps you created them when you were experimenting with different Web techniques. In any case, you can get rid of those extra Webs and save yourself a little disk space. To delete a Web, open it in the Folders view, right-click on the top folder icon, and choose Delete from the shortcut menu. When the Confirm Delete dialog box appears, click the Yes button.

Creating Nested Sub-Webs

Suppose you and your co-workers are working together to create a single Web. You're working on the product catalog, Jim is working on order forms, and Mary is working on all that marketing mumbo jumbo. All of your pages will be available on the same Web site, but none of you wants the others to make any changes to your pages. FrontPage lets you create nested sub-Webs, which are part of the main Web site but can also be published separately from the rest of the Web. You can even set different access levels, as covered later in this chapter.

Nested sub-Webs are especially useful when you're working on an intranet. You'll find out more about intranets in Chapter 29, "It Doesn't Take a Village to Build an Intranet: Publishing, Sharing, and Updating Files."

You create a nested sub-Web just like you would create any new Web in FrontPage (see Chapter 2, "Instant Web-Site-O-Matic: Spinning FrontPage Webs"). Okay, it's a *little* bit different. Let's say that you've created a Web called Projects and now you want to create a nested sub-Web for the new project, code-named Purple. Open the Projects Web and select New from the File menu, and then select Web. When the New dialog box appears, as shown in the following figure, choose the type of Web you want to create from the Web Sites list, select the Add to Current Web check box, and click OK. FrontPage creates a new Web and puts it inside the current Web.

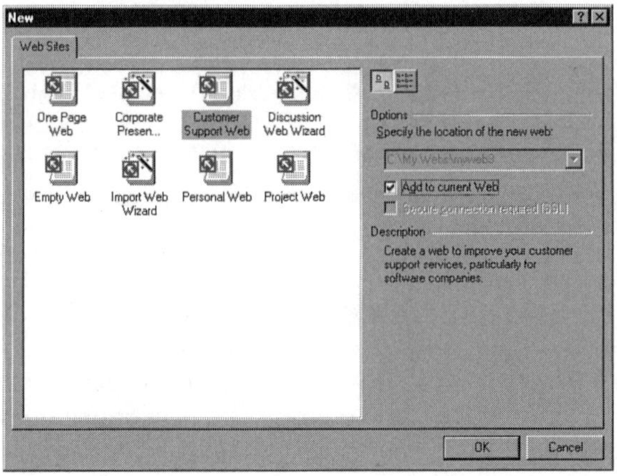

The New dialog box.

Creating a Sub-Web from a Folder

Okay, you've been using FrontPage for a while now, and you've made sure to organize your files and folders within a Web. Now you're hearing all this about sub-Webs. Don't worry, you don't have to re-create anything. FrontPage 2000 lets you turn any folder into its own FrontPage Web. Just right-click the folder in the Folders view, choose Convert to Web from the shortcut menu, and click Yes when the Microsoft FrontPage confirmation dialog box appears. FrontPage will do all the work for you.

Co-workers, Kids, and Visitors: Giving People Access Rights

Too many cooks spoil the broth, as the saying goes. Sure, you want to help people get their work done, but you don't necessarily need to give everyone full access rights to your Webs. Access rights let you decide how much control different people should have over the pages on your Web site.

With FrontPage, you can set up three different levels of access rights:

- *Full Access* This allows users to set access rights for a Web site, create and remove Webs and sub-Webs, publish Webs, and create, edit, and delete Web pages.
- *Read Only* This allows users to view Web pages in a browser, but they can't make any changes.
- *Custom* This allows you to choose the access permissions you want your users to have.

How Permissions Work

When you set permissions for the root Web (the top-level Web on your Web server), all of the sub-Webs within that root Web inherit those permissions. That means that you (as the administrator) get permission for everything, visitors with Read Only permission on the root Web can view pages on all other Webs, and a user who has custom permissions that allow them to create and delete pages on the root Web can change pages on all sub-Webs too. If you want to control the access to a sub-Web differently, you'll need to open the sub-Web and change the permissions there.

Giving Users Access to a Web

To give people access to a Web, open it, select Security from the Tools menu, and then select Permissions. When the Permissions dialog box appears, select the Users tab and then click the Add button to display the Add Users dialog box, as shown in the following figure. Type the name of the new user in the Name box (or select a user from the Name list if you're using Microsoft's NT Security Manager). Then, depending on the level of access you want to assign to that person, click the Read Only, Full Access, or Custom button. As you give each user a set of access rights, his or her name will appear in the appropriate Read Only, Full Access, or Custom list. Click OK to return to the Permissions dialog box. Keep in mind that you and others who work on the Web site should have full access, and everyone else (including The World—which appears as an item on the Name list) should have Read Only privileges. Anyone else can be assigned a set of custom permissions.

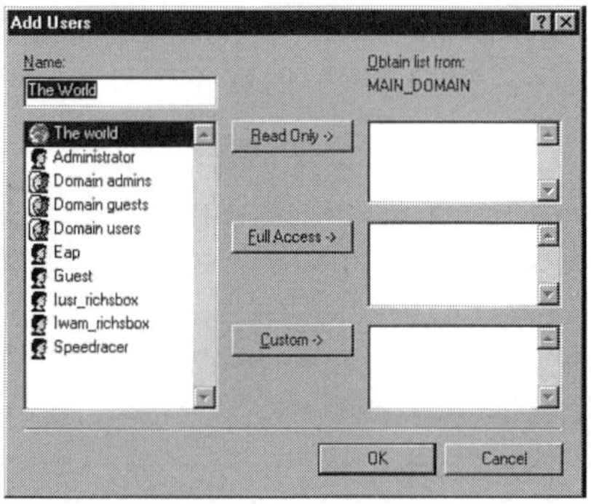

Add Users dialog box.

Giving Access to Workgroups

You can also assign access levels to entire workgroups—as long as they work on computers with a common *IP address*. An IP address is kind of like a URL, except that it's a group of numbers. In fact, all URLs (as in `http://www.myWebsite.com`) are actually pointers to these IP addresses. After all, words are usually easier to remember than numbers. On the Internet, IP addresses are servers. On a local network, IP addresses are computers on the network.

To give access to a workgroup, display the Permissions dialog box, click the Computers tab, and then click the Add button. When the Add Computer dialog box appears, enter an IP mask (IP address) in the text box and then choose an access level from the Computer can list. All of your coworkers who use computers with the specified IP address will be able to access the FrontPage Web.

Take a Load Off!

Make sure to give at least one other person administrator rights for Webs. After all, life goes on when you take a vacation or a sick day.

Editing a User's Access Rights

To edit a user's access rights, display the Add Users dialog box, select a user, and click a different button. The user's name will then appear on the corresponding list.

Deleting Permissions

To remove a user, display the Add Users dialog box, select a user, and click the button.

Limiting Browse Access for a Web

Most of the time, you'll give just about everyone at least Read Only access to your Webs. After all, most people *want* others to visit their Web pages. But sometimes you might not want just *anyone* to browse your Web. Perhaps you've set up a discussion Web for a department that contains confidential information. Or maybe you're just plain snooty.

If you want to keep some pages confidential, you should create them in their own Web or sub-web. From the Permissions dialog box, select users one by one from the Name list to whom you want to give access, and then click the Read Only, Full Access, or Custom button to add them to the appropriate list. You should also check and make sure that The World (meaning everybody) doesn't appear on the Read Only List.

Setting Access Levels for Webs and Web Pages

You can set access levels for different users to determine who can do what to which pages and which Webs. Chapter 27 tells you how to create users and allow them to browse, edit, or administer your Web.

The Least You Need to Know

- The person who installs FrontPage and creates a name and password during the setup routine is the Web site administrator.
- You can create nested sub-Webs that are integrated with the main Web site, and yet allow different access levels and publishing settings.
- With FrontPage, there are three levels of access rights that you can set for users: Administrator, Author, and Browse.
- You can also give groups of computers access to a Web. This applies the same levels of access to people who work on the same group of computers.

Chapter 28

Keeping Track of It All with the Task List

In This Chapter

- Viewing the task list
- Adding, removing, and marking tasks complete
- Viewing the task history
- Spell checking your Web pages
- Searching and replacing text throughout your Web site
- Five cool task list tips

Think of FrontPage's task list as a sort of "things to do" list, except that you don't have to worry about losing those little scraps of paper. A quick glance at the Tasks views reminds you of unfinished business, and you can also add your own items to the task list and remove items when you complete them.

A Tisket, A Tasket, No Need to Be a Basket (Case): Using the Task List

When you create a FrontPage Web with one of the Web Wizards, as covered in Chapter 2, "Instant Web-Site-O-Matic: Spinning FrontPage Webs," FrontPage creates a list of tasks so you'll remember to finish creating all of the pages on your Web. The task list can also help you out at any time. When you start something but don't finish it (like a spell check), FrontPage automatically adds an item to the task list.

Take a peek at your own task list right now by clicking the Tasks icon in the Views list. The Tasks view appears with a list of things to do, kind of like the one shown in the following figure.

A list of tasks displayed in the Tasks view.

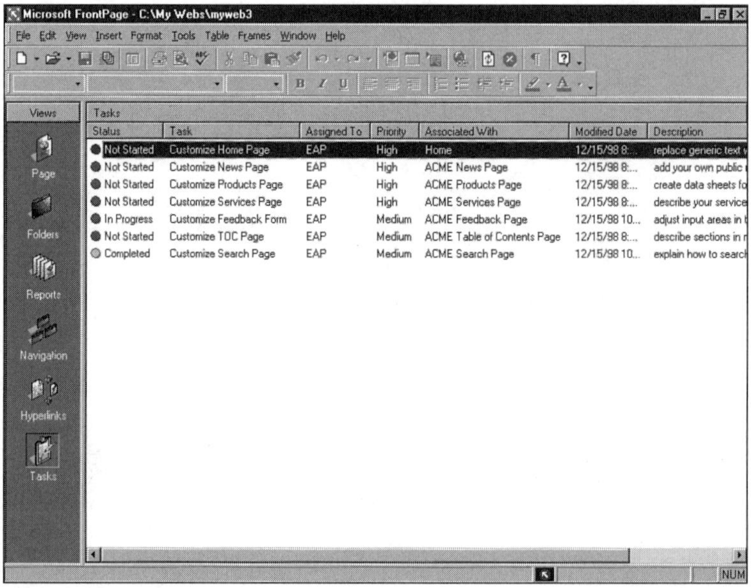

The information about each list item is organized into the following columns:

- *Status* Tells you whether a task is in progress, has been completed, or has not been started.
- *Task* Gives you a brief description of what you need to do.
- *Assigned to* Displays the username of the person responsible for completing the task. By default, FrontPage uses the name of the Web administrator (as covered in Chapter 27, "You're the Boss! Becoming a Web Site Administrator").
- *Priority* Ranks items in priority, on a scale of high to low.
- *Associated With* Tells you which page or pages the task relates to.
- *Modified Date* Provides the date and time that the page was last edited.
- *Description* Offers a more detailed explanation of the task.

Viewing and Editing Task Details

From the Task Details dialog box, you can view more information about a task on your list or edit the task details. To display your task details, right-click a task and select Edit Task from the shortcut menu. Or, you can select a task and then select Properties from the File menu. When the Task Details dialog box appears, as shown in the following figure, make your changes and click OK to return to the Tasks view.

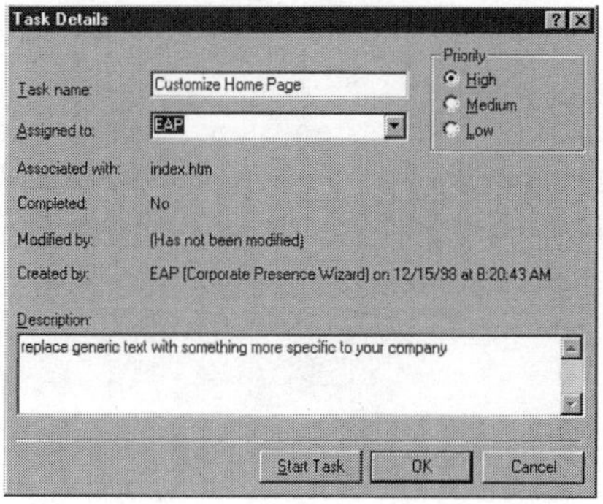

The Task Details dialog box.

You can edit the following items:

- *Task Name* You can type a new name for the task.
- *Assigned To* Change the name of the person the task is assigned to, select a name from the list, or type a new name.
- *Priority* Select a radio button to assign a different priority level to the task.
- *Description* Change the description or add more information by typing your text in the scrolling Description box.

You can also click the Start Task button to open the Web page and complete your task, or click Cancel to return to the Tasks view without changing the task details.

Adding a New Task

Just remembered something that needs more work? You can add a new task to your list without changing the current Web site view. Select New from the File menu and then select Task from the cascading menu. When the New Task dialog box appears, type in your information, select a priority level, and click OK.

Starting a Task from the Task List

You're looking at all the stuff on the task list, and you feel kind of energetic today. You can tackle your work, one task at a time, straight from the task list. And FrontPage gives you two ways to do it: right-click a task and select Start Task from the shortcut menu, or double-click the task and select Start Task. Either way, FrontPage opens the related Web page in the Page view so that you can make your changes.

When you make your changes and save the Web page, the Microsoft FrontPage dialog box appears and asks if you want to mark the task as completed (as shown in the following figure). Click the Yes button to mark the task as completed. If you still have unfinished business, click the No button to mark the task as being in progress. The next time you return to the Tasks view, you'll find that FrontPage has changed the task's status for you. How convenient.

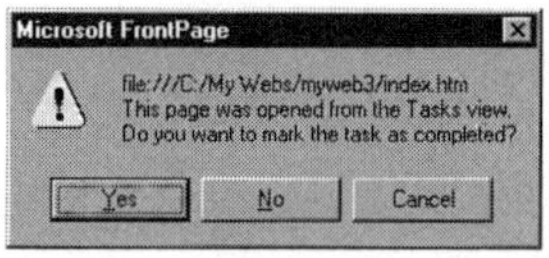

The Microsoft FrontPage task dialog box.

Deleting Tasks and Marking Them as Completed

When you complete tasks, FrontPage marks them as completed but does not remove them from your list. After all, completed tasks give you a sense of accomplishment! Plus, completed tasks help you keep track of your projects. At some point, though, you may want to delete these old tasks. To remove a task from the list, right-click the task and select Delete from the Shortcut menu. You can also remove a task by selecting it and pressing the Delete key.

You can also mark tasks as completed to give yourself a feeling of accomplishment (although it's probably a good idea to complete the task first!). If you complete a task without opening the page from the task list first (as explained in the previous section), FrontPage won't know that you've done anything. Some tasks may not involve opening a particular Web page, so you'll sometimes need to mark tasks as completed yourself. To do this, display the task list, right-click a task, and select Mark as completed from the shortcut menu.

Spell Checking Your Web Site

Chapter 5, "Entering Text and Fiddling with Fonts," told you how to check for spelling errors on individual pages, but did you know that FrontPage will help you check the spelling on your whole site at once? Even better, it adds all of the errors to your task list so that you can keep track of them.

To spell check your entire Web site, go to the Folders view and select Spelling from the Tools menu to display the Spelling dialog box, shown in the following figure. Select the Entire Web radio button to check all the pages in the current FrontPage Web. Then click the Start button to begin the spell check, and select the Add a task for each page with misspellings check box to add each of the misspellings to your task list.

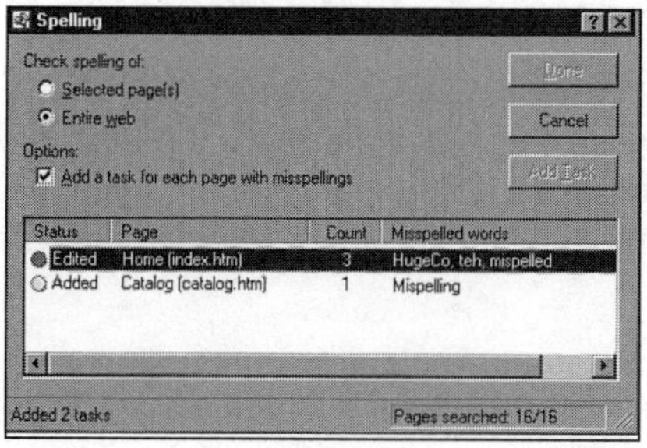

The Spelling dialog box with errors displayed and added to the task list.

Correcting Your Spelling Mistakes

When the spell checker finishes catching your spelling boo-boos (or what it *thinks* are spelling boo-boos), a list of pages appears. To correct the spelling mistakes, double-click an item on the page list to display the Web page and the Spelling dialog box. You can then correct the errors the way you do with individual pages (if you've forgotten, Chapter 5 tells you how).

When you finish the current page, you see the Continue with the next document? dialog box. Leave the Close the current document check box selected to close the page, and click the Next Document button to go to the next page. If you can't finish your spell check right now, click the Cancel button. You can always resume it by selecting another item from the task list.

If you didn't select the Add a task for each page with misspellings check box before running the spell check, you can add pages to your task list by selecting them from the errors list and clicking the Add Task button. When you finish spell checking a page, select the page from the list and click the Done button so FrontPage knows you've corrected the page.

The Spelling dialog box's page list displays information for each page in the following columns:

- *Status* Tells you the status of each page, such as whether FrontPage has added it to the task list and whether you've edited (corrected) the page.
- *Page* Displays the title and filename of each Web page.

- *Count* Indicates the number of misspelled words on each Web page.
- *Misspelled Words* Lists the misspelled words on each page.

In addition, the status bar tells you the number of tasks added to your task list and the number of pages that have been spell checked.

Oops! That's Harold, Not Harry: Finding and Replacing Text on Your Whole Web Site

Yikes! You've referred to the president of your company as "Harry Smith" throughout the Web site, but it turns out that he prefers "Harold Smith." And now you have to change 32 pages! Not to worry. FrontPage can help you search and replace text on your entire Web site.

To do this, go to the Folders view and select Replace from the Edit menu. When the Replace dialog box appears, click the All Pages radio button, type the text you want to replace in the Find What box and the replacement text in the Replace With box, and then click the Find in Web button.

When the list of pages appears, as shown in the following figure, double-click a list item to open a Web page. When you open the item, the Replace dialog box changes so you can replace the text as explained in Chapter 5. When you finish, click the Back to Web button to display the page list again. If you'd rather work on the pages later, you can add them to your task list by selecting them from the list and clicking the Add Task button. As with the spell checker, the Replace dialog box's page list tells you the page's status, its title and filename, and the number of items found there.

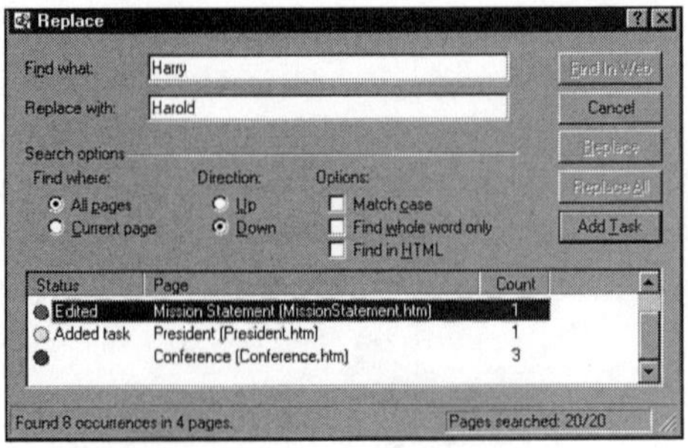

The Replace dialog box with errors displayed and added to the task list.

Five Cool Task List Tips

The task list is like an online "in box." You need to stay on top of it so things don't get out of hand! The following tips can help you manage your task list so it won't manage you:

Find and Replace Source Code, Too!

If you know HTML, you can select the Find in HTML check box in the Replace dialog box to locate and change snippets of source code.

- *Let FrontPage keep track of your tasks* When you work with pages on your task list, always open them from the task list. That way you don't have to worry about whether or not you've marked the status for your task items correctly.
- *Clean up your task list now and then* FrontPage doesn't automatically delete items from your task list, so it can get awfully long. When you finish a project, take a little time to delete old tasks.
- *Add tasks from the Reports view* If your reports tell you that some pages need work, you can add the pages to your task list straight from the Reports view. Right-click a list item and choose Add Task from the shortcut menu.
- *Show those columns who's boss!* Remember how Chapter 24, "You and Your Web Files," told you how to resize columns and click column headings to sort list items? These tricks work with the task list, too.
- *Lay down the law!* The task list won't do much good unless your co-workers follow the rules. Show them how to use the task list and make sure they *use* it!

The Least You Need to Know

- FrontPage's task list displays a list of things you need to do on your Web pages and displays the status of each task. To display the task list, click the Tasks icon from the Views list.
- You can edit tasks and view more information from the Task Details dialog box.
- When you create a new Web, FrontPage automatically adds items to your task list. You can also add your own tasks from the New Task dialog box.
- To ensure that FrontPage keeps track of your tasks, you should complete your tasks by opening Web pages from the task list.
- When you complete a task by opening pages from the task list, FrontPage marks the task as completed. You can also manually mark items on the task list as completed.
- You can also delete old items from the task list so it doesn't get too long.

Chapter 29

It Doesn't Take a Village to Build an Intranet: Publishing, Sharing, and Updating Files

In This Chapter

- About intranets and servers
- Browsing intranet Web sites
- FrontPage intranet features
- Using Web wizards to build an intranet Web site
- Sharing and collaborating on files
- Generating workflow reports
- Five cool places to learn more about intranets

What's the difference between the *Inter*net and an *intra*net? An intranet is an office network that acts just like the Internet—except that only you and your co-workers can use it. Before the Web came along, organizations all had their own ways of publishing files and sending them to people. Sometimes it took a week or two just to learn how to send a file to a co-worker—let alone get any work done! Intranets make it much easier to get up and running. After all, many people already know how to browse Web pages.

So what are you waiting for? With FrontPage, you can set up an intranet for your business or department in no time!

Why Build an Intranet?

How do most of us spend our time during a typical workday (besides sneaking in the occasional game of Solitaire)? Communicating with people. We spend hours attending meetings, talking on the phone, composing letters and memos, waiting for today's FedEx delivery, and sending faxes and email messages. And that's a good thing—we humans do need to interact with each other from time to time.

However, with today's telecommuting and flextime hours, getting in touch with a *particular* human isn't always so simple. FrontPage makes it easy to create and manage intranet Web sites that help you and your co-workers keep track of who's doing what, communicate via discussion groups, and publish Web pages with links to files that others need.

The following examples show how intranets save time on telephone and email messages, allow for different work schedules, and encourage everyone to work productively as a team:

- *On the road again* John meets with an important client and clinches the sale. But the meeting runs later than expected, and he still has to check on some marketing data prepared by his assistant. He stops by the office (everyone else has gone home), launches his browser, follows the link to the spreadsheet, makes a few corrections, and marks the file as completed so his assistant will know to look it over when she arrives in the morning.
- *Not another meeting!* Sandy is in charge of preparing the company's annual report, and she needs to meet with different department heads. She gets frustrated when everyone's hectic schedules make it impossible to set a meeting time, but she doesn't give up. Instead, she sets up a discussion Web, publishes the agenda, and invites her co-workers to post their messages. Within a couple of days, they've hashed out all the details and Sandy has all the information she needs.
- *Job sharing* Tom is a new father. He tells his manager that he plans to leave the company and find a part-time job so he can spend more time with his family. Tom's manager wants him to stay, suggests a part-time job-sharing arrangement, and hires Tanya. Tom and Tanya both come in three days a week, and are both in the office on Wednesdays. They set up a project Web so they can keep track of their assignments, update each other's files, and stay in touch during the rest of the week.
- *Freeing up some time* Marie heads up the Human Resources department. She spends so much time answering phone calls and email messages about company policies, benefits, and vacation days that she barely has time for her other work. Finally, she asks her assistant to set up a Web site with answers to the most frequently asked questions (also known as a FAQ). Now everyone checks the Web site when they need basic information, and Marie is free to tackle more challenging tasks.

Browsing a FrontPage Intranet Web Site

An intranet Web site isn't terribly useful unless you tell your co-workers how to access it. Intranet Webs and sub-Webs have URLs just like Web sites on the Internet (as in `http://NameofServer/NameofWeb/`). In order to view your Web pages properly in a browser, your co-workers need to enter a URL in the browser's location window rather than opening pages as files through the Open dialog box. When you publish a new Web, you can send email messages with the URL to your co-workers.

Planning an Intranet Web Site

Before you get started, think about which features you would like to include on your intranet Web site. As with regular old Internet Web sites, intranet sites require a little advanced planning. But keep in mind that you don't have to do everything at once. Once you've got your intranet up and running, you can get feedback from people and add features and pages as time goes on.

Here are some useful FrontPage features that you can add to your intranet:

- *Automatic file updates* Table of contents and other pages that display a list of Web pages and other files, with links and brief descriptions of files. FrontPage gathers these descriptions from the file summaries and Web page comments. (For more on summaries and Web page comments, see Chapters 18, "A Match Made in Redmond: FrontPage and Microsoft Office 2000," and 24, "You and Your Web Files.")
- *Reserved files* You can use FrontPage's document check-in and check-out feature to ensure that only people with the right access permissions can change files on your Web (see Chapter 27, "You're the Boss! Becoming a Web Site Administrator"). We'll talk more about reserving files later in this chapter.
- *Web forms* Chapter 13, "Form and Function: Building Online Forms," tells you how to create Web forms to gather feedback from visitors. The FrontPage Web Wizards also generate forms that are tailored for intranets, such as a discussion Web form. These types of forms make it easy for you and your co-workers to tell each other when you're working different schedules, and to post announcements.
- *Discussion Webs* Allow you and your co-workers to read messages and fill out a form to send replies. A discussion Web displays an automatically updated list of messages, organized by subject, and also has a search form. For more on discussion Webs, see Chapter 23, "Switchboard Central: Setting Up a Discussion Web."
- *File exchange* You can subscribe files on your Web site to files on your co-workers' computers. When your co-workers edit the files, FrontPage automatically updates them.
- *Private Webs* You can create Webs that allow only authorized users (see Chapter 27) to read them. This way you can limit access to discussion groups, pages, or Webs with confidential information.

- *Status checking* Users can track the status of files and projects through reports (Chapter 25, "Testing, Testing, One, Two, Three: Checking Your Web Site") and the task list (Chapter 28, "Keeping Track of It All with the Task List"), or through a file's Properties dialog box with the Workgroup tab selected (as explained later in this chapter).
- *Access rights* You can assign different levels of access to Webs and files, as covered in Chapter 27.

Building an Intranet Web Site

Oh, you've never set up an intranet Web site before? Join the club! Luckily, the FrontPage Web Wizards can help you with the tough stuff. First, think about which features you'd like to include on your intranet Web site. You can then create a new Web from the New dialog box, as shown in the following figure, and go through the Web Wizard's steps, as covered in Chapter 2, "Instant Web-Site-O-Matic: Spinning FrontPage Webs."

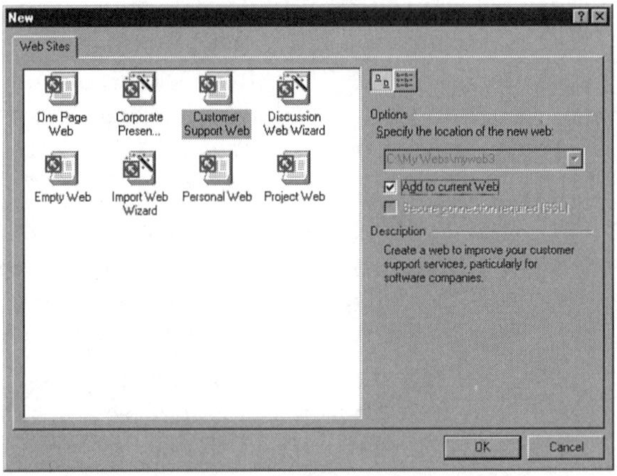

New dialog box with the Web Wizard options displayed.

The following types of FrontPage Webs are ideal for intranet Web sites:

- *Corporate presence Web* For publishing general information and a table of contents with links that is automatically updated when files are added or removed.
- *Project Web* Gives you everything you need for planning projects, working together on files, and tracking the status of different assignments. You can assign members to a group and set up an automatically updated archives page with links to files and pages. In addition, a project Web includes a search page and a discussion group page.
- *Discussion Web* Think of it as your online bulletin board. You can create a discussion Web (see Chapter 23) so that you and your co-workers can keep in touch and leave messages for each other.

- *Customer service Web* Includes a discussion group, a page for frequently asked questions (FAQ), and a download page.
- *Mix and match!* You can use any combination of Webs on your intranet site. Create a main Web, set up the other Webs as nested sub-Webs within the main Web site (see Chapter 27), and create links and navigation bars (see Chapter 7, "Think Links: Adding Links to Your Pages") to tie everything together.

Be Creative!

Once you've used a Web Wizard to whip up a Web site that meets your basic needs, you can customize your pages and navigation elements to suit your office.

Sharing Files Through Your Web Site

FrontPage intranets sure make it easy for people to view and edit each other's files. Too easy, perhaps. Keeping your co-workers from stepping on each other's toes is a big part of a Web administrator's job. For example, Janine would get pretty mad if Frank changed her presentation without telling her and she wound up making a fool of herself at the next meeting.

Luckily, with FrontPage you can set different access levels (as discussed in Chapter 27) for pages and files so people don't add and change files willy-nilly.

Uploading Files to the Server

Once you've given users the right to edit and upload files on your Web (see Chapter 27), they can publish their changes and new files to your Web site in the following ways:

- *Use the FrontPage Publisher* If your co-workers also have FrontPage, they can use it to upload files to your Web, as explained in Chapter 26, "Don't Just Let It Sit There! Publishing Your Web Site." Windows users can use FrontPage Express, a slimmed-down version of FrontPage that comes free with Windows 98, to do their publishing.
- *Save files straight to your Web* Microsoft Office users can save their Office files directly into an Internet or intranet Web site if you give them access permissions. First they'll need to create your Web as a Web folder, as covered in Chapter 18. Web folders let you save files to a remote Web site as you would to your own hard drive. When you install an Office 2000 application (or several), the setup program creates the Web folder as a new drive that you can view, along with other available drives, by double-clicking the MyComputer icon on your desktop.

- *Use an FTP program* Anyone with a username and password can also use a File Transfer Protocol (FTP) program like Cute FTP or WS FTP to upload files to your Web. The Tucows shareware site at `http://www.tucows.com/` offers a variety of good FTP applications. These programs are very useful if your co-workers aren't using Microsoft Office to create their files.

Automatic Updates

So how do you keep track of all the files on your Web? You don't. FrontPage does everything for you. When someone edits a file, the table of contents modification date changes. When a co-worker posts a new file, FrontPage adds a new item, link, and file information to the table of contents page. If you don't have a table of contents page on your Web, see Chapter 19, "A Grab Bag of Helpful Doodads: FrontPage Components."

Checking Files In and Out

Every now and then it happens: Two people open the same file at the same time, and they both make changes. You can set up your Web so users can check files in and out. When a co-worker reserves a file, others cannot work on that file until it's checked back in again.

So how does it work? First you'll need to enable the check-in/check-out feature. Open your Web and select Web Settings from the Tools menu. At the bottom of the General tab in the Web Settings dialog box, click the check box called Use document check in and check out, as shown in the following figure.

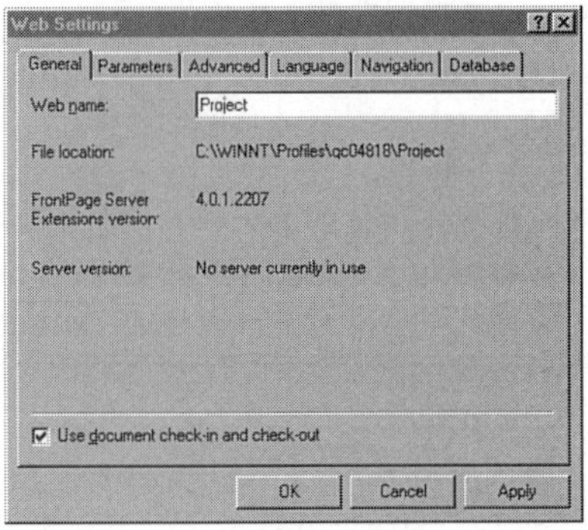

The Web Settings dialog box.

FrontPage puts a status indicator next to every file in your Web. In the following figure, a dot next to a filename indicates that the file can be edited. A check mark next to a filename indicates that someone else is already editing that file. This way, you know not to make any changes to that file until it's checked in again.

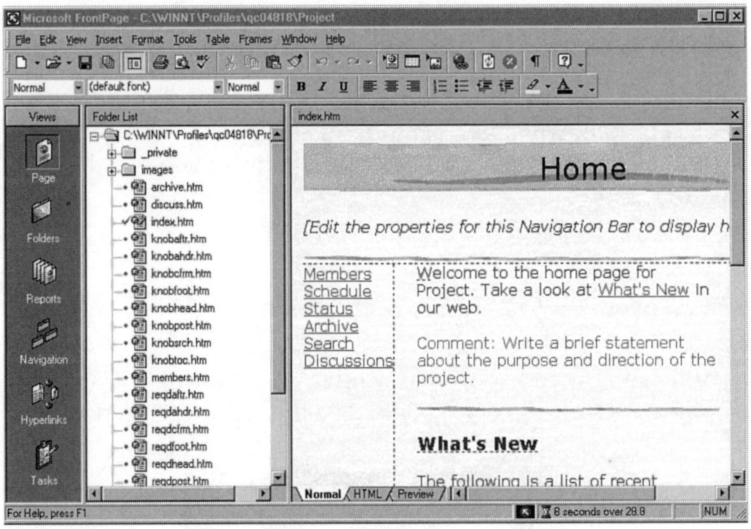

The document check-in status indicator shown in the Page view.

Whenever you open a file with the document check-in feature enabled, FrontPage will display a confirmation notice (shown in the following figure) to tell you that you're checking out a file. Pretty neat, huh?

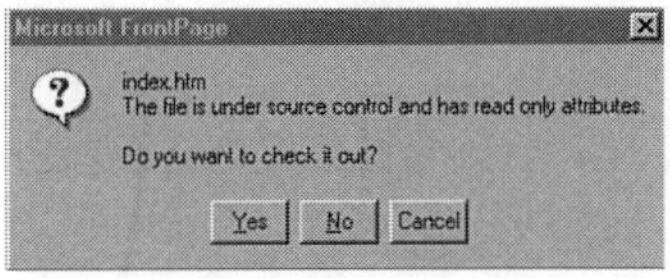

The document check-out notice.

Teamwork: Creating Workflow Reports

Remember how you learned to display reports in Chapter 25? You can also set up files to generate workflow reports for individual Web pages and other files. This feature helps everyone stay on top of who's responsible for a file, as well as its status. To create workflow reports for your Web, you'll first need to set up the information for each of your files through the Properties dialog box.

Adding Workflow Report Information to a File

To add a file to the FrontPage workflow report, go to the Folders view, right-click a file, and select Properties from the shortcut menu. Or you can select the file and choose Properties from the File menu. The Workgroup Properties dialog box, as mentioned in Chapter 18, allows users to designate who's assigned to pages and the stage of production for each page.

When the Properties dialog box appears, click the Workgroup tab, choose options for the following items, and then click OK:

- *Select categories for the Web page* You can assign categories to a Web page by clicking the checkboxes on the Available Categories list. When you assign categories to a Web page, you can use the AutoLinks component to generate links for you, as explained in Chapter 19.
- *Assign a file to someone* You can assign a file to a user by selecting his or her name from the Assigned To list.
- *Review status* Select an item that best describes the current file's stage of development from the Review Status list.
- *Add new list items* You can also add your own list items by clicking the Categories, Names, or Statuses button, as explained in the following section.

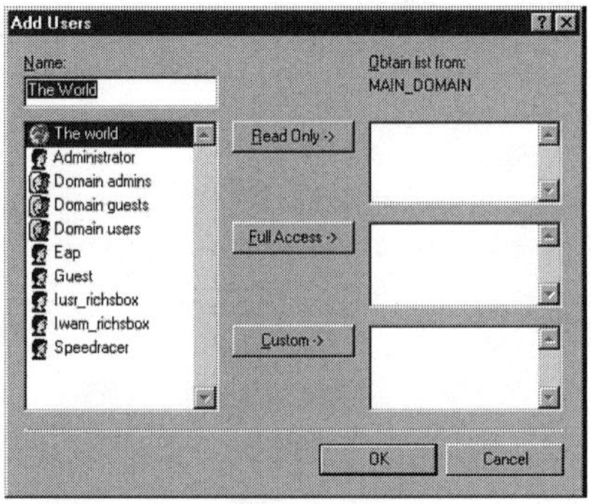

The Properties dialog box with the Workgroup tab selected.

Changing Your Categories, Names, and Statuses Lists

You don't have to use the categories and statuses that FrontPage gives you. But you'll need to add your own category names, because even a smart program like FrontPage can't create a list of names for you!

To edit your lists, click the Categories, Names, or Statuses button to the right of the list. When the Master List dialog box appears, you can do the following:

- *Add a list item* Type an entry in the New (Category, Name, or Status) box and click the Add button.
- *Remove a list item* Select a list item and click the Delete button.
- *Restore the defaults* You can restore the list that comes with FrontPage by clicking the Reset button.
- *Apply your changes* To return to the Properties dialog box and apply your changes, click OK. You can also click Cancel to close the dialog box without making any changes.

Do Not Publish!

Yikes! How do you keep FrontPage from publishing a file before you and your co-workers have finished working on it? It's easy. Display the Properties dialog box, click the Workgroup tab, and select the Exclude this file when publishing the rest of the Web check box. Now you can tweak your file to perfection and rest assured that nobody will see it before you're ready.

Editing Workflow Information for Files

"Garbage in, garbage out," the old saying goes. Your workflow reports won't tell you much unless the users keep up with their files. Most importantly, you and your co-workers need to update the status information as a file goes through different stages of a project. To edit a file's workflow information, display the Properties dialog box for the file with the Workgroup tab selected. You can then select a new item from the Statuses list, or make other changes. Available Review Status options include Code Review (making sure the page works properly), Content Review (making suggestions, edits, and changes), Legal Review (clearing material with the legal department), and Manager Review (getting the go-ahead from the person in charge).

Displaying a Workflow Report

Once you've assigned properties to your files, you can generate workflow reports, as covered in Chapter 25. Go to the Reports view and then select Review Status from the Reports toolbar list.

Remember the Task List

FrontPage's task list also helps you and your co-workers keep track of what needs to be done. In addition, you can add workflow report items to the task list. For more about working with tasks, see Chapter 28.

Five Cool Resources for Learning More About Intranets

FrontPage makes it easy to set up a basic intranet. However, if you want to add more advanced features, you'll need to learn some technical stuff. The following Web sites provide general information about setting up and maintaining intranets:

- *Microsoft's FrontPage Intranet page* A step-by-step guide to setting up an intranet in an hour, and more (`http://www.microsoft.com/office/intranet/solutions.htm`).
- *Web 66 NT Resource Center* Web 66 is a community that helps educators set up servers and Web pages for their schools. Their Windows NT section uses plain language and step-by-step tutorials on how to set up a Windows NT server. And while you're there, you can learn about lots of other things, too (`http://web66.coled.umn.edu/WinNT/Default.html`).

- *Intranet Journal* Techie stuff, along with tips and tricks (`http://www.intranetjournal.com/`).
- *Builder.Com* CNet's Builder site offers lots of helpful articles on the latest Web technologies, including servers and intranets (`http://www.builder.com/`).
- *Complete Intranet Resource* A general Web site that covers everything about intranets, including the basics, discussion groups, articles, techie stuff, and demos (`http://www.intrack.com/intranet/`).

The Least You Need to Know

- Intranets are Web sites that run on private office networks. They make it easy for co-workers with different schedules to work together and share files through a Web site.
- You can use the FrontPage Web Wizards to set up your intranet. Intranet Web sites have URLs (as in `http://yourServer/yourWeb/`) just like regular Web sites on the Internet. When you create your intranet Web, you'll need to email the URL to your co-workers so they can find it.
- You can maintain control over your intranet Web site and keep people from stepping on each other's toes by setting access levels for Webs and pages, as covered in Chapter 27.
- Your co-workers can use FrontPage or FrontPage Express' Publisher (or an FTP program) to publish files to your Web, as covered in Chapter 26. Microsoft Office users can also save a remote Web site as a folder and save files to it through the Save dialog box, as covered in Chapter 18.
- When you assign workgroup properties to the pages and files on your Web site, you can generate workflow reports from the Reports view, as covered in Chapter 25.

Chapter 30

Building a Web Site That Fits Your Ego

In This Chapter

- Publishing an e-zine
- Launching a Web discussion group
- Working at home
- Starting an online store
- Five other cool things you can try

So. Now that you're a FrontPage whiz kid, where do you go from here? Like the proverbial 800-pound gorilla, you can go anywhere you want. Have you always dreamed of starting a home business, launching a magazine, working at home, promoting a cause that you care about, or finding like-minded folks to chat with about a favorite topic or hobby? Go for it! FrontPage gives you the tools you need.

If you tend to feel overwhelmed by large projects, that's okay. The great thing about having a Web site is that you can start off small and grow the site at your own pace. When you print out a few hundred brochures, you're stuck with them for a while. But you can change or update your Web pages as often as you like.

Publish an Online Zine

Watch out, Tina Brown! Nowadays, anyone who's got a way with words and something to say can be a publishing mogul. Whether you want to publish for fun or profit, FrontPage can help you with everything from design to managing all your articles. You can even create a private Project Web to work with the people who write articles for you and contribute pictures. So go ahead—be a pundit. The Web is your soapbox.

When you're planning an online zine (also called an *e-zine*), think about what sort of information you want to publish, how often you want to update your articles (weekly? monthly?), and where you'll get content (articles and pictures). E-zines can also get pretty large in a hurry, so you should think about how you want to organize and manage your issues and articles. For example, some e-zines organize articles by topic and others by issue.

You can also explore the Web for ideas and inspiration—here's an e-zine sampling:

- *Salon Magazine* The mother of all e-zines is a great place to start out when looking for ideas. They publish articles on current topics and also have discussion groups so visitors can comment and talk amongst themselves (`http://www.salonmagazine.com/`).
- *Inklings* An e-zine with resources and articles galore for writers (`http://www.inkspot.com/inklings/`).
- *Parent's Council* Reviews of children's books and publications for concerned parents (`http://www.parentcouncil.com/`).
- *Zines* Take a walk on the wild side. The authors of the book *Zines* have a Web site with all sorts of links and resources for counterculture e-zine publishers (`http://www.zinebook.com/`).

Can't Pay Your E-Zine Contributors?

Of course, writers and artists have to make a living like everyone else. But if your online magazine covers topics that interest them (and which paying publications don't talk about), they might welcome a chance to air their views. You also may have friends, family, or co-workers who write, illustrate, or take photos as a hobby. Just make sure to give them credit, link back to their Web sites, and promote them when you can.

You can also ask for content from other Webmasters who publish related articles and artwork. They might let you run an article or picture in exchange for credit and a link back to their Web site.

The Virtual Coffee Klatch

Has anyone ever told you that you should have been a talk show host? Or do you want a forum to discuss issues in your community, or a favorite hobby or topic? With the FrontPage Discussion Web Wizard, you can start your own online coffee klatch where people can post messages and exchange ideas. You can also use FrontPage tools that require people to sign in with a password and that help you moderate discussions to make sure messages stay on topic and are appropriate.

The Web abounds with discussion groups on anything and everything, including fan clubs, current events, local happenings, health, collectibles, finance, and more. Many companies also run discussion groups so their customers can find information and get help when they need it. Chapter 23, "Switchboard Central: Setting Up a Discussion Web," tells you more about setting up and running a FrontPage Discussion Web.

Discussion Groups Need Care and Feeding

FrontPage makes it easy to set up and manage your Discussion Web. But if you want your discussion group to succeed, you'll need to put some work into it. Lively, informative discussions keep people coming back. Otherwise, your online community will quickly degenerate into messages that say "Hello? Is anyone there?" or "Make $1000 a week working at home!" You also need to delete or archive messages now and then and remove messages that are offensive or inappropriate.

The following discussion groups draw lots of visitors and are well run:

- *FrontPage User Group* Do a little discussion group research while getting help with FrontPage (`http://www.fpug.com/`).
- *Forum One* If you want to visit a few discussion groups that talk about similar topics, you can search for them on Forum One (`http://www.forumone.com/`).
- *The Garden Web Forums* Helpful information on planting and maintaining all sorts of gardens. Beginners are welcome (`http://www.gardenweb.com/forums/`).
- *Homework Help* The Minneapolis/St. Paul *Star Tribune* runs discussion groups organized by subject to help kids of all ages with their homework. Maybe you can start a discussion group for your kids' school (`http://www.startribune.com/stonline/html/special/homework/`).

Work at Home

Wouldn't it be nice to work at home? No morning commute, and you could work in your jammies if you wanted. With today's technologies, it's easier than ever to start a home business (and promote it on the Web, as explained in Chapter 26, "Don't Just Let It Sit There! Publishing Your Web Site"). With FrontPage, you can set up a spiffy-looking professional Web site and tell people about what you do, show them projects you've worked on, let them look at your resume, link them to your references' email addresses, and more. If you like your job but are considering telecommuting a couple days a week, the Project and Discussion Webs can help you keep in touch with your co-workers.

Of course, you might want to read up a little before you quit your day job:

- *Poor Richard's Web Site* The book that goes with this site is a must-have if you're creating a Web site for your small business or home business. The site also has tons of useful information. Plus, the author works at home and uses FrontPage too (`http://www.poorrichard.com/`).
- *Small Business Resources* A resource and help center for small business and home business owners, or people thinking of starting one (`http://small-bizhelp.net/`).
- *Mother's Home Business Network* Advice, recommended books and products, home business opportunities, advice on telecommuting, and more (`http://www.homeworkingmom.com/`).
- *Gil Gordon Associates Telecommuting* Information for people who telecommute or who want to. You can also find links to other resources, read reviews of helpful books, and more (`http://www.gilgordon.com/`).

Start an Online Store

Got something you'd like to sell? Try setting up an online store. Lots of people run online storefronts to sell greeting cards, crafts, artwork, toys, collectibles, healthcare products, and more. Or, if you run a bed-and-breakfast or plan events for a living, you can offer visitors the convenience of registering and paying from your Web site.

You can start off simply—all you really need is a merchant account (so you can accept credit cards), a Web host with a secure server (so people can order safely), and an order form. Once you get up and running, you'll probably want your Web site to add up the orders, sales tax, and shipping for your customers. Shopping cart software and services make it easy to do this too. Many Web hosts also offer shopping cart software.

Need More Information?

For more on starting an online store, visit Poor Richard's Directory of Shopping Cart Software and Services at `http://www.poorrichard.com/freeinfo/shop.htm`. There you'll find a long list of software and services in all price ranges.

Five Other Cool Things You Can Try

Sure, FrontPage has lots of great stuff, but nobody has *everything*. You can add all sorts of nifty doodads that make your Web site more fun and useful. Best of all, you can do it for free.

Check out the following possibilities:

- *Your own chat room* How would you like to host a chat room? Chat rooms work differently than Web discussion groups because people can talk in *real-time*—meaning that what you type appears in the chat room as soon as you send it. Talk City at `http://www.talkcity.com/` gives you everything you need to run a free Web chat room.
- *Online postcards* Here's the deal. You choose your favorite pictures and set them up as postcards. Visitors can choose a picture, fill out a special form, and send the postcard to a friend. The friend receives an email message with a URL, which they can click to view their postcard. Pretty neat, huh? Go to `http://mypostcards.com` and they'll tell you how to set everything up. The service is free.
- *A virtual bookstore* If you love books and want to publish book reviews, or would like to recommend a few titles that relate to your Web site, you can set up a virtual bookstore. Amazon.com Books (`http://www.amazon.com/`) and other online booksellers have affiliate programs that you can sign up for. When you join, they'll tell you how to set up links to books on their Web site so you can earn a little commission on the books referred by you.
- *Instant messages and more* Have you taken ICQ for a spin yet? ICQ (pronounced "I seek you") is a program that tells you when friends are online, lets you exchange instant messages, and allows visitors to "page" you (send instant messages) from your Web site. You can download ICQ at `http://www.icq.com`.
- *Free advertising* If you have no advertising budget yet, join a banner ad exchange program, like the Link Exchange at `http://www.linkexchange.com/`. Here's how it works: You create a banner ad (FrontPage's Banner Ad Manager can help you do it, as explained in Chapter 20, "Gee-Whiz Pages with Animated Special Effects") and upload it to your Web site. When you sign up with a program, you give them the URL for your ad and they give you instructions for inserting a snippet of code on your page. The banner ad program then rotates your ad between other pages and displays other people's ads on yours.

The Least You Need to Know

- As explained in Chapter 23, FrontPage's Discussion Web Wizard makes it easy to build an online discussion forum.
- FrontPage's Project Web (see Chapter 2, "Instant Web-Site-O-Matic: Spinning FrontPage Webs") can help you manage projects and work with other people. You can use the Project Web to manage an online magazine or track projects with coworkers.
- If your Web hosting company offers access to a secure server, you can set up an online store and take orders with FrontPage forms. Chapter 13, "Form and Function: Building Online Forms," tells you how to set up forms.

Speak Like a Geek

accessibility Refers to the various issues involved with ensuring that the handicapped can view Web pages and navigate Web sites.

action In DHTML and scripting, an action is what happens when an event occurs. *See also* **event** and **object**.

active graphics In FrontPage themes, refers to navigation buttons that change in appearance when the user passes the mouse pointer over them, and that provide navigational cues (for example, a button is highlighted to indicate the current page).

active server pages (ASP) A technology developed by Microsoft that allows users whose servers have ASP capabilities to easily script Web pages.

active Web pages Web pages enhanced with programs, scripts, and other Web technologies that respond to user input or contain animated special effects.

ActiveX A Microsoft technology that enables Web developers to take bits and pieces of programming code and put them together to create programs that run on Web pages. ActiveX only works in Internet Explorer.

ActiveX control An ActiveX program that loads in a Web browser.

alternative text Text that appears when a visitor's Web browser cannot display a picture or embedded object.

animated GIF A group of GIF images that are assembled into simple animations that run in a Web browser.

article A message posted to a discussion Web or newsgroup.

aspect ratio The width-to-height ratio of a picture. Most image programs have an aspect ratio feature to ensure that pictures are resized proportionally.

audio Sound on your computer. Common audio file formats include AU, WAV, and MIDI.

AVI Audio Video Interleaved, Microsoft's popular video format.

background image An image that repeats across a Web page to form a patterned background.

background sound An audio file that plays when a Web page loads in a Web browser.

bandwidth The amount of data transferred over the Internet or via a particular connection. Bandwidth is measured in kilobites per second. *See also* **Kbps**.

banner In FrontPage themes, the text graphic that appears near the top of a Web page that contains the page's topic.

banner ad An advertisement that appears on a Web site (usually at the top of a page).

bookmark In FrontPage, a target on a Web page that links to a particular section on that Web page. In Netscape Navigator, a favorite Web page that you can visit by pulling it down from a list instead of having to type the URL. *See also* **internal links** and **target**.

browse To surf the Web or to look for a file on your computer through a dialog box, such as the Open dialog box.

browser An application, such as Internet Explorer or Netscape Navigator, for viewing Web pages.

browser compatibility Issues involved with making sure pages appear correctly in different Web browsers and different versions of Web browsers.

browser-safe colors 216 colors that are displayed correctly in a Web browser, regardless of the computer or operating system the visitor is using.

bullet list An indented list of items preceded by a decorative character that calls attention to each item.

bulletin board A Web site that allows users to have ongoing discussions. Bulletin boards generally contain a table of contents page with links to individual messages, pages with the text for each message, and a page with a Web form so users can post and reply to messages. *See also* **discussion Web**.

cascading style sheets (CSS) A Web technology that allows you to create a document with built-in custom formatting styles that you can apply to pages throughout a Web site. Style sheets work similarly to the styles in desktop publishing and word processing documents.

CGI script A script that runs on a server and enables you to program a Web page. The most common example of a CGI script is a form processor that gathers data from a Web form. FrontPage components allow users to do things that used to require CGI scripting. *See also* **scripting language**.

child level In objects and Web pages, child level elements are lower in the hierarchy. For example, when you create FrontPage navigation bars in the Navigation view, child level pages are represented as pages that fall under a main section page.

client A computer that connects to a server to access a network, the Internet, or other data. Also refers to browsers, email programs, and other applications that allow users to get information and services from a server.

client-side Refers to technologies like DHTML, cascading style sheets, Java applets, and ActiveX controls, which rely on a Web browser or other client application. For example, only version 4.0 browsers and higher support DHTML.

closed network A group of computers within an organization that are connected to each other (usually through a server) so people within the organization can communicate and exchange files. Closed networks can only be accessed by authorized users.

collapsible list A list of items that allows Web page visitors to click an item and display additional list items.

color depth The number of colors that a computer screen can display or that an image can include. Options include millions of colors (16.7 million colors, true color, 24-bit color), thousands of colors (67,000 colors, high color, 16-bit color), and 256 colors (8-bit color). Higher color depths generally enable better-quality image displays.

color scheme The colors of a Web page's background, text, and links.

common gateway interface (CGI) A set of commands and scripting languages that can run on most standard servers. Perl is a popular CGI scripting language. *See also* **CGI script**.

components In FrontPage, menu items that add features to a Web page that would otherwise require programming or scripting.

continuous tone image An image with complex shading and gradation of colors, like a photograph or an oil painting. On the Web, these images work best when formatted as JPEGs.

CSS *See* **cascading style sheets**.

data Web pages, email messages, pictures, documents, and anything else that is stored on your computer or transferred over networks or over the Internet.

data access pages In FrontPage, a set of Web pages that allows visitors to search (and sometimes add entries to) a database stored on the server.

default The automatic setting that determines the behavior of an application or an element that is created or manipulated within an application. Most defaults can be changed by clicking a toolbar button, selecting a menu item, or changing settings in a dialog box. For example, FrontPage automatically aligns text and images to the left, but you can realign them to the center.

definition description The indented text that follows a definition term in a definition list. *See also* **definition list**.

definition list A list consisting of main entries followed by indented items with additional information. This type of list is generally used in tables of contents and other documents that contain titles or definitions followed by an explanation or description.

definition term The main entry in a definition list, which is followed by a definition description in a definition list. *See also* **definition list**.

delay In animation, the amount of time that elapses between frames and, in video and audio, the amount of time that elapses between loops. *See also* **loop**.

DHTML *See* **Dynamic HTML**.

dialog box A box with a message or set of options that appears on the computer screen after you perform an action, click a toolbar button, or select a menu item.

directory path The location of a file in relation to a computer or Web.

directory server A type of server that allows users to conference online with NetMeeting.

discussion Web A type of FrontPage Web where visitors can read and post messages to each other. *See also* **bulletin board.**

display settings The resolution and color depth of a computer screen's display. Common settings are 640×480 at 256 colors (8-bit) or 800×600 at millions of colors (24-bit).

docking a toolbar Anchoring a floating toolbar to the top, right, bottom, or left of the application window.

domain name The address of a server or group of servers, as in `mydomain.com`. *See also* **virtual domain**.

double-click To click the mouse button twice in quick succession.

download To get data from a server.

dynamic database An online database that visitors can interact with via the Web and that is updated automatically when the data changes.

Dynamic HTML (DHTML) A Web technology that enables Web developers to position, layer, and animate Web page elements, set up collapsible lists, and load special fonts to a Web browser.

dynamic Web pages *See* **active Web pages**.

email link A link that enables the visitor to send email to a specified address.

embedded files A file and plug-in application (complete with toolbar buttons) that appears as part of your Web page layout, such as a QuickTime movie with player controls. FrontPage also uses the term *embed* when you save Web pages that contain images that you've edited with the Picture toolbar. In this context, *embed* means adding the pictures to your Web page. *See also* **inline files**.

event In DHTML and scripting, an event is something that happens to a Web page or object that triggers an action. *See also* **action** and **object**.

Extensible Markup Language (XML) An up-and-coming Web technology that enables Web developers to create custom HTML tags that add greater Web page capabilities and better integrate Web pages with databases. Version 5.0 Web browsers support XML.

external files Files that are launched separately from a Web page when a visitor clicks a link, rather than appearing as embedded or inline files that are part of the Web page layout. *See also* **inline files** and **embedded files**.

external links Hyperlinks to pages on other Web sites. *See also* **hyperlinks**.

filename extension A period and a string of characters added to a filename that tell computers and Web browsers the file type. For example, `image.jpeg` designates a JPEG file.

flame An angry message sent by email or posted to a discussion Web or newsgroup.

floating toolbar A toolbar that floats in the middle of an application window when displayed. You can anchor a floating toolbar by dragging it to the top, bottom, left, or right of the application window. *See also* **docking a toolbar**.

form On the Web, a page with form fields that allows users to enter information, select options, and post data to the server.

form field A text box, scrolling list, button, or other page element that appears on a Web form so visitors can enter information, select options, and send data.

form handler A CGI script or FrontPage component installed on a server that processes form data, such as by adding the information to a database or sending it to an email address.

frames Divide a Web page into separate areas with individual Web documents.

frameset document A Web page that tells which pages to display in which frames.

FrontPage navigation bar A type of navigation bar that you can generate automatically with FrontPage. *See also* **navigation bar**.

FrontPage server extensions Special software that extends a server's capabilities so FrontPage users can do things that would normally require programming. Many FrontPage features only work on a server with FrontPage server extensions.

FrontPage Web A Web site created in FrontPage.

GIF Graphic Interchange Format, an image file format for the Web that works well for line art and flat-color pictures. The GIF format also allows you to create animations from GIF files and create transparent GIFs. *See also* **animated GIF** and **transparent GIF**.

GIF animation *See* **animated GIF**.

graphical bullets Bullets that are created as images, rather than text.

graphical text An image that contains text.

horizontal line A Web page element that inserts a line on the Web page. Horizontal lines are commonly used to create separators for different types of information or sections on a Web page. Some people also use the terms *horizontal rule* or *page divider*.

horizontal spacing The amount of space between the left and right sides of an image or other page.

hot spot An area on an image map that functions as a link.

hover button In FrontPage, an image or text link that changes in appearance when a visitor passes their mouse pointer over it or clicks it.

HTML Hypertext Markup Language, a coding language used for creating Web pages.

HTTP Hypertext Transfer Protocol, the set of server, communications, and browser technologies that enables Web pages to be used on the Internet.

hyperlink rollover A piece of text or an image that changes its appearance when a visitor passes the cursor over it.

hyperlinks Text or pictures on a Web page that you can click on to jump to another Web page or download a file.

Hypertext Markup Language (HTML) *See* **HTML**.

Hypertext Transfer Protocol *See* **HTTP**.

icon A graphic that represents a concept or action. For example, in most computer applications a folder icon represents a directory that contains files, or a button that you can click to open a file.

image map A picture with clickable hot spots that function as links. *See also* **hot spot**.

inheritance A programming and Web concept in which child level elements (objects that are lower in the hierarchy) inherit characteristics from parent elements. For example, level 2 headings are generally smaller than level 1 headings, but still appear in the same font as the level 1 headings. *See also* **child level** and **parent level**.

inline files Files that appear on a Web page, such as images or embedded movies or soundtracks. *See also* **external files**.

internal links Links to targets within the same Web page. *See also* **bookmark** and **target**.

Internet A vast global network that allows people to view Web pages, send and receive email messages, participate in newsgroups, join chat rooms, and more.

Internet service provider (ISP) A company or organization that allows you to connect to the Internet through their server. In general, these ISPs charge a flat monthly rate and also host Web sites.

intranet A closed office network that works similarly to the Internet and uses Internet programs like Web browsers and email programs to share information among co-workers.

ISP *See* **Internet service provider**.

Java Sun Microsystems' popular programming language for creating applications that run in a Web browser.

Java applets Programs written in Java.

JavaScript Netscape's popular client-side scripting language for programming Web pages. *See also* **scripting language** and **client-side**.

JPEG Joint Picture Experts Group. A Web image file format that works well for continuous tone images. *See also* **continuous tone image**.

JScript Microsoft's answer to JavaScript. JScript works with Internet Explorer, or in any browser when the Web server supports active server pages.

jump map A visual flowchart that shows the structure of a Web site. In FrontPage, you can create a jump map in the Navigation view.

Kbps Kilobits per second, the unit of measurement for modem and connection speeds on the Internet, as in 56.6Kbps. The faster the modem, the more quickly you can download data.

key combination A shortcut that allows the user to press a combination of keys instead of selecting commands from a menu.

keyword A descriptive word entered when using a search engine form to search for information on the Web or on an individual Web site.

layer To arrange text and images so they overlap, or to position them one on top of one another.

line art Images with simple lines and solid colors. On the Web, these images work best when formatted as GIFs.

links *See* **hyperlinks**.

local files Files on the same computer, or on a computer on a local network to which you're directly connected.

local links Links to pages on the same Web site. *See also* **external links**, **internal links**, and **hyperlinks**.

local network A group of computers that are directly connected to each other, usually through a local server. Most offices and other organizations have local networks. *See also* **intranet** and **closed network**.

local server A server that hosts a local network.

loop In multimedia, a loop occurs each time the file plays.

low-res image A low-quality image with a small file size that appears as a placeholder on a Web page until the larger, higher-quality image finishes loading.

main page The Web page that visitors automatically go to when they enter a URL that doesn't point to a specific document(as in `http://www.byteit.com/work/` rather than `http://www.byteit.com/work/books.htm`). Each Web folder, Web, and sub-Web should contain one (and only one) main page that is named either `index.htm`, `index.html`, `default.htm`, or `default.html`.

marquee An animated text message that scrolls on a Web page.

meta-information Information about a Web page. Meta-information can't be displayed in Web browsers, but it gives search engine spiders and other applications important information, including a summary and keywords for the Web page. *See also* **spider**.

modem A device used to connect a computer to a telephone line.

moderator The person who runs a discussion Web or newsgroup.

monitor settings *See* **display settings**.

mouse over When a visitor passes the mouse pointer over a text or image link. *See also* **hyperlink rollover**.

navigation bar A row of graphics or text links that appears consistently throughout a Web site (or sections within a Web site) to help visitors navigate the site.

navigation map *See* **jump map**.

nested sub-Web A FrontPage Web within a Web that can have individual settings apart from the root Web.

newsgroup An online forum that allows people to post text-only messages and read other people's messages. Netscape Navigator and Internet Explorer both come with newsreader applications for participating in newsgroups. Now, you can do the same thing through a Web page. *See also* **discussion Web** and **bulletin board**.

numbered list An indented list of items, each preceded by a number.

object In DHTML and scripting, a picture, block of text, or other Web page element that performs an action when an event occurs. *Object* is also used as a general term for a page element or a snippet of programming code. *See also* **action**, **event**, and **page elements**.

Office viewers Browser plug-ins that allow visitors to view Microsoft Word, Excel, and PowerPoint files even if they don't have those applications.

operating system The software that runs your computer and tells it how to work with other applications.

overlay A page layout with overlapping or layered text and image elements. *See also* **layer**.

page elements A general term for Web files and things that you put on a Web page, including text, images, embedded files, scripts, and FrontPage components.

page title Text that appears in the browser's title bar when a page appears in a Web browser.

parent level In Web pages and programming, the top elements in a hierarchy. In the FrontPage Navigation view, a parent level page is generally the main page for a section, with child level pages organized beneath it. *See also* **child level** and **same level**.

Perl A popular CGI scripting language. *See also* **CGI script** and **common gateway interface**.

permissions In server administration, sets of passwords and access levels that allow co-workers to administer, edit, or view Web pages.

photorealistic image *See* **continuous tone image**.

pixel Short for "picture element." Computer screens display words, pictures, and other elements as little dots that blend together. Each dot is a pixel.

plug-in An application that extends a Web browser's capabilities so it can launch files that browsers don't normally support. For example, the Shockwave plug-in allows you to view Shockwave movies on a Web page.

PNG Portable Network Graphic, an up-and-coming Web image format supported by 5.0 Web browsers, FrontPage, and newer versions of imaging programs.

Portable Document Format (PDF) Adobe's technology for creating online Acrobat documents that retain their fonts and layouts and that can be viewed with the Acrobat Reader plug-in.

positioning Placing an image or block of text in an exact location for a precise page layout.

processor Another name for the central processing unit (CPU), the device that determines how quickly your computer runs.

programming language A language like C++, Java, or Visual Basic that allows programmers to write powerful software applications.

properties Details about a Web page, image, or other type of file or Web page element.

publish To upload files from a FrontPage Web to a server. *See also* **upload**.

QuickTime Apple's popular video format.

ratings On the Web, meta-information intended for programs that block out inappropriate Web pages. Web site ratings are somewhat like movie ratings.

remote files Files on a computer that you can connect to by dialing up an Internet account. *See also* **local files**.

remote server A server that you can connect to by dialing up your Internet account. *See also* **local server**.

repeating page elements Pictures, links, and text that appear on pages throughout a Web site, such as a navigation bar.

reports Lists of Web site details generated automatically by FrontPage in the Reports view.

resample In FrontPage, the process of using the Picture toolbar to change the dimensions of the image itself, rather than simply telling the Web browser to display the image at a different size through the Image Properties dialog box.

resolution The number of dots (pixels) per inch used to render an image, or the display resolution for a computer screen. On the Web, images are formatted at 72 or 96 dots per inch (DPI). Standard computer display resolutions include 640×480, 800×600, and 1280×1024 (Super VGA). *See also* **display settings** and **pixel**.

right-click To click an object on the computer screen with the right mouse button to display a shortcut menu.

rollover *See* **hyperlink rollover** and **mouse over**.

root Web The main Web that contains all of the files and folders for a FrontPage Web.

round-trip HTML Microsoft's term for FrontPage and Microsoft Office's capability to convert files to Web pages and back to the original format for editing without losing any information.

same level In Web pages and programming, elements that occupy the same level in a hierarchy. In the FrontPage Navigation view, parent level pages appear on the same level, with child level pages organized beneath them. *See also* **child level** and **parent level**.

screen real estate The amount of available space on a computer screen for displaying application windows.

scripting language A simplified programming language that allows even non-programmers to create Web pages. Scripting languages rely on another application—such as a Web browser or a server application—in order to run. Popular scripting languages include JavaScript and Perl.

search engine A technology that enables people to search databases on the Web. This term is also used for search sites like Yahoo!, WebCrawler, and HotBot.

search form A text field with a Submit button. Visitors can type keywords and click the button to display a list of links that meet the search criteria. Some search forms also include pull-down lists or items with check boxes so users can select additional items to narrow down the search.

search page A Web page with a search form.

server A computer that stores data and serves it up to users who request it or that allows users to connect to the Internet.

server-side Technologies that rely on a server's capabilities. For example, many FrontPage features require a server with FrontPage extensions.

shared borders A FrontPage feature that makes it easy to create repeating page elements on the top, right, bottom, or left page border, and to apply them to other pages.

Shockwave movie A multimedia file created with one of Macromedia's applications, including Director and Flash.

shortcut menu A menu that appears when you click a page element with the right mouse button.

site search engine A search engine that only searches the contents of a particular Web site, rather than the entire Web. The FrontPage Search component allows users to create a searchable Web site.

slow pages Pages that take a long time to load in the browser due to large (or many) images, large quantities of text, elaborate animations, and other factors. A Web page should take no longer than 20-30 seconds to load. The FrontPage status bar displays the estimated download time for the current Web page.

source code The HTML code behind the Web pages. In FrontPage you can click the HTML tab in the Page view to see the source code. *See also* **HTML**.

spam Advertisements and promotional announcements sent by email or posted to a discussion Web or newsgroup.

spider Programs used by search engine companies like Lycos and AltaVista to automatically find and catalog Web pages. Spiders are also called *robots*.

static database Information from a database that is formatted as a set of Web pages and that doesn't allow visitors to retrieve information or otherwise interact with the database itself.

static Web pages Web pages that contain no animated elements, programmed components, collapsible lists, hover buttons, or other elements that the user interacts with. *See also* **active Web pages**.

style sheets *See* **cascading style sheets**.

table A Web page element consisting of rows, columns, and cells that helps Web designers arrange images, text, and other page elements.

target An area of a Web page that is defined so you can create a link to it from within the same Web page. In FrontPage, targets are called bookmarks. *See also* **bookmark** and **internal links**.

tasks In FrontPage, items that appear in the Tasks view as reminders of work that needs to be done on a Web site.

themes In FrontPage, professional, prefab Web page designs that you can apply to a Web site.

thread Articles posted to a discussion Web or newsgroup in response to a particular message.

toolbar A row of buttons in an application window that users can click to perform tasks.

transparent GIF A GIF image with the background color removed so it appears to float against the Web page's background.

uniform resource locator (URL) An Internet address, as in `http://www.website.com/`.

upload To send files to a server or publish files to a FrontPage Web site. *See also* **download** and **publish**.

VBScript Microsoft's scripting language for Internet Explorer or Active Server Pages.

vertical spacing The amount of space between the top and bottom of a Web page element and the surrounding text.

video Movies. Popular video formats include AVI and QuickTime.

virtual domain A domain that is hosted on another server. Many people sign up for a domain name, as in `mydomain.com`, but host it on their ISP's or Web hosting company's server instead of their own.

Web *See* **World Wide Web** or **FrontPage Web**.

Web hosting company A company that provides Web hosting services but not dial-up Internet access.

Web-safe colors *See* **browser-safe colors**.

Web server A program that enables a server to host, manage, and serve up Web pages.

Web site address *See* **uniform resource locator**.

whitespace The amount of empty space on a Web page that contains no text, images, or other elements. A reasonable amount of whitespace is essential for good design, readability, and an uncluttered look.

wizard An application built into a program that takes users through the steps of a complicated process, such as setting up a FrontPage Web.

workgroup A group of people who work together, or groups of people who share the same FrontPage Web access privileges.

World Wide Web The part of the Internet devoted to Web pages.

WYSIWYG What you see is what you get, an expression describing computer software with an intuitive graphical display.

XML *See* **Extensible Markup Language**.

ZIP A popular file compression format for Windows.

Index

Symbols

A

B

C

D

I

N

O

P

Q-R

S

T

X-Y-Z